10 0460495 4

A survey carried out by the Office for National Statistics on behalf of the Department of Health and the Scottish Executive

Mental health of children and young people in Great Britain, 2004

Authors: Hazel Green

Áine McGinnity

Howard Meltzer

Tamsin Ford

Robert Goodman

palgrave
macmillan

First published 2005 by
PALGRAVE MACMILLAN
Houndmills, Basingstoke, Hampshire RG21 6XS and
175 Fifth Avenue, New York, NY 10010
Companies and representatives throughout the world.

PALGRAVE MACMILLAN is the global academic imprint of the Palgrave Macmillan division of St. Martin's Press, LLC and of Palgrave Macmillan Ltd. Macmillan® is a registered trademark in the United States, United Kingdom and other countries. Palgrave is a registered trademark in the European Union and other countries.

ISBN 1-4039-8637-1

This book is printed on paper suitable for recycling and made from fully managed and sustained forest sources.

A catalogue record for this book is available from the British Library.

10   9   8   7   6   5   4   3   2   1
14   13   12   11   10   09   08   07   06   05

Printed and bound in Great Britain by Ashford Colour Press Ltd, Gosport.

A National Statistics publication

National Statistics are produced to high professional standards as set out in the National Statistics Code of Practice. They are produced free from political influence.

About the Office for National Statistics

The Office for National Statistics (ONS) is the government agency responsible for compiling, analysing and disseminating economic, social and demographic statistics about the United Kingdom. It also administers the statutory registration of births, marriages and deaths in England and Wales.

The Director of ONS is also the National Statistician and the Registrar General for England and Wales.

For enquiries about this publication, contact Hazel Green.
Tel: 020 7533 5374
E-mail: hazel.green@ons.gsi.gov.uk

For general enquiries, contact the National Statistics Customer Contact Centre.
Tel: **0845 601 3034** (minicom: 01633 812399)
E-mail: info@statistics.gov.uk
Fax: 01633 652747
Post: Room D115, Government Buildings,
            Cardiff Road, Newport NP10 8XG

You can also find National Statistics on the Internet at
www.statistics.gov.uk

Contents

5: Emotional disorders 71

6: Conduct disorders 113

7: Hyperkinetic disorders 155

8: Autistic spectrum disorder and other less common disorders 187

List of tables

5: Emotional disorders

6: Conduct disorders

7: Hyperkinetic disorders

8: Autistic spectrum disorder and other less common disorders

9: Children with multiple disorders

10: Mental disorders in Scotland

Appendices

List of figures

Acknowledgements

We would like to thank all the children and their parents and teachers who participated in the survey and the ONS interviewers who conducted the fieldwork.

The research team were supported by specialist staff in ONS and expert advisers who contributed to the sampling, fieldwork and computing stages. A special thank you is extended to Anne Klepacz who provided expert advice on the handling of the interview based on her many years experience of surveys of psychiatric morbidity. Thanks also to Tamara Taylor who managed the research during its fieldwork stage.

The project was steered by a group comprising the following, to whom thanks are due for assistance and specialist advice at various stages of the survey:

Department of Health:
Dr R Jezzard (chair)
Mr A Glanz
Mr R Bond
Mr J O'Shea (secretariat)

Scottish Executive:
Ms A Hallam

Department for Education and Skills:
Ms L Hertzmann
Ms L Bridson

Expert advisers:
Prof R Goodman (Institute of Psychiatry, London)
Dr T Ford
Dr P Moran

Office for National Statistics:
Dr H Meltzer
Ms H Green
Ms Á McGinnity
Dr R Harker

Notes

1 Tables showing percentages

The row or column percentages may add to 99% or 101% because of rounding.

The varying positions of the percentage signs and bases in the tables denote the presentation of different types of information. Where there is a percentage sign at the head of a column and the base at the foot, the whole distribution is presented and the individual percentages add to between 99% and 101%. Where there is no percentage sign in the table and a note above the figures, the figures refer to the proportion of people who had the attribute being discussed, and the complementary proportion, to add to 100%, is not shown in the table.

The following conventions have been used within tables showing percentages:

..	data not available
-	no cases
0	values less than 0.5%
0.0	values less than 0.05%

2 Small bases

Very small bases have been avoided wherever possible because of the relatively high sampling errors that attach to small numbers. Often, where the numbers are not large enough to justify the use of all categories, classifications have been condensed. However, an item within a classification is occasionally shown separately, even though the base is small, because to combine it with another large category would detract from the value of the larger category. In general, percentage distributions are shown if the base is 30 or more. Where the base is lower, percentages are shown in brackets

3 Significant differences

Unless otherwise stated, all differences noted in the text are statistically significant at the 95 per cent confidence level ($p < 0.05$).

This report first describes the prevalence of mental disorders among 5- to 16- year-olds in 2004 and notes any changes since the previous survey in 1999. It then provides profiles of children in each of the main disorder categories (emotional, conduct, hyperkinetic and autistic spectrum disorders) and, where the sample size permits, profiles subgroups within these categories. The final chapters examine the characteristics of children with multiple disorders and present a selection of analyses for Scotland. Causal relationships should not be assumed for any of the results presented in this report.

Summary of main findings

Background, aims and coverage (Chapter 1)

- The main aims of the survey were:

- To examine whether there were any changes between 1999 and 2004 in the prevalence of the three main categories of mental disorder: conduct disorders, emotional disorders and hyperkinetic disorders.

- To describe the characteristics and behaviour patterns of children in each main disorder category and subgroups within those categories.

- To extend the coverage in the 1999 survey of children with autistic spectrum disorder to provide more detailed information for this group.

- To examine the relationship between mental disorder and aspects of children's lives not covered in the previous national survey carried out in 1999, for example, medication, absence from school, empathy and social capital.

- To collect baseline information to enable identification of the protective and risk factors associated with the main categories of disorder and the precursors of personality disorder through future follow-up surveys.

- The surveyed population consisted of children and young people, aged 5–16, living in private households in Great Britain.

- Fieldwork for the survey took place between March and June 2004.

Concepts and methods (Chapter 2)

- This report uses the term 'mental disorders', as defined by the ICD-10, to imply a clinically recognisable set of symptoms or behaviour associated in most cases with considerable distress and substantial interference with personal functions.

- The assessment of mental disorder was based on both structured and open-ended questions. When definite symptoms were identified by the structured questions, interviewers used open-ended questions and supplementary prompts to get informants to describe the child's problems in their own words.

- Data collection included information gathered from parents, teachers and the young people themselves (if aged 11–16).

- A case vignette approach was used for analysing the survey data in which clinicians reviewed the responses to the precoded questions and the transcripts of informants' comments, particularly those which asked about the child's significant problems.

Sampling and survey procedures (Chapter 3)

- The sample was drawn from Child Benefit Records held by the Child Benefit Centre (CBC).

- 12,294 opt out letters were despatched by the Child Benefit Centre on behalf of ONS.

- After removing those addresses that opted out or were ineligible, 10,496 addresses were allocated to ONS interviewers.

- Information was collected for 76 per cent of the children approached, resulting in 7,977 achieved interviews.

- Among the co-operating families, almost all the parents and most of the children took part. Teacher questionnaires were obtained for 78 per cent of the children interviewed.

New topics in 2004 (Chapters 5–9)

Medication

The use of psychotropic drugs was largely confined to children with a hyperkinetic disorder of whom 43 per cent were taking some kind of medication, mainly Methylphenidate. Only seven per cent of the children with an emotional disorder and nine per cent of those with a conduct disorder were taking some form of medication and many of these had a hyperkinetic disorder as well. The very limited use of medication for children with non-hyperkinetic disorders suggests that clinicians are mainly using non-pharmacological approaches with these families.

Absence from school

Children with mental disorders were much more likely than other children to have had time off school: 17 per cent of those with emotional disorders, 14 per cent of those with conduct disorders and 11 per cent of those with hyperkinetic disorders had been away from school for over 15 days in the previous term. Among other children, the proportion was just 4 per cent. Children with mental disorders tended to have poorer general health than other children and at least some of these absences will have been health related. However, children with emotional disorders and those with conduct disorders were much more likely than other children to have had unauthorised absences and high proportions in all three disorder groups were thought by their teachers to have played truant at some time. As many as one in three children with a conduct disorder had been excluded from school and nearly a quarter had been excluded more than once.

Social aptitude

Parents were asked to assess the child's social aptitude to provide a measure of his or her ability to empathise with others (see Chapter 2). Children in all three of the main disorder groups had much lower scores than other children on this scale indicating poor ability to empathise. About a half (48 per cent) of those with emotional disorders, about two-thirds (69 per cent) of those with conduct disorders and over four-fifths (83 per cent) of those with hyperkinetic disorders scored in the bottom quartile.

Social networks and social support

The 2004 survey showed that the relationship between availability of social support and mental health, which is well established for adults, also existed for young people.

For example, 42 per cent of children with emotional disorders and 54 per cent of those with conduct or hyperkinetic disorders scored in the bottom quartile on a scale measuring the extent of the network of family and friends to whom the child felt close. Similarly, about one-fifth (22 per cent) of children with emotional disorders, one third (33 per cent) of those with conduct disorders and about one-half (44 per cent) of those with hyperkinetic disorders found it more difficult than average to keep friends compared with only 5 per cent of other children. Moreover, the parents of children with mental disorders were much more likely than other parents to express some reservations about their child's friends.

Prevalence of mental disorders[1] (Chapter 4)

Prevalence in 2004

- In 2004, one in ten children and young people (10 per cent) aged 5–16 had a clinically diagnosed mental disorder: 4 per cent had an emotional disorder (anxiety or depression), 6 per cent had a conduct disorder, 2 per cent had a hyperkinetic disorder, and 1 per cent had a less common disorder (including autism, tics, eating disorders and selective mutism). Some children (2 per cent) had more than one type of disorder (see Chapter 9).

Changes between 1999 and 2004

- There were no differences in prevalence between 1999 and 2004 in the overall proportions of children with a mental disorder.

- There were no changes between 1999 and 2004 in the prevalence of conduct or hyperkinetic disorders among children aged 5–15 as a whole. The only change that was statistically significant was a decrease in the proportion of boys aged 5–10 who had an emotional disorder, which declined from 3 per cent in 1999 to 2 per cent in 2004.

Socio-demographic variations in prevalence (2004)

- Boys were more likely to have a mental disorder than girls. Among 5- to 10-year- olds, 10 per cent of boys and 5 per cent of girls had a mental disorder. In the older age group (11- to 16-year-olds), the proportions were 13 per cent for boys and 10 per cent for girls.

- The prevalence of mental disorders was greater among children:

  - in lone parent (16 per cent) compared with two parent families (8 per cent);

  - in reconstituted families (14 per cent) compared with families containing no stepchildren (9 per cent);

  - whose interviewed parent had no educational qualifications (17 per cent) compared with those who had a degree level qualification (4 per cent);

  - in families with neither parent working (20 per cent) compared with those in which both parents worked (8 per cent);

  - in families with a gross weekly household income of less than £100 (16 per cent) compared with those with an income of £600 or more (5 per cent);

  - in households in which someone received disability benefit (24 per cent) compared with those that received no disability benefit (8 per cent);

  - in families where the household reference person was in a routine occupational group (15 per cent) compared with those with a reference person in the higher professional group (4 per cent);

  - living in the social or privately rented sector (17 per cent and 14 per cent) compared with those who owned accommodation (7 per cent); and

  - living in areas classed as 'hard pressed' (15 per cent) compared with areas classed as 'wealthy achievers' or 'urban prosperity' (6 per cent and 7 per cent).

---

1. *Prevalence rates are based on the ICD-10 Classification of Mental and Behavioural Disorders with strict impairment criteria – the disorder causing distress to the child or having a considerable impact on the child's day to day life.*

Children with emotional disorders (Chapter 5)

Demographic and socio-economic characteristics

- Children with emotional disorders were more likely than those with no emotional disorders to be girls (54 per cent compared with 49 per cent) and to be in the older age group, 11–16 (62 per cent compared with 46 per cent).

- The proportion of children with emotional disorders living with a widowed, divorced or separated lone parent was twice that among those with no such disorder (31 per cent compared with 15 per cent).

- Among children with generalised anxiety disorder, 19 per cent lived in a family containing stepchildren compared with 11 per cent among children with no emotional disorder.

- Children with emotional disorders were more likely than other children to have parents who had no educational qualifications (35 per cent compared with 20 per cent) and to live in low income families: 54 per cent lived in households with gross incomes under £300 per week compared with 33 per cent of other children.

- There was a fairly consistent pattern for children with separation anxiety to live in the poorest economic circumstances across a range of measures.

Child's general, physical and mental health

- The parents of children with an emotional disorder were more than four times as likely as other parents to say that their child's general health was fair or bad (23 per cent compared with 5 per cent) and a higher proportion reported that their child had a specific physical or developmental problem (72 per cent compared with 53 per cent).

- Over a quarter (27 per cent) of children with an emotional disorder also suffered from another of the main types of clinically recognisable mental disorder, most commonly conduct disorder.

Use of services

- In the year before interview, nearly three-quarters (73 per cent) of parents of children with an emotional disorder had sought some form of advice or help because of concerns about their child's mental health. Just under two-thirds (64 per cent) had contacted a professional source, usually a teacher (47 per cent).

Scholastic ability and attendance at school

- Over two-fifths (44 per cent) of children with an emotional disorder were behind in their intellectual development with 23 per cent 2 or more years behind, compared with 24 per cent and 9 per cent of other children.

- Children with an emotional disorder were twice as likely as other children to have special educational needs (35 per cent compared with 16 per cent).

- Children with an emotional disorder had more time off school than other children: 43 per cent had had more than 5 days absence and 17 per cent had had more than 15 days absence in the previous term. Among those with no disorder, these proportions were much lower (21 per cent and 4 per cent).

- Children with generalised anxiety disorder and those with depression had the most days away from school – a quarter had had more than 15 days absence in the previous term. These groups were much more likely than other children to be considered definite or possible truants (26 per cent and 33 per cent compared with 3 per cent among those with no disorder).

Social functioning of the family

- Parents of children with an emotional disorder were more than twice as likely as other parents to have a score on the General Health Questionnaire (GHQ-12) indicative of an emotional disorder (51 per cent compared with 23 per cent among other parents).

- One-third (33 per cent) of families containing children with an emotional disorder were assessed as having unhealthy functioning. Among other families, the proportion was 18 per cent.

- Over a half (55 per cent) of children with an emotional disorder had experienced their parents' separation and over a quarter (28 per cent) had a parent who had had a serious mental illness. For other children the proportions were 30 per cent and 7 per cent.

Child's social functioning

- Over a half (58 per cent) of parents of children with an emotional disorder rated their child in the lowest quartile on a scale measuring their strengths (that is, their positive attributes and behaviour). About a half (48 per cent) rated their child in the lowest quartile on a scale measuring their social aptitude.

- Parents of children with an emotional disorder were four times as likely as other parents to give a negative assessment when asked about their child's ability to make and keep friends: 35 per cent compared with 9 per cent said it was harder than average for their child to make friends and 22 per cent compared with 5 per cent said it was harder than average for him or her to keep friends.

Smoking, drinking and drug use

- Among young people aged 11–16, those with an emotional disorder were more likely to smoke, drink and use drugs than other children. The largest differences were for smoking and drug use. Among young people with an emotional disorder, 23 per cent were smokers and 20 per cent had taken drugs at some time. Among other young people, the proportions were 8 per cent for both.

Self-harm

- Among young people aged 11–16 who had an emotional disorder, 28 per cent said that they had tried to harm or kill themselves.

Children with conduct disorders (Chapter 6)

Demographic and socio-economic characteristics

- Children with a conduct disorder were more likely than other children to be boys (69 per cent compared with 50 per cent) and more likely to be in the older age group, 11–16 (55 per cent compared with 47 per cent).

- Among children with conduct disorders, the proportions living with cohabiting, single or previously married lone parents were higher than those among children with no such disorder (12 per cent compared with 8 per cent, 14 per cent compared with 7 per cent and 27 per cent compared with 15 per cent).

- Children with conduct disorders were more likely than other children to live in households containing a large number of children: 17 per cent lived in households containing 4 or more children compared with 10 per cent of children with no conduct disorder.

- Children with unsocialised conduct disorder were particularly likely to have a large number of siblings: 26 per cent lived in households containing 4 or more children.

- Children with conduct disorders were more likely than other children to have parents with no educational qualifications (39 per cent compared with 20 per cent) and to live in low-income families: 58 per cent of children with a conduct disorder lived in households with a gross weekly income of less than £300 compared with 33 per cent of other children.

- Children with unsocialised conduct disorder lived in the most economically disadvantaged circumstances, as indicated by a range of measures. Well over a half (57 per cent) had parents with no educational qualifications and nearly a third (31 per cent) lived in households which received a disability benefit.

Child's general, physical and mental health

- The parents of children with a conduct disorder were more than three times as likely as other parents to say that their child's general health was fair or bad (17 per cent compared with 5 per cent) and a higher proportion reported that their child had a specific physical or developmental problem (65 per cent compared with 53 per cent).

- About one-third (35 per cent) of children with a conduct disorder had another clinically recognisable disorder as well. This group was fairly evenly split between those who had an emotional disorder and those who had a hyperkinetic disorder.

Use of services

- In the year before interview, over three-quarters (81 per cent) of parents of children with a conduct disorder had sought some form of advice or help because of concerns about their child's mental health. The majority of these (76 per cent) had approached a professional source, most commonly a teacher (60 per cent) but substantial minorities had sought specialist advice, 28 per cent from a mental health specialist and 24 per cent from special educational services such as psychologists.

Scholastic ability and attendance at school

- 59 per cent of children with conduct disorders were rated as being behind with their schooling, with 36 per cent 2 or more years behind. For other children, these proportions were 24 per cent and 9 per cent.

- About a half (52 per cent) of children with conduct disorders were considered by their teachers to have special educational needs.

- Children with conduct disorders had more time away from school than other children: 42 per cent had had more than 5 days absence and 14 per cent had had more than 15 days absence in the previous term. Among those with no such disorder, these proportions were much lower, 21 per cent and 4 per cent.

- Nearly one-quarter (22 per cent) of children with a conduct disorder had possibly or certainly played truant. The corresponding proportion for other children was just 3 per cent.

- Absenteeism and truancy rates were particularly high among those with socialised conduct disorder: 87 per cent had been absent in the previous term; 55 per cent had had an unauthorised absence; and 55 per cent were considered by their teachers to be definite or possible truants.

- A third (33 per cent) of children with conduct disorders had been excluded from school at some time and nearly a quarter (22 per cent) had been excluded more than once. For children with no conduct disorder, these proportions were 2 per cent and 1 per cent.

- Among children with unsocialised or socialised conduct disorders, nearly a half (46 per cent and 48 per cent) had been excluded and over a quarter had been excluded more than once (27 per cent and 28 per cent).

Social functioning of the family

- Nearly a half (48 per cent) of the parents of children with conduct disorders had a score on the General Health Questionnaire (GHQ-12) indicative of an emotional disorder, twice the proportion among other parents (23 per cent).

- Children with conduct disorders were much more likely than other children to live in families classified as having unhealthy functioning (42 per cent compared with 17 per cent).

- Over a half (54 per cent) of children with conduct disorders had experienced their parents' separation compared with less than a third of those with no such disorder (30 per cent). There were also large differences in the proportions whose parents had experienced a major financial crisis (22 per cent and 13 per cent), who had been in trouble with the police (15 per cent and 5 per cent), or who had had a serious mental illness (17 per cent and 7 per cent).

- A fifth (21 per cent) of the parents of children with unsocialised conduct disorder had been in trouble with the police and a quarter (24 per cent) had had a serious mental illness.

Child's social functioning

- About three-quarters (77 per cent) of children with conduct disorders had scores in the bottom quartile on a scale measuring their strengths. About two thirds (69 per cent) had scores in the bottom quartile on a scale measuring their social aptitude.

- A quarter (24 per cent) of children with a conduct disorder found it harder than average to make friends and a third (33 per cent) found it harder than average to keep friends. The proportions for children with no conduct disorder were 9 per cent and 4 per cent.

- Children with unsocialised conduct disorders who tended to have solitary behaviour patterns, fared particularly badly on measures of friendship. About a half had difficulty making and keeping friends (47 per cent and 54 per cent).

Smoking, drinking and drug use

- Young people with conduct disorders were much more likely than other young people to smoke, drink and take drugs. As was the case with emotional disorders, the largest differences were in smoking and drug taking. Among those aged 11–16, 30 per cent of young people with conduct disorders were regular smokers and 28 per cent had taken drugs at some time. Among other young people, these proportions were 5 per cent and 8 per cent.

Self-harm

- Among young people aged 11–16 who had a conduct disorder, 21 per cent said that they had tried to harm or kill themselves.

Children with hyperkinetic disorders (Chapter 7)

Demographic and socio-economic characteristics

- Children with hyperkinetic disorders were predominantly boys (86 per cent compared with 50 per cent of other children) and almost all were white (97 per cent compared with 89 per cent of other children).

- Children with hyperkinetic disorders were more likely than other children to live with single or previously married lone parents (38 per cent compared with 24 per cent).

- Over a third (36 per cent) of children with hyperkinetic disorders had parents with no educational qualifications compared with about a fifth (21 per cent) of other children and over half (52 per cent) lived in households with a gross weekly income of less than £300 compared with a third (34 per cent) of other children.

- The proportions of children with hyperkinetic disorders living in a household in which no parent was working was over twice that among those with no such disorder (31 per cent compared with 14 per cent).

- Children with hyperkinetic disorders were more likely than other children to live in households in which someone received a disability benefit (27 per cent compared with 8 per cent).

Child's general, physical and mental health

- Parents of children with hyperkinetic disorders were more than twice as likely as other parents to report that their child's general health was fair or bad (18 per cent compared with 7 per cent). Just over two-thirds (70 per cent) reported that their child had a specific physical or developmental problem compared with just over a half (54 per cent) of other children.

- Two-thirds (66 per cent) of children with a hyperkinetic disorder also suffered from another of the main types of clinically diagnosed mental disorder, most commonly conduct disorder (62 per cent). One in eight (12 per cent) also had an emotional disorder.

Use of services

- Almost all (95 per cent) parents of children with hyperkinetic disorders had sought some form of help in the past year because of concerns about their child's mental health. Most (93 per cent) had contacted a professional source, usually a teacher (70 per cent).

Scholastic ability and attendance at school

- Almost two-thirds (65 per cent) of children with hyperkinetic disorders were rated as being behind in their overall scholastic ability and 18 per cent were three or more years behind, compared with 24 per cent and 4 per cent of other children.

- Children with hyperkinetic disorders were more than 4 times as likely as other children to have officially recognised special educational needs (71 per cent compared with 16 per cent).

- Children with hyperkinetic disorders were more likely than other children to have been absent from school for long periods: 11 per cent had missed more than fifteen days, compared with 5 per cent of other children.

Social functioning of the family

- Over two-fifths (43 per cent) of parents of children with hyperkinetic disorders had a score on the General Health Questionnaire (GHQ-12) indicative of an emotional disorder (compared with 24 per cent among other parents).

- Over one-third (36 per cent) of families containing children with a hyperkinetic disorder were assessed as having unhealthy family functioning. Among other families, the proportion was 18 per cent.

- Almost half (49 per cent) of children with hyperkinetic disorders had experienced their parents' separation and almost a quarter (23 per cent) had had a serious mental illness that required a stay in hospital. The proportions for other children were 31 per cent and 13 per cent.

Child's social functioning

- Over four-fifths (84 per cent) of the parents of children with hyperkinetic disorders rated their child in the lowest quartile

on a scale measuring strengths. A similar proportion of parents (83 per cent) rated their child in the lowest quartile on a scale measuring social aptitude.

- Almost a third (32 per cent) of children with hyperkinetic disorders found it harder than average to make friends and two-fifths (44 per cent) found it harder to keep friends.

- Young people aged 11–16, who had a hyperkinetic disorder were about twice as likely as other young people to have a score in the lowest quartile on a scale measuring social support (54 per cent compared with 28 per cent).

Smoking, drinking and drug use

- Young people with hyperkinetic disorders were more likely than other young people to smoke and take drugs. However, they were no more likely than other young people to drink alcohol. Among young people with a hyperkinetic disorder, 21 per cent were smokers and 23 per cent had taken drugs at some time. Among other young people 9 per cent were smokers and 8 per cent had taken drugs.

Self-harm

- Among young people aged 11–16 who had a hyperkinetic disorder, 18 per cent said they had tried to harm or kill themselves.

Children with autistic spectrum disorder (Chapter 8)

Demographic and socio-economic characteristics

- Children with autistic spectrum disorder were predominantly boys, 82 per cent.

- Unlike children with the more common disorders, autistic children tended to have more highly qualified parents than other children: 46 per cent had parents with qualifications above GCSE compared with 35 per cent of other children. Similarly, autistic children were slightly less likely to live in low income families: only 9 per cent compared with 20 per cent of other children lived in households with a gross weekly income of less than £200 per week.

- Autistic children were, however, similar to children with other types of disorder in that a relatively high proportion lived in families in which neither parent worked (30 per cent compared with 14 per cent of other children). The unusual combination of high educational status and low economic activity rate among the parents of autistic children probably reflects their heavy caring responsibilities.

- Over a half (56 per cent) of families containing autistic children were receiving a disability benefit.

Child's general, physical and mental health

- The parents of children with autistic spectrum disorder were much more likely than the parents of other children to say that their child's health was fair or bad (24 per cent compared with 7 per cent) and almost all the children had a physical or developmental problem as well (89 per cent compared with 54 per cent of other children).

- Just under one-third (30 per cent) of autistic children had another clinically recognisable mental disorder: 16 per cent had an emotional disorder, usually an anxiety disorder; and 19 per cent had an additional diagnosis of conduct disorder, often made on the basis of severely challenging behaviour.

Use of services

- Nine out of ten parents (89 per cent) of children with autistic spectrum disorder had sought help for their child's mental health problems and almost all of these had approached professional sources for advice (86 per cent).

Scholastic ability and attendance at school

- Autistic children were three times as likely as other children to be behind in terms of their scholastic ability (72 per cent compared with 24 per cent). Two-fifths (39 per cent) were more than two years behind.

- Almost all children with autistic spectrum disorder were reported to have special educational needs (97 per cent compared with 16 per cent of other children).

- Over a quarter (27 per cent) of autistic children had been excluded from school at some point and most of these (23 per cent overall) had been excluded on more than one occasion.

Social functioning of the family

- The parents of autistic children were almost twice as likely as other parents to have scores on the General Health Questionnaire (GHQ-12) indicative of an emotional disorder (44 per cent compared with 24 per cent).

- Autistic children were twice as likely as other children to live in families classified as having unhealthy functioning (37 per cent compared with 18 per cent).

Child's social functioning

- Almost all of the children with autistic spectrum disorder fell into the bottom quartiles on scales measuring strengths (96 per cent compared with 25 per cent of other children) and social aptitude (96 per cent compared with 24 per cent)

- Over two-thirds of autistic children found it harder than average to make and keep friends, 71 and 73 per cent compared with 10 and 5 per cent of other children. Two-fifths (42 per cent) had no friends whereas hardly any other children (1 per cent) were in this position.

Self-harm

- A quarter (25 per cent) of parents of autistic children reported that their child had tried to harm or kill themselves.

Children with multiple disorders (Chapter 9)

Prevalence of multiple disorders

- One in five of the children with a disorder were diagnosed with more than one of the main categories of mental disorder (emotional, conduct, hyperkinetic or less common disorders). This figure represents 1.9 per cent of all children.

- The most common combinations were conduct and emotional disorder and conduct and hyperkinetic disorder (0.7 per cent in each case).

Characteristics and behaviour patterns of children with multiple disorders

- Nearly three-quarters (72 per cent) of children with multiple disorders were boys reflecting the high proportion of children with conduct disorder in this group.

- About three-quarters (76 per cent) of children with multiple disorders had a physical or developmental problem as well compared with two-thirds (66 per cent) of those with a single disorder

- Almost all parents of children with multiple disorders had sought help with their child's mental health problems (96 per cent) and most had sought some form of professional advice (93 per cent).

- Nearly two-thirds (63 per cent) of children with multiple disorders were behind with their schooling and 40 per cent were more than a year behind. Among children with a single disorder, these proportions were 49 per cent and 27 per cent.

- Nearly four-fifths (88 per cent) of children with multiple disorders had scores in the bottom quartile on a scale measuring strengths compared with three-fifths (61 per cent) of those with a single disorder. The pattern for scores on an empathy scale was similar.

The six-month follow-up study (Chapters 3, 5–9)

- Samples of the children interviewed in the 1999 and 2004 surveys were followed up six months later by means of a postal questionnaire sent to their parents. The analysis compared the total symptoms, the disorder specific symptoms and the impact of the symptoms at the main interview and at follow-up.

- Over the six months between main survey and follow up, the gap between the children with a disorder and those with no disorder narrowed by 10–50 per cent but did not disappear. Improvement in disorder specific symptoms was most marked for children with an emotional disorder and least marked for children with an autistic spectrum disorder.

Background, aims and coverage of the survey

Chapter 1

Background

The survey of the mental health of children and young people living in private households in Great Britain 2004, is the second national survey on this topic carried out by ONS. It was commissioned by the Department of Health and the Scottish Executive Health Department.

The first survey, carried out in 1999, obtained information about the mental health of 10,500 young people living in private households in Great Britain. (Meltzer *et al*, 2000). The results from the 1999 survey highlighted the key public health significance of psychiatric disorders in childhood. Almost one in ten 5- to 15-year-olds were assessed as having a clinically recognisable mental disorder – with significant impact on the child's life and burden on the child's family (Meltzer *et al*, 2000). Longitudinal evidence has confirmed that many child psychiatric disorders persist, increasing risks for mental health problems and difficulties in social functioning well into adult life (Maughan, 2004).

Between 1999 and 2004, four additional mental health surveys were carried out by ONS focussing on particular groups of young people.

- Persistence, onset, risk factors and outcomes of childhood mental disorders (Meltzer *et al*, 2003a):
  - Fieldwork period: January 2002 to April 2002.
  - Achieved sample size: 2,587.

- The mental health of young people looked after by local authorities in England, (Meltzer *et al*, 2003b):
  - Fieldwork period: October 2001 to June 2002.
  - Achieved sample size: 1,038.

- The mental health of young people looked after by local authorities in Scotland, (Meltzer *et al*, 2004a):
  - Fieldwork period: October 2002 to June 2003.
  - Achieved sample size: 350.

- The mental health of young people looked after by local authorities in Wales (Meltzer *et al*, 2004b):
  - Fieldwork period: October 2002 to June 2003.
  - Achieved sample size: 150.

All these surveys represented the first tranche of studies whose aim was to describe the mental health of young people in Great Britain.

Aims of the 2004 survey

From a policy perspective, the 2004 private household survey was commissioned with a view to taking forward a number of key initiatives:

- To inform strategic service planning with health, social service and educational agencies.
- To examine protective as well as risk factors in relation to childhood mental disorders.
- To identify training and support requirements for parents, teachers and health and child welfare professionals.
- To monitor health inequality targets.
- To improve health outcomes of all children.

From a research perspective, the focus was on the extent to which the prevalence of the three common groups of childhood mental disorders changed over the five-year period between surveys, namely:

- Emotional problems involving anxiety, depression and obsessions.
- Conduct problems involving awkward and troublesome behaviour and aggressive and antisocial behaviours.
- Hyperactivity disorders involving inattention, impulsiveness and aggression.

Where there have not been substantial changes since the 1999 survey, data from the two surveys can be combined thereby increasing the sample size. With a larger sample, it is possible to examine the characteristics and behaviour of different subgroups of children within the main disorder categories.

The second survey in 2004 was also regarded as an opportunity to look more carefully and more systematically at the less common, childhood mental disorders and their co-morbidity with other disorders.

- Autistic spectrum (developmental) disorders.
- Tic disorders (motor and vocal tics).
- Eating disorders (anorexia nervosa and bulimia).

Protective and contextual factors were included for the first time in the 2004 survey relating to current governmental concerns on social inclusion and mental health improvement. These included questions measuring the child's resilience (for example, the extent of their social support networks), their ability to empathise with others and possible precursors of personality disorder. It was planned that the effectiveness of these factors would be determined by following up children interviewed in the main survey.

Other topics included for the first time in 2004 were:

- Medication commonly prescribed for childhood mental disorders.
- Services used by all children irrespective of psychopathology.
- Educational issues: number of schools attended, absences and exclusions.
- Deviant peer group pressure.

- Social context of drinking and smoking.
- Mental health of other children in the family.[1]

Review of previous research

A literature review of previous epidemiological research on childhood psychopathology up to the end of the 1990s was included in the report of the first survey (Meltzer et al, 2000). Therefore, the review of previous research included here focuses on cross-sectional studies which compare psychiatric morbidity among young people over two time periods.

Repeated, national, cross-sectional studies focussing on the childhood mental health problems are far rarer than prospective or longitudinal studies. The latter are essential for examining the course of psychiatric problems and investigating persistence of disorders. Cross-sectional studies at different points in time answer a different question – what is the stability of childhood psychopathology in the population across decades or generations?

Achenbach and Howell (1993) looked at whether the prevalence of children's behavioural or emotional problems changed significantly over a 13-year period. Problems reported by parents and teachers for a random sample of 7- to 16-year-olds assessed in 1989 were compared with those reported by parents for a 1976 sample and by teachers for a 1981/1982 sample. Parent reports were obtained with the Child Behaviour Checklist; teacher reports were obtained with the Teacher's Report Form. They found problem scores were higher in 1989 than in the earlier assessments. The changes were small and did not differ significantly by age, gender, socio-economic status or black/white ethnicity.

Achenbach, Dumenci and Rescorla (2003) carried out another assessment in 1999 in order to comment on changes to the mental health of children over a 23-year period. Thus, Child Behaviour Checklists (Achenbach and Edelbrock) were completed in home interviews by parents of 7- to 16-year-olds in 1976, 1989, and 1999. Problem scores increased from 1976 to 1989 and decreased in 1999 but remained higher than in 1976. For the 114 problem items that were common to the 1976, 1989, and 1999 assessments, the Q correlation was 0.98 between the mean scores on the 114 items in 1976 versus 1989 and was 0.94 between the mean scores on the 114 items in 1976 compared with 1999. This indicated very high stability in the rank ordering of item scores across intervals up to 23 years. For all children, the 1-year prevalence rate for mental health services use was 13.2 per cent in 1989 versus 12.8 per cent in 1999.

The 10-year time trends in competencies and problem scores in children and young people were assessed by Verhulst, van der Ende and Rietbergen (1997). Children and young people randomly selected from the Dutch general population in 1983 were assessed with the Child Behaviour Checklist and the Teacher's Report Form. Their problem scores and competence scores were compared with those obtained by the same method 10 years later. No significant differences were found between the 1983 and 1993 total problem scores obtained from parents or teachers. On the level of problem items and scales, a few differences indicating an increase in problems were found. However, the magnitude of these differences was very small. The researchers concluded that their results did not provide evidence for a clear secular increase in malfunctioning of Dutch children and young people.

More recently, Sourander et al, (2004) studied the differences in children's psychiatric symptoms and child mental health service use at two time points: 1989 and 1999. Two cross-sectional representative samples of 8- to 9-year-old children from southern Finland were compared. The 1989 sample consisted of 985 children, of whom 95 per cent participated, and the 1999 sample consisted of 962 children, of whom 86 per cent participated. Information was gathered from parents and teachers using Rutter's questionnaires and other related determinants of service use, and from children using the Child Depression Inventory (Kovacs, 1985).

The overall rate of children's problems assessed by parents did not increase during the ten-year period. Boys had fewer psychiatric symptoms in 1999 than in 1989, whereas no clear change had occurred in girls' symptoms, except that, according to parents, girls in 1999 had more hyperactive symptoms. However, children themselves reported more depressive symptoms in the 1999 than in the 1989 sample. In 1989, 2.3 per cent and in 1999, 5.3 per cent of children had used child mental health services. The increase in service use among girls was fourfold. Parents preferred to seek help for their children's problems from teachers, school nurses, and school psychologists rather than from specialised child psychiatric services.

They concluded that there has been an increase in mental health service use especially among girls as well as a convergence of symptom levels by gender.

All four studies above indicate that the **overall** rate of childhood psychopathology has not changed considerably since the 1970s although there may have been small changes in specific symptomatology.

---

1. *This data has not been analysed for this report.*

Timetable

Although the 2004 survey was the second national survey in Great Britain a considerable amount of feasibility and pilot work was required because of the development of the sections on the less common disorders (pervasive developmental disorder, tics and eating disorders). Not only were new sections extensively piloted in the general population, they were also tested on clinical samples owing to the rarity of the conditions.

Figure 1.1 summarises the timetable for whole programme of research.

Figure 1.1 Timetable for survey

From	To	Activity
April 2003	Oct. 2003	Survey development – sample design and questionnaire, MREC application, selection of primary sampling units, design pilot survey – questionnaire and field documents.
Oct. 2003	Apr 2004	Pilot survey – interviews completed, report written and debriefing carried out; design of mainstage questionnaire and field documents.
Apr. 2004	Jul. 2004	Mainstage interviewing
Jun. 2004	Sep. 2004	Clinical assessment of survey data
Sep. 2004	Mar. 2005	Analysis, interpretation and report writing of main survey.

Coverage of the survey

Region

The surveyed population comprised young people living in private households in England, Scotland (including the Highlands and Islands) and Wales.

Age

The survey focused on the prevalence of mental disorders among young people aged 5–16. (The 1999 survey had the same minimum age but a maximum age of 15 rather than 16.) Young adults, aged 17 and above were included in the national adult psychiatric surveys in 1993 and 2000 (Meltzer *et al*, 1994; Singleton *et al*, 2001). Children under the age of 5 were still excluded in 2004 primarily because the assessment instruments for these children are different and not so well developed as those for older children.

The feasibility study for the 1999 survey which took place in January to March 1997 included a questionnaire for parents of 3- and 4-year-olds. The questions were based on the Richman questionnaire revised by Nichol for a study of pre-school children (Nichol *et al*, 1987). Fifty-seven families of 3- to 4-year-olds were interviewed.

The data were presented in terms of case studies which highlighted the areas where parents expressed concern about their children: eating habits, potty training, bedtime, indoor play etc. Discussions of the report on the feasibility study by an expert group recommended that 3- and 4-year-olds should not be included in the main survey because of the problems in finding an appropriately sensitive instrument.

Childhood psychopathology

Though children and young people can be affected by many different mental health problems, most of these are rare. As in the original 1999 survey, the three common groups of disorders were covered:

- Emotional disorders such as anxiety, depression and obsessions.
- Conduct disorders characterised by awkward, troublesome, aggressive and antisocial behaviours.
- Hyperactivity disorders involving inattention and overactivity.

However, in 2004 a greater effort was made to assess the less common disorders, including:

- Autistic spectrum disorders.
- Vocal and motor tics.
- Eating disorders.

Additional questions were included in the survey to measure the precursors to personality disorder, the aim being to follow up children in future surveys so as to identify those who develop this disorder.

Content of the survey

A brief summary of the sections of the questionnaire is shown below, subsumed under the headings of questionnaire content for parents, children and teachers. The rationale behind using three sources of information is described in Chapter 2.

Questionnaire content for parents

The interview schedule for parents was asked of a parent of all selected children. It included the following sections:

Household composition and demographic characteristics

Details of child:

- General health.
- Social aptitudes.
- Friendships.
- Strengths and Difficulties Questionnaire (SDQ).
- Developmental disorders.
- Separation anxiety.
- Specific phobias.

- Social phobias.
- Panic attacks and agoraphobia.
- Post Traumatic Stress Disorder (PTSD).
- Compulsions and obsessions.
- Generalised anxiety.
- Depression.
- Attention and activity.
- Awkward and troublesome behaviour.
- Dieting, weight and body shape.
- Tics.
- Other concerns.
- Personality.
- Significant problems.
- Service use.
- Stressful life events.
- Education of young person.
- Strengths.

Details of interviewed parent/family:

- Education and employment (parent and partner).
- State Benefits.
- GHQ12 (Self-Completion).
- Family functioning (Self-Completion).

Questionnaire content for children and adolescents

Questions for children aged 11–16, by face-to-face interview, included the following topics:

- Strengths and Difficulties Questionnaire (SDQ).
- Separation anxiety.
- Specific Phobias.
- Social Phobia.
- Panic attacks and agoraphobia.
- Post Traumatic Stress Disorder (PTSD).
- Compulsions and Obsessions.
- Generalised Anxiety.
- Depression.
- Attention and activity.
- Awkward and troublesome behaviour.
- Dieting, Weight and Body shape.
- Less Common Disorders.
- Significant problems.
- Strengths.
- Social life (Neighbourhood, Trust , Care, Clubs).
- Social support.
- Educational attainment.
- Looked after by LA.

The self-completion element for the 11- to 16-year-olds included:

- Awkward and troublesome behaviour.
- Smoking cigarettes.
- Use of alcohol.
- Experience with drugs.

Questionnaire content for teachers

A postal questionnaire was sent to teachers covering scholastic achievement as well as assessments of behaviour and emotional well-being.

- Scholastic achievement and special needs.
- Strengths and Difficulties Questionnaire (SDQ).
- Emotions.
- Attention, activity and impulsiveness.
- Awkward and troublesome behaviour.
- Other concerns.
- Help from school.

Coverage of the report

One of the main purposes of this report is to examine the stability of the prevalence of mental disorders among children and young people aged 5–16 in Great Britain during the first half of 2004. Data for 1999 and 2004 are presented in Chapter 4.

In order to interpret these results, it is important to have an understanding of the concepts and methods adopted for this study; these are described in Chapter 2. Chapter 3 describes the sampling and interview procedures.

Each of the next three chapters focuses on a broad category of disorder: emotional disorders (Chapter 5), conduct disorders (Chapter 6) and hyperkinetic disorders (Chapter 7). Chapter 8 describes children with the less common disorders, in particular, autistic spectrum disorder and Chapter 9 presents a profile of those with multiple disorders. The last chapter provides selected analyses for Scotland.

The final part of the report contains the technical appendices and has five sections. The first gives details of the sampling design and shows how the data were weighted. The second section gives examples of standard errors from the prevalence tables. Section 3 describes the statistical terms used in the report and their interpretation. The last two sections comprise the survey documents and a glossary of terms.

Access to the data

Anonymised data from the survey will be lodged with the ESRC Data Archive, University of Essex, within three months of the publication of this report. Independent researchers who wish to carry out their own analyses should apply to the Archive for access (www.data-archive.ac.uk)

Notes and References

Achenbach T M, Dumenci L and Rescorla LA (2003) Are American children's problems still getting worse? A 23-year comparison. *J Abnorm Child Psychol.* **Feb, 31(1)**, 1–11.

Achenbach T M and Edelbrock C S (1983) *Manual for the Child Behaviour Checklist and Revised Child Behaviour Profile*, University of Vermont, Department of Psychiatry: Burlington, Vermont.

Achenbach T M and Howell C T (1993) Are American children's problems getting worse? A 13-year comparison. *J Am Acad Child Adolesc Psychiatry.* **Nov, 32(6)**, 1145–1154.

American Psychiatric Association (1994) *Diagnostic and Statistical Manual of Mental Disorders (4th edn)*, American Psychiatric Association: Washington, DC.

Kovacs M (1985) The Children's Depression Inventory (CDI). *Psychopharmocology Bulletin* **21**, 995–1124.

Maughan B (2004) 'Chapter 12, Mental Health' in *The health of children and young people*, http://www.statistics.gov.uk/Children/downloads/mental_health.pdf

Meltzer H, Gatward R, Corbin T, Goodman R and Ford T (2003a) *Persistence, onset, risk factors and outcomes of childhood mental disorders,* TSO: London.

Meltzer H, Gatward R, Corbin T, Goodman R and Ford T (2003b) *The mental health of young people looked after by local authorities in England,* TSO: London.

Meltzer H, Gatward R, Goodman R and Ford T (2000) *Mental health of children and adolescents in Great Britain*, TSO: London.

Meltzer H, Gill B, Petticrew M and Hinds K (1995) *The prevalence of psychiatric morbidity among adults living in private households*, OPCS Surveys of Psychiatric Morbidity in Great Britain, Report 1, HMSO: London.

Meltzer H, Lader D, Corbin T, Gooodman and Ford T (2004a) *The mental health of young people looked after by local authorities in Scotland*, TSO: London.

Meltzer H, Lader D, Corbin T, Gooodman and Ford T (2004b) *The mental health of young people looked after by local authorities in Wales*, TSO: London.

Nicol A R, Stretch D D, Fundundis T, Smith I and Davidson I (1987) The nature of mother and toddler problems – I Development of a multiple criterion screen. *J. Child Psychol. Psychiatry* **28**, 739–754.

Singleton N, Bumpstead R, O'Brien M, Lee A and Meltzer H (2001) *Psychiatric morbidity among adults living in private households,* 2000, TSO: London.

Sourander A, Santalahti P, Haavisto A, Piha J, IkAheimo K and Helenius H (2004) Have there been changes in children's psychiatric symptoms and mental health service use? A 10-year comparison from Finland. *J Am Acad Child Adolesc Psychiatry.* **Sep 43(9)**, 1134–1145.

Verhulst F C, van der Ende J and Rietbergen A (1997) Ten-year time trends of psychopathology in Dutch children and adolescents: no evidence for strong trends. *Acta Psychiatr Scand.* **Jul, 96(1)**, 7–13.

World Health Organisation (1993) *The ICD-10 classification of mental and behavioural disorders: diagnostic criteria for research*, World Health Organisation: Geneva.

Assessing mental disorders and their correlates

Chapter 2

Introduction

Estimates of the prevalence of psychiatric morbidity among young people depend on the choice of concepts as well as how they are operationalised. These, in turn, depend on the particular purposes and aims of the study. This point needs emphasising because it means that estimates from this survey will not necessarily be comparable with those obtained from other studies using different concepts, sampling designs, assessment instruments or analytic methods. However, estimates from this 2004 study can be directly compared with those from the 1999 survey as all the methodological components were identical.

Therefore, this chapter begins with a discussion about the use of the term, mental disorder, in relation to young people and how it is defined in this report. This is followed by a description of the advantages of gathering information from multiple informants (parent, teacher and child) within a one-phase interview strategy. The third section of the chapter looks at the validity and reliability of the screening and diagnostic instruments used in the survey with a brief review of their use nationally and internationally. The chapter ends with a description of how a clinical input was added to the interpretation of the survey data.

Definitions of mental disorder

The Health Advisory Committee report (1995) stated that it was important to define terms relating to the mental health of children and young people because the lack of terminological clarity can lead to confusion and uncertainty about the suffering involved, the treatability of problems and disorders and the need to allocate resources.

This survey report deliberately uses the term, mental disorder, as distinct from psychiatric disorders or mental health problems. However, this should not be taken to indicate that the problem is entirely within the child. Disorders arise for a variety of reasons, often interacting. In certain circumstances, a mental disorder, which describes a constellation or syndrome of features, may indicate the reactions of a young person to external circumstances, which, if changed, could largely resolve the problem.

Because the questionnaires used in this survey were based on ICD10 diagnostic research criteria, mental disorders are defined for this report to imply a clinically recognisable set of symptoms or behaviour associated in most cases with considerable distress and substantial interference with personal functions.

Instruments used for clinical assessments of psychiatric disorders often allow for several possible diagnoses to be made. Although it would be possible to impose a hierarchy among different disorders, the prevalence rates presented in subsequent chapters of this report do not have a hierarchy imposed on them. Thus children rated as having more than one disorder can be represented in several parts of a table. Nevertheless, the last section of Chapter 4 and Chapter 9 focus on the co-occurrences of childhood mental disorders.

Single versus multiple informants

While single-informant investigation characterised nearly all of the early epidemiological studies, more recent studies have broadened data collection to include information gathered from parents, teachers, and the subjects themselves. Hodges (1993) has pointed out that young people can respond to direct questions aimed at enquiring about their mental status and that there is no indication that asking these direct questions has any morbidity or mortality risks.

A well-established fact is that information from many sources is a better predictor of disorder than just one source. Many experienced clinicians and researchers in child psychiatry believe that information gleaned from multiple informants facilitates the best estimate of diagnosis in the individual case (Young et al, 1987). At the population level, information from multiple informants enhance the specificity of prevalence estimates.

Angold (1989) states:

"In general, parents often seem to have a limited knowledge of children's internal mental states and to report less in the way of depressive and anxiety symptoms than their children would report. On the other hand adults seem to be better informants about externalised or conduct disorder items such as fighting and disobedience. Teachers are good informants about school behaviour and performance, whilst parents are informative about home life."

Hodges (1993) comments that agreement between child and parent has varied depending on type of pathology:

"There appears to be more agreement for behavioural symptoms, moderate agreement for depressive symptoms, and poor agreement for anxiety"

One of the problems of collecting information from various sources is finding the best way to integrate the information which may show a lack of agreement. One method has been to accept a diagnosis irrespective of its source (Bird et al, 1992). Others have promoted 'case vignette' assessments where clinical judgements are made on detailed case histories from several sources. (Goodman et al, 1996)

Methods of assessing mental disorders

About half of the national surveys that have been carried out in other countries have used the multimethod-multiphase approach of Rutter et al (1970) to ascertain potential cases. In this approach, rating scales completed by children above a certain age and/or parents and/or teachers are used as first stage screening instruments. Subjects with scores above the cut-off score are identified as potential cases and further evaluated. A small sample of individuals with scores below the cut-off threshold are also selected for interview to assess the frequency of false negatives, i.e., those who have problems but whose rating scale scores were below the cut-off score.

In the second stage, children with scores above the cut-off score and a sample of those with scores below this value are interviewed using semi-structured or structured psychiatric interview instruments. At this stage categorical diagnoses are made. The overall prevalence of disorder is determined at the conclusion of this two-stage process.

The other method does not base caseness upon the multimethod-multiphase approach. All children and young people identified through the initial sampling procedure are eligible for diagnostic assessment. This approach was adopted in 1999 and was repeated in 2004. There are many advantages of such an approach:

- Detailed information is collected on all children. A sample distribution can be produced on all subscales even though only those with above-threshold score will have psychopathology.

- Because the survey aims to investigate service use, risk factors and protective factors, one needs to have information for all children to calculate relative risk.

- With the possibility of a longitudinal element in the survey, there is a large pool of children from which to select controls who could be matched on several characteristics to the children who exhibit significant psychiatric symptoms during the first interview stage.

- A one-stage design undoubtedly increases the overall response rate compared with a two-stage (screening plus clinical assessment) design.

- A one-stage design also reduces the burden put on respondents. Ideally, a two-stage design would require a screening questionnaire to be asked of a parent, a teacher as well as the child, followed up with an assessment interview administered to the child and the parent. A one-stage design only requires an interview with the parent and child and, if possible, the administration of a teacher questionnaire.

- A key advantage of a one-stage over a two-stage design is

that its implementation is cheaper and can be carried out in a far shorter time scale.

Screening instruments

The 1999 survey report (Meltzer et al 2000) included a review of the instruments commonly used for the first-stage, screening process in community-based studies of children: Goodman's Strengths and Difficulties Questionnaire, SDQ, (Goodman 1997) the Rutter Scales: A and B (Rutter et al, 1970) and the Child Behaviour Checklist (Achenbach and Edelbrock, 1983). The report also outlines the reasons for selecting the SDQ for the national survey in Great Britain.

The Strengths and Difficulties Questionnaire (SDQ) is a brief behavioural screening questionnaire that can be administered to the parents and teachers of 4- to 16-year-olds and also to 11- to 16-year-olds themselves. It covers common areas of emotional and behavioural difficulties, also enquiring whether the informant thinks that the child has a problem in these areas, and if so asking about resultant distress and social impairment.

Recent research on the Strengths and Difficulties Questionnaire (SDQ) is described in Appendix D.

Diagnostic instruments

Structured versus unstructured interviews

Hodges (1993) reviewed many structured interviews for assessing psychiatric morbidity among children: CAPA, CAS, DICA, DISC, ISC, K-SADS. She looked at their validity and reliability and what lessons had been learnt from their use. These were regarded as unsuitable for use in the GB studies because they required considerable clinical knowledge, were lengthy (some were estimated to last three to four hours) and were not validated for the whole age range covered here.

Therefore, the instrument used in the 2004 survey to produce the prevalence of clinically recognisable mental disorders among children was the Development and Well-Being Assessment (DAWBA). It was designed for use in the first national survey of childhood mental disorders in Great Britain in 1999. It was constructed in order to combine some of the best features of structured and semi-structured measures. Using existing semi-structured measures for a large national survey would have been impractical and prohibitively expensive since it would have required recruiting a team of several hundred clinically trained interviewers or providing prolonged additional training and supervision to lay interviewers. Therefore, it was clear that the main interview would need to be fully structured. However, we were aware at that time that the disadvantage of relying entirely upon existing structured interviews was that the results are far less clinically convincing than the results of surveys based on semi-structured interviewing To circumvent this problem, the new structured interview was supplemented with open-ended questions. When definite symptoms were identified by the structured questions, interviewers used open-ended questions and supplementary prompts to get parents to describe the problems in their own words. The specific prompts used were:

- Description of the problem.
- How often does the problem occur?
- How severe is the problem at it's worst?
- How long has it been going on for?
- Is the problem interfering with the child's quality of life? If so, how?
- Where appropriate, what does the parent/child think the problem is due to and what have they done about it?

Answers to these questions and any other information given were transcribed verbatim by the interviewers but not rated by them. Interviewers were also given the opportunity to make additional comments, where appropriate, on the respondents' understanding and motivation.

A small team of experienced clinicians reviewed the transcripts and interviewers' comments to ensure that the answers to structured questions were not misleading. The same clinical reviewers also considered clashes of information between different informants, deciding which account to prioritise. Furthermore, children with clinically relevant problems that did not quite meet the operationalised diagnostic criteria were assigned suitable diagnoses by the clinical raters.

In a study to test how well the DAWBA worked (Goodman et al, 2000), the questionnaire was administered to community (N = 491) and clinic (N = 39) samples. They found excellent discrimination between community and clinic samples in rates of diagnosed disorder. Within the community sample, subjects with and without diagnosed disorders differed markedly in external characteristics and prognosis. In the clinic sample, there was substantial agreement between DAWBA and case note diagnoses, though the DAWBA diagnosed more comorbid disorders. Overall, the DAWBA successfully combined the cheapness and simplicity of respondent-based measures with the clinical persuasiveness of investigator-based diagnoses.

Case vignettes in diagnostic assessment

One of the problems of collecting information from various sources is finding the best way to integrate the information which may show a lack of agreement. One method has been to accept a diagnosis irrespective of its source (Bird et al, 1992).

Others have promoted 'case vignette' assessments where clinical judgements are made on detailed case histories from several sources. (Goodman et al, 1996)

This case vignette approach for analysing survey data uses clinician ratings based on a review of all the information of each subject. This information includes not only the questionnaires and structured interviews but also any additional comments made by the interviewers, and the transcripts of informants' comments to open-ended questions particularly those which ask about the child's significant problems. The case vignette approach was extensively tested among community and clinical samples in the pre-pilot and pilot phases of the survey.

The clinical raters perform four major tasks. Firstly, they use the transcripts to check whether respondents appear to have understood the fully structured questions. This is particularly valuable for relatively unusual symptoms such as obsessions and compulsions – even when parents or young people say "yes" to items about such symptoms, their own description of the problem often makes it clear that they are not describing what a clinician would consider to be an obsession or compulsion.

Secondly, the clinical raters consider how to interpret conflicts of evidence between informants. Reviewing the transcripts and interviewers' comments often helps decide whose account to prioritise. Reviewing all of the evidence, it may be clear that one respondent gives a convincing account of symptoms, whereas the other respondent minimises all symptoms in a defensive way. Conversely, one respondent may clearly be exaggerating.

Thirdly, the clinical raters aim to catch those emotional, conduct and hyperactivity disorders that slip through the 'operationalised' net. When the child has a clinically significant problem that does not meet operationalised diagnostic criteria, the clinician can assign a 'not otherwise specified' diagnosis such as 'anxiety disorder, NOS' or 'disruptive behaviour disorder, NOS.'

Finally, the clinical raters rely primarily on the transcripts to diagnose less common disorders such as mutism, mania or schizophrenia. The relevant symptoms are so distinctive that respondents' descriptions are often unmistakable.

The following case vignettes from the pilot study provide illustrative examples of subjects where the clinical rating altered the diagnosis. In each case the 'computer-generated diagnosis' is the diagnosis arrived at by a computer algorithm based exclusively on the answers to fully structured questions. In these two illustrative instances, the computer-generated diagnoses were changed by the clinical raters.

Subject 1: overturning a computer-generated diagnosis. A 13-year-old boy was given a computer diagnosis of a specific phobia because he had a fear that resulted in significant distress and avoidance. In his open-ended description of the fear, he explained that boys from another school had threatened him on his way home on several occasions. Since then, he had been afraid of this gang and had taken a considerably longer route home every day in order to avoid them. The clinical rater judged his fear and avoidance to be appropriate responses to a realistic danger and not a phobia.

Subject 2: including a diagnosis not made by the computer. A 7-year-old girl fell just short of the computer algorithm's threshold for a diagnosis of ADHD because the teacher reported that the problems with restlessness and inattentiveness resulted in very little impairment in learning and peer relationships at school. A review of all the evidence showed that the girl had officially recognised special educational needs as a result of hyperactivity problems, could not concentrate in class for more than 2 minutes at a time even on activities she enjoyed, and had been offered a trial of medication. The clinician concluded that the teacher's report of minimal impairment was an understatement, allowing a clinical diagnosis of ADHD to be made.

Measurement of correlates of mental disorders

Risk and protective factors can be regarded as key correlates of childhood psychopathology. Rather than describing the construction of these analytical variables in each chapter (where a scale has been constructed from answers to several questions) they are listed here for reference purposes.

Physical complaints

To what extent are physical complaints more commonly found in children with mental disorders, and conversely, to what extent are mental disorders more prevalent among children with specific physical complaints? In order to answer these two questions the parent was asked to say "yes" if the child had the health problem or condition presented on three lists. No further information was gathered on their onset, severity or chronicity. When constructing the measure 'any physical disorder', positive responses to the mental health conditions in list two were omitted.

Asthma	Hyperactivity	Diabetes
Eczema	Behavioural problems	Obesity
Hay fever	Emotional problems	Cystic fibrosis
Glue ear or otitis media or grommets	Learning difficulties	Spina bifida
Bed wetting	Dyslexia	Kidney, urinary tract problems
Soiling pants	Cerebral palsy	Missing fingers, hands, arms, toes, feet or legs
Stomach or digestive problems or tummy pains	Migraine or severe headaches	Any stiffness or deformity of the foot, leg, fingers, arms or back
A heart problem	Chronic Fatigue Syndrome	Any muscle disease or weakness
Any blood disorder	Eye or sight problems	Any difficulty with co-ordination
Epilepsy	Speech or language problems	A condition present since birth such as club foot or cleft palate
Food allergy	Hearing problems	Cancer
Some other allergy		

Mental health of parent

The parent who was interviewed about the child's mental health, in most cases the mother, was also asked about her own mental health by means of the GHQ-12 (General Health Questionnaire, Goldberg and Williams, 1988). The GHQ-12 is a self administered screening test of twelve questions designed to detect non-psychotic psychiatric disorders in community settings.

1. Have you recently been able to concentrate on whatever you're doing?
2. Have you recently lost much sleep over worry?
3. Have you recently felt that you are playing a useful part in things?
4. Have you recently felt capable about making decisions about things?
5. Have you recently felt constantly under strain?
6. Have you recently felt you couldn't overcome your difficulties?
7. Have you recently been able to enjoy your day to day activities?
8. Have you recently been able to face up to your problems?
9. Have you recently been feeling unhappy or depressed?

10. Have you recently been losing confidence in yourself?

11. Have you recently been thinking of yourself as a worthless person?

12 Have you recently been feeling happy, all things considered?

Each item is scored with a 1 according to whether it applied more than usual (for a negative item) or less than usual (for a positive item). A score in the range of 0 (no problem) to 12 (severe problem) was calculated for each person. In the present survey the threshold score was set at 3, i.e. all those with a score of 3 or more were deemed to have screened positive for an emotional disorder.

Family functioning

The instrument used to estimate family functioning was the General Functioning Scale of the MacMaster Family Activity Device (FAD). It comprises 12 statements that parents rate on a four point scale: strongly agree, agree, disagree and strongly disagree. The scale has been shown to have good reliability, internal consistency and validity in distinguishing between non-clinical families and families attending a psychiatric service. (Miller *et al*, 1985; Byles *et al*, 1988; Fristad M A, 1989).

1. Planning family activities is difficult because we misunderstand each other.
2. In times of crisis we can turn to each other for support.
3. We can not talk to each other about the sadness we feel.
4. Individuals are accepted for what they are.
5. We avoid discussing our fears and concerns.
6. We can express feelings to each other.
7. There is lots of bad feeling in the family.
8. We feel accepted for what we are.
9. Making decisions is a problem for our family.
10. We are able to make decisions on how to solve problems.
11. We don't get along well together.
12. We confide in each other.

A scoring system was used to calculate 'healthy' or 'unhealthy' family functioning. First, the answer to each question was scored on a scale of 1–4. Questions 2, 4, 6, 8, 10 and 12 are 'positive' items and were scored as follows: strongly agree = 1, agree = 2, disagree = 3 and strongly disagree = 4. Questions 1, 3, 5, 7, 9 and 11 are 'negative' items and the scores were therefore reversed. The scores for all twelve questions were then summed and divided by 12 to get an average family functioning score for each respondent. If the respondent's average score was between 0 and 2 they were considered to

have 'healthy' family functioning and if their average score was above 2.01 they were considered to have 'unhealthy' family functioning.

Child's social aptitudes

Parents were asked to rate their children in terms of how they compared with other children of their age on the following abilities:[1]

1. Able to laugh around with others, for example accepting light-hearted teasing and responding appropriately.
2. Easy to chat with, even if it isn't on a topic that specially interests him/her.
3. Able to compromise and be flexible.
4. Finds the right thing to say or do in order to calm a tense or embarrassing situation.
5. Gracious when he/she doesn't win or get his/her own way. A good loser.
6. Other people feel at ease around him/her.
7. By reading between the lines of what people say, he/she can work out what they are really thinking and feeling.
8. After doing something wrong, he/she's able to say sorry and sort it out so that there are no hard feelings.
9. Can take the lead without others feeling they are being bossed about.
10. Aware of what is and isn't appropriate in different social situations.

Parents were asked to rate each item in terms of: (0) a lot worse than average, (1) a bit worse than average, (2) about average, (3) a bit better than average, (4) a lot better than average. A score in the range of 0–40 was calculated for each person by summing their responses to the ten items. These scores where then grouped into quartiles.

Child's social networks and social support

Adults who have extensive social networks or have people in whom they can confide are less likely to experience common mental disorders than those with less than three close friends or relatives or little or no social support (Brugha *et al*, 1993; Meltzer *et al*, 1995). To test whether these relationships exist for young people, questions on these topics were included in the 2004 survey. They were asked of young people aged 11–16.

Two sets of questions were asked to establish (a) the extent of the child's social networks, and (b) the child's support network. The latter questions were taken from the Health and Lifestyle Survey 1987 and were also asked in the Health Survey for England, 1992.

---

1. *This scale is copyright to Robert Goodman at the Institute of Psychiatry, London.*

- Questions about social networks

1. How many relatives in same household does child feel close to.
2. How many other relatives does child feel close to
3. How many friends would child describe as close or good friends.

The answer categories were 'None'(0), 'One'(1) and 'Two or more'(2).

- Statements about the availability of social support:

1. There are people I know who do things to make me feel happy.
2. There are people I know who make me feel loved.
3. There are people I know who can be relied on no matter what happens.
4. There are people I know who would see that I am taken care of if I need to be.
5. There are people I know who accept me just as I am.
6. There are people I know who make me feel an important part of their lives.
7. There are people I know who give me support and encouragement.

The answer categories for these questions were: 'Not true'(0), 'Partly true'(1) and 'Certainly true'(2).

Scores to the ten items were summed to create a scale ranging from 0–20, the total scores were then grouped into quartiles.

Child's strengths

Strengths may act as protective factors for young people in adverse circumstance, that is, factors or situations which are associated with increased odds of childhood mental disorder. Parents were asked to rate their children on two sets of 12 items, with response categories: (0) 'no', (1) 'a little', (2) 'a lot'.

1. Generous.
2. Lively.
3. Keen to learn.
4. Affectionate.
5. Reliable and responsible.
6. Easy-going.
7. Good fun, good sense of humour.
8. Interested in many things.
9. Caring, kind-hearted.
10. Bounces back quickly after set-backs.
11. Grateful, appreciative of what he/she gets.
12. Independent.

1. Helps around the home.
2. Gets on well with the rest of the family.
3. Does homework without needing to be reminded.
4. Creative activities: art, acting, music, making things.
5. Likes to be involved in family activities.
6. Takes care of his/her appearance.
7. Good at school work.
8. Polite.
9. Good at sports.
10. Helps keep his/her bedroom tidy.
11. Good with friends.
12. Well-behaved.

A score in the range of 0–48 was calculated for each person by summing their responses to the twenty-four items. These scores where then grouped into quartiles.

Young people aged 11–16 were also given the opportunity to rate what they thought were their own strengths on subsets of the above items, using the same response categories: (0) 'no', (1) 'a little', (2) 'a lot'.

1. Generous.
2. Out-going, sociable.
3. Nice personality.
4. Reliable and responsible.
5. Easy-going.
6. Good fun, good sense of humour.
7. Caring, kind-hearted.
8. Independent.

1. Good at sport.
2. Good with friends.
3. Helpful at home.
4. Good at music.
5. Well behaved.
6. Good with computers.
7. Good at drama, acting.
8. Raising money for charity, helping others.
9. Good at art, making things.
10. Polite.
11. Good at school work.

A score in the range of 0–38 was calculated for each young person by summing their responses to the nineteen items. These scores where then grouped into quartiles.

Stressful life events

Goodyer (1990) has suggested that moderately or highly undesirable recent life events exert potential or causal effects on the onset of emotional and behavioural symptoms in school aged children.

Parents were asked if their child experienced any of ten stressful life events with response categories (1) 'yes' and (2) 'no'. The items were chosen because they were thought to be highly (psychologically) threatening for the child.

1. Since child was born, parent had a separation due to marital difficulties or broken off a steady relationship.
2. Since child was born, parent (or partner) had a major financial crisis such as losing the equivalent to at least three months income.
3. Since child was born, parent (or partner) had a problem with the police involving a court appearance.
4. At some stage in the child's life, s/he had a serious illness which required a stay in hospital.
5. At any stage in the child's life, s/he had been in a serious accident or badly hurt in an accident.
6. At any stage in the child's life, a parent, brother or sister died.
7. At any stage in the child's life, a close friend died.
8. Since child was born, parent (or partner) had a serious physical illness such as cancer or a major heart attack.
9. Since child was born, parent (or partner) had a serious mental illness such as schizophrenia or major depression.
10. In the past year, close friendship has ended for child e.g. has broken off a steady relationship with a boy or girl friend or falling out with a best friend. *(applies if aged 13 or above)*
11. In the past year, close friendship has ended for child e.g. falling out with a best friend. *(applies if aged under 13)*

In the 1999 survey items 8 and 9 referred to the death of a grandparent and the death of a pet. Analysis of the 1999 data showed that these two life events lacked predictive power so in 2004 they were omitted and replaced with two events that seemed more likely to have a significant impact on the child's emotional wellbeing.

A stressful life event score in the range of 0–10 was calculated for each respondent by summing their responses to the 10 items.

Self-harm

Questions on self-harm were asked of all parents and young people aged 11–16. Different questions were asked depending on whether or not the child was feeling depressed, irritable or showing a lack of interest.

Parents of all children/children aged 11–16 who were feeling depressed, irritable or showing a lack of interest:

Over the whole of (child's) lifetime, has (child) ever tried to harm or kill him/herself?

During the period when (child) was sad, irritable or lacking in interest, did (child) ever try to harm or kill him/herself?

Other parents/other children aged 11–16:

Over the whole of (child's) lifetime, has (child) ever tried to harm or hurt him/herself?

During the last 4 weeks, has (child) ever try to harm or hurt him/herself?

Parents and children who answered 'Yes' to any of the above questions were counted as having harmed themselves. The questions do not distinguish between self-harm with the intention of taking one's life and that carried out for other reasons, such as self-mutilation.

Notes and References

Achenbach T M and Edelbrock C S (1983) *Manual for the Child Behaviour Checklist and Revised Child Behaviour Profile,* University of Vermont, Department of Psychiatry: Burlington, Vermont.

Angold A (1989) Structured assessments of psychopathology in children and adolescents, in Thompson C (ed), *The Instruments of Psychiatric Research,* John Wiley & Sons Ltd.

Bird H R, Gould M S and Staghezza B (1992) Aggregating data from multiple informants in child psychiatry epidemiological research. *J. Am. Acad. Child Adol. Psychiatry* **31**, 78–85.

Brugha T S, Wing J K, Brewin C R, MacCarthy B and lesage A (1993) The relationship of social network deficits with deficits in social functioningin long-term psychiatric disorders. *Social Psychiatry and Psychiatric Epidemiology* **28**, 218–224.

Breeze E *et al* (1987) *Health Survey for England,* Her Majesty's Stationery Office: London.

Byles J, Byrne C, Boyle M H and Offord D R (1988) Ontario Child Health Study: Reliability and validity of the General Functioning Scale of the MacMaster Family Assessment Device. *Family Process* **30(1)**, 116–23.

Cox BD *et al* (1987). *Health and Lifestyle Survey,* Health Promotion Research Trust: London.

Goodman R (1997) The Strengths and Difficulties Questionnaire: A research note. *Journal of Child Psychology and Psychiatry* **38**, 581–586.

Goodman R, Yude C, Richards H and Taylor E (1996) Rating child psychiatric caseness from detailed case histories. *Journal of Child Psychology and Psychiatry* **37**, 369–379.

Goodyer I M, Wright C and Altham P M E (1990) The Friendships and Recent Life Events of Anxious and Depressed School-Age-Children. *British Journal of Psychiatry* **156 (May)**, 689–698.

Fristad M A (1989) A comparison of the MacMaster and circumplex family assessment instruments. *Journal of Marital and Family Therapy* **15**, 259–269.

Hodges K (1993) Structured Interviews for Assessing Children. *J. Child Psychol.* **34**, 49–68.

Meltzer H and Gatward R (2000) *The mental health of children and adolescents in Great Britain,* TSO: London.

Meltzer H, Gill B, Petticrew M and Hinds K (1995) *Economic activity and social functioning of adults with psychiatric disorders*, OPCS Surveys of Psychiatric Morbidity in Great Britain, Report 3, HMSO: London.

Miller I W, Epstein N B, Bishop D S and Keitner G I (1985) The MacMaster Family Assessment Device: reliability and Validity. *Journal of Marital and Family Therapy* **11**, 345–356.

Rutter M, Tizard J and Whitmore K (1970) *Education, health and behaviour*, Longmans: London.

Young J G, O'Brien J D, Gutterman E M and Cohen P (1987) Research on the clinical interview. *J. Am. Acad. Child Adol. Psychiatry* **26**, *5*, 613–620.

Sampling and survey procedures

Chapter 3

Introduction

This chapter describes the main features of the survey methodology: the sample design, operational procedures and response.

Sample design

The sample design was essentially the same as that used in the 1999 survey. The main difference was that the 2004 survey covered children aged 5–16 while the 1999 survey had a cut-off at age 15. The sample was drawn from Child Benefit records held by the Department for Work and Pensions' Child Benefit Centre (CBC). The use of centralised records as a sampling frame was preferred to the alternative designs of carrying out a large scale postal sift of the general population or sampling through schools. The design used enabled direct access to parents, which would not have been possible with a school-based sample, and it was more efficient than a sift.

The sample design consisted of a sample of postal sectors and, within these, a sample of addresses. The postal sectors were selected by ONS. In order to preserve the confidentiality of the respondents, the CBC selected the addresses following ONS instructions and then despatched a letter on behalf of ONS to each selected household explaining the purpose of the survey and giving parents an opportunity to opt-out.

There are some minor limitations to the use of Child Benefit records as a sampling frame. Over 98 per cent of the records have postcodes attributed to addresses. The DWP had no evidence that records with postcodes were different from those without. The addresses with missing postcodes probably represent a mixture of people who did not know their postcode at the time of applying for Child Benefit or simply forgot to enter the details on the form. There may be other factors which differentiate between households with and without postcoded addresses but, because these factors are not known, we do not know whether any biases have been introduced by omitting the non-postcoded addresses.

We also excluded from the original sampling frame those cases where 'action' was being invoked by the CBC, for example, because of the death of the child, a change of address, or the case was considered sensitive. These are simply administrative actions as distinct from some legal process concerning the child and hence should not bias the sample in any way.

The planned sample consisted of 29 children in each of 426 postal sectors. However, five of the postal sectors contained fewer than 29 families with children in the required age range.

In these sectors, all the eligible households were selected. These 'small' sectors gave an overall shortfall of 60 families. Therefore, the set sample consisted of 12,294 families.

The interviews

The first stage of the fieldwork was a face-to-face interview with the parent, which included a five minute self-completion component (GHQ-12 and Family Functioning Scale). If the parent had difficulties with the English language, a special two page self-completion questionnaire containing the Strengths and Difficulties Questionnaire was available in 40 languages as a replacement.

After the parent interview, permission was sought to ask questions of the sampled child if they were aged 11–16. These children then had a face-to-face interview and entered details of their smoking, drinking and drug-taking experiences via a self-completion questionnaire on a laptop. The subject matter was considered to be too complicated for younger children.

When the parent and, if appropriate, child interviews were completed, parents were asked for written consent to contact the child's teacher. Parents were asked to nominate the teacher who they felt knew the child best. Consent was only requested if an interview had been achieved with the parent (including cases where the parent completed the translated version of the questionnaire only). Contact names for teachers were still sought if the child had been expelled or excluded from school within the last few months.

Most of the psychiatric assessment was designed for children with a mental and language age of at least 3 or 4, and was therefore unsuitable for assessing children who are functioning below this level. (Also, it is distressing to parents of these children to be asked lots of questions that are inappropriate to someone of their child's ability level.) Consequently, the parent interview was adjusted so that when the initial questioning revealed that a child was severely disabled, parents were only asked those parts of the psychiatric interview that would be appropriate, for example, the section on developmental difficulties including autistic spectrum difficulties. No suitable teacher questionnaire was available for this group, and therefore teachers were not approached if the child was severely disabled.

Survey response rates

Table 3.1 shows the response among parents and children. Table 3.2 shows the response among teachers.

Table **3.1**

Final response: Parents and children

	Number	Per cent of all cases	Per cent of cases approached
Set Sample	**12,294**	**100**	
Not approached for interview			
Opt-outs	1,085	9	
Moved no trace	631	5	
Ineligible	82	1	
All not approached	1,798	15	
Approached for interview	**10,496**	**85**	**100**
Refusals			
Refusal to ONS HQ	401	3	4
Refusal to interviewer	1,733	14	17
Other (language/comprehension difficulties / ill health)	49	0	0
All refusals	**2,183**	**18**	**21**
Non-contact	**313**	**3**	**3**
Interviews achieved[1]			
Adult and child	3,344	27	32
Adult only (child under 11)	3,834	31	37
Adult only (child refused/unable to be interviewed)	579	5	6
Other partial interviews	221	2	2
All interviews	**7,977**	**65**	**76**

1. Due to missing information we were unable to produce disorder classifications for 23 cases.

Families not approached for interview

Of the 12,294 sampled families 9 per cent contacted ONS via a freephone number to opt-out. This group includes parents who telephoned the DWP to opt-out, as well as those who were considered by DWP to have sensitive circumstances and for whom an interview for this study was judged inappropriate. This proportion is higher than that recorded in the 1999 survey (6 per cent).

A further 5 per cent of the sample had moved and could not be traced. It had been hoped that the accuracy of the Child Benefit Register (CBR) would have been improved due to recent work to link claimants receiving different benefits. However, the proportion with untraceable addresses was actually slightly higher than in 1999 (4 per cent). A small number of sampled families were ineligible because the child was in foster care, outside the age criteria of 5–16, had died, or

the family had emigrated. Therefore, just under 10,500 addresses were allocated to interviewers.

Parents and children

Information was collected from up to three sources (parents, children and teachers) on 76 per cent of the 10,496 families approached for interview, resulting in 8,000 achieved interviews. However, these included 23 cases for whom there was insufficient information for a diagnostic classification so the analysis is based on 7,977 cases.

Among the co-operating families, almost all the parents and most of the children (93 per cent) took part and the great majority provided full information (97 per cent). The information from the remaining 3 per cent was usable although incomplete. They include the following situations:

- The parent completed a full interview but the child only completed a part of the interview due to difficulties in comprehension.
- The parent completed a translated SDQ questionnaire – with either a child interview, a teacher questionnaire or both.
- The parent completed the assessment part of the interview but chose to terminate the interview before the remainder was complete.
- The interview was terminated very early because the child was severely disabled, therefore making the interview inappropriate.

Refusals

Of the 10,496 families approached for interview, 3 per cent contacted ONS headquarters to say that they did not wish to participate and 14 per cent refused to take part when the interviewer called. Many of the refusals to ONS headquarters were from parents who claimed that they had not received the opt-out letter from the DWP but would certainly have opted-out if they had. There were also a number of cases where the parent called the field office claiming that they had opted-out but were contacted by an interviewer anyway. It is therefore likely that the true number of opt-outs is greater than the 9 per cent stated in Table 3.1.

A small number of respondents (less than 1 per cent) could not be interviewed because they had learning or language difficulties. The SDQ questionnaire had been translated into 40 different languages but this still did not cover all those required and could not be used by respondents who were not literate in their own language.

Teachers

Before the teachers' questionnaires were posted out, various steps were taken to maximise response:

- A paragraph describing the survey was inserted into a journal which goes to all teachers.
- Chief Education Officers were notified of the plans for the survey and the extent of teachers' involvement.
- A week before any postal questionnaires were sent out, the head teachers in all schools of the sampled children were notified that some of their teachers would be asked to complete a questionnaire.
- The sample was designed so that most teachers would not have to fill in more than two questionnaires.
- A reminder letter was sent two weeks after the initial mail out.

Table 3.2

Final response: Teachers

	Number	Per cent of all interviews	Per cent of all teachers contacted
All interviews	7,977	100	
Parental consent not sought	36	1	
Parental consent sought	7,965	99	
Parental consent received	7,521	94	100
Questionnaire Returned	6,236	78	83

The majority of parents interviewed (94 per cent) gave consent for their child's teacher to be contacted and only 5 per cent refused. Consent to the teacher questionnaire was not sought for children who did not attend school or any other educational institution (1 per cent) and for children for whom the parent interview was incomplete (0.5 per cent).

Of the 7,521 teachers contacted 83 per cent returned a completed questionnaire. Teacher information was therefore available for 78 per cent of all interviews. Within the past year, teachers have become more limited in the amount of administrative work which their contracts permit them to do. Comments from head teachers indicated that this is the reason why some teachers did not complete the questionnaire. In these circumstances, the response achieved was very high.

Interviewing procedures

Choice of parent to interview

In over 95 per cent of interviews, the parent interview was carried out with the mother as she tended to be available when the interviewer called. In some of the cases where the father was interviewed, the mother did not speak sufficient English to cope with the interview. The remainder were lone fathers or situations where the father was more accessible than the mother.

Interview length

The length of the parent's interview was highly variable, with most interviews ranging from 90 to 120 minutes. On average, the young person's interview lasted around 45 minutes.

Privacy

It was very important for parents and children to be interviewed alone. A technique successfully used by interviewers when parents refused to leave the room when their child was being interviewed, was to sit side by side with the child, reading out the questions but then asking the child to key in their own answers into the laptop computer.

Self-completion using laptop computers was particularly useful for questions addressed to children about awkward and troublesome behaviour, smoking, drinking and drug taking. However, the previous ONS Survey of Childhood Mental Disorders found that the usage of all types of substance use and abuse was under-reported compared with the national surveys of smoking and drinking carried out by group administration in school settings (Goddard and Higgins, 1999a; Goddard and Higgins, 1999b).

Follow-up study

Background and aims

A follow-up procedure using a self-completion postal questionnaire was incorporated into the study to examine the persistence or chronicity of disorders at about 6 months after the main interview.

The strength of follow up surveys is "that they allow a focus on chronic or persistent psychiatric disorders…. This is potentially important because a high proportion of otherwise normal children exhibit transient disorders at some time during their development" (Rutter, 1989). Emotional and behavioural problems which resolve rapidly and spontaneously are far less relevant for service planning than problems that persist unless help is provided.

A prospective approach to determine the prevalence of persistent disorders, asking parents on two separate occasions about symptoms and resultant impairments was regarded as preferable to asking them to recall how long symptoms (and resultant impairments) had been present at the time of interview.

Sampling strategy

The sample was selected from parents who had agreed to recall (96 per cent overall). The parents of all children who were diagnosed with a disorder at the main interview and who had agreed to recall (705 cases and a sample of those whose child had no disorder (926 cases) were allocated for follow up.

Content of interview

The self-completion questionnaire designed for the follow-up survey included a repeat of the two-sided Strengths and Difficulties Questionnaire (SDQ) and a question asking about any help or advice about the child's behaviour and emotions that had been received from professional or informal sources over the last six months.

Response to the follow up procedures

In order to increase response, three reminder letters with replacement copies of the questionnaire were sent to non-respondents. Overall, 72 per cent of the parents approached returned a completed questionnaire. The response rate among those whose child had a disorder, 66 per cent was lower than that among other parents, 77 per cent.   (Table 3.3)

Table **3.3**

Response to follow-up survey

	Questionnaires sent out	Questionnaires returned	Response rate
Children with a disorder	705	465	66%
Children with no disorder	926	709	77%
All children	**1,631**	**1,174**	**72%**

Analysis and results

For the analysis, data from the 2004 follow-up survey were combined with data from the 6 month follow-up to the 1999 survey (Meltzer). The research design of the latter was different to that of the 2004 follow-up. A random sample of one in three parents who had agreed to recall were asked to complete an SDQ and questionnaires were also sent to their children and a subsample of teachers. This means that the sample for the 1999 follow-up was larger than that of the 2004 survey but it contained a much lower proportion of children with a disorder.

The findings for children in each disorder category and for those with multiple disorders are presented at the end of the chapter pertaining to the disorder (Chapters 5–9). The graphs show the total symptoms, the disorder specific symptoms and the impact of the symptoms at the main interview and at follow-up. In general, the level of symptoms and impact was low for the children who did not have a disorder initially, and this low level was maintained over the next six months. By contrast, the level of symptoms and impact was high for the children who did initially have a disorder. Over the following 6 months, this gap between them and the children without a disorder narrowed by 10–50 per cent but did not disappear. Improvement in disorder specific symptoms was most marked for children with an emotional disorder and least marked for children with an autistic spectrum disorder.

References

Goddard E and Higgins V (1999a) *Smoking, drinking and drug use among teenagers, Volume 1, England*, TSO: London.

Goddard E and Higgins V (1999b) *Smoking, drinking and drug use among teenagers, Volume 2*, Scotland, TSO: London.

Meltzer H and Gatward R (2000) Appendix D in *The mental health of children and adolescents in Great Britain*, TSO: London.

Rutter M (1989) *Isle of Wight Revisited: Twenty five years of Child Psychiatric Epidemiology*, American Academy of Child and Adolescent Psychiatry.

Prevalence of
mental disorders

Chapter 4

Introduction

This chapter describes the prevalence of mental disorders among children and young people aged 5–16 in 2004 and examines any changes in the prevalence of childhood psychopathology since the previous ONS survey in 1999.

The first set of tables show four broad categories of childhood mental disorder and the subgroups within them, analysed by age and sex. The remaining tables show rates for the main categories only, analysed by other socio-demographic variables such as economic status and area classification. The last two tables show the results of modelling analyses to determine the significant factors associated with each of the main types of disorder.

Prevalence was based on a clinical evaluation of parent, child and teacher data collected by ONS interviewers from questionnaires designed by the Department of Child and Adolescent Psychiatry, Institute of Psychiatry, London. Chapter 2 describes the assessment process in detail and the questionnaires are reproduced in Appendix E.

Prevalence rates for all disorders are presented in the tables as percentages to one decimal point so that rates per thousand can be derived. The percentages in the text and figures which refer to numbers in the tables are usually rounded to the nearest integer. Sampling errors around these estimates are shown in Appendix C.

The figures in the tables are weighted to represent the age, sex and region structure of the total population and to correct for unequal sampling probabilities. They are also adjusted to account for missing teacher data. The weighting and adjustment procedures are described in Appendix A.

Prevalence of mental disorders by personal characteristics

In 2004, one in ten children and young people (10 per cent) aged 5–16 had a clinically diagnosed mental disorder. These include: 4 per cent with an emotional disorder (3 per cent anxiety disorders and 1 per cent depression), 6 per cent with a conduct disorder, 2 per cent with a hyperkinetic disorder, and 1 per cent with a less common disorder (including autism, tics, eating disorders and mutism). Some children had more than one type of disorder. (Table 4.1)

Sex and Age

Boys were more likely than girls to have a mental disorder (11 per cent compared with 8 per cent). While boys were more

likely than girls to have a conduct disorder (8 per cent compared with 4 per cent), or a hyperkinetic disorder (3 per cent compared with 0.4 per cent), they were slightly less likely than girls to have an emotional disorder (3 per cent compared with 4 per cent). (Figure 4.1 and Table 4.1)

Overall, older children were more likely than younger children to have a mental disorder (12 per cent compared with 8 per cent). This variation was apparent for emotional (5 per cent and 2 per cent) and conduct disorders (7 per cent and 5 per cent) but there was no difference between older and younger children in the proportions with hyperkinetic and less common disorders. (Figure 4.1 and Table 4.1)

Figure 4.1
Prevalence of any mental disorder by age and sex, 2004

Great Britain

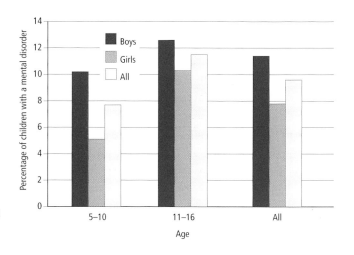

Changes in prevalence between 1999 and 2004 by sex and age

Table 4.2 shows prevalence rates for the three main disorder categories in 1999 and 2004 analysed by age and sex. Tables 4.3–4.5 show trends for the subcategories of these disorders. The tables refer to children aged 5–15 as 16-year-olds were not included in the 1999 survey. Therefore, the rates differ slightly from those presented in Table 4.1.

Data are not shown for the less common disorders because different questions were used to identify them in the two surveys and the prevalence figures are therefore not comparable. In 2004, more detailed questions were included to identify children with an Autistic Spectrum Disorder (ASD).[1] This change affects the prevalence rates for both the 'common' disorders (emotional, conduct and hyperkinetic) and those for the less common disorders which include ASD. To understand

---

1. *More detailed questioning was also used to diagnose tics and eating disorders but the additional number of children identified in 2004 was very small.*

the way that the more detailed questioning about ASDs in 2004 will have affected comparability with the 1999 results, it is worth thinking about four different groups of children with ASDs:

Group 1

These children would only have been diagnosed as having a common disorder in 1999, and this would switch in 2004 to only being diagnosed as having an ASD. For example, in 1999 they might have been diagnosed as having hyperkinesis, whereas in 2004 they might have been diagnosed as having autism. This happens because, in the international diagnostic systems, ASD takes precedence over all hyperkinesis diagnoses and some behavioural and emotional diagnoses. *Such children would lead to lower rates of common disorders in 2004 than 1999*, but would not affect rates of total disorder (because the child would obtain a diagnosis, albeit a different one, in both 1999 and 2004).

Group 2

These children would only have been diagnosed as having a common disorder in 1999, but would have been diagnosed as having *both* a common disorder and an ASD in 2004. For example, in 1999 they might just have been diagnosed as having depression, whereas in 2004 they might have been diagnosed as having depression and autism. (This combination is permitted by the international classifications.) Such children would not lead to any difference between 1999 and 2004 in the apparent prevalence of either common disorders or total disorders (because the child would only be counted once in the overall prevalence rate for total disorders whether they have one or two disorders).

Group 3

These children would not have received any diagnosis in 1999, but would have been diagnosed as having just an ASD in 2004 on the basis of the expanded interview. *Such children would lead to a higher rate of total disorders in 2004 than 1999*, but would not affect rates for the common disorders.

Group 4

These children would have received a diagnosis of an ASD (and nothing else) both in 1999 in 2004, reflecting symptoms that were sufficiently marked that the ASD was diagnosable even with the more restricted questioning used in 1999. Such children would not lead to any difference between 1999 and 2004 in the apparent prevalence of either common disorders or total disorders.

We cannot therefore produce totals with 'Any mental disorder'

that are strictly comparable in the two years. For the trend tables, we have provided two overall total figures. The first represents the proportion with an emotional, conduct or hyperkinetic disorder (i.e. excluding less common disorders). The 2004 figure will understate the proportion compared with 1999 because of the transfer of some children with common disorders to the ASD subgroup within the less common disorder category in 2004 (Group 1 above). This comparison does not show a statistically significant difference between 1999 and 2004 in the proportions with an emotional, conduct or hyperkinetic disorder (9.1 per cent and 8.7 per cent). To be absolutely comparable with 1999, the 2004 figure would be a little higher than 8.7 per cent so the actual difference is even smaller. Therefore, it is very unlikely that there was a change in the overall prevalence of the three main categories of disorder between 1999 and 2004.

The second total is the proportion with any disorder. In this case, the 2004 figure (9.6 per cent) overstates the proportion compared with 1999 (9.5 per cent) because of the additional children with ASD who were identified through the more extensive questioning (Group 3 above). The difference was not statistically significant. Thus, again, it is very unlikely that there was a change between 1999 and 2004 in the overall proportions of children with any mental disorder.

To summarise, there was not a statistically significant change in the rates either of common disorders or total disorders over the 5 years between 1999 and 2004. The small (statistically non-significant) changes that did occur were in opposite directions, namely an increase in total disorders but a decrease in common disorders – changes that can most straightforwardly be explained by increased detection of ASDs in 2004 as a result of improvements to the 2004 interview. Research by Collishaw *et al* (2004) indicates that rates of mental health problems among young people probably rose markedly between 1974 and 1999. The data presented here suggest that this upward trend was halted in the period between the 1999 and 2004 surveys.

Turning to the main categories of disorder, there were no changes between 1999 and 2004 in the prevalence of conduct or hyperkinetic disorders among children aged 5–15 as a whole. The only change that was statistically significant was a decrease in the proportion of boys aged 5–10 who had an emotional disorder which declined from 3 per cent in 1999 to 2 per cent in 2004. There was a corresponding decrease among girls of this age but the difference was not statistically significant. Table 4.3 shows that the decrease in emotional disorders among younger boys was attributable to a decrease in the proportion with anxiety disorders, particularly separation anxiety. There are no clinical reasons for expecting such a decrease and the diagnostic classification method was the same in both years. However, the questions on anxiety disorders were positioned later in the interview in 2004 and this may have affected the reporting rate.   (Tables 4.2–4.5)

In general, prevalence rates in 2004 showed similar patterns of variation with socio-demographic variables as those in 1999. Any differences are noted in the commentary.

Ethnicity

Ethnic differences are difficult to interpret because of the small numbers of minority ethnic children in the survey. When the ethnic differences are analysed by age and sex the bases are smaller still and make the differences between distributions correspondingly more difficult to interpret. Also, the diagnoses for some minority ethnic children with non-English speaking parents are based on less complete information than those for white children and English-speaking minorities because their parents were not able to answer the detailed diagnostic questions (although they were able to complete the SDQ in their own language). This affects particularly children of Bangladeshi and African origin.

The ethnicity question in the 2004 survey was the same as that used in the 2001 Census and was different from the question used in 1999. In particular, in 2004 various categories of 'Mixed origin' were specified on the show card (e.g. 'mixed white and black Caribbean'). In 1999, it is likely that the children of mixed origin will have been split across several of the other categories (for example, parents of mixed white and black Caribbean children could have classified them as being of 'White', 'Black Caribbean' or 'Other' origin.). This means that the 1999 and 2004 data are not comparable.

The data suggest that Indian children had a relatively low rate of mental disorder (3 per cent compared with 7–10 per cent in other groups). The prevalence of hyperkinetic disorders was low among all the non-white groups. Similar findings for Indian children and hyperkinesis were reported in 1999 and have been observed in clinical practice, suggesting that they are real variations.   (Figure 4.2 and Table 4.6)

Figure 4.2
Prevalence of mental disorders by ethnicity, 2004

Great Britain

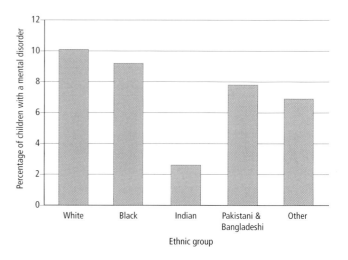

Prevalence of mental disorders by family characteristics

Family type and marital status

Children from lone parent and cohabiting couple families were about twice as likely as the children of married couples to have a mental disorder (16 per cent and 13 per cent compared with 7 per cent). This pattern was evident for girls and boys, both age groups and the three main types of disorder. However, the difference between the children of married and cohabiting couples is attributable to other factors. The modelling analysis at the end of the chapter shows that, when other variables are taken into account, children of cohabiting couples are no more likely to have a mental disorder than those of married couples.

Within the lone parent group, children whose parent was previously married were more likely to have an emotional disorder than those whose parent was single (8 per cent compared with 5 per cent) but there was no corresponding difference in the prevalence rates for conduct or hyperkinetic disorders.   (Figure 4.3 and Table 4.7)

Almost one in five boys (18 per cent) living in lone parent families had a mental disorder, of whom about two thirds had a conduct disorder. The corresponding proportion for girls was 13 per cent, equally divided between emotional and conduct disorders.   (Figure 4.3 and Table 4.7)

Figure **4.3**
Prevalence of mental disorders by family type, 2004

Great Britain

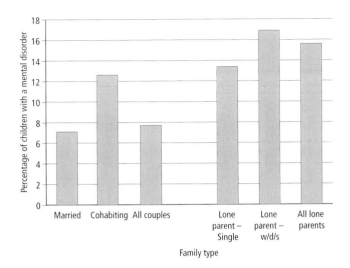

Number of children in the household

There was no consistent pattern of variation in the overall prevalence of mental disorder according to the number of children in the household. There are, however, indications that children in larger households were more likely to have a conduct disorder than those in smaller households (7 per cent and 9 per cent among children in households with three and four children compared with 5 per cent among those with one or two children). The figure for the largest households, with five or more children, was somewhat out of line at 7 per cent. More detailed inspection showed that the prevalence of conduct disorders among younger boys in such households was particularly low. The 1999 data showed a more consistent pattern suggesting that there is probably a genuine relationship between the presence of conduct disorders and the number of children in the household, though this may reflect socio-economic characteristics rather than household size *per se*.

(Figure 4.5 and Table 4.9)

Reconstituted families

A family was regarded as 'reconstituted' if stepchildren were present. Overall, about one in ten children (11 per cent) lived in a reconstituted family.

Children living in reconstituted families were more likely to have a mental disorder than those living in a family without stepchildren (14 per cent compared with 9 per cent). The disparity was mainly due to differences in the proportions of children with conduct disorders (10 per cent compared with 5 per cent). This was apparent for boys and girls and for both age groups.

(Figure 4.4 and Table 4.8)

Figure **4.4**
Prevalence of mental disorders by whether family contains stepchildren, 2004

Great Britain

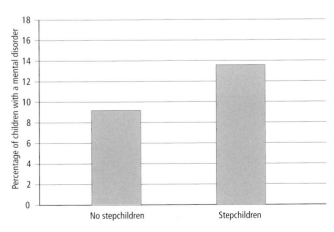

Figure **4.5**
Prevalence of mental disorders by number of children in household, 2004

Great Britain

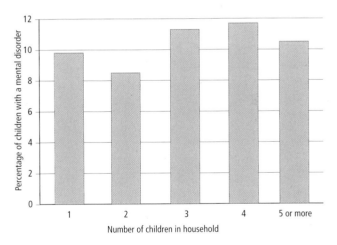

Educational qualifications of parent

There was a strong association between the presence of a mental disorder and the educational level of the interviewed parent, usually the mother. Similar relationships have been reported in the 1999 survey and other research. The overall prevalence of mental disorder increased from 4 per cent among children whose parent was educated to degree level to 17 per cent for those whose parent had no educational qualifications. There was not a consistent pattern of decrease between successive educational levels. However, there was a clear difference in prevalence rates between children whose interviewed parent had a qualification of some kind and those whose parent had no qualifications. This general pattern was observed among boys and girls and in both age groups. The 1999 survey showed the same variation although the differential between the children whose parent had a degree and those whose parent had no qualification was not quite so large (6 per cent and 15 per cent)   (Figure 4.6 and Table 4.10)

Figure **4.6**
Prevalence of mental disorders by educational qualifications of parent, 2004

Great Britain

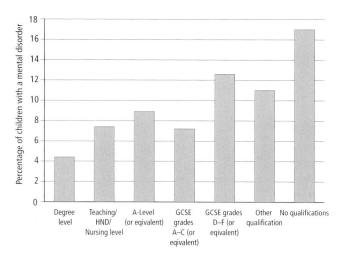

Prevalence of mental disorders by household characteristics

Family's employment situation

The relationship between unemployment and mental disorder among adults is well documented (Meltzer *et al*, 1995). The 2004 survey (and the previous survey) shows a similar association for the children of unemployed parents. Thus, in 2004, one-fifth (20 per cent) of children in families without a working parent had a mental disorder, more than twice the proportion among children with one or both parents working (9 per cent and 8 per cent). This pattern was repeated for all categories of mental disorder, for both boys and girls and for younger and older children. The highest prevalence was found among boys aged 11–16 with neither parent working of whom one quarter (25 per cent) had a mental disorder. Among boys of a similar age with both parents working, the proportion with a mental disorder was 10 per cent. For girls aged 11–16, prevalence rates were lower but the ratio was about the same, 21 per cent and 8 per cent.   (Figure 4.7 and Table 4.11)

Figure **4.7**
Prevalence of mental disorders by family's employment, 2004

Great Britain

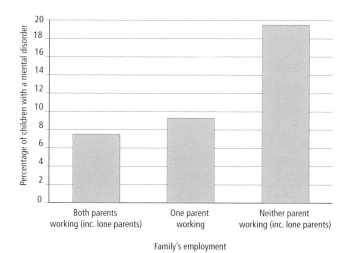

Household income

The close association between mental disorder and economic disadvantage is clearly illustrated in the income analysis. The proportion of children with a mental disorder decreased from 16 per cent among families with a gross weekly income of under £100 to 5 per cent for those earning £600 a week or more. This trend occurred for boys and girls, both age groups and the three main disorder categories. Thus, for example, among children aged 11–16 living in families with gross weekly incomes of less than £200, about 20 per cent had a mental disorder compared with 6 per cent of their contemporaries in families with incomes of at least £600.

(Figure 4.8 and Table 4.12)

Figure **4.8**
Prevalence of mental disorders by gross weekly household income, 2004

Great Britain

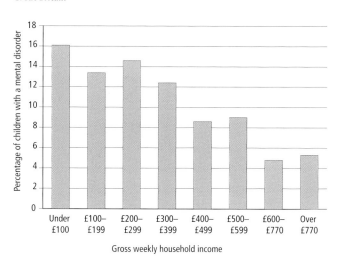

State Benefits

The benefits shown in Table 4.13 (Carers Allowance, Disability Living/Attendance Allowance and Incapacity Allowance) have been chosen to indicate disability among a member of the child's household. The prevalence rate of mental disorders in children in relation to means-tested benefits (e.g. lone parent benefit and working family credit) are not shown in the table as equivalent data have been presented earlier – for example, on family type and household income.

Children living in households who received one of these disability benefits were three times as likely as other children to have a mental disorder, 24 per cent compared with 8 per cent. Prevalence was high among children in families receiving Carers Allowance (29 per cent), and Disability Living Allowance/Attendance Allowance (28 per cent). In some cases it would have been the sampled child who was receiving the disability benefit so it would be expected that the rate of receipt would be higher among the children with a disorder. Since these cases cannot be distinguished from those in which another household member was receiving a disability benefit, we cannot conclude that children with a disorder were more likely to live in households in which another member was disabled.

(Figure 4.9 and Table 4.13)

Figure **4.9**
Prevalence of mental disorders by receipt of disability benefits, 2004

Great Britain

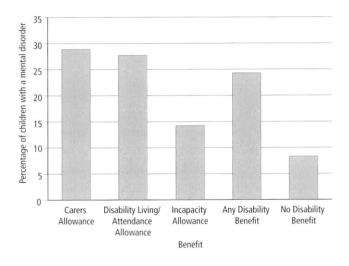

Socio-economic classification

The National Statistics Socio-economic Class (NS-SEC) was measured by the occupation of the household reference person, usually the child's father. Children in families where the reference person was in semi-routine or routine occupational groups were about three times as likely to have a mental disorder as children whose reference person was in a higher professional group (13 per cent and 15 per cent compared with 4 per cent). Among children whose reference person was long-term unemployed or had never worked, 16 per cent had a mental disorder. The socio-economic gradient was observed among boys and girls, younger and older children and for the three main disorder categories but was particularly marked for conduct disorder. The proportion of children with a conduct

Figure **4.10**
Prevalence of mental disorders by socio-economic classification, 2004

Great Britain

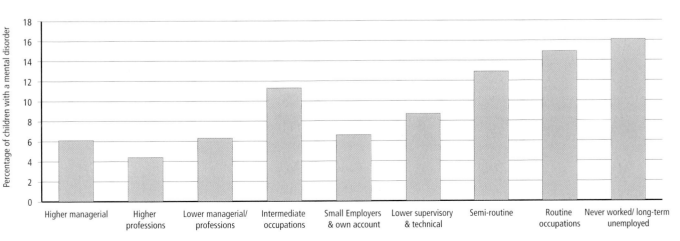

disorder in families whose reference person was in a routine occupational group was about five times that of children in families whose reference person was in a higher professional group (10 per cent and 2 per cent). (Figure 4.10 and Table 4.14)

Although there was an overall negative association between the prevalence of mental disorder and socio-economic class, it was not a completely smooth gradient. In particular, the rates for older children whose family reference person was in the Intermediate occupational group had a disproportionately high rate of mental disorder. Further investigation showed that this was mainly due to a high prevalence rate among boys aged 11–16 in this group. A different social classification was used in 1999 so it is not possible to determine whether this is a persistent variation. (Figure 4.10 and Table 4.14)

Tenure

Tenure provides another socio-economic indicator and shows the expected relationship with mental disorder. Children living in rented accommodation, whether social or private sector, were twice as likely to have a mental disorder as those in owned accommodation (17 per cent and 14 per cent compared with 7 per cent). This general trend was evident for the three main disorders but the prevalence of conduct disorders was particularly high among older children, both boys and girls, living in social rented accommodation (17 per cent and 12 per cent). The corresponding proportions for boys and girls living in owned accommodation were 6 per cent and 3 per cent.

(Figure 4.11 and Table 4.15)

Figure 4.11
Prevalence of mental disorders by tenure, 2004

Great Britain

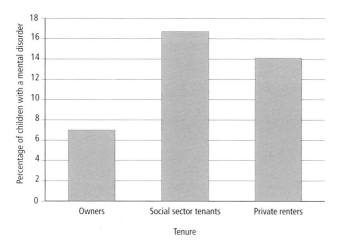

Type of accommodation

Variations in the prevalence of mental disorder by accommodation type again reflect affluence. The overall rate of mental disorder was lower among children living in detached houses, 6 per cent, than among those living in terraced or semi-detached houses and flats and maisonettes who had similar prevalence rates, 10–12 per cent.

(Figure 4.12 and Table 4.16)

Figure 4.12
Prevalence of mental disorders by accommodation type, 2004

Great Britain

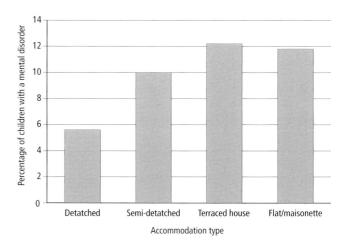

Prevalence of mental disorders by area characteristics

Region

Table 4.17 shows prevalence rates for England and Scotland in 1999 and 2004 for the three main disorder types – emotional, conduct and hyperkinetic, for children aged 5–15.[2] In England, the only difference in the rates recorded by the two surveys was a decrease in emotional disorders among 5- to 10-year-olds. The decrease was small, however, from 3 per cent to 2 per cent, and only just reached statistical significance at the 95 per cent confidence level. In Scotland, there was also a decrease in the proportion with an emotional disorder, from 5 per cent to 3 per cent, but only among 11- to 15-year-old girls.

(Table 4.17)

There were no differences in the prevalence of mental disorders between the metropolitan and non-metropolitan areas of England in 2004. A similar finding was reported in the 1999 survey. Some variations might have been expected given the associations between prevalence rates and socio-economic

2. The sample was not designed to provide separate data for Wales (see Appendix A).

measures discussed above. It may be that the area groupings cover such a heterogeneous range of areas that any variations with type of area are masked. Analysis by the ACORN classification in the following section provides a more direct examination of the relationship between mental disorder and area type. (Figure 4.13 and Table 4.18)

Figure **4.13**
Prevalence of mental disorders by region, 2004

Great Britain

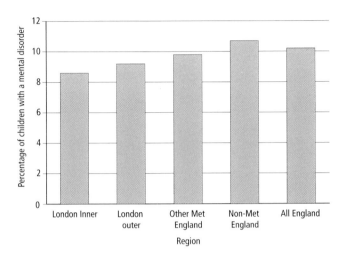

Type of area (ACORN)

ACORN (A Classification of Residential Neighbourhoods) is a geo-demographic classification combining geographical and demographic characteristics to distinguish different types of people in different areas of Great Britain. The ACORN classification has five categories, 17 groups and 56 types. For the comparative analyses in this report, the highest level, i.e. the five broad categories, has been used.

Table 4.19 shows the pattern of variation that would be expected from previous analyses in this report. Children living in areas classed as 'Hard pressed' were the most likely to be assessed as having a mental disorder (15 per cent). This proportion was about twice as high as that for children living in areas classed as 'Wealthy achievers' or 'Urban prosperity' (6 per cent and 7 per cent). This trend was evident for the three main types of disorder, boys and girls and for younger and older children although, as with the socio-economic measure, the relationship was particularly strong for conduct disorders.

(Figure 4.14 and Table 4.19)

Figure **4.14**
Prevalence of mental disorders by ACORN classification, 2004

Great Britain

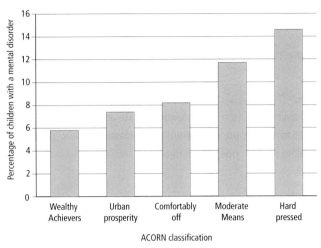

Odds ratios of socio-demographic correlates of mental disorders

The previous sections have shown variations in the prevalence of mental disorders according to a range of socio-demographic variables. Many of these variables are inter-related – for example, we have presented analyses by various measures of affluence. Modelling analysis (logistic regression) allows the independent effects of predictor variables to be measured, that is, controlling for all other factors. The regression produces an odds ratio which shows the increase in odds that a child in a particular group (for example, an age or social group) will have a disorder when compared with a reference group.

Models were produced to identify the socio-demographic correlates of any disorder, the three principal subgroups – emotional disorders, conduct disorders and hyperkinetic disorders – and the two main types of emotional disorders: anxiety and depression.

Odds of having any mental disorder

The statistically significant odds ratios for the socio-demographic correlates of the child having any mental disorder (compared with no disorder) were: age, sex, ethnic group, family type, whether living in a reconstituted family, family's employment situation, socio-economic classification, household income, parental educational qualifications, type of area and country. In 1999, slightly fewer variables were entered into the model but all but one of the statistically significant variables in 1999 were also statistically significant in 2004.[3]

---

3. *Number of children in the household was not significant in 2004. As explained earlier, this variable had an inconsistent distribution in 2004.*

The odds of having any mental disorder increased by around 50 per cent for boys compared with girls (OR = 1.52) and by almost 75 per cent for older compared with younger children (OR = 1.73). Children of Black African, Indian or Pakistani ethnic origin had markedly lower odds of having a mental disorder than white children (ORs = 0.11, 0.21 and 0.47).

(Table 4.20)

The simple tabular analyses presented earlier showed marked variations in the prevalence of mental disorder by family type. The logistic regression analysis confirms the impact of living with a widowed, divorced or separated lone parent. The odds of having a mental disorder increased by 75 per cent for children of lone parents who had been previously married compared with children living with married parents (OR = 1.75). However, there were no differences in the odds for children living with married, cohabiting or single parents. This suggests that the variations between these groups that were apparent in the simple tables were due to other factors rather than to marital status per se. The presence of stepchildren in a family increased the odds of having a mental disorder by around 50 per cent compared with being in a family with no stepchildren (OR = 1.52). (Table 4.20)

The modelling analysis confirmed the association between economic characteristics and mental disorder. The odds of having a mental disorder for children living in families in which both parents were working were 60 per cent of those for children who had neither parent working (OR = 0.61). Conversely, living in a family in which the gross weekly household income was less than £400 increased the odds of having a mental disorder by about a half compared with living in a family with an income of more than £600 per week (OR = 1.46). The effect of parental educational qualifications was also significant. The odds of having a mental disorder among children for whom the responding parent had no educational qualifications were one and a half times those of children whose parent had some qualifications (OR = 1.55). (Table 4.20)

Type of area had a particularly large impact on the odds. Living in areas classified as 'Moderate means' or 'Hard pressed' increased the odds of having a mental disorder by up to three-quarters compared with living in 'Wealthy achiever' areas (ORs = 1.74 and 1.64). (Table 4.20)

In the next sections, we look at the odds of having each of the three main types of disorder. In many cases the patterns are the same and the commentary focuses on differences from the pattern for any disorder.

Emotional disorder

Variables which had a significant effect on the odds of having an emotional disorder were: age, sex, family type, family's employment situation and parental educational qualifications.

The pattern for older children to have higher odds of having any mental disorder was particularly marked in relation to emotional disorders. Children aged 11–16 had more than twice the odds of those aged 5-10 (OR = 2.28). However, boys had lower odds than girls (OR = 0.70), reversing the overall pattern.

(Table 4.21)

Family type had a marked effect on the odds of having an emotional disorder. The odds for children living with a previously married lone parent were 2.5 times as high and those for children living with a single lone parent were 1.7 times as high as those for children living with a couple (ORs = 2.48 and 1.71) (Table 4.21)

Separate analyses were run to model the odds for anxiety disorders and depression. These showed the same general pattern as those for emotional disorders overall. However, the higher odds for older children to have an emotional disorder was very marked in the case of depression (OR=6.20).

(Table 4.21)

Conduct disorders

All the variables entered into the model had a significant effect on the odds of having a conduct disorder: age, sex, ethnic group, family type, whether living in a reconstituted family, family's employment situation, parental educational qualifications, household income, type of area and country.

The odds of having a conduct disorder for boys were almost twice those for girls (OR=1.91). Children of Indian or Pakistani origin had considerably lower odds than those of white children (ORs = 0.13 and 0.37). The presence of stepchildren in the family almost doubled the odds compared with being in a family with no stepchildren. (OR=1.92). (Table 4.20)

Type of area had a marked impact on the odds of having a conduct disorder. The odds for children living in areas classified as 'Moderate means' or 'Hard pressed' were more than twice those of children living in 'Wealthy achiever' areas (ORs =2.13 and 2.10). (Table 4.20)

Hyperkinetic disorders

Only three variables had a significant effect on the odds of having a hyperkinetic disorder: sex, family's employment situation and household income.

The most notable feature of this model was the sex variation. The odds of having a hyperkinetic disorder for boys were six times those for girls (OR = 6.10). (Table 4.20)

References

CACI Information Services (1993) *ACORN User Guide*, CACI Limited 1994. All Rights Reserved. Source: ONS and GRO (S) © Crown Copyright 1991. All Rights Reserved.

Collishaw S, Maughan B, Goodman R and Pickles A (2004) Time trends in adolescent mental health. *Journal of Child Psychology and Psychiatry* **45**, 1350–1362.

Meltzer H, Gatward R, Goodman R and Ford T (2000) *The mental health of children and adolescents in Great Britain*, TSO: London.

Table **4.1**

Prevalence of mental disorders by age and sex, 2004

All children

	5- to 10-year-olds			11- to 16-year-olds			All children		
	Boys	Girls	All	Boys	Girls	All	Boys	Girls	All
	Percentage of children with each disorder								
Emotional disorders	**2.2**	**2.5**	**2.4**	**4.0**	**6.1**	**5.0**	**3.1**	**4.3**	**3.7**
Anxiety disorders	2.1	2.4	2.2	3.6	5.2	4.4	2.9	3.8	3.3
Separation anxiety	0.4	0.7	0.6	0.3	0.4	0.3	0.3	0.5	0.4
Specific phobia	0.8	0.7	0.7	0.8	0.9	0.9	0.8	0.8	0.8
Social phobia	0.1	0.1	0.1	0.5	0.6	0.5	0.3	0.3	0.3
Panic	-	-	-	0.2	0.5	0.4	0.1	0.3	0.2
Agoraphobia	-	-	-	0.2	0.4	0.3	0.1	0.2	0.1
Post traumatic stress	-	0.1	0.0	0.1	0.5	0.3	0.0	0.3	0.2
Obsessive compulsive	0.1	0.2	0.2	0.3	0.2	0.2	0.2	0.2	0.2
Generalised anxiety	0.2	0.3	0.3	0.9	1.6	1.2	0.6	1.0	0.8
Other anxiety	0.6	0.7	0.7	0.9	1.5	1.2	0.8	1.1	0.9
Depression	0.2	0.3	0.2	1.0	1.9	1.4	0.6	1.1	0.9
Depressive episode (full ICD criteria)	0.1	0.2	0.2	0.8	1.4	1.1	0.5	0.8	0.6
Other depressive episode	0.0	0.1	0.1	0.3	0.5	0.4	0.2	0.3	0.2
Conduct disorders	**6.9**	**2.8**	**4.9**	**8.1**	**5.1**	**6.6**	**7.5**	**3.9**	**5.8**
Oppositional defiant disorder	4.5	2.4	3.5	3.5	1.7	2.6	4.0	2.0	3.0
Unsocialised conduct disorder	0.9	0.3	0.6	1.2	0.8	1.0	1.1	0.5	0.8
Socialised conduct disorder	0.6	-	0.3	2.6	1.9	2.2	1.6	0.9	1.3
Other conduct disorder	0.9	0.1	0.5	0.7	0.8	0.8	0.8	0.4	0.6
Hyperkinetic disorder	**2.7**	**0.4**	**1.6**	**2.4**	**0.4**	**1.4**	**2.6**	**0.4**	**1.5**
Less common disorders	**2.2**	**0.4**	**1.3**	**1.6**	**1.1**	**1.4**	**1.9**	**0.8**	**1.3**
Autistic Spectrum Disorder	1.9	0.1	1.0	1.0	0.5	0.8	1.4	0.3	0.9
Tic disorders	0.0	0.1	0.1	-	-	-	0.0	0.1	0.0
Eating disorders	0.5	0.2	0.3	0.6	0.1	0.4	0.5	0.1	0.3
Mutism	-	0.1	0.0	0.1	0.4	0.3	0.0	0.2	0.1
Any disorder	**10.2**	**5.1**	**7.7**	**12.6**	**10.3**	**11.5**	**11.4**	**7.8**	**9.6**
Base (weighted)	*2010*	*1916*	*3926*	*2101*	*1950*	*4051*	*4111*	*3866*	*7977*

Table **4.2**

Prevalence of mental disorders by age and sex, 1999 and 2004

All children aged 5–15   Great Britain

	Boys		Girls		All	
	1999	2004	1999	2004	1999	2004
	Percentage of children with each disorder					
Children aged 5–10						
Emotional disorders	3.3	2.2	3.3	2.5	3.3	2.4
Conduct disorders	6.5	6.9	2.7	2.8	4.6	4.9
Hyperkinetic disorder	2.6	2.7	0.4	0.4	1.5	1.6
Any emotional, conduct or hyperkinetic disorder	9.7	8.6	5.8	4.8	7.7	6.7
Any disorder	10.4	10.2	5.9	5.1	8.2	7.7
Base (weighted)	*2909*	*2010*	*2921*	*1916*	*5830*	*3926*
Children aged 11–15						
Emotional disorders	5.1	3.9	6.1	6.0	5.6	4.9
Conduct disorders	8.6	8.8	3.8	5.1	6.2	7.0
Hyperkinetic disorder	2.3	2.6	0.5	0.3	1.4	1.5
Any emotional, conduct or hyperkinetic disorder	12.5	12.1	9.2	9.8	10.8	11.0
Any disorder	12.8	13.1	9.6	10.2	11.2	11.7
Base (weighted)	*2310*	*1783*	*2299*	*1654*	*4609*	*3437*
All children aged 5–15						
Emotional disorders	4.1	3.0	4.5	4.1	4.3	3.5
Conduct disorders	7.4	7.8	3.2	3.8	5.3	5.9
Hyperkinetic disorder	2.4	2.7	0.4	0.4	1.4	1.5
Any emotional, conduct or hyperkinetic disorder	10.9	10.2	7.3	7.1	9.1	8.7
Any disorder[1]	11.4	11.6	7.6	7.5	9.5	9.6
Base (weighted)	*5219*	*3793*	*5219*	*3570*	*10438*	*7363*

The shaded boxes indicate figures where the difference between the 1999 and 2004 prevalence is statistically significant at the 95% confidence level.
1. Includes less common disorders not shown in the table.

Table **4.3**

Prevalence of subcategories of mental disorders: children aged 5–10, 1999 and 2004

Children aged 5–10   Great Britain

	Boys		Girls		All	
	1999	2004	1999	2004	1999	2004
	Percentage of children with each disorder					
Emotional disorders	**3.3**	**2.2**	**3.3**	**2.5**	**3.3**	**2.4**
Anxiety disorders	3.2	2.1	3.1	2.4	3.1	2.2
Separation anxiety	1.0	0.4	1.0	0.7	1.0	0.6
Specific phobia	1.1	0.8	1.1	0.7	1.1	0.7
Social phobia	0.4	0.1	0.2	0.1	0.3	0.1
Panic	-	-	-	-	-	-
Agoraphobia	-	-	-	-	-	-
Post traumatic stress	0.0	-	-	0.1	0.0	0.0
Obsessive compulsive	0.1	0.1	0.1	0.2	0.1	0.2
Generalised anxiety	0.3	0.2	0.4	0.3	0.4	0.3
Other anxiety	0.9	0.6	0.5	0.7	0.7	0.7
Depression	0.2	0.2	0.3	0.3	0.2	0.2
Depressive episode (full ICD criteria)	0.2	0.1	0.2	0.2	0.2	0.2
Other depressive episode	-	0.0	0.1	0.1	0.1	0.1
Conduct disorders	**6.5**	**6.9**	**2.7**	**2.8**	**4.6**	**4.9**
Oppositional defiant disorder	4.8	4.5	2.1	2.4	3.5	3.5
Unsocialised conduct disorder	0.5	0.9	0.2	0.3	0.4	0.6
Socialised conduct disorder	0.6	0.6	0.0	-	0.3	0.3
Other conduct disorder	0.6	0.9	0.3	0.1	0.4	0.5
Hyperkinetic disorder	**2.6**	**2.7**	**0.4**	**0.4**	**1.5**	**1.6**
Any emotional, conduct or hyperkinetic disorder	**9.7**	**8.6**	**5.8**	**4.8**	**7.7**	**6.7**
Any disorder[1]	**10.4**	**10.2**	**5.9**	**5.1**	**8.2**	**7.7**
Base (weighted)	*2909*	*2010*	*2921*	*1916*	*5830*	*3926*

The shaded boxes indicate figures where the difference between the 1999 and 2004 prevalence is statistically significant at the 95% confidence level.
1. Includes less common disorders not shown in the table.

37

Table **4.4**

Prevalence of subcategories of mental disorders: children aged 11–15, 1999 and 2004

Children aged 11–15   Great Britain

	Boys		Girls		All	
	1999	2004	1999	2004	1999	2004
	Percentage of children with each disorder					
Emotional disorders	**5.1**	**3.9**	**6.1**	**6.0**	**5.6**	**4.9**
Anxiety disorders	3.9	3.5	5.3	5.3	4.6	4.4
Separation anxiety	0.7	0.3	0.3	0.4	0.5	0.4
Specific phobia	0.7	0.8	1.1	1.0	0.9	0.9
Social phobia	0.3	0.3	0.4	0.5	0.4	0.4
Panic	0.4	0.2	0.3	0.4	0.3	0.3
Agoraphobia	0.1	0.1	0.2	0.4	0.2	0.2
Post traumatic stress	0.2	0.1	0.5	0.4	0.4	0.2
Obsessive compulsive	0.5	0.2	0.5	0.2	0.5	0.2
Generalised anxiety	0.8	1.0	1.1	1.4	0.9	1.2
Other anxiety	1.3	1.0	2.3	1.6	1.8	1.3
Depression	1.7	1.0	1.9	1.6	1.8	1.3
Depressive episode (full ICD criteria)	1.2	0.7	1.4	1.2	1.3	1.0
Other depressive episode	0.5	0.2	0.5	0.4	0.5	0.3
Conduct disorders	**8.6**	**8.8**	**3.8**	**5.1**	**6.2**	**7.0**
Oppositional defiant disorder	2.8	3.9	1.3	1.8	2.1	2.9
Unsocialised conduct disorder	1.0	1.5	0.3	0.8	0.6	1.2
Socialised conduct disorder	2.8	2.6	1.1	1.6	1.9	2.1
Other conduct disorder	2.0	0.9	0.7	0.7	1.4	0.8
Hyperkinetic disorder	**2.3**	**2.6**	**0.5**	**0.3**	**1.4**	**1.5**
Any emotional, conduct or hyperkinetic disorder	**12.5**	**12.1**	**9.2**	**9.8**	**10.8**	**11.0**
Any disorder[1]	**12.8**	**13.1**	**9.6**	**10.2**	**11.2**	**11.7**
Base (weighted)	*2310*	*1783*	*2299*	*1654*	*4609*	*3437*

1. *Includes less common disorders not shown in the table.*

Table **4.5**

Prevalence of subcategories of mental disorders: all children, 1999 and 2004

All children aged 5–15   Great Britain

	Boys		Girls		All	
	1999	2004	1999	2004	1999	2004
	Percentage of children with each disorder					
Emotional disorders	**4.1**	**3.0**	**4.5**	**4.1**	**4.3**	**3.5**
Anxiety disorders	3.5	2.8	4.0	3.7	3.8	3.2
Separation anxiety	0.9	0.4	0.7	0.6	0.8	0.5
Specific phobia	0.9	0.8	1.1	0.8	1.0	0.8
Social phobia	0.4	0.2	0.3	0.3	0.3	0.2
Panic	0.2	0.1	0.1	0.2	0.1	0.1
Agoraphobia	0.1	0.1	0.1	0.2	0.1	0.1
Post traumatic stress	0.1	0.1	0.2	0.2	0.2	0.1
Obsessive compulsive	0.3	0.1	0.2	0.2	0.2	0.2
Generalised anxiety	0.5	0.6	0.7	0.8	0.6	0.7
Other anxiety	1.1	0.8	1.3	1.1	1.2	1.0
Depression	0.9	0.6	1.0	0.9	0.9	0.7
Depressive episode (full ICD criteria)	0.6	0.4	0.7	0.7	0.7	0.5
Other depressive episode	0.2	0.1	0.3	0.3	0.2	0.2
Conduct disorders	**7.4**	**7.8**	**3.2**	**3.8**	**5.3**	**5.9**
Oppositional defiant disorder	3.9	4.2	1.8	2.1	2.9	3.2
Unsocialised conduct disorder	0.7	1.2	0.2	0.5	0.5	0.9
Socialised conduct disorder	1.5	1.5	0.5	0.8	1.0	1.1
Other conduct disorder	1.2	0.9	0.5	0.4	0.9	0.7
Hyperkinetic disorder	**2.4**	**2.7**	**0.4**	**0.4**	**1.4**	**1.5**
Any emotional, conduct or hyperkinetic disorder	**10.9**	**10.2**	**7.3**	**7.1**	**9.1**	**8.7**
Any disorder[1]	**11.4**	**11.6**	**7.6**	**7.5**	**9.5**	**9.6**
Base (weighted)	*5219*	*3793*	*5219*	*3570*	*10438*	*7363*

The shaded boxes indicate figures where the difference between the 1999 and 2004 prevalence is statistically significant at the 95% confidence level.
1. Includes less common disorders not shown in the table.

Table **4.6**

Prevalence of mental disorders by ethnicity, age and sex, 2004

All children   Great Britain

| | Ethnic Group | | | | | |
	White	Black[1]	Indian	Pakistani and Bangladeshi	Other	All
	Percentage of children with each disorder					
BOYS						
5- to 10-year-olds						
Emotional disorders	2.3	1.3	-	3.3	-	2.2
Conduct disorders	7.1	6.7	3.0	6.5	3.8	6.9
Hyperkinetic disorder	3.2	-	-	-	-	2.7
Less common disorders	2.3	1.3	2.5	1.2	1.8	2.2
Any disorder	10.6	7.6	5.4	9.6	5.5	10.2
Base (weighted)	*1736*	*86*	*42*	*85*	*59*	*2008*
11- to 16-year-olds						
Emotional disorders	4.0	3.4	2.4	3.1	7.0	4.0
Conduct disorders	8.5	7.7	-	4.7	5.3	8.1
Hyperkinetic disorder	2.6	1.3	-	-	3.6	2.4
Less common disorders	1.7	1.2	-	-	3.5	1.6
Any disorder	13.0	11.9	2.4	7.6	15.9	12.6
Base (weighted)	*1827*	*91*	*49*	*71*	*62*	*2100*
All boys						
Emotional disorders	3.2	2.3	1.3	3.2	3.6	3.1
Conduct disorders	7.9	7.2	1.4	5.7	4.6	7.5
Hyperkinetic disorder	2.9	0.7	-	-	1.8	2.6
Less common disorders	2.0	1.2	1.2	0.7	2.7	1.9
Any disorder	11.8	9.8	3.8	8.7	10.8	11.4
Base (weighted)	*3562*	*178*	*92*	*156*	*121*	*4108*
GIRLS						
5- to 10-year-olds						
Emotional disorders	2.6	2.1	-	3.8	1.9	2.5
Conduct disorders	3.0	1.3	-	2.6	2.0	2.8
Hyperkinetic disorder	0.4	-	-	-	2.0	0.4
Less common disorders	0.5	-	-	-	-	0.4
Any disorder	5.5	3.3	-	6.4	1.9	5.1
Base (weighted)	*1604*	*112*	*53*	*88*	*59*	*1916*
11- to 16-year-olds						
Emotional disorders	6.2	7.6	3.1	7.5	2.0	6.1
Conduct disorders	5.3	9.9	-	1.7	-	5.1
Hyperkinetic disorder	0.4	1.5	-	-	-	0.4
Less common disorders	1.1	-	-	1.1	1.8	1.1
Any disorder	10.6	17.1	3.2	7.6	3.8	10.3
Base (weighted)	*1707*	*68*	*56*	*63*	*55*	*1949*

1. The black ethnic group includes people of mixed origin.

Table **4.6** (contd)

Prevalence of mental disorders by ethnicity, age and sex, 2004

All children   Great Britain

	Ethnic Group					
	White	Black[1]	Indian	Pakistani and Bangladeshi	Other	All
	Percentage of children with each disorder					
All girls						
Emotional disorders	4.5	4.2	1.6	5.4	1.9	4.3
Conduct disorders	4.2	4.5	-	2.2	1.0	3.9
Hyperkinetic disorder	0.4	0.6	-	-	1.0	0.4
Less common disorders	0.8	-	-	0.5	0.9	0.8
Any disorder	8.1	8.5	1.6	6.9	2.8	7.8
Base (weighted)	*3311*	*181*	*109*	*151*	*114*	*3865*
ALL						
5- to 10-year-olds						
Emotional disorders	2.5	1.7	-	3.6	0.9	2.4
Conduct disorders	5.1	3.6	1.3	4.5	2.9	4.9
Hyperkinetic disorder	1.8	-	-	-	1.0	1.6
Less common disorders	1.4	0.6	1.1	0.6	0.9	1.3
Any disorder	8.1	5.2	2.4	8.0	3.7	7.7
Base (weighted)	*3340*	*199*	*96*	*172*	*118*	*3924*
11- to 16-year-olds						
Emotional disorders	5.1	5.2	2.8	5.1	4.7	5.0
Conduct disorders	7.0	8.6	-	3.3	2.8	6.6
Hyperkinetic disorder	1.5	1.4	-	-	1.9	1.4
Less common disorders	1.4	0.7	-	0.5	2.7	1.4
Any disorder	11.9	14.1	2.8	7.6	10.2	11.5
Base (weighted)	*3534*	*160*	*105*	*134*	*117*	*4049*
All children						
Emotional disorders	3.8	3.3	1.4	4.3	2.8	3.7
Conduct disorders	6.1	5.9	0.6	4.0	2.9	5.8
Hyperkinetic disorder	1.7	0.6	-	-	1.4	1.5
Less common disorders	1.4	0.6	0.5	0.6	1.8	1.3
Any disorder	10.1	9.2	2.6	7.8	6.9	9.6
Base (weighted)	*6873*	*358*	*201*	*306*	*235*	*7973*

1. The black ethnic group includes people of mixed origin.

Table **4.7**

Prevalence of mental disorders by family type, age and sex, 2004

All children   Great Britain

				Child's family type			
	Married	Cohabiting	All couples	Lone parent – Single	Lone parent – widowed, divorced, separated	All lone parents	All
				Percentage of children with each disorder			
BOYS							
5- to 10-year-olds							
Emotional disorders	1.0	2.6	1.2	2.9	7.8	5.6	2.2
Conduct disorders	5.4	8.2	5.7	8.3	12.7	10.7	6.9
Hyperkinetic disorder	2.3	3.5	2.4	3.4	4.0	3.7	2.7
Less common disorders	2.0	2.9	2.1	1.0	3.5	2.4	2.2
Any disorder	7.9	13.4	8.6	11.8	18.5	15.5	10.2
Base (weighted)	*1361*	*183*	*1543*	*211*	*256*	*466*	*2010*
11- to 16-year-olds							
Emotional disorders	2.5	4.3	2.7	6.7	8.3	7.8	4.0
Conduct disorders	5.2	13.5	6.0	12.8	14.4	13.9	8.1
Hyperkinetic disorder	1.5	3.6	1.7	5.3	4.3	4.6	2.4
Less common disorders	1.5	0.7	1.4	2.6	1.9	2.1	1.6
Any disorder	9.0	17.9	9.9	17.9	21.7	20.5	12.6
Base (weighted)	*1399*	*156*	*1555*	*163*	*383*	*546*	*2101*
All Boys							
Emotional disorders	1.8	3.4	1.9	4.6	8.1	6.8	3.1
Conduct disorders	5.3	10.7	5.9	10.2	13.7	12.4	7.5
Hyperkinetic disorder	1.9	3.5	2.1	4.2	4.2	4.2	2.6
Less common disorders	1.8	1.9	1.8	1.7	2.5	2.2	1.9
Any disorder	8.4	15.5	9.2	14.4	20.4	18.2	11.4
Base (weighted)	*2760*	*339*	*3098*	*374*	*639*	*1013*	*4111*
GIRLS							
5- to 10-year-olds							
Emotional disorders	1.8	2.2	1.8	3.9	5.4	4.7	2.5
Conduct disorders	1.9	3.5	2.1	5.8	4.2	4.9	2.8
Hyperkinetic disorder	0.3	0.6	0.3	0.5	0.8	0.6	0.4
Less common disorders	0.4	0.7	0.5	0.9	-	0.4	0.4
Any disorder	3.7	5.2	3.9	8.5	9.0	8.8	5.1
Base (weighted)	*1261*	*186*	*1447*	*215*	*254*	*469*	*1916*
11- to 16-year-olds							
Emotional disorders	4.5	8.3	4.9	8.1	10.4	9.8	6.1
Conduct disorders	3.0	9.3	3.8	14.6	7.4	9.1	5.1
Hyperkinetic disorder	0.4	-	0.3	1.0	0.3	0.5	0.4
Less common disorders	0.9	0.5	0.8	2.6	1.7	1.9	1.1
Any disorder	7.3	15.0	8.2	19.4	16.1	16.9	10.3
Base (weighted)	*1304*	*173*	*1476*	*112*	*361*	*474*	*1950*

Table **4.7** (contd)

Prevalence of mental disorders by family type, age and sex, 2004

All children

	Married	Cohabiting	All couples	Lone parent – Single	Lone parent – widowed, divorced, separated	All lone parents	All
Percentage of children with each disorder							
All Girls							
Emotional disorders	3.1	5.2	3.4	5.3	8.3	7.3	4.3
Conduct disorders	2.5	6.3	2.9	8.8	6.0	7.0	3.9
Hyperkinetic disorder	0.3	0.3	0.3	0.7	0.5	0.6	0.4
Less common disorders	0.6	0.6	0.6	1.5	1.0	1.2	0.8
Any disorder	5.6	9.9	6.1	12.2	13.2	12.9	7.8
Base (weighted)	*2564*	*359*	*2923*	*328*	*615*	*943*	*3866*
ALL							
5- to 10-year-olds							
Emotional disorders	1.4	2.4	1.5	3.4	6.6	5.1	2.4
Conduct disorders	3.7	5.8	4.0	7.0	8.5	7.8	4.9
Hyperkinetic disorder	1.3	2.1	1.4	1.9	2.4	2.2	1.6
Less common disorders	1.3	1.8	1.3	1.0	1.8	1.4	1.3
Any disorder	5.9	9.2	6.3	10.1	13.8	12.1	7.7
Base (weighted)	*2621*	*369*	*2990*	*426*	*509*	*936*	*3926*
11- to 16-year-olds							
Emotional disorders	3.4	6.4	3.8	7.3	9.3	8.8	5.0
Conduct disorders	4.1	11.3	4.9	13.5	11.0	11.7	6.6
Hyperkinetic disorder	1.1	1.9	1.2	2.6	2.4	2.4	1.5
Less common disorders	1.2	0.6	1.1	2.6	1.8	2.0	1.4
Any disorder	8.2	16.4	9.1	18.5	19.0	18.8	11.5
Base (weighted)	*2702*	*329*	*3031*	*275*	*745*	*1020*	*4051*
All children							
Emotional disorders	2.4	4.3	2.6	4.9	8.2	7.0	3.7
Conduct disorders	3.9	8.4	4.4	9.6	10.0	9.8	5.8
Hyperkinetic disorder	1.1	1.9	1.2	2.6	2.4	2.4	1.5
Less common disorders	1.2	1.2	1.2	1.6	1.8	1.7	1.3
Any disorder	7.1	12.6	7.7	13.4	16.9	15.6	9.6
Base (weighted)	*5324*	*697*	*6021*	*702*	*1254*	*1956*	*7977*

Child's family type

Table **4.8**

Prevalence of mental disorders by whether family contains stepchildren, age and sex, 2004

All children   Great Britain

	No stepchildren	Stepchildren	All
		Percentage of children with each disorder	
BOYS			
5- to 10-year-olds			
Emotional disorders	2.3	1.0	2.2
Conduct disorders	6.4	11.2	6.9
Hyperkinetic disorder	2.5	5.5	2.7
Less common disorders	2.0	3.8	2.2
Any disorder	9.7	14.4	10.2
Base (weighted)	*1820*	*189*	*2010*
11- to 16-year-olds			
Emotional disorders	4.2	2.8	4.0
Conduct disorders	7.7	11.4	8.1
Hyperkinetic disorder	2.4	2.7	2.4
Less common disorders	1.6	1.7	1.6
Any disorder	12.2	16.2	12.6
Base (weighted)	*1862*	*239*	*2101*
All Boys			
Emotional disorders	3.3	2.0	3.1
Conduct disorders	7.1	11.3	7.5
Hyperkinetic disorder	2.4	3.9	2.6
Less common disorders	1.8	2.7	1.9
Any disorder	11.0	15.4	11.4
Base (weighted)	*3683*	*428*	*4111*
GIRLS			
5- to 10-year-olds			
Emotional disorders	2.4	4.1	2.5
Conduct disorders	2.5	5.7	2.8
Hyperkinetic disorder	0.4	0.7	0.4
Less common disorders	0.4	0.6	0.4
Any disorder	4.8	8.3	5.1
Base (weighted)	*1742*	*174*	*1916*
11- to 16-year-olds			
Emotional disorders	5.9	7.3	6.1
Conduct disorders	4.3	10.3	5.1
Hyperkinetic disorder	0.4	-	0.4
Less common disorders	1.1	0.7	1.1
Any disorder	9.7	14.3	10.3
Base (weighted)	*1694*	*256*	*1950*

Table **4.8** (contd)

Prevalence of mental disorders by whether family contains stepchildren, age and sex, 2004

All children

Great Britain

	No stepchildren	Stepchildren	All
	Percentage of children with each disorder		
All Girls			
Emotional disorders	4.1	6.0	4.3
Conduct disorders	3.4	8.4	3.9
Hyperkinetic disorder	0.4	0.3	0.4
Less common disorders	0.8	0.7	0.8
Any disorder	7.2	11.9	7.8
Base (weighted)	*3436*	*430*	*3866*
ALL			
5- to 10-year-olds			
Emotional disorders	2.4	2.5	2.4
Conduct disorders	4.5	8.6	4.9
Hyperkinetic disorder	1.4	3.2	1.6
Less common disorders	1.2	2.3	1.3
Any disorder	7.3	11.4	7.7
Base (weighted)	*3562*	*364*	*3926*
11- to 16-year-olds			
Emotional disorders	5.0	5.1	5.0
Conduct disorders	6.0	10.8	6.6
Hyperkinetic disorder	1.5	1.3	1.4
Less common disorders	1.4	1.2	1.4
Any disorder	11.0	15.2	11.5
Base (weighted)	*3556*	*495*	*4051*
All children			
Emotional disorders	3.7	4.0	3.7
Conduct disorders	5.3	9.9	5.8
Hyperkinetic disorder	1.4	2.1	1.5
Less common disorders	1.3	1.7	1.3
Any disorder	9.2	13.6	9.6
Base (weighted)	*7119*	*858*	*7977*

Table **4.9**

Prevalence of mental disorders by number of children in household, age and sex, 2004

All children   Great Britain

	Number of children in household					
	1	2	3	4	5 or more	All
	Percentage of children with each disorder					
BOYS						
5- to 10-year-olds						
Emotional disorders	2.6	1.7	3.0	2.6	1.9	2.2
Conduct disorders	5.2	5.6	9.7	10.8	4.1	6.9
Hyperkinetic disorder	4.3	2.1	3.1	2.9	2.2	2.7
Less common disorders	2.3	1.8	3.0	2.7	-	2.2
Any disorder	10.7	8.1	13.5	13.5	6.0	10.2
Base (weighted)	*308*	*1017*	*484*	*152*	*50*	*2010*
11- to 16-year-olds						
Emotional disorders	4.4	3.9	3.8	3.2	4.4	4.0
Conduct disorders	7.3	6.7	10.4	15.7	11.2	8.1
Hyperkinetic disorder	2.9	2.3	2.5	1.0	-	2.4
Less common disorders	0.9	2.3	1.7	-	4.1	1.6
Any disorder	12.0	11.9	14.5	15.8	15.0	12.6
Base (weighted)	*785*	*818*	*352*	*100*	*47*	*2101*
All Boys						
Emotional disorders	3.8	2.6	3.4	2.8	3.1	3.1
Conduct disorders	6.7	6.1	10.0	12.7	7.6	7.5
Hyperkinetic disorder	3.3	2.2	2.9	2.2	1.1	2.6
Less common disorders	1.3	2.0	2.4	1.6	2.0	1.9
Any disorder	11.6	9.8	13.9	14.5	10.4	11.4
Base (weighted)	*1093*	*1835*	*835*	*252*	*97*	*4111*
GIRLS						
5- to 10-year-olds						
Emotional disorders	2.1	1.9	3.6	3.2	5.0	2.5
Conduct disorders	2.3	2.0	3.1	6.0	7.0	2.8
Hyperkinetic disorder	0.3	0.4	-	0.7	1.7	0.4
Less common disorders	0.4	0.4	0.5	-	1.6	0.4
Any disorder	4.2	4.3	6.3	7.0	10.1	5.1
Base (weighted)	*319*	*948*	*422*	*168*	*59*	*1916*
11- to 16-year-olds						
Emotional disorders	6.0	5.3	7.5	7.8	6.4	6.1
Conduct disorders	3.7	6.0	5.4	5.8	6.8	5.1
Hyperkinetic disorder	0.3	0.4	0.3	-	1.6	0.4
Less common disorders	1.3	0.9	1.1	1.7	-	1.1
Any disorder	9.5	10.4	11.2	12.5	11.1	10.3
Base (weighted)	*701*	*739*	*338*	*108*	*64*	*1950*

Table **4.9** (contd)

Prevalence of mental disorders by number of children in household, age and sex, 2004

All children   Great Britain

	Number of children in household					
	1	2	3	4	5 or more	All
	Percentage of children with each disorder					
All Girls						
Emotional disorders	4.8	3.4	5.3	5.0	5.7	4.3
Conduct disorders	3.3	3.7	4.1	5.9	6.9	3.9
Hyperkinetic disorder	0.3	0.4	0.1	0.4	1.7	0.4
Less common disorders	1.0	0.6	0.7	0.7	0.8	0.8
Any disorder	7.8	7.0	8.4	9.1	10.6	7.8
Base (weighted)	*1020*	*1687*	*760*	*276*	*123*	*3866*
ALL						
5- to 10-year-olds						
Emotional disorders	2.3	1.8	3.3	2.9	3.6	2.4
Conduct disorders	3.7	3.9	6.6	8.2	5.7	4.9
Hyperkinetic disorder	2.3	1.3	1.7	1.7	1.9	1.6
Less common disorders	1.4	1.2	1.8	1.3	0.9	1.3
Any disorder	7.4	6.3	10.1	10.1	8.2	7.7
Base (weighted)	*626*	*1965*	*906*	*320*	*109*	*3926*
11- to 16-year-olds						
Emotional disorders	5.2	4.5	5.6	5.6	5.5	5.0
Conduct disorders	5.6	6.3	8.0	10.6	8.7	6.6
Hyperkinetic disorder	1.7	1.4	1.4	0.5	0.9	1.4
Less common disorders	1.1	1.6	1.4	0.9	1.7	1.4
Any disorder	10.8	11.2	12.9	14.1	12.8	11.5
Base (weighted)	*1487*	*1557*	*689*	*207*	*111*	*4051*
All children						
Emotional disorders	4.3	3.0	4.3	3.9	4.5	3.7
Conduct disorders	5.0	5.0	7.2	9.2	7.2	5.8
Hyperkinetic disorder	1.8	1.3	1.6	1.2	1.4	1.5
Less common disorders	1.2	1.4	1.6	1.1	1.3	1.3
Any disorder	9.8	8.5	11.3	11.7	10.5	9.6
Base (weighted)	*2113*	*3522*	*1595*	*527*	*220*	*7977*

Table **4.10**

Prevalence of mental disorders by educational qualifications of parent, age and sex, 2004

All children Great Britain

	Degree level	Teaching/ HND/ Nursing level	A-Level (or eqivalent)	GCSE grades A-C (or eqivalent)	GCSE grades D-F (or eqivalent)	Other qualification	No qualification	All
				Percentage of children with each disorder				
BOYS								
5- to 10-year-olds								
Emotional disorders	1.0	0.4	3.0	1.5	2.8	1.5	4.9	2.2
Conduct disorders	3.7	4.0	7.2	5.0	10.4	12.4	11.4	6.8
Hyperkinetic disorder	1.1	1.3	2.4	2.6	3.0	5.1	5.3	2.8
Less common disorders	1.1	2.2	2.7	1.6	2.4	-	2.8	2.0
Any disorder	5.4	6.4	11.2	7.9	13.3	13.4	16.3	9.9
Base (weighted)	*297*	*241*	*227*	*598*	*207*	*64*	*341*	*1974*
11- to 16-year-olds								
Emotional disorders	1.1	2.5	6.3	3.7	2.1	8.0	6.3	3.9
Conduct disorders	4.9	4.0	6.6	6.2	9.6	6.4	16.5	8.2
Hyperkinetic disorder	1.3	1.2	1.6	1.6	3.7	5.2	4.4	2.4
Less common disorders	2.4	1.7	2.7	0.8	1.7	-	1.5	1.5
Any disorder	7.3	8.8	13.1	9.6	13.4	17.5	21.3	12.5
Base (weighted)	*272*	*268*	*199*	*587*	*239*	*64*	*394*	*2023*
All Boys								
Emotional disorders	1.1	1.5	4.5	2.6	2.4	4.7	5.6	3.1
Conduct disorders	4.2	4.0	6.9	5.6	10.0	9.4	14.1	7.5
Hyperkinetic disorder	1.2	1.3	2.0	2.1	3.4	5.2	4.8	2.6
Less common disorders	1.8	1.9	2.7	1.2	2.0	-	2.1	1.8
Any disorder	6.3	7.7	12.1	8.8	13.4	15.4	19.0	11.2
Base (weighted)	*569*	*509*	*426*	*1185*	*445*	*128*	*735*	*3997*
GIRLS								
5- to 10-year-olds								
Emotional disorders	0.3	2.7	1.7	2.2	3.0	1.7	6.0	2.6
Conduct disorders	0.8	2.4	1.9	2.6	3.9	1.9	5.7	2.8
Hyperkinetic disorder	-	0.5	-	0.4	-	-	1.4	0.4
Less common disorders	0.9	-	0.9	0.2	0.5	-	0.3	0.4
Any disorder	1.6	4.1	3.9	4.4	6.7	3.5	11.1	5.2
Base (weighted)	*273*	*222*	*233*	*586*	*202*	*59*	*298*	*1873*
11- to 16-year-olds								
Emotional disorders	2.7	7.3	5.3	3.6	12.0	4.2	8.8	6.0
Conduct disorders	0.3	4.9	2.9	4.2	7.5	2.1	9.8	5.0
Hyperkinetic disorder	0.4	0.4	0.4	0.2	1.1	-	0.3	0.4
Less common disorders	-	1.2	1.0	0.2	1.8	2.2	1.4	0.8
Any disorder	3.4	10.0	7.8	6.9	17.4	8.4	17.8	10.2
Base (weighted)	*262*	*241*	*221*	*551*	*183*	*51*	*383*	*1892*

Table **4.10** (contd)

Prevalence of mental disorders by educational qualifications of parent, age and sex, 2004

All children

	Educational level (interviewed parent)							
	Degree level	Teaching/ HND/ Nursing level	A-Level (or eqivalent)	GCSE grades A–C (or eqivalent)	GCSE grades D–F (or eqivalent)	Other qualification	No qualification	All
	Percentage of children with each disorder							
All Girls								
Emotional disorders	1.5	5.1	3.5	2.9	7.3	2.9	7.6	4.3
Conduct disorders	0.5	3.7	2.4	3.4	5.6	2.0	8.0	3.9
Hyperkinetic disorder	0.2	0.5	0.2	0.3	0.5	-	0.8	0.4
Less common disorders	0.4	0.6	0.9	0.2	1.1	1.0	0.9	0.6
Any disorder	2.5	7.2	5.8	5.6	11.8	5.8	14.9	7.7
Base (weighted)	536	463	454	1137	385	110	681	3764
ALL								
5- to 10-year-olds								
Emotional disorders	0.7	1.5	2.3	1.8	2.9	1.6	5.4	2.4
Conduct disorders	2.3	3.2	4.5	3.8	7.2	7.4	8.8	4.9
Hyperkinetic disorder	0.6	0.9	1.2	1.5	1.5	2.6	3.5	1.6
Less common disorders	1.0	1.1	1.8	0.9	1.5	-	1.6	1.2
Any disorder	3.5	5.3	7.5	6.2	10.0	8.6	13.9	7.6
Base (weighted)	570	463	461	1184	409	122	639	3847
11- to 16-year-olds								
Emotional disorders	1.9	4.8	5.8	3.7	6.4	6.3	7.5	4.9
Conduct disorders	2.6	4.6	4.7	5.2	8.7	4.5	13.2	6.6
Hyperkinetic disorder	0.8	0.9	1.0	0.9	2.6	2.9	2.4	1.4
Less common disorders	1.2	1.4	1.8	0.5	1.7	1.0	1.5	1.2
Any disorder	5.4	9.4	10.3	8.3	15.1	13.5	19.6	11.4
Base (weighted)	534	509	420	1138	421	115	777	3915
All children								
Emotional disorders	1.3	3.2	4.0	2.7	4.7	3.9	6.6	3.7
Conduct disorders	2.4	3.9	4.6	4.5	8.0	6.0	11.2	5.8
Hyperkinetic disorder	0.7	0.9	1.1	1.2	2.1	2.8	2.9	1.5
Less common disorders	1.1	1.3	1.8	0.7	1.6	0.5	1.5	1.2
Any disorder	4.4	7.4	8.9	7.2	12.6	11.0	17.0	9.5
Base (weighted)	1104	972	881	2322	830	238	1415	7762

Table **4.11**

Prevalence of mental disorders by family's employment, age and sex, 2004

All children   Great Britain

	Family's employment			
	Both parents working (inc. lone parents)	One parent working	Neither parent working (inc. lone parents)	All
	Percentage of children with each disorder			
BOYS				
5- to 10-year-olds				
Emotional disorders	1.3	1.2	7.0	2.2
Conduct disorders	5.1	6.5	14.6	6.9
Hyperkinetic disorder	2.3	1.7	5.9	2.8
Less common disorders	1.7	2.1	3.7	2.1
Any disorder	8.1	8.2	20.5	10.1
Base (weighted)	*1267*	*389*	*326*	*1982*
11- to 16-year-olds				
Emotional disorders	2.8	3.4	11.0	4.1
Conduct disorders	5.9	9.6	17.5	8.2
Hyperkinetic disorder	2.0	1.7	5.3	2.5
Less common disorders	1.8	0.7	2.0	1.6
Any disorder	10.1	12.9	25.2	12.8
Base (weighted)	*1433*	*305*	*302*	*2039*
All Boys				
Emotional disorders	2.1	2.2	8.9	3.2
Conduct disorders	5.5	7.9	16.0	7.6
Hyperkinetic disorder	2.2	1.7	5.6	2.6
Less common disorders	1.7	1.5	2.9	1.9
Any disorder	9.2	10.3	22.7	11.5
Base (weighted)	*2700*	*693*	*628*	*4021*
GIRLS				
5- to 10-year-olds				
Emotional disorders	1.6	3.3	5.5	2.6
Conduct disorders	1.3	3.0	8.4	2.8
Hyperkinetic disorder	0.2	0.6	1.0	0.4
Less common disorders	0.3	0.5	0.6	0.4
Any disorder	3.1	5.9	12.0	5.2
Base (weighted)	*1165*	*400*	*313*	*1877*
11- to 16-year-olds				
Emotional disorders	5.2	6.5	10.7	6.2
Conduct disorders	3.3	5.7	12.8	5.1
Hyperkinetic disorder	0.2	0.6	0.8	0.4
Less common disorders	0.5	0.9	3.3	0.9
Any disorder	7.9	11.5	20.8	10.4
Base (weighted)	*1318*	*307*	*277*	*1902*

Table **4.11** (contd)

Prevalence of mental disorders by family's employment, age and sex, 2004

All children   Great Britain

	Family's employment			
	Both parents working (inc. lone parents)	One parent working	Neither parent working (inc. lone parents)	All
	Percentage of children with each disorder			
All Girls				
Emotional disorders	3.5	4.7	7.9	4.4
Conduct disorders	2.4	4.2	10.5	4.0
Hyperkinetic disorder	0.2	0.6	0.9	0.4
Less common disorders	0.4	0.7	1.9	0.7
Any disorder	5.7	8.3	16.1	7.8
Base (weighted)	*2483*	*707*	*589*	*3779*
ALL				
5- to 10-year-olds				
Emotional disorders	1.4	2.3	6.3	2.4
Conduct disorders	3.3	4.7	11.6	4.9
Hyperkinetic disorder	1.3	1.1	3.5	1.6
Less common disorders	1.0	1.3	2.2	1.3
Any disorder	5.7	7.1	16.3	7.7
Base (weighted)	*2432*	*789*	*639*	*3859*
11- to 16-year-olds				
Emotional disorders	3.9	5.0	10.9	5.1
Conduct disorders	4.7	7.7	15.2	6.7
Hyperkinetic disorder	1.2	1.2	3.1	1.4
Less common disorders	1.1	0.8	2.6	1.3
Any disorder	9.1	12.2	23.1	11.6
Base (weighted)	*2751*	*612*	*578*	*3940*
All children				
Emotional disorders	2.8	3.4	8.5	3.8
Conduct disorders	4.0	6.0	13.3	5.8
Hyperkinetic disorder	1.2	1.1	3.3	1.5
Less common disorders	1.1	1.1	2.4	1.3
Any disorder	7.5	9.3	19.5	9.7
Base (weighted)	*5183*	*1400*	*1217*	*7800*

Table **4.12**

Prevalence of mental disorders by household income, age and sex, 2004

All children   Great Britain

	Gross weekly household income								
	Under £100	£100– £199	£200– £299	£300– £399	£400– £499	£500– £599	£600– £770	Over £770	All
	Percentage of children with each disorder								
BOYS									
5- to 10-year-olds									
Emotional disorders	1.7	3.7	5.2	0.5	2.4	0.6	1.6	1.0	2.1
Conduct disorders	11.5	8.0	13.3	5.8	8.2	3.6	2.5	3.9	6.4
Hyperkinetic disorder	9.9	2.0	4.0	2.0	4.2	3.4	0.9	1.6	2.6
Less common disorders	-	-	2.1	2.8	2.6	4.6	1.6	1.3	1.9
Any disorder	16.8	9.0	15.6	9.3	11.9	9.2	5.7	6.2	9.3
Base (weighted)	*56*	*220*	*243*	*213*	*196*	*162*	*243*	*487*	*1820*
11- to 16-year-olds									
Emotional disorders	11.4	6.7	6.6	6.4	3.5	2.7	1.7	1.5	3.9
Conduct disorders	13.2	13.7	15.1	13.8	4.8	7.1	3.2	3.8	8.1
Hyperkinetic disorder	3.5	4.2	4.9	4.3	0.8	1.9	1.2	1.2	2.4
Less common disorders	6.2	1.3	2.3	2.5	1.2	1.2	0.8	1.9	1.7
Any disorder	21.1	18.5	20.2	20.7	8.9	11.8	6.3	7.2	12.5
Base (weighted)	*33*	*230*	*223*	*202*	*262*	*184*	*240*	*474*	*1849*
All Boys									
Emotional disorders	5.3	5.2	5.9	3.3	3.0	1.7	1.6	1.3	3.0
Conduct disorders	12.2	10.9	14.2	9.7	6.3	5.5	2.9	3.8	7.2
Hyperkinetic disorder	7.5	3.1	4.4	3.2	2.2	2.6	1.1	1.4	2.5
Less common disorders	2.3	0.7	2.2	2.7	1.8	2.8	1.2	1.6	1.8
Any disorder	18.4	13.9	17.8	14.8	10.2	10.6	6.0	6.7	10.9
Base (weighted)	*89*	*450*	*466*	*416*	*459*	*346*	*483*	*961*	*3668*
GIRLS									
5- to 10-year-olds									
Emotional disorders	2.9	3.8	4.8	1.2	3.3	3.2	1.7	0.7	2.5
Conduct disorders	2.9	6.1	5.6	1.9	1.0	2.1	-	1.6	2.6
Hyperkinetic disorder	2.8	0.4	1.3	-	-	0.8	-	-	0.4
Less common disorders	-	0.4	0.4	0.6	0.5	-	0.4	0.6	0.4
Any disorder	5.6	8.5	9.7	3.5	4.4	4.6	2.2	2.5	4.9
Base (weighted)	*38*	*260*	*231*	*179*	*203*	*153*	*248*	*411*	*1724*
11- to 16-year-olds									
Emotional disorders	12.9	8.5	8.3	9.2	6.2	4.6	3.0	3.7	5.9
Conduct disorders	13.7	13.5	6.8	7.6	3.1	5.1	2.6	1.6	5.2
Hyperkinetic disorder	-	0.7	0.4	-	-	2.5	-	0.2	0.4
Less common disorders	-	2.6	1.2	1.5	0.5	-	0.4	0.5	0.9
Any disorder	21.1	19.6	13.2	15.5	9.3	9.6	5.2	5.1	10.2
Base (weighted)	*39*	*176*	*245*	*197*	*197*	*162*	*257*	*456*	*1728*

Table **4.12** (contd)

Prevalence of mental disorders by household income, age and sex, 2004

All children

| | \multicolumn{9}{c}{Gross weekly household income} | | | | | | | | |
	Under £100	£100– £199	£200– £299	£300– £399	£400– £499	£500– £599	£600– £770	Over £770	All
	\multicolumn{9}{c}{*Percentage of children with each disorder*}								
All Girls									
Emotional disorders	7.9	5.7	6.6	5.4	4.8	3.9	2.4	2.2	4.2
Conduct disorders	8.3	9.1	6.2	4.9	2.1	3.7	1.3	1.6	3.9
Hyperkinetic disorder	1.4	0.5	0.8	-	-	1.6	-	0.1	0.4
Less common disorders	-	1.3	0.8	1.1	0.5	-	0.4	0.5	0.6
Any disorder	13.4	13.0	11.5	9.8	6.8	7.1	3.7	3.9	7.5
Base (weighted)	*77*	*437*	*476*	*376*	*400*	*315*	*505*	*866*	*3452*
ALL									
5- to 10-year-olds									
Emotional disorders	2.2	3.8	5.0	0.8	2.9	1.9	1.6	0.9	2.3
Conduct disorders	8.0	7.0	9.5	4.0	4.6	2.9	1.3	2.8	4.5
Hyperkinetic disorder	7.0	1.1	2.7	1.1	2.1	2.1	0.4	0.9	1.5
Less common disorders	-	0.2	1.3	1.8	1.5	2.4	1.0	0.9	1.2
Any disorder	12.3	8.8	12.7	6.7	8.1	7.0	3.9	4.5	7.2
Base (weighted)	*94*	*480*	*475*	*392*	*399*	*315*	*491*	*897*	*3544*
11- to 16-year-olds									
Emotional disorders	12.2	7.5	7.5	7.7	4.7	3.6	2.4	2.6	4.9
Conduct disorders	13.5	13.6	10.7	10.8	4.1	6.2	2.9	2.7	6.7
Hyperkinetic disorder	1.6	2.7	2.5	2.2	0.5	2.1	0.6	0.7	1.4
Less common disorders	2.8	1.9	1.8	2.0	0.9	0.6	0.6	1.2	1.3
Any disorder	21.1	19.0	16.5	18.1	9.1	10.8	5.7	6.1	11.4
Base (weighted)	*72*	*406*	*467*	*399*	*459*	*346*	*497*	*930*	*3576*
All children									
Emotional disorders	6.5	5.5	6.2	4.3	3.8	2.8	2.0	1.7	3.6
Conduct disorders	10.4	10.0	10.1	7.4	4.3	4.6	2.1	2.8	5.6
Hyperkinetic disorder	4.7	1.8	2.6	1.7	1.2	2.1	0.5	0.8	1.5
Less common disorders	1.2	1.0	1.5	1.9	1.2	1.5	0.8	1.1	1.2
Any disorder	16.1	13.4	14.6	12.4	8.6	9.0	4.8	5.3	9.3
Base (weighted)	*166*	*887*	*942*	*791*	*858*	*661*	*987*	*1827*	*7120*

Table **4.13**

Prevalence of mental disorders by receipt of disability benefits, age and sex, 2004

All children

Great Britan

	Carers Allowance	Disability Living/ Attendance Allowance	Incapacity Allowance	Any disability benefit	No disability benefit	All
				Receipt of disability benefits		
			Percentage of children with each disorder			
BOYS						
5- to 10-year-olds						
Emotional disorders	8.8	7.7	5.3	6.8	1.7	2.2
Conduct disorders	19.2	18.4	8.8	16.7	5.9	6.9
Hyperkinetic disorder	9.4	9.9	3.0	8.5	2.1	2.7
Less common disorders	20.0	18.4	-	13.8	1.0	2.2
Any disorder	36.6	38.1	13.8	31.8	7.9	10.2
Base (weighted)	56	141	37	189	1821	2010
11- to 16-year-olds						
Emotional disorders	18.2	12.7	10.2	12.1	3.3	4.0
Conduct disorders	31.0	20.6	15.2	18.0	7.2	8.1
Hyperkinetic disorder	10.2	5.3	-	4.9	2.2	2.4
Less common disorders	7.6	7.8	-	5.9	1.2	1.6
Any disorder	44.1	31.6	22.3	29.3	11.1	12.6
Base (weighted)	54	120	42	175	1926	2101
All Boys						
Emotional disorders	13.4	10.0	7.9	9.3	2.5	3.1
Conduct disorders	25.0	19.4	12.2	17.3	6.5	7.5
Hyperkinetic disorder	9.8	7.8	1.4	6.8	2.2	2.6
Less common disorders	14.0	13.5	-	10.0	1.1	1.9
Any disorder	40.3	35.1	18.3	30.6	9.6	11.4
Base (weighted)	110	261	79	365	3747	4111
GIRLS						
5- to 10-year-olds						
Emotional disorders	8.4	3.8	4.5	5.0	2.3	2.5
Conduct disorders	6.1	9.7	4.9	8.8	2.3	2.8
Hyperkinetic disorder	3.9	2.4	-	2.2	0.2	0.4
Less common disorders	1.9	1.1	-	0.7	0.4	0.4
Any disorder	10.5	10.8	6.8	10.6	4.7	5.1
Base (weighted)	52	90	42	147	1769	1916
11- to 16-year-olds						
Emotional disorders	10.2	11.0	10.8	12.0	5.6	6.1
Conduct disorders	13.8	9.8	2.9	8.7	4.7	5.1
Hyperkinetic disorder	1.6	4.6	-	3.2	0.1	0.4
Less common disorders	3.3	4.7	2.7	4.5	0.8	1.1
Any disorder	24.0	24.2	13.8	22.5	9.3	10.3
Base (weighted)	60	110	40	159	1790	1950

Table **4.13** (contd)

Prevalence of mental disorders by receipt of disability benefits, age and sex, 2004

All children   Great Britan

	Receipt of disability benefits					
	Carers Allowance	Disability Living/ Attendance Allowance	Incapacity Allowance	Any disability benefit[1]	No disability benefit	All
	Percentage of children with each disorder					
All Girls						
Emotional disorders	9.3	7.8	7.6	8.7	4.0	4.3
Conduct disorders	10.2	9.8	3.9	8.7	3.5	3.9
Hyperkinetic disorder	2.7	3.6	-	2.7	0.2	0.4
Less common disorders	2.6	3.1	1.3	2.6	0.6	0.8
Any disorder	17.7	18.2	10.2	16.8	7.0	7.8
Base (weighted)	*112*	*200*	*81*	*307*	*3559*	*3866*
ALL						
5- to 10-year-olds						
Emotional disorders	8.6	6.2	4.9	6.0	2.0	2.4
Conduct disorders	12.9	15.0	6.8	13.2	4.1	4.9
Hyperkinetic disorder	6.7	7.0	1.4	5.7	1.2	1.6
Less common disorders	11.3	11.7	-	8.0	0.7	1.3
Any disorder	24.0	27.4	10.1	22.5	6.3	7.7
Base (weighted)	*108*	*231*	*79*	*336*	*3589*	*3926*
11- to 16-year-olds						
Emotional disorders	14.0	11.9	10.5	12.1	4.4	5.0
Conduct disorders	22.0	15.4	9.3	13.5	6.0	6.6
Hyperkinetic disorder	5.7	4.9	-	4.1	1.2	1.4
Less common disorders	5.3	6.3	1.3	5.2	1.0	1.4
Any disorder	33.5	28.0	18.2	26.1	10.2	11.5
Base (weighted)	*114*	*230*	*82*	*335*	*3716*	*4051*
All children						
Emotional disorders	11.4	9.0	7.7	9.0	3.2	3.7
Conduct disorders	17.6	15.2	8.0	13.4	5.1	5.8
Hyperkinetic disorder	6.2	6.0	0.7	4.9	1.2	1.5
Less common disorders	8.2	9.0	0.7	6.6	0.9	1.3
Any disorder	28.9	27.7	14.2	24.3	8.3	9.6
Base (weighted)	*222*	*461*	*161*	*671*	*7306*	*7977*

1. The 'Any disability benefit' category includes a small number of households receiving Severe Disablement Allowance not shown in the table.

Table **4.14**

Prevalence of mental disorders by socio-economic classification, age and sex, 2004

All children

Great Britain

	Higher managerial	Higher professions	Lower managerial /professions	Intermediate occupations	Small Employers and own account	Lower supervisory and technical	Semi-routine	Routine occupations	Never worked/ long-term unemployed	All
					Socio-economic classification[1]					

Percentage of children with each disorder

BOYS

5- to 10-year-olds

Emotional disorders	1.2	2.3	0.8	0.5	1.2	2.3	3.2	4.3	3.7	2.1
Conduct disorders	2.1	4.1	4.3	5.4	8.5	6.8	10.1	7.9	14.2	6.7
Hyperkinetic disorder	1.4	0.6	1.5	4.0	2.1	2.4	3.9	4.8	5.9	2.8
Less common disorders	2.6	0.5	1.1	2.9	1.7	0.7	2.0	2.7	5.9	1.9
Any disorder	6.5	5.0	6.0	9.6	8.9	8.7	13.7	14.1	21.1	9.9
Base (weighted)	*160*	*172*	*374*	*182*	*243*	*129*	*348*	*297*	*53*	*1960*

11- to 16-year-olds

Emotional disorders	2.7	3.4	3.4	5.5	2.1	1.6	4.5	5.1	14.0	4.0
Conduct disorders	4.5	3.2	3.6	12.8	4.2	6.4	11.7	16.5	11.9	8.3
Hyperkinetic disorder	0.8	0.6	1.0	5.4	2.2	0.8	2.5	5.2	3.8	2.4
Less common disorders	2.0	1.4	1.0	3.8	0.9	1.4	1.2	1.7	3.4	1.6
Any disorder	8.5	6.7	7.9	19.7	8.3	9.1	15.1	22.0	20.0	12.7
Base (weighted)	*150*	*177*	*412*	*167*	*255*	*138*	*354*	*304*	*53*	*2010*

All Boys

Emotional disorders	2.0	2.8	2.2	2.9	1.6	1.9	3.8	4.7	8.8	3.1
Conduct disorders	3.3	3.7	3.9	8.9	6.3	6.6	10.9	12.3	13.1	7.5
Hyperkinetic disorder	1.1	0.6	1.2	4.7	2.1	1.6	3.2	5.0	4.8	2.6
Less common disorders	2.3	1.0	1.1	3.3	1.3	1.1	1.6	2.2	4.7	1.7
Any disorder	7.4	5.9	7.0	14.5	8.6	8.9	14.4	18.1	20.5	11.3
Base (weighted)	*310*	*350*	*787*	*349*	*499*	*267*	*702*	*601*	*106*	*3969*

GIRLS

5- to 10-year-olds

Emotional disorders	1.7	1.1	1.5	3.7	1.5	3.8	3.2	3.6	4.2	2.6
Conduct disorders	2.0	1.3	1.4	1.2	2.6	4.0	3.1	4.9	7.2	2.8
Hyperkinetic disorder	1.0	-	0.3	-	-	-	-	1.4	1.4	0.4
Less common disorders	1.7	-	0.6	0.6	-	-	-	0.4	1.4	0.4
Any disorder	3.6	2.4	3.0	4.9	4.0	7.0	5.5	8.6	9.8	5.1
Base (weighted)	*119*	*166*	*366*	*173*	*249*	*128*	*291*	*294*	*71*	*1858*

11- to 16-year-olds

Emotional disorders	4.1	2.5	5.4	4.3	3.0	7.4	9.2	8.7	8.6	6.0
Conduct disorders	1.5	0.6	3.3	8.3	2.1	3.7	7.7	8.5	11.2	5.0
Hyperkinetic disorder	-	0.7	-	1.1	0.8	0.9	-	0.4	-	0.4
Less common disorders	-	0.7	0.5	0.5	0.4	0.8	2.0	1.3	-	0.8
Any disorder	5.5	3.2	8.1	11.3	5.0	10.2	16.4	14.7	15.8	10.1
Base (weighted)	*153*	*152*	*388*	*180*	*245*	*110*	*304*	*285*	*60*	*1878*

1. This is the National Statistics socio-economic classification (NS-SEC).

Table **4.14** (contd)

Prevalence of mental disorders by socio-economic classification, age and sex, 2004

All children   Great Britain

| | Socio-economic classification[1] | | | | | | | | | |
	Higher managerial	Higher professions	Lower managerial /professions	Intermediate occupations	Small Employers and own account	Lower supervisory and technical	Semi-routine	Routine occupations	Never worked/ long-term unemployed	All
	Percentage of children with each disorder									
All Girls										
Emotional disorders	3.0	1.8	3.5	4.0	2.2	5.5	6.3	6.1	6.2	4.3
Conduct disorders	1.7	1.0	2.4	4.8	2.4	3.9	5.4	6.7	9.0	3.9
Hyperkinetic disorder	0.4	0.3	0.1	0.6	0.4	0.4	-	0.9	0.8	0.4
Less common disorders	0.7	0.3	0.6	0.5	0.2	0.4	1.0	0.8	0.7	0.6
Any disorder	4.7	2.8	5.6	8.2	4.5	8.5	11.1	11.6	12.5	7.6
Base (weighted)	*271*	*318*	*754*	*354*	*493*	*239*	*596*	*579*	*131*	*3736*
ALL										
5- to 10-year-olds										
Emotional disorders	1.4	1.7	1.2	2.1	1.3	3.1	3.2	3.9	4.0	2.3
Conduct disorders	2.0	2.7	2.9	3.4	5.5	5.4	6.9	6.4	10.2	4.8
Hyperkinetic disorder	1.2	0.3	0.9	2.1	1.1	1.2	2.1	3.1	3.3	1.6
Less common disorders	2.2	0.3	0.9	1.8	0.9	0.4	1.1	1.5	3.3	1.2
Any disorder	5.2	3.7	4.5	7.3	6.4	7.9	10.0	11.4	14.6	7.5
Base (weighted)	*279*	*339*	*740*	*356*	*492*	*257*	*640*	*590*	*124*	*3817*
11- to 16-year-olds										
Emotional disorders	3.4	3.0	4.4	4.9	2.5	4.1	6.6	6.9	11.1	4.9
Conduct disorders	3.0	2.0	3.5	10.5	3.2	5.2	9.8	12.6	11.5	6.7
Hyperkinetic disorder	0.4	0.6	0.5	3.2	1.5	0.9	1.3	2.9	1.8	1.4
Less common disorders	1.0	1.1	0.8	2.1	0.7	1.1	1.5	1.5	1.6	1.2
Any disorder	7.0	5.1	8.0	15.3	6.7	9.6	15.7	18.5	17.8	11.4
Base (weighted)	*302*	*329*	*800*	*347*	*500*	*248*	*658*	*589*	*113*	*3888*
All children										
Emotional disorders	2.5	2.3	2.8	3.5	1.9	3.6	5.0	5.4	7.4	3.6
Conduct disorders	2.5	2.4	3.2	6.9	4.4	5.3	8.4	9.5	10.8	5.8
Hyperkinetic disorder	0.8	0.5	0.7	2.6	1.3	1.0	1.7	3.0	2.6	1.5
Less common disorders	1.6	0.7	0.8	1.9	0.8	0.7	1.3	1.5	2.5	1.2
Any disorder	6.1	4.4	6.3	11.3	6.6	8.7	12.9	14.9	16.1	9.5
Base (weighted)	*581*	*668*	*1541*	*703*	*992*	*506*	*1298*	*1180*	*237*	*7705*

1. This is the National Statistics Socio-economic classification (NS–SEC).

Table **4.15**

Prevalence of mental disorders by tenure, age and sex, 2004

All children   Great Britain

	Tenure			
	Owners	Social sector tenants	Private renters	All
	Percentage of children with each disorder			
BOYS				
5- to 10-year-olds				
Emotional disorders	1.4	4.0	4.3	2.2
Conduct disorders	5.0	11.8	9.4	6.9
Hyperkinetic disorder	2.3	3.5	4.5	2.7
Less common disorders	2.1	2.2	3.1	2.2
Any disorder	8.1	15.0	14.4	10.2
Base (weighted)	*1396*	*452*	*160*	*2009*
11- to 16-year-olds				
Emotional disorders	2.6	7.5	8.6	4.0
Conduct disorders	5.6	16.7	8.5	8.1
Hyperkinetic disorder	1.6	4.0	6.3	2.4
Less common disorders	1.4	1.9	2.8	1.6
Any disorder	9.2	22.6	19.1	12.6
Base (weighted)	*1516*	*433*	*151*	*2100*
All Boys				
Emotional disorders	2.0	5.7	6.4	3.1
Conduct disorders	5.3	14.2	9.0	7.5
Hyperkinetic disorder	1.9	3.7	5.4	2.6
Less common disorders	1.7	2.1	3.0	1.9
Any disorder	8.7	18.7	16.7	11.4
Base (weighted)	*2912*	*885*	*312*	*4108*
GIRLS				
5- to 10-year-olds				
Emotional disorders	1.8	4.8	2.0	2.5
Conduct disorders	1.3	7.0	3.5	2.8
Hyperkinetic disorder	0.1	1.0	1.3	0.4
Less common disorders	0.5	0.5	-	0.4
Any disorder	3.3	10.6	5.2	5.1
Base (weighted)	*1321*	*435*	*159*	*1914*
11- to 16-year-olds				
Emotional disorders	4.6	9.1	13.1	6.1
Conduct disorders	3.1	11.7	5.9	5.1
Hyperkinetic disorder	0.2	0.8	0.7	0.4
Less common disorders	0.8	1.2	4.2	1.1
Any disorder	7.1	18.8	18.9	10.3
Base (weighted)	*1413*	*409*	*128*	*1950*

Table **4.15** (contd)

Prevalence of mental disorders by tenure, age and sex, 2004

All children

	Tenure			
	Owners	Social sector tenants	Private renters	All
	Percentage of children with each disorder			
All Girls				
Emotional disorders	3.3	6.9	7.0	4.3
Conduct disorders	2.2	9.3	4.6	3.9
Hyperkinetic disorder	0.1	0.9	1.1	0.4
Less common disorders	0.6	0.8	1.9	0.8
Any disorder	5.3	14.6	11.3	7.8
Base (weighted)	*2734*	*844*	*287*	*3864*
ALL				
5- to 10-year-olds				
Emotional disorders	1.6	4.4	3.2	2.4
Conduct disorders	3.2	9.5	6.5	4.9
Hyperkinetic disorder	1.2	2.3	2.9	1.6
Less common disorders	1.3	1.4	1.6	1.3
Any disorder	5.8	12.9	9.8	7.7
Base (weighted)	*2718*	*887*	*319*	*3923*
11- to 16-year-olds				
Emotional disorders	3.5	8.3	10.7	5.0
Conduct disorders	4.4	14.3	7.3	6.6
Hyperkinetic disorder	0.9	2.4	3.8	1.4
Less common disorders	1.1	1.5	3.4	1.4
Any disorder	8.2	20.7	19.0	11.5
Base (weighted)	*2928*	*842*	*279*	*4049*
All children				
Emotional disorders	2.6	6.3	6.7	3.7
Conduct disorders	3.8	11.8	6.9	5.8
Hyperkinetic disorder	1.1	2.4	3.3	1.5
Less common disorders	1.2	1.4	2.4	1.3
Any disorder	7.0	16.7	14.1	9.6
Base (weighted)	*5646*	*1729*	*598*	*7973*

Table **4.16**

Prevalence of mental disorders by accommodation type, age and sex, 2004

All children   Great Britain

	Accomodation type				
	Detatched	Semi-detatched	Terraced house	Flat/ maisonette	All
	Percentage of children with each disorder				
BOYS					
5- to 10-year-olds					
Emotional disorders	1.2	2.5	1.9	5.1	2.2
Conduct disorders	4.9	6.4	9.1	6.7	6.9
Hyperkinetic disorder	2.0	3.3	2.9	1.9	2.7
Less common disorders	1.9	2.3	2.7	0.7	2.2
Any disorder	7.2	10.0	12.8	10.3	10.2
Base (weighted)	*493*	*735*	*616*	*161*	*2010*
11- to 16-year-olds					
Emotional disorders	3.3	3.6	4.9	6.1	4.0
Conduct disorders	3.2	9.2	11.4	8.4	8.1
Hyperkinetic disorder	1.2	2.8	2.9	3.5	2.4
Less common disorders	2.0	1.3	1.4	2.5	1.6
Any disorder	8.2	13.1	16.0	15.1	12.6
Base (weighted)	*594*	*780*	*590*	*132*	*2101*
All Boys					
Emotional disorders	2.3	3.1	3.4	5.5	3.1
Conduct disorders	4.0	7.9	10.2	7.5	7.5
Hyperkinetic disorder	1.6	3.1	2.9	2.6	2.6
Less common disorders	1.9	1.8	2.1	1.5	1.9
Any disorder	7.7	11.6	14.4	12.5	11.4
Base (weighted)	*1086*	*1514*	*1207*	*293*	*4111*
GIRLS					
5- to 10-year-olds					
Emotional disorders	1.2	2.6	3.0	4.2	2.5
Conduct disorders	0.7	3.3	3.4	4.3	2.8
Hyperkinetic disorder	0.2	0.3	0.3	1.5	0.4
Less common disorders	0.5	0.3	0.3	1.5	0.4
Any disorder	1.9	5.8	6.0	8.4	5.1
Base (weighted)	*453*	*712*	*612*	*134*	*1916*
11- to 16-year-olds					
Emotional disorders	2.4	6.8	8.5	6.6	6.1
Conduct disorders	2.1	4.6	7.6	9.1	5.1
Hyperkinetic disorder	0.2	0.2	0.5	1.1	0.4
Less common disorders	0.6	1.3	1.3	0.8	1.1
Any disorder	4.5	10.6	14.4	14.5	10.3
Base (weighted)	*511*	*738*	*590*	*106*	*1950*

The total includes a small number of children living in 'other' types of accommodation.

Table **4.16** (contd)

Prevalence of mental disorders by accommodation type, age and sex, 2004

All children   Great Britain

	Accommodation type				
	Detatched	Semi-detatched	Terraced house	Flat/ maisonette	All
	Percentage of children with each disorder				
All Girls					
Emotional disorders	1.9	4.7	5.7	5.3	4.3
Conduct disorders	1.4	4.0	5.4	6.4	3.9
Hyperkinetic disorder	0.2	0.3	0.4	1.3	0.4
Less common disorders	0.6	0.8	0.8	1.2	0.8
Any disorder	3.3	8.2	10.1	11.1	7.8
Base (weighted)	*964*	*1450*	*1203*	*241*	*3866*
ALL					
5- to 10-year-olds					
Emotional disorders	1.2	2.6	2.4	4.7	2.4
Conduct disorders	2.9	4.9	6.3	5.6	4.9
Hyperkinetic disorder	1.1	1.8	1.6	1.7	1.6
Less common disorders	1.2	1.4	1.5	1.0	1.3
Any disorder	4.7	7.9	9.4	9.4	7.7
Base (weighted)	*946*	*1447*	*1229*	*295*	*3926*
11- to 16-year-olds					
Emotional disorders	2.9	5.1	6.7	6.3	5.0
Conduct disorders	2.7	7.0	9.5	8.7	6.6
Hyperkinetic disorder	0.8	1.6	1.7	2.4	1.4
Less common disorders	1.3	1.3	1.3	1.7	1.4
Any disorder	6.5	11.9	15.2	14.8	11.5
Base (weighted)	*1105*	*1518*	*1181*	*238*	*4051*
All children					
Emotional disorders	2.1	3.9	4.5	5.4	3.7
Conduct disorders	2.8	6.0	7.8	7.0	5.8
Hyperkinetic disorder	0.9	1.7	1.7	2.0	1.5
Less common disorders	1.3	1.3	1.4	1.4	1.3
Any disorder	5.6	10.0	12.2	11.8	9.6
Base (weighted)	*2051*	*2965*	*2410*	*533*	*7977*

The total includes a small number of children living in 'other' types of accommodation.

Table **4.17**

Prevalence of mental disorders by country, 1999 and 2004

All children aged 5–15   Great Britain

	England		Scotland	
	1999	2004	1999	2004
	Percentage of children with each disorder			
Children aged 5–10				
Emotional disorders	3.3	2.4	4.3	2.9
Conduct disorders	4.7	5.0	3.6	4.8
Hyperkinetic disorder	1.5	1.7	1.0	1.0
Any emotional, conduct or hyperkinetic disorder	7.9	6.9	7.4	6.6
Any disorder	8.3	8.1	7.7	6.6
Base (weighted)	*5070*	*3387*	*481*	*332*
Children aged 11–15				
Emotional disorders	5.5	5.5	4.8	2.0
Conduct disorders	6.3	7.3	5.8	6.4
Hyperkinetic disorder	1.5	1.3	1.3	2.3
Any emotional, conduct or hyperkinetic disorder	10.9	11.6	9.2	9.6
Any disorder	11.3	12.3	9.4	10.3
Base (weighted)	*3948*	*2977*	*411*	*287*
Boys				
Emotional disorders	4.2	3.2	3.4	2.2
Conduct disorders	7.5	8.1	6.7	6.6
Hyperkinetic disorder	2.5	2.7	2.0	2.1
Any emotional, conduct or hyperkinetic disorder	11.2	10.6	8.8	8.8
Any disorder	11.8	12.1	9.0	9.2
Base (weighted)	*4494*	*3278*	*461*	*318*
Girls				
Emotional disorders	4.3	4.5	5.8	2.9
Conduct disorders	3.3	4.0	2.5	4.4
Hyperkinetic disorder	0.5	0.3	0.2	1.0
Any emotional, conduct or hyperkinetic disorder	7.2	7.5	7.6	7.1
Any disorder	7.5	7.8	8.0	7.4
Base (weighted)	*4524*	*3086*	*432*	*300*
All children				
Emotional disorders	4.3	3.9	4.6	2.5
Conduct disorders	5.4	6.1	4.6	5.5
Hyperkinetic disorder	1.5	1.5	1.1	1.6
Any emotional, conduct or hyperkinetic disorder	9.2	9.1	8.2	8.0
Any disorder[1]	9.6	10.1	8.5	8.3
Base (weighted)	*9018*	*6364*	*892*	*618*

The shaded boxes indicate figures where the difference between the 1999 and 2004 prevalence is statistically significant at the 95% confidence level.
1. Includes less common disorders not shown in the table.

Table **4.18**

Prevalence of mental disorders by region, age and sex, 2004

All children

England

	Region				
	London Inner	London Outer	Other Met England	Non-Met England	All England
	Percentage of children with each disorder				
BOYS					
5- to 10-year-olds					
Emotional disorders	1.3	1.3	2.3	2.4	2.2
Conduct disorders	4.4	2.9	6.4	8.7	7.1
Hyperkinetic disorder	2.9	0.7	2.9	3.4	2.9
Less common disorders	1.3	1.4	2.4	3.0	2.5
Any disorder	8.1	5.5	10.2	11.9	10.5
Base (weighted)	85	175	621	856	1736
11- to 16-year-olds					
Emotional disorders	4.9	5.0	3.2	5.1	4.5
Conduct disorders	7.8	10.0	8.0	8.9	8.6
Hyperkinetic disorder	2.6	4.6	1.0	2.8	2.3
Less common disorders	1.2	3.6	1.5	1.8	1.8
Any disorder	13.6	16.7	11.5	14.2	13.4
Base (weighted)	91	154	637	934	1816
All Boys					
Emotional disorders	3.1	3.0	2.8	3.8	3.4
Conduct disorders	6.2	6.2	7.2	8.8	7.9
Hyperkinetic disorder	2.7	2.5	2.0	3.1	2.6
Less common disorders	1.3	2.4	1.9	2.4	2.2
Any disorder	11.0	10.7	10.9	13.1	12.0
Base (weighted)	175	329	1258	1790	3552
GIRLS					
5- to 10-year-olds					
Emotional disorders	2.9	2.5	2.6	2.8	2.7
Conduct disorders	1.7	0.9	2.5	3.7	2.9
Hyperkinetic disorder	-	-	0.2	0.7	0.4
Less common disorders	-	0.9	0.9	0.1	0.5
Any disorder	4.6	4.3	5.2	6.1	5.5
Base (weighted)	84	161	589	818	1652
11- to 16-year-olds					
Emotional disorders	3.5	6.5	7.2	6.6	6.7
Conduct disorders	3.7	2.7	6.6	4.8	5.2
Hyperkinetic disorder	1.9	-	0.3	0.2	0.3
Less common disorders	-	1.5	1.3	0.9	1.1
Any disorder	7.1	10.7	12.1	10.2	10.8
Base (weighted)	62	172	606	850	1689

Table **4.18** (contd)

Prevalence of mental disorders by region, age and sex, 2004

All children

England

	Region				
	London Inner	London Outer	Other Met England	Non-Met England	All England
	Percentage of children with each disorder				
All Girls					
Emotional disorders	3.2	4.6	4.9	4.7	4.7
Conduct disorders	2.6	1.8	4.6	4.3	4.1
Hyperkinetic disorder	0.8	-	0.3	0.4	0.3
Less common disorders	-	1.2	1.1	0.5	0.8
Any disorder	5.7	7.6	8.7	8.2	8.2
Base (weighted)	*146*	*332*	*1194*	*1668*	*3341*
ALL					
5- to 10-year-olds					
Emotional disorders	2.1	1.9	2.5	2.6	2.4
Conduct disorders	3.1	1.9	4.5	6.2	5.0
Hyperkinetic disorder	1.4	0.4	1.6	2.0	1.7
Less common disorders	0.7	1.1	1.6	1.6	1.5
Any disorder	6.4	4.9	7.8	9.1	8.1
Base (weighted)	*169*	*335*	*1210*	*1674*	*3387*
11- to 16-year-olds					
Emotional disorders	4.3	5.8	5.2	5.9	5.5
Conduct disorders	6.2	6.2	7.3	7.0	7.0
Hyperkinetic disorder	2.3	2.2	0.7	1.6	1.4
Less common disorders	0.7	2.5	1.4	1.4	1.4
Any disorder	11.0	13.6	11.8	12.3	12.2
Base (weighted)	*153*	*325*	*1243*	*1784*	*3505*
All children					
Emotional disorders	3.1	3.8	3.8	4.3	4.0
Conduct disorders	4.5	4.0	5.9	6.6	6.0
Hyperkinetic disorder	1.8	1.3	1.1	1.8	1.5
Less common disorders	0.7	1.8	1.5	1.5	1.5
Any disorder	8.6	9.2	9.8	10.7	10.2
Base (weighted)	*321*	*661*	*2453*	*3458*	*6893*

Table **4.19**

Prevalence of mental disorders by ACORN classification, age and sex, 2004

Great Britain

	ACORN classification					
	Wealthy Achievers	Urban prosperity	Comfortably off	Moderate Means	Hard pressed	All
	Percentage of children with each disorder					
BOYS						
5- to 10-year-olds						
Emotional disorders	0.8	2.5	2.3	1.6	3.5	2.1
Conduct disorders	3.8	3.1	6.6	9.4	9.8	6.9
Hyperkinetic disorder	1.4	0.7	2.8	3.6	4.3	2.8
Less common disorders	1.1	2.8	2.2	3.0	2.4	2.2
Any disorder	5.5	7.3	9.3	13.3	14.4	10.1
Base (weighted)	*488*	*177*	*502*	*355*	*475*	*1998*
11- to 16-year-olds						
Emotional disorders	2.8	2.1	3.0	5.3	6.2	4.0
Conduct disorders	3.3	7.1	6.9	10.1	13.7	8.1
Hyperkinetic disorder	2.2	4.6	1.2	2.4	3.5	2.5
Less common disorders	1.7	0.8	1.7	1.5	1.6	1.6
Any disorder	8.3	11.0	10.3	15.1	19.0	12.7
Base (weighted)	*552*	*147*	*538*	*353*	*495*	*2085*
All Boys						
Emotional disorders	1.9	2.3	2.7	3.5	4.9	3.1
Conduct disorders	3.6	4.9	6.7	9.8	11.8	7.5
Hyperkinetic disorder	1.8	2.5	2.0	3.0	3.9	2.6
Less common disorders	1.4	1.9	2.0	2.3	2.0	1.9
Any disorder	7.0	9.0	9.8	14.2	16.8	11.5
Base (weighted)	*1041*	*324*	*1040*	*708*	*970*	*4083*
GIRLS						
5- to 10-year-olds						
Emotional disorders	1.4	2.2	2.1	2.4	3.7	2.4
Conduct disorders	0.9	1.3	1.8	2.6	6.3	2.8
Hyperkinetic disorder	0.4	-	0.5	-	0.7	0.4
Less common disorders	0.5	-	0.5	0.6	0.4	0.4
Any disorder	2.5	3.5	3.9	5.6	8.6	5.0
Base (weighted)	*462*	*151*	*481*	*327*	*477*	*1898*
11- to 16-year-olds						
Emotional disorders	4.5	3.6	5.9	7.8	8.0	6.2
Conduct disorders	1.8	4.6	4.0	6.1	9.8	5.1
Hyperkinetic disorder	0.2	-	0.3	0.7	0.5	0.4
Less common disorders	1.1	-	1.4	0.9	1.1	1.0
Any disorder	6.5	8.1	8.7	12.2	16.4	10.4
Base (weighted)	*517*	*144*	*526*	*315*	*434*	*1936*

Table **4.19** (contd)

Prevalence of mental disorders by ACORN classification, age and sex, 2004

	ACORN classification					
	Wealthy Achievers	Urban prosperity	Comfortably off	Moderate Means	Hard pressed	All
	Percentage of children with each disorder					
All Girls						
Emotional disorders	3.0	2.9	4.1	5.1	5.8	4.3
Conduct disorders	1.4	2.9	2.9	4.3	7.9	4.0
Hyperkinetic disorder	0.3	-	0.4	0.3	0.6	0.4
Less common disorders	0.8	-	0.9	0.8	0.7	0.7
Any disorder	4.6	5.7	6.4	8.8	12.3	7.7
Base (weighted)	*978*	*296*	*1007*	*641*	*911*	*3834*
ALL						
5- to 10-year-olds						
Emotional disorders	1.1	2.4	2.2	2.0	3.6	2.3
Conduct disorders	2.4	2.3	4.2	6.2	8.0	4.9
Hyperkinetic disorder	0.9	0.4	1.7	1.9	2.5	1.6
Less common disorders	0.8	1.5	1.4	1.8	1.4	1.3
Any disorder	4.1	5.5	6.7	9.6	11.5	7.6
Base (weighted)	*950*	*328*	*983*	*682*	*953*	*3896*
11- to 16-year-olds						
Emotional disorders	3.6	2.8	4.4	6.5	7.1	5.1
Conduct disorders	2.6	5.8	5.5	8.3	11.9	6.7
Hyperkinetic disorder	1.2	2.3	0.8	1.6	2.1	1.4
Less common disorders	1.4	0.4	1.6	1.3	1.4	1.3
Any disorder	7.4	9.6	9.5	13.7	17.8	11.6
Base (weighted)	*1069*	*292*	*1064*	*668*	*929*	*4021*
All children						
Emotional disorders	2.4	2.6	3.4	4.2	5.3	3.7
Conduct disorders	2.5	4.0	4.9	7.2	9.9	5.8
Hyperkinetic disorder	1.1	1.3	1.2	1.7	2.3	1.5
Less common disorders	1.1	1.0	1.5	1.6	1.4	1.3
Any disorder	5.8	7.4	8.2	11.7	14.6	9.6
Base (weighted)	*2019*	*619*	*2047*	*1350*	*1881*	*7916*

Table 4.20

Odds Ratios for socio-demographic correlates of mental disorders, 2004

All children   Great Britain

Variable	Emotional disorders Adjusted Odds ratio	95% C.I.	Conduct disorders Adjusted Odds ratio	95% C.I.	Hyperkinetic disorders Adjusted Odds ratio	95% C.I.	Any disorder[1] Adjusted Odds ratio	95% C.I.
Age					NS			
5–10	1.00		1.00				1.00	
11–15	2.28***	(1.71–3.03)	1.62***	(1.29–2.03)			1.73***	(1.45–2.07)
Sex								
Female	1.00		1.00		1.00		1.00	
Male	0.70**	(0.54–0.90)	1.91***	(1.52–2.40)	6.10***	(3.39–10.99)	1.52***	(1.28–1.80)
Ethnic group	NS				NS			
White			1.00				1.00	
Black Caribbean			0.36				0.58	
Black African			0.01				0.11*	(0.02–0.79)
Indian			0.13*	(0.02–0.96)			0.21**	(0.07–0.67)
Pakistani			0.37*	(0.15–0.95)			0.47*	(0.24–0.92)
Bangladeshi			0.31				0.38	
Mixed			1.01				1.08	
Other			0.31				0.36	
Family type					NS			
Married	1.00		1.00				1.00	
Cohabiting	1.50		1.09				1.20	
Lone parent – single	1.71*	(1.03–2.86)	1.34				1.23	
Lone parent–previously married	2.48***	(1.68–3.68)	1.59**	(1.14–2.22)			1.75***	(1.35–2.26)
Reconstituted families	NS				NS			
No stepchildren			1.00				1.00	
Stepchildren present			1.92***	(1.37–2.69)			1.52**	(1.16–2.00)
Family's employment								
Neither parent working	1.00		1.00		1.00		1.00	
One parent working	0.85		0.68*	(0.46–1.00)	0.47		0.74	
Both parents working	0.56**	(0.39–0.81)	0.51***	(0.38–0.70)	0.47*	(0.26–0.85)	0.61***	(0.48–0.79)
Weekly household income								
More than £600	NS		1.00		1.00		1.00	
Between £400–£600			1.27		2.12*	(1.10–4.05)	1.3*	(1.0–1.69)
Less than £400			1.79**	(1.24–2.60)	1.88		1.46**	(1.11–1.93)
Parent's educational qualifications					NS			
Any qualification	1.00		1.00				1.00	
No qualification	1.52**	(1.11–2.07)	1.43**	(1.10–1.84)			1.55***	(1.26–1.91)

*** $p<0.001$, ** $p<0.01$, * $p<0.05$
Variables which were not significant predictors of the disorder are denoted as 'NS'.
Confidence intervals are shown only for categories that were significantly different from the reference category
   (ie the category with an odds ratio of 1.00).
1. *Includes less common disorders not shown in the table.*

Table **4.20** (contd)

Odds Ratios for socio-demographic correlates of mental disorders

All children   Great Britain 2004

Variable	Emotional disorders		Conduct disorders		Hyperkinetic disorders		Any disorder[1]	
	Adjusted Odds ratio	95% C.I.	Adjusted Odds ratio	95% C.I.	Adjusted Odds ratio	95% C.I.	Adjusted Odds ratio	95% C.I.
ACORN Group	NS				NS			
Wealthy achievers			1.00				1.00	
Urban prosperity			1.14				1.10	
Comfortably off			1.63*	(1.10–2.42)			1.26	
Moderate means			2.13***	(1.40–3.23)			1.74***	(1.29–2.35)
Hard pressed			2.10***	(1.41–3.13)			1.64***	(1.23–2.18)
Country	NS				NS			
England			1.00				1.00	
Scotland			0.80				0.77	

*** $p<0.001$, ** $p<0.01$, * $p<0.05$
Variables which were not significant predictors of the disorder are denoted as 'NS'.
Confidence intervals are shown only for categories that were significantly different from the reference category
   (ie the category with an odds ratio of 1.00).
1. Includes less common disorders not shown in the table.

Table **4.21**

Odds ratios for socio-demographic correlates of emotional disorders, 2004

All children   Great Britain

Variable	Anxiety disorders		Depressive disorders		All emotional disorders	
	Adjusted Odds ratio	95% C.I.	Adjusted Odds ratio	95% C.I.	Adjusted Odds ratio	95% C.I.
Age						
5–10	1.00		1.00		1.00	
11–16	2.07***	(1.53–2.79)	6.20***	(2.89–13.3)	2.28***	(1.71–3.03)
Sex						
Female	1.00		1.00		1.00	
Male	0.75*	(0.57–0.99)	0.51*	(0.30–0.88)	0.70**	(0.54–0.90)
Family type						
Married	1.00		1.00		1.00	
Cohabiting	1.66*	(1.02–2.73)	0.97		1.50	
Lone parent – single	1.74*	(1.01–2.99)	1.75		1.71*	(1.03–2.86)
Lone parent – previously married	2.55***	(1.68–3.86)	2.83**	(1.28–6.28)	2.48***	(1.68–3.68)
Family's employment						
Neither parent working	1.00		1.00		1.00	
One parent working	0.9		0.87		0.85	
Both parents working	0.56**	(0.38–0.83)	0.40*	(0.19–0.85)	0.56**	(0.39–0.81)
Parent's educational qualifications			NS			
Any qualification	1.00				1.00	
No qualification	1.50*	(1.08–2.08)			1.52**	(1.11–2.07)

*** p<0.001, ** p<0.01, * p<0.05
Variables which were not significant predictors of the disorder are denoted as 'NS' .
Confidence intervals are shown only for categories that were significantly different from the reference category
   (ie the category with an odds ratio of 1.00).
1. Includes less common disorders not shown in the table.

Emotional
disorders

Chapter 5

Introduction

This chapter begins by describing the types of behaviour patterns typically found among children and young people who have an emotional disorder. It goes on to describe the characteristics of these children and young people, looking at their:

- demographic characteristics;
- family situation;
- socio-economic characteristics;
- geographic distribution;
- general, physical and mental health;
- use of services;
- scholastic ability and attendance at school;
- family's social functioning;
- their own social functioning; and
- lifestyle behaviours.

As Chapter 4 noted, there was little change between 1999 and 2004 in the prevalence rates of emotional disorders among children and young people, either overall or within different subgroups. It is therefore possible to combine the two sets of data so as to increase the sample base. This allows us to analyse the larger subcategories of emotional disorders:

- Separation anxiety.
- Specific phobia.
- Social phobia.
- Generalised anxiety disorder.
- Depression.

The remaining subgroups (Panic, Agoraphobia, Post-traumatic Stress disorder, Obsessive Compulsive Disorder and Other anxiety disorders) are too small for separate analysis and are not shown as separate categories in the tables. However, they are included in the 'Any emotional disorder' total.

As far as possible, the same questions and classifications were used in both the 1999 and the 2004 surveys. However, some changes were necessary to improve the questions or to cover new topics. In these cases, data are presented for 2004 only and hence the bases in some subgroups are very small. We have not commented on the characteristics of these very small groups.

Within each topic, the text generally follows the same pattern: first, children with any form of emotional disorder are compared with those who have no such disorder; then, any variations from the overall pattern within the subcategories of emotional disorders are reported. The shaded boxes summarise the main features of the group as a whole followed by those for each subgroup including any characteristics on which they differ from the overall pattern. The commentary is descriptive, the aim being to provide a profile of children who have different types of emotional disorder. It therefore takes no account of the inter-relationships between the characteristics. The analysis at the end of Chapter 4 described the factors which had the largest independent effects on prevalence and this gives an indication of the key variables.

Typical behaviour patterns

A description of typical symptoms displayed by children with different types of emotional disorders is given below. As noted in Chapter 2, many children display the symptoms listed to some degree. To count as a disorder symptoms have to be sufficiently severe to cause distress to the child or impairment in functioning. In order to illustrate the impact of the disorder on the child's life and that of his or her family, the symptoms are followed by a case vignette of a fictitious child.[1]

Separation anxiety

Typical symptoms are concerns about: separation from an attachment figure, for example, because of loss of or harm to that person or the child being taken away; not wanting to go to school; being afraid of sleeping or being at home alone. The child may feel sick, anxious or have nightmares about the possibility of separation.

He gets frantic if left on his own at all – he follows me from room to room, he doesn't want me to have my own life. He won't stay with his friends or even stay the night with his gran like all his cousins do. He won't even stay over with his dad (we're divorced and I've remarried). It is not always easy to get him to go to school and he has to phone me at lunch time to check up on me. I feel like a prisoner at times, with him as my warder. He is reluctant to let me go to the bathroom by myself, waiting outside the door until I come out. He gets upset if I want to go out with my new husband, and needs to know when I'll be back, and waits up for me.

Specific phobia

This disorder is characterised by excessive fears about particular objects or situations, for example: animals, storms, the dark, loud noises, blood, infections or injuries, dentists or doctors, vomiting, choking or diseases, types of transport, enclosed spaces, toilets, people who look unusual, monsters, etc. The child becomes very upset each time the stimulus is triggered

---

1. *The symptoms and vignettes are based on descriptions of a 'made up' child created by Youthinmind to illustrate the diagnostic classification system.*

and tries to avoid such situations.

He is really terrified of dogs. I know lots of children are afraid of big dogs or aggressive dogs, but this is different. He is afraid of any dog, no matter how friendly or well-behaved it is. He doesn't want one to come near him and if one does, then he screams and grabs me tight or tries to run away. On several occasions, he has run into the road without looking just to get out of the way. He won't go to the house of his best friend or his grandparents because they have dogs. He's old enough to go places on his own, but he won't just in case he meets a dog.

Social phobia

Typical symptoms are anxiety about: meeting new or large groups of people, eating, reading or writing in front of others, speaking in class. The child may be able to socialise with familiar people in small numbers but is frightened of interacting with other adults or children. The anxiety is typically due to fear of embarrassment. The child becomes distressed (for example, blushes or feels sick) and tries to avoid such social situations.

She doesn't like being with people she doesn't know, she is extremely shy. Once she's used to people, she's alright with them, just so long as she's with them one-to-one. But she doesn't even like family parties with her cousins and uncles and aunts, even though she's OK with them individually. At school, she doesn't want to do anything that will make her noticed. She's never yet acted in a school play, or anything like that. Her teacher says she's very quiet in class.

Generalised anxiety

The child worries about a wide range of past, present or future events and situations, for example: past behaviour, school work and exams, disasters and accidents, his/her own health, weight or appearance, bad things happening to others, the future, making and keeping friends, death and dying, being bullied and teased. The anxiety is accompanied by physical symptoms such as restlessness, fatigue, poor concentration, irritability, muscular tension or insomnia.

I can't think of anything that he doesn't worry about. If it's not worry about his health, it's worry about whether he might have upset people at school, or about his homework, or about asteroids hitting the earth, or about them burning down the rainforest. He'll worry himself sick about the slightest little thing, like whether he might have made a spelling mistake in a school essay he's just handed in. Just that will stop him going to sleep – I'll be going to bed and he'll call me into his room needing yet more reassurance before he can get to sleep.

Depression

Depression is characterised by feelings of sadness, irritability and loss of interest which last for most of the day and persist over a period of time. Associated features may be: tiredness, changed appetite, weight loss or gain, insomnia, hypersomnia, agitation, feelings of worthlessness or guilt, poor concentration, thoughts of death, recent talk or experience of deliberate self harm.

This last month or so she seems really down in the dumps. She has been crying about the slightest little thing. If you say anything to her, she is likely to snap back at you. A few times I've heard her being really grumpy with her friends when they have called up to speak to her. They don't call up any more. She used to have many interests, like her favourite soap operas, playing on the computer, listening to her music. But now she's just not interested in any of it. She just stays in her room and only comes down if we insist. She is waking up really early in the morning, and she then often wakes the rest of us up too. She's stopped eating even her favourite meals, and she looks a lot thinner. I don't know if it's due to being tired or eating less, but she doesn't have her usually energy any more. It's hard getting her off to school, and when she's home again, I doubt if she gets much homework done since she's tired and she can't seem to focus on anything.

Demographic, socio-economic and area characteristics

Demographic characteristics

Children with an emotional disorder were more likely to be girls and more likely to be aged 11–16 than those with no such disorder (54 per cent compared with 49 per cent and 62 per cent compared with 46 per cent). Within the emotional disorder subgroups, the generalised anxiety category contained a particularly high proportion of girls compared with children with no emotional disorder (59 per cent). The preponderance of older children was evident in most subgroups. However, as might be expected, those with separation anxiety tended to be young: 68 per cent were aged 5–10. There were no ethnic variations between children who had and those who had no emotional disorders. (Figure 5.1 and Table 5.1)

Family characteristics

Children with emotional disorders were twice as likely as those with no such disorder to live with a widowed, divorced or separated lone parent (31 per cent compared with 15 per cent). Conversely, they were much less likely to live in a married couple household (51 per cent compared with 69 per cent).

Figure **5.1**
Age by type of emotional disorder, 1999 and 2004 combined

Great Britain

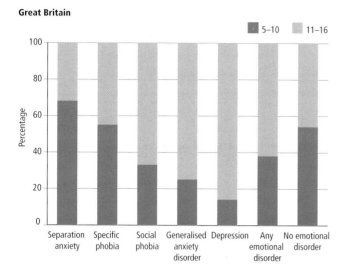

This pattern was evident across all types of disorder. Among children with separation anxiety, the proportion living with a single lone parent was also relatively high, 16 per cent compared with 8 per cent among children with no emotional disorder. (Figure 5.2 and Table 5.2)

Children with an emotional disorder tended to have more siblings than other children: 37 per cent of the former lived in households with three or more other children compared with 32 per cent of the latter. However, only those with generalised anxiety disorder were more likely to live in a family containing stepchildren, 19 per cent compared with 11 per cent among children with no emotional disorder. (Table 5.2)

Figure **5.2**
Family type by type of emotional disorder, 1999 and 2004 combined

Great Britain

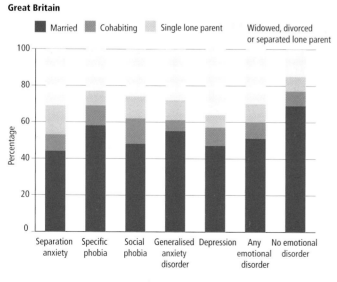

Parental education and socio-economic characteristics

Children with an emotional disorder were more likely than other children to have parents with no educational qualifications and to live in low-income families.

Over a third (35 per cent) of children with an emotional disorder had parents who had no educational qualifications compared with only a fifth (20 per cent) of those with no such disorder. The same variation occurred in all the subgroups.

(Table 5.3)

Children with an emotional disorder were twice as likely as other children to live in households in which neither parent was working (30 per cent compared with 14 per cent). Conversely, only a half (51 per cent) lived in households with both parents working compared with two-thirds (68 per cent) of children with no such disorder. Likewise, with respect to the socio-economic classification of the household reference person: 48 per cent of the children with an emotional disorder had a parent in the semi-routine or routine occupational group compared with 38 per cent of other children. (Table 5.3)

Housing and income

The economic disadvantages of children with an emotional disorder are also reflected in housing and income differentials. Only a half (49 per cent) lived in owned accommodation compared with over two-thirds (70 per cent) of other children. Similarly, over a half (54 per cent) of children with an emotional disorder lived in households with gross incomes under £300 per week whereas only a third (33 per cent) of other children were in this position.

One-fifth of children with an emotional disorder lived in households in which someone received a disability benefit (20 per cent compared with 8 per cent for other children).

(Table 5.4)

Area characteristics

The tendency for children with an emotional disorder to live in less affluent circumstances than other children was also evident from the type of area in which they lived. One third (34 per cent) lived in areas classified (by ACORN) as 'Hard pressed' compared with less than a quarter (23 per cent) of children with no emotional disorder. (Table 5.5)

The trend for children with emotional disorders to live in less affluent households prevailed in all subgroups. In general, differences between the subgroups were not statistically significant. However, there was a fairly consistent pattern for children with separation anxiety to live in the poorest economic circumstances across a range of measures. Thus, 62 per cent lived in households with gross incomes of less than £300 per week, 34 per cent had neither parent working and 45 per cent

lived in areas classified as 'Hard pressed'. This is mainly because a relatively high proportion of these children lived in one parent families. (Tables 5.3 – 5.5)

Among children with emotional disorders:

- 54 per cent were girls *(compared with 49 per cent for children with no emotional disorder)*
- 62 per cent were aged 11–16 *(46 per cent)*
- 31 per cent lived with a widowed, divorced or separated lone parent *(15 per cent)*
- 51 per cent lived in a married couple family *(69 per cent)*
- 37 per cent lived in households containing 3 or more children *(32 per cent)*
- 35 per cent had parents with no educational qualifications *(20 per cent)*
- 49 per cent lived in owned accommodation *(70 per cent)*
- 54 per cent lived in households with gross incomes under £300 per week *(33 per cent)*
- 20 per cent lived in households in which someone received a disability benefit *(8 per cent)*
- 34 per cent lived in areas classified as 'Hard pressed' *(23 per cent)*

Among children with separation anxiety:

- 49 per cent were girls
- 32 per cent were aged 11–16
- 31 per cent lived with a widowed, divorced or separated lone parent and 16 per cent lived with a single lone parent
- 62 per cent lived in households with gross incomes under £300 per week

Among children with specific phobias:

- 52 per cent were girls
- 45 per cent were aged 11–16
- 24 per cent lived with a widowed, divorced or separated lone parent
- 49 per cent lived in households with gross incomes under £300 per week

Child's general, physical and mental health

General health

The parents of children with an emotional disorder were more than four times as likely as other parents to say that their child's general health was fair or bad (23 per cent compared with 5 per cent). (Figure 5.3 and Table 5.6)

Among children with social phobias:

- 47 per cent were girls
- 67 per cent were aged 11–16
- 26 per cent lived with a widowed, divorced or separated lone parent and 14 per cent lived in a cohabiting couple family
- 45 per cent had a parent with no educational qualifications
- 44 per cent lived in households with gross incomes under £300 per week

Among children with generalised anxiety disorders:

- 59 per cent were girls
- 75 per cent were aged 11–16
- 28 per cent lived with a widowed, divorced or separated lone parent
- 19 per cent lived in a family containing stepchildren
- 51 per cent lived in households with gross incomes under £300 per week

Among children with depression:

- 57 per cent were girls
- 86 per cent were aged 11–16
- 37 per cent lived with a widowed, divorced or separated lone parent
- 57 per cent lived in households with gross incomes under £300 per week

Figure 5.3
Child's general health by type of emotional disorder, 1999 and 2004 combined

Great Britain

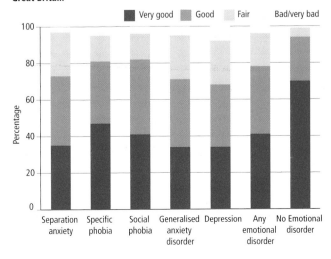

Physical and developmental problems

Parents of children with an emotional disorder were also more likely than other parents to report that their child had a specific complaint (72 per cent and 53 per cent). The largest differences were for: asthma (23 per cent and 14 per cent), stomach or digestive problems (14 per cent and 5 per cent) and migraine or severe headaches (12 per cent and 4 per cent). (Table 5.7)

The poorer general health of children with emotional disorders was evident in all subgroups as was their greater propensity to report specific complaints. There were, however, no differences between the subgroups nor any consistent pattern of variation across the complaints.

Mental disorders

A substantial minority (27 per cent) of children with an emotional disorder also suffered from another of the main types of clinically recognisable mental disorder, most commonly conduct disorder (23 per cent). In most subgroups, children with emotional disorders who were also diagnosed with a conduct disorder generally had oppositional defiant disorder. However, among those with depression and a conduct disorder, the majority had some other form of conduct disorder (26 per cent). (Figure 5.4 and Table 5.8)

Figure 5.4

Proportion of children with an emotional disorder who had another type of mental disorder, 1999 and 2004 combined

Great Britain

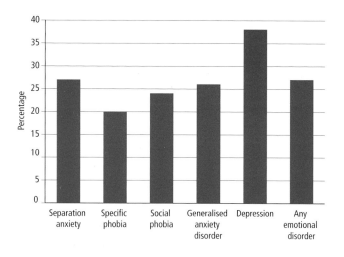

Parents were asked whether their child had any emotional problems, behavioural problems or hyperactivity. As would be expected, the parents of children with an emotional disorder were much more likely than other parents to report such problems (40 per cent compared with 9 per cent) but still less than a third (29 per cent) considered that their child had emotional problems. Almost as many, 23 per cent, mentioned behavioural problems – the same proportion as were clinically assessed as having a conduct disorder as well. Ten per cent considered that their child was hyperactive but only 4 per cent were clinically assessed as such. The low reporting rate for emotional problems among the parents of the children classified as having such disorders probably occurs because the symptoms have less impact on other family members and are less readily observable than behavioural problems and hyperkinesis. And, of course, parents do not classify symptoms in the same way as professionals. (Table 5.9)

Medication

The survey data suggests that there is no evidence that psychotropic drugs are being prescribed inappropriately for children with emotional disorders. First, the use of such medication is by no means widespread and rarely involves young children. Only seven per cent of the children with an emotional disorder were taking any form of medication at the time of interview and this includes 3 per cent who were taking Methylphenidate, all of whom had another type of disorder, usually hyperkinesis. Nearly three-quarters of all children on medication were aged 10 or over. Second, only one child with an emotional disorder was taking a trycyclic antidepressant whose effectiveness has not been proved for this group. And third, the Committee on the Safety of Medicines recommends that the only antidepressant that should be taken by children under 18 with depression is Fluoxetine. In fact, only three children with emotional disorders were taking this, all of whom had depression and only four children were taking other SSRI (selective serotonin re-uptake inhibitors) antidepressants (Citalopram/Cimpramil), of whom two had depression. (Table 5.10)

Among the parents of children with emotional disorders:

- 23 per cent reported that the child's general health was fair or bad *(compared with 5 per cent for children with no emotional disorder)*
- 72 per cent reported that the child had a specific physical or developmental problem *(53 per cent)*
- 23 per cent reported that the child suffered from asthma, 14 per cent reported stomach and digestive problems and 12 per cent reported migraine or severe headaches *(14 per cent, 5 per cent and 4 per cent)*
- 40 per cent reported that the child had mental health problems *(9 per cent)*
- 29 per cent reported that the child had emotional problems, 23 per cent reported behavioural problems and 10 per cent reported hyperactivity *(3 per cent, 5 per cent and 3 per cent)*
- 27 per cent of the children had another main type of clinically recognisable disorder *(5 per cent)*

Among the parents of children with separation anxiety:

- 27 per cent reported that the child's general health was fair or bad
- 80 per cent reported that the child had a physical or developmental problem
- 44 per cent reported that the child had mental health problems
- 27 per cent of the children had another main type of clinically recognisable disorder

Among the parents of children with specific phobias:

- 18 per cent reported that the child's general health was fair or bad
- 72 per cent reported that the child had a physical or developmental problem
- 29 per cent reported that the child had mental health problems
- 20 per cent of the children had another main type of clinically diagnosed disorder

Among the parents of children with social phobias:

- 18 per cent reported that the child's general health was fair or bad
- 73 per cent reported that the child had a physical or developmental problem
- 40 per cent reported that the child had mental health problems
- 24 per cent of the children had another main type of clinically recognisable disorder

Among the parents of children with generalised anxiety disorders:

- 29 per cent reported that the child's general health was fair or bad
- 73 per cent reported that the child had a physical or developmental problem
- 54 per cent reported that the child had mental health problems including 39 per cent who considered that the child had emotional problems
- 26 per cent of the children had another main type of clinically recognisable disorder

Among the parents of children with depression:

- 32 per cent reported that the child's general health was fair or bad
- 73 per cent reported that the child had a physical or developmental problem
- 53 per cent reported that the child had mental health problems including 40 per cent who considered that the child had emotional problems
- 38 per cent of the children had another main type of clinically recognisable disorder including 33 per cent who had a conduct disorder

Use of services

Parents were asked whether, in the last year, they had had contact with a range of specialist and non-professional services because they were worried about their child's emotions, behaviour or concentration. These questions were new for 2004. In the previous survey, the questioning covered different services and was directed only at those for whom significant problems had been reported in the interview. The questions in the 2004 survey were asked about all children.

In the year before interview, nearly three-quarters (73 per cent) of parents of children with an emotional disorder had sought some form of advice or help because of concerns about their child's mental health. Just under two-thirds (64 per cent) had contacted a professional source. The corresponding proportions for children with no disorder were 26 per cent and 21 per cent. (Table 5.11)

Teachers, were the most commonly used source, contacted by nearly a half (47 per cent) of the parents of children with an emotional disorder. Next were family members and friends (34 per cent) and primary health care professionals, such as GPs and practice nurses, (29 per cent). About a quarter (24 per cent) had contacted, or been referred to, a mental health service, usually a specialist in children's mental health. This group includes a small number, 2 per cent, who used a specialist in adult mental health. (Table 5.11)

Among the parents of children with emotional disorders:

- 73 per cent had sought help or advice in the last year because of worries about their child's mental health *(compared with 26 per cent for children with no emotional disorder)*
- 64 per cent had contacted a professional service *(21 per cent)*
- The most commonly used services were: teachers (47 per cent), family members or friends (34 per cent), primary health care (29 per cent) and mental health specialists *(24 per cent)*

Parents who had mentioned a problem with their child's emotions, attention or behaviour during the course of the interview and who had not seen a specialist were asked whether there was anything that had stopped them seeking such help. They were shown a card listing various obstacles that they might have encountered. Fewer than a third (30 per cent) had had any of the problems prompted and there were no differences between those whose children had a clinically diagnosed emotional disorder and other parents in this respect. Overall, the most common obstacles mentioned were a belief that a specialist would not be able to help (8 per cent), lack of awareness of the services available (7 per cent) and difficulty getting a referral (5 per cent). The latter two problems were also mentioned by those who were actually seeing a specialist (12 per cent and 10 per cent overall). (Tables not shown)

As these questions were based on 2004 data only, the bases for many of the subcategories of emotional disorder are small and summary boxes for types of emotional disorder have therefore not been presented.

Scholastic ability and attendance at school

Teachers were asked to rate the child's abilities in reading, mathematics and spelling compared with an average child of the same age and to estimate at what age the child was in terms of their scholastic ability. They were also asked to say whether the child had officially recognised special educational needs.

Basic skills

Children with emotional disorders were more likely than other children to be rated as having difficulty on each of the three skills assessed: 40 per cent had difficulty with reading, 45 per cent with mathematics and 46 per cent with spelling. For children with no emotional disorder, the proportions were 23 per cent, 24 per cent and 30 per cent. Likewise, with respect to

Figure 5.5

Proportion of children who were behind in their overall scholastic ability by whether they had an emotional disorder, 1999 and 2004 combined

Great Britain

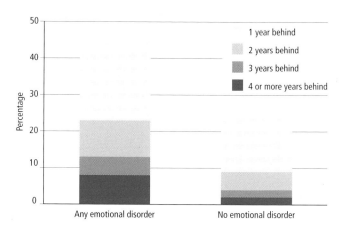

overall scholastic ability, as measured by subtracting the child's actual age from their functioning age: 44 per cent of those with an emotional disorder were behind in their overall intellectual development and 13 per cent were more than 2 years behind compared with 24 per cent and 4 per cent of other children. (Figure 5.5 and Table 5.12)

Looking at specific emotional disorders, differences on basic skills were generally not statistically significant and there was no difference between any of the groups on overall ability. (Table 5.12)

Special educational needs

Teachers reported that one in six children (17 per cent) had officially recognised needs, the same proportion as reported by the Department for Education and Skills for England (January 2004). Children with an emotional disorder were twice as likely as other children to be in this position (35 per cent compared with 16 per cent). Among the former, children with separation anxiety were most likely to have special educational needs (51 per cent) (Table 5.13)

Nearly a half (47 per cent) of all children with special needs had a written statement but there was no difference between those with, and those with no emotional disorder in this respect. (Based on 2004 data, Table not shown)

Absence from school

The majority of children had had some time away from school in the previous term but those with an emotional disorder were more likely to have been absent than other children (81 per cent compared with 68 per cent). The former were also away for longer periods – 43 per cent had had more than 5 days absence and 17 per cent had had more than 15 days absence in the previous term. Among those with no disorder, these proportions were much lower, 21 per cent and 4 per cent.

(Table 5.14)

It was noted earlier, that children with emotional disorders had poorer general health than other children and at least some of these absences will have been health related. In 2004, teachers were asked specifically about unauthorised absences. Children with emotional disorders were more than twice as likely as other children to have had these (21 per cent compared with 9 per cent). (Table not shown)[2]

Further evidence that some of the time away from school was unofficial comes from information on truancy. Teachers reported that one in six children (16 per cent) with an emotional disorder certainly or possibly played truant. For other children the proportion was only 3 per cent. (Table 5.14)

Children with generalised anxiety disorder and those with depression had the most days away from school – a quarter (25 per cent and 26 per cent) had had more than 15 days absence in the previous term. At least some of this time off was probably unauthorised - these groups were much more likely than other children to be considered definite or possible truants (26 per cent and 33 per cent).

(Figure 5.6 and Table 5.14)

In 2004, parents were asked about exclusions from school and other absences. Looking first at the latter, the parents' reports follow the same pattern as those of the teachers: over a half (54 per cent) of children with an emotional disorder had missed school for reasons other than exclusion in the previous term compared with a third (33 per cent) of other children.

(Table 5.15)

We would not expect the parents' data to match the teachers' reports because the latter were asked about all absences (including exclusions and truancies of which the parent might not be aware) and the figures in Tables 5.14 and 5.15 relate to different populations.

Among both groups of children, the most common reason for absence was illness, mentioned by three-quarters (78 per cent) of the parents of children who had been absent in the previous term. However, among the parents of those with an emotional disorder who had been absent, 15 per cent said that the child had refused to attend school or had a school phobia compared with only 2 per cent of other parents. One tenth (10 per cent) of the children who had been absent from school had received some form of educational provision and there were no differences between children with and those with no emotional disorder in this respect.

(Table 5.15)

Turning to exclusions from school, children with an emotional disorder were more likely than other children to have been excluded (12 per cent compared with 4 per cent) and 5 per cent had been excluded on three or more occasions. However, two-thirds of those excluded had another disorder, mainly conduct disorder. Among all excluded children, the majority of exclusions were fixed term but those with an emotional disorder were the more likely to have had some form of help following their exclusion (36 per cent compared with 14 per cent). (Tables not shown).

(Table 5.16)

Figure 5.6
Proportion of children whose teacher thought that they played truant by type of emotional disorder, 1999 and 2004 combined

Great Britain

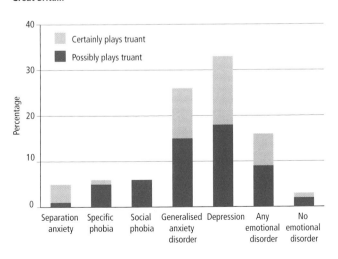

Among children with emotional disorders:

- 44 per cent were behind in their overall intellectual development *(compared with 24 per cent for children with no emotional disorder)*
- 35 per cent had officially recognised special educational needs *(16 per cent)*
- 43 per cent had more than 5 days away from school in the previous term and 17 per cent had had more than 15 days absence *(21 per cent and 4 per cent)*
- 16 per cent were considered by teachers to be definite or possible truants *(3 per cent)*
- 12 per cent had been excluded from school and 30 per cent had changed schools apart from normal transitions *(4 per cent and 19 per cent)*

2. The bases are too small to show a detailed breakdown.

Among children with separation anxiety:

- 44 per cent were behind in their overall intellectual development
- 51 per cent had officially recognised special educational needs
- 44 per cent had had more than 5 days away from school in the previous term and 14 per cent had had more than 15 days absence
- 5 per cent were considered by teachers to be definite or possible truants

Among children with specific phobias:

- 34 per cent were behind in their overall intellectual development
- 32 per cent had officially recognised special educational needs
- 36 per cent had had more than 5 days away from school in the previous term and 12 per cent had had more than 15 days absence
- 6 per cent were considered by teachers to be definite or possible truants

Among children with generalised anxiety disorders:

- 41 per cent were behind in their overall intellectual development
- 31 per cent had officially recognised special educational needs
- 56 per cent had had more than 5 days away from school in the previous term and 25 per cent had had more than 15 days absence
- 26 per cent were considered by teachers to be definite or possible truants

Among children with depression:

- 46 per cent were behind in their overall intellectual development
- 27 per cent had officially recognised special educational needs
- 65 per cent had had more than 5 days away from school in the previous term and 26 per cent had had more than 15 days absence
- 33 per cent were considered by teachers to be definite or possible truants

(Figures for children with social phobias are not shown because of the small base)

Another indicator of interrupted schooling is given by the number of times a child has changed school apart from the normal transitions between primary, junior and secondary school. Again, this was more common among those with an emotional disorder – 30 per cent had changed schools compared with 19 per cent of other children. This variation was not attributable to the higher rate of exclusions among those with an emotional disorder since none of these children had changed schools following their exclusion.   (Table 5.17)

Social functioning of the family

This section looks at various aspects of parental health, attitudes and behaviour which provide indicators of the social functioning of the family.

Mental health of parent

The parent who was interviewed about the child's behaviour, usually the mother, was asked about her own mental health using the General Health Questionnaire (GHQ-12 –see Chapter 2 for details). Scores range from 0 (no psychological distress) to 12 (severe psychological distress). A score of 3 is generally taken as the threshold with scores at this level or higher being considered indicative of an emotional disorder.

Overall, about one quarter of parents scored at or over the threshold which is similar to the proportion usually found in general population surveys. However, parents of children with an emotional disorder were more than twice as likely to have a score of 3 or more (51 per cent compared with 23 per cent among other parents). Almost one in five had very high scores of 9–12 (18 per cent compared with 4 per cent). This pattern occurred in all the disorder subgroups, the proportion scoring at or over the threshold ranging from 44 per cent among the

Figure 5.7

Proportion of children whose parent scored 3 or more on the GHQ-12, 1999 and 2004 combined

Great Britain

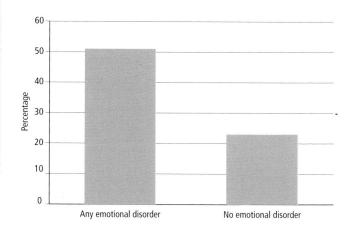

parents of children with a specific phobia to 61 per cent among the parents of those with depression.

(Figure 5.7 and Table 5.18)

Family functioning

Family functioning was measured using the FAD-GFS scale in which parents rated 12 statements about family relationships (see Chapter 2 for details). For this survey, families which scored over 2.00 on this scale were considered to have unhealthy family functioning.

One-third (33 per cent) of families containing children with an emotional disorder were assessed as having unhealthy functioning on this measure. Among other families, the proportion was 18 per cent. The functioning scores were relatively high for families with children in all the disorder subgroups except for those in which the child had a social phobia.

(Table 5.19)

Stressful life events

It has been suggested (Goodyer, 1990) that moderately or highly undesirable life events can cause the onset of emotional and behavioural symptoms in children of school age. Parents were asked whether their child had experienced any of 10 potentially stressful events. The list in the 2004 survey was slightly different to that used in 1999 so the data are presented for 2004 only.

Children with emotional disorders were more likely than other children to have experienced each of the 10 events listed. Over a half (55 per cent) had experienced their parents' separation and over a quarter (28 per cent) had a parent who had had a serious mental illness. For other children the proportions were 30 per cent and 7 per cent. Looking at the number of stressful life events, children with an emotional disorder were more than twice as likely as other children to have had two or more stressful events (59 per cent compared with 25 per cent)

(Tables 5.20 and 5.21)

Child's social functioning

A large part of the interview was concerned with various types of problems that children experienced. For 2004, new questions were introduced to examine the child's strengths, the rationale being that these might provide protection against the onset and course of mental disorder as well as providing parents with the opportunity to describe their child's good points. The section goes on to discuss other features of social functioning which might also affect the child's resilience: their relationships with friends, their social aptitudes and various measures of social capital.

Most of the findings presented in this section are based on new questions in the 2004 survey. The bases for the disorder subgroups are quite small and the commentary and summary boxes therefore focus on the differences between children with any emotional disorder and other children.

Strengths

Both parents and young people were asked to rate the child on a series of items covering various qualities (see Chapter 2 for details). Scores on the adult scale ranged from 0–48 and those on the children's scale ranged from 0–38. Table 5.22 shows the scores on each scale grouped into quartiles. Looking first at the parent's assessment, children with an emotional disorder were more than twice as likely as other children to have scores in the lowest quartile, 58 per cent compared with 24 per cent. The children's scale did not include all the items on the parent's scale and was asked only of young people aged 11–16 so the

Among children with emotional disorders:
- 51 per cent of parents had an emotional disorder (compared with 23 per cent for the parents of children with no emotional disorder)
- 33 per cent lived in families with unhealthy functioning *(18 per cent)*
- 59 per cent had had two or more stressful life events *(25 per cent)*

Among children with separation anxiety:
- 56 per cent of parents had an emotional disorder
- 37 per cent lived in families with unhealthy functioning
- 47 per cent had had two or more stressful life events

Among children with specific phobias:
- 44 per cent of parents had an emotional disorder
- 29 per cent lived in families with unhealthy functioning
- 49 per cent had had two or more stressful life events

Among children with social phobias:
- 50 per cent of parents had an emotional disorder
- 23 per cent lived in families with unhealthy functioning
(Stressful life event figures omitted because of small base)

Among children with generalised anxiety disorders:
- 59 per cent of parents had an emotional disorder
- 36 per cent lived in families with unhealthy functioning
- 63 per cent had had two or more stressful life events

Among children with depression:
- 61 per cent of parents had an emotional disorder
- 43 per cent lived in families with unhealthy functioning
- 67 per cent had had two or more stressful life events

scores are not directly comparable. However, the proportions scoring in the lowest quartile showed the same pattern as for the parent's assessment but the differential was much smaller, 34 per cent of young people with an emotional disorder were in this quartile compared with 23 per cent of other young people.

(Table 5.22)

Social aptitude

The social aptitude scale consisted of 10 questions addressed to parents designed to measure the child's ability to empathise with others (see Chapter 2 for details). Scores ranged from 0–40 and were grouped into quartiles. Those with an emotional disorder were again twice as likely as other children to have a score in the lowest quartile (48 per cent compared with 24 per cent)

(Table 5.23)

Social capital

'Social capital' is a multi-faceted concept which has been defined as 'networks together with shared norms, values and understandings that facilitate co-operation within and among groups' (Cote and Healey, 2001). It is believed that high levels of social capital have a positive effect on health. The aspects of social capital covered in this report are:

- relationships with friends;
- social support;
- views about the neighbourhood;
- help provided to others; and
- participation in clubs and groups.

Many of the questions are taken from the children and young person modules included in the 2003 Home Office Citizenship Survey. The questions on friends were asked of all parents. The remaining topics were asked of young people aged 11 or over only because previous research has shown that younger children were not able to cope with some of the more complex questioning. The analysis of these questions is not presented for the subcategories of emotional disorders because of the small bases.

Relationships with friends

Questions on friendships were asked of the interviewed parent and covered:

- the child's ability to make and keep friends;
- number of friends;
- common interests and shared activities;
- emotional support; and
- parent's approval of child's friends.

On the first three measures, children with an emotional disorder were four times as likely as those with no disorder to

have a negative assessment. For example, among the former, 35 per cent found it harder than average to make friends, 22 per cent found it harder to keep friends, and 11 per cent did not engage in shared activities. For other children, the proportions were 9 per cent, 5 per cent and 3 per cent. Similarly, 20 per cent of children with an emotional disorder had fewer than two friends compared with only 5 per cent of other children. The ratio was smaller in relation to whether the child could talk things over with a friend if they were worried: 29 per cent of the children with an emotional disorder had no such confidante compared with 21 per cent of other children.

(Table 5.24)

The parents of children with an emotional disorder were less likely to give their full approval to their child's friends: 35 per cent said that they did not approve at all or only approved a little compared with 15 per cent of other parents. Likewise, the former were more likely to say that many or all of their child's friends got into trouble, 7 per cent compared with 1 per cent.

(Table 5.24)

Social support

This scale, completed by young people aged 11–16, was designed to assess the extent of the network of family and friends to whom they felt close. Scores ranged from 0 to 20 and were grouped into rough quartiles. Those with an emotional disorder were one and a half times as likely as other young people to have a score in the lowest quartile (42 per cent compared with 27 per cent).

(Table 5.25)

Views about the neighbourhood

Young people with an emotional disorder were more likely than other young people to express negative views about their neighbourhood. For example, 23 per cent did not enjoy living there, 18 per cent felt unsafe walking alone in the daytime, 37 per cent felt that few or none of their neighbours could be trusted and 62 per cent thought it unlikely that a lost bag would be returned. The proportions among other young people were much lower: 7 per cent, 6 per cent, 17 per cent and 42 per cent.

(Table 5.26)

It may be that the nature of the young people's disorders coloured their attitudes, leading them to be, for example, more despondent about their surroundings or more fearful about safety. However, we noted earlier that a relatively high proportion of children with emotional disorders lived in areas classified (by ACORN) as 'Hard pressed' so it may be that their views partly reflect the type of neighbourhood in which they lived. Further analysis showed, however, that the variation persisted within each type of area. (Table not shown)

Help provided to others

Young people were asked separately about types of help that they provided to relatives and non-relatives. Almost all young people gave help to relatives but those with an emotional disorder were more likely than others to give help to non-relatives (52 per cent compared with 39 per cent). The former were more likely to give most of the different types of help specified. Of particular interest are the proportions who looked after a sick relative – 42 per cent compared with 33 per cent. As was discussed earlier, children with an emotional disorder were the more likely to have had a parent with a mental disorder and it may be that some of the young people were providing care for them. Among those who gave help, 76 per cent provided help to relatives at least once a week and there was no difference between those with and those with no emotional disorder in this respect. However, among those helping non-relatives, young people with an emotional disorder provided help more frequently – 51 per cent helped at least once a week compared with 37 per cent of other young people.

(Table 5.27)

There were no differences between young people with and those with no emotional disorder in the proportions who received payment for helping non-relatives – overall 63 per cent were sometimes or always paid. Thus, the greater propensity of young people with a disorder to help others is not due to the poorer financial situations of their families. (Table not shown). There were also no differences in the proportion doing regular paid work (that is, at least once a month) – 22 per cent overall.

(Table 5.28)

Participation in groups, clubs and organisations

Young people with an emotional disorder were less likely than other young people to have taken part in a group, club or organisation in the last year: 68 per cent compared with 79 per cent had taken part in a school-based group and 55 per cent compared with 67 per cent had taken part in a group outside school. Membership of sports groups and teams was the most common group activity, both inside and outside school. There was a marked variation in participation rates in sports groups between young people with and those with no emotional disorder: 35 per cent compared with 52 per cent for school-based groups and 20 per cent versus 38 per cent for other groups. One reason for this could be the poorer general health of children with disorders. The proportions mentioning barriers to participation showed the opposite pattern with 74 per cent of young people with a disorder mentioning a barrier, in particular, not wanting to participate, 28 per cent. For other young people these proportions were 58 per cent and 15 per cent. There was, however, little variation in the proportions

who had given unpaid help to a group, club or organisation, which is consistent with findings on the provision of help to individuals.

(Tables 5.29 and 5.31)

Among children with emotional disorders:

- 35 per cent found it harder than average to make friends *(compared with 9 per cent for children with no emotional disorder)*
- 35 per cent of parents did not fully approve of their child's friends *(15 per cent)*
- 23 per cent did not enjoy living in their neighbourhood *(7 per cent)*
- 97 per cent gave help to relatives and 52 per cent helped non- relatives *(93 per cent and 39 per cent)*
- 42 per cent looked after a sick relative *(33 per cent)*
- 68 per cent had taken part in a school-based group and 55 per cent had taken part in a group outside school in the last year *(79 per cent and 67 per cent)*

Smoking, drinking and drug use

Questions on smoking, drinking and drug use were included in both the 1999 and 2004 surveys. They were addressed to children aged 11–16 and were based on questions used in the national surveys of smoking, drinking and drug use among schoolchildren. A comparison of the data from the 1999 Children's Mental Health Survey with the 1999 Schools Survey showed that children interviewed at home systematically under-reported their smoking, drinking and drug use compared with those interviewed in school. Tables presented in this report should not therefore be taken as true estimates of prevalence. Their main value is in enabling comparisons to be made between children with a disorder and other children. Percentages are shown separately for young people aged 11–13 and those aged 14–16 and so the bases are not large enough to show figures for the subcategories of emotional disorder.

Young people with an emotional disorder were more likely to smoke, drink and take drugs than other children. The largest differences were for smoking and drug use where they were apparent among both age groups. Among all young people with an emotional disorder, 23 per cent were smokers and most of these (19 per cent) were classified as 'regular smokers' (smokes at least one cigarette a week). For other young people, the proportions were 8 per cent and 5 per cent. Likewise for drug use: 20 per cent of young people with an emotional disorder had used drugs, mainly cannabis, compared with 8 per cent of other young people. Drinking behaviour showed the same pattern but the difference was not so large and occurred only among the older age group: 23 per cent of young people aged 14–16 who had an emotional disorder were classified as 'regular drinkers' (drinking at least once a week) compared with 17 per cent of other young people.

(Figure 5.8 and Tables 5.32–5.34)

Figure 5.8

Smoking, drinking and drug use by whether has an emotional disorder: children aged 11–16, 1999 and 2004 combined

Great Britain 1999 & 2004 combined

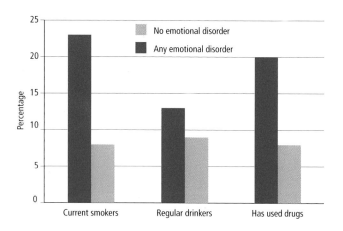

In the 2004 survey, young people were asked about the social context of the last occasions on which they had smoked, drunk alcohol and taken drugs. Table 5.35 shows the results for the last drinking occasion which had the largest base size. There were no differences between young people with an emotional disorder and other young people in terms of where and with whom they had last had a drink. Overall, young people were most likely to have drunk with friends (53 per cent) or family (44 per cent), in a small group of 3-6 people (45 per cent). The child's own home was the most popular venue (42 per cent), followed by someone else's home (28 per cent).

(Table 5.35)

The patterns for smoking and drug use were slightly different in that young people generally engaged in these behaviours with friends and rarely with family and the most common venue was outside in a public place. Again, however, there were no differences between young people with, and those with no, emotional disorder on these measures. (Tables not shown because the base sizes for the groups with no emotional disorder were small).

Among children aged 11–16 with emotional disorders:

- 19 per cent were regular smokers *(compared with 5 per cent for children with no emotional disorder)*
- 13 per cent were regular drinkers *(9 per cent)*
- 20 per cent had taken drugs at some time *(8 per cent)*

Self-harm

All parents were asked whether the child had ever tried to hurt, harm or kill themselves and the same question was asked of older children aged 11–16 (see Chapter 2 for details). Looking first at parents' reports for children of all ages, those whose child had an emotional disorder were much more likely to say that the child had tried to harm themselves, 14 per cent compared with 2 per cent. Young people aged 11–16 were more likely to report instances of self-harm than their parents but, among both groups, the rates were much higher for those with an emotional disorder, 28 per cent and 6 per cent based on self-reports and 19 per cent and 2 per cent based on parents' reports.

(Table 5.36)

Results from the six-month follow-up survey

Samples of the parents of children interviewed in the 1999 and 2004 surveys were sent a self-completion questionnaire six months after the interview in order to establish whether there had been any change in their symptoms (see Chapter 3).

The average levels of total and emotional symptoms among the children with emotional disorders did fall slightly over the six months following the survey. However, as Figures 5.9 and 5.10 show, the gap between children with and those with no emotional disorder only narrowed a little as a result. The symptoms of emotional disorders were typically persistent, at least in the short term. By contrast, the impact of these symptoms fell by about a half over the six months, as shown in Figure 5.11. At first glance, it seems surprising that impact halved although the level of symptoms was fairly steady. The most likely explanation is that the impact of symptoms depends not just on the symptoms themselves but on everything else in the child's life. Changes at home or at school may make symptoms easier or harder to live with. (Figures 5.9–5.11)

Since a diagnosis of an emotional disorder is only made when a child experiences both emotional symptoms and resultant impact, children can move in and out of having a diagnosable disorder according to whether or not their symptoms have a substantial impact at any given time. Some of the children who had a diagnosis of an emotional disorder at the time of the main survey would not have warranted a diagnosis six months later because their symptoms were not having a substantial impact. Conversely, some children who did not quite warrant a diagnosis at the time of the main survey would have met the criteria six months later because their symptoms were then having a substantial impact. The frontier between normality and disorder is somewhat arbitrary, so it not surprising that some children cross and re-cross the boundary as a result of the ups and downs of life (not to mention the imprecision of the diagnostic process itself).

Figure **5.9**
Total symptoms[1] at main interview and at six-month follow-up by whether child had an emotional disorder at main interview, 1999 and 2004 combined

Great Britain

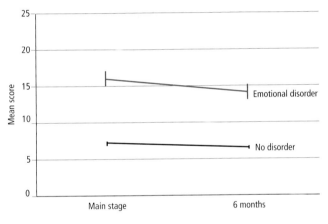

1. Total symptoms is the 'total difficulties score' on the parent-reported SDQ, reflecting the sum of the subscale scores for emotional symptoms, conduct problems, hyperactivity and peer problems.

Figure **5.10**
Emotional symptoms at main interview and at six-month follow-up by whether child had an emotional disorder at main interview, 1999 and 2004 combined

Great Britain

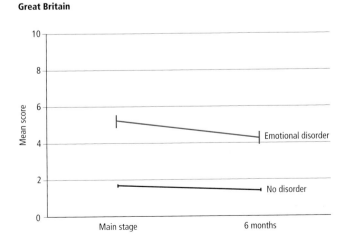

Figure **5.11**
Impact of symptoms at main interview and at six-month follow-up by whether child had an emotional disorder at main interview, 1999 and 2004 combined

Great Britain

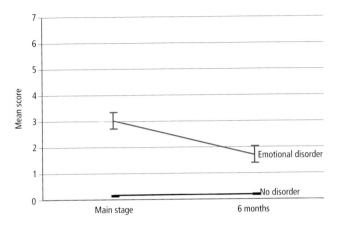

References

Committee on Safety of Medicines and the Medicines and Healthcare Regulatory Agency. (September 2003) .*SSRI factsheet*. Info@mhra.gsi.gov.uk or www.mca.gov.uk

Department for Education and Skills (January 2004) *Special Educational needs in England,* January 2004, National Statistics First Release, SFR 44/2004.

Goddard E and Higgins V (1999) *Smoking, drinking and drug use among young teenagers in 1998, Volume 1: England,* TSO: London.

Goodyer I M, Wright C and Altham P M E (1990) The friendships and recent life events of anxious and depressed school-age-children. *British Journal of Psychiatry,* **156 (May),** 689–698.

Home Office (December 2004) *2003 Home Office Citizenship Survey.* Home Office Research, Development and Statistics Directorate.

Meltzer H, Gatward R, Goodman R, and Ford T (2000) *The mental health of children and adolescents in Great Britain,* TSO: London.

Table **5.1**

Age, sex and ethnicity of child by type of emotional disorder, 1999 and 2004 combined

All children

Great Britain

| | Type of emotional disorder | | | | | | | |
	Separation anxiety	Specific phobia	Social phobia	Generalised anxiety disorder	Depression	Any emotional disorder[1]	No emotional disorder	All
	%	%	%	%	%	%	%	%
Sex								
Boys	51	48	54	41	43	46	51	51
Girls	49	52	47	59	57	54	49	49
Age								
5–10	68	55	33	25	14	38	54	53
11–16	32	45	67	75	86	62	46	47
Ethnicity								
White	91	91	93	92	90	90	89	89
Black[2]	4	3	2	1	2	3	3	3
Indian	-	1	-	1	4	1	2	2
Pakistani/ Bangladeshi	3	3	3	4	2	3	3	3
Other	3	2	2	3	2	3	3	3
Base (weighted)	115	164	57	121	161	732	17683	18415

1. The 'Any emotional disorder category' includes children with other types of emotional disorder.
2. Includes people of mixed black and white origin.

Table **5.2**

Family characteristics by type of emotional disorder, 1999 and 2004 combined

All children   Great Britain

| | Type of emotional disorder | | | | | | | |
	Separation anxiety	Specific phobia	Social phobia	Generalised anxiety disorder	Depression	Any emotional disorder[1]	No emotional disorder	All
	%	%	%	%	%	%	%	%
Family type								
Married	44	58	48	55	47	51	69	68
Cohabiting	9	11	14	6	10	9	8	8
Lone parent – single	16	8	12	11	7	10	8	8
Lone parent – widowed, divorced or separated	31	24	26	28	37	31	15	16
Number of children in household								
1	28	21	20	23	25	26	23	23
2	38	41	47	37	36	38	45	45
3	23	26	17	24	23	24	22	22
4	3	10	8	10	11	9	7	7
5 or more	8	2	7	6	4	4	3	3
Base (weighted 1999 and 2004 data)	*115*	*164*	*57*	*121*	*161*	*732*	*17683*	*18415*
If stepchildren in family								
Yes	12	9	(5)	19	14	12	11	11
No	88	91	(95)	81	86	88	89	89
Base (weighted 2004 data)[2]	*33*	*61*	*23*	*57*	*65*	*282*	*7695*	*7977*

1. The 'Any emotional disorder category' includes children with other types of emotional disorder.
2. The 1999 data had a different classification for whether or not a family contained stepchildren.

Table **5.3**

Parent's education and socio-economic characteristics by type of emotional disorder, 1999 and 2004 combined

All children

Great Britain

	Type of emotional disorder							
	Separation anxiety	Specific phobia	Social phobia	Generalised anxiety disorder	Depression	Any emotional disorder[1]	No emotional disorder	All
	%	%	%	%	%	%	%	%
Parent's highest educational qualification								
Degree level	6	6	3	5	7	6	13	13
Teaching/HND/Nursing	8	7	6	9	10	9	11	11
A /AS level or equivalent	7	10	9	10	9	10	11	11
GCSE Grades A–C or equivalent	25	26	21	23	21	24	30	30
GCSE Grades D–F or equivalent	14	15	11	11	14	13	11	11
Other qualification	3	2	5	3	2	3	3	3
No qualification	38	34	45	39	36	35	20	21
Parents' employment status								
Both working/lone parent working	49	53	45	58	47	51	68	67
One parent working	17	23	29	13	18	19	19	19
Neither working/lone parent not working	34	24	26	29	35	30	14	15
Base (weighted 1999 and 2004 data)	*114*	*163*	*56*	*119*	*159*	*716*	*17340*	*18056*
Family's socio-economic classification[2]								
Large employers and higher managerial	3	3	(-)	3	1	1	2	2
Higher professional	-	-	(-)	1	3	1	3	3
Lower managerial and professional	9	13	(9)	7	16	12	21	20
Intermediate occupations	20	29	(8)	13	13	18	19	19
Small employers and own account	3	6	(13)	2	3	5	7	7
Lower supervisory and technical	-	2	-	-	3	2	1	1
Semi-routine	33	24	(26)	40	30	30	26	26
Routine occupations	17	17	(26)	22	19	18	12	13
Never worked/ long-term unemployed	15	5	(14)	9	10	8	5	5
FT student/inadequate description	-	2	(5)	3	3	5	4	4
Base (weighted 2004 data)[3]	*33*	*61*	*23*	*57*	*65*	*282*	*7695*	*7977*

1. The 'Any emotional disorder category' includes children with other types of emotional disorder.
2. This is the National Statistics socio-economic classification (NS-SEC).
3. The 1999 data had a different social classification

Table **5.4**

Housing and income by type of emotional disorder, 1999 and 2004 combined

All children

Great Britain

	Separation anxiety	Specific phobia	Social phobia	Generalised anxiety disorder	Depression	Any emotional disorder[1]	No emotional disorder	All
	%	%	%	%	%	%	%	%
Type of accommodation								
Detached	10	20	16	11	18	16	25	25
Semi-detached	39	35	37	38	35	36	38	38
Terraced house	37	33	41	40	38	38	30	30
Flat/maisonette	13	12	6	11	8	10	6	7
Tenure								
Owners	41	50	45	46	50	49	70	69
Social sector tenants	49	38	46	41	38	41	23	24
Private renters	10	11	9	12	12	10	7	7
Base (weighted 1999 and 2004 data)	*115*	*164*	*57*	*121*	*161*	*731*	*17673*	*18404*
Gross weekly household income								
Under £100	12	2	5	6	7	7	4	4
£100–£199	32	25	29	22	26	26	15	16
£200–£299	18	22	10	23	24	21	14	14
£300–£399	10	10	24	17	12	12	12	12
£400–£499	7	10	10	8	9	9	11	11
£500–£599	5	10	6	6	4	6	10	10
£600–£770	5	11	6	7	6	7	13	13
Over £770	11	12	11	10	12	11	21	20
Base (weighted 1999 and 2004 data)	*106*	*146*	*54*	*112*	*144*	*657*	*16239*	*16896*
Receipt of disability benefits								
Carers allowance	6	13	(8)	10	7	9	3	3
Severe Disablement allowance	12	17	(4)	15	15	14	5	6
Disability living/attendance allowance			(4)	3	3	1	0	0
Incapacity allowance	3	3	(5)	8	8	4	2	2
Any disability allowance	**15**	**27**	**(17)**	**27**	**22**	**20**	**8**	**8**
No disability allowance	85	73	(83)	73	78	80	92	92
Base (weighted 2004 data)[2]	*33*	*61*	*23*	*57*	*65*	*282*	*7695*	*7977*

1. The 'Any emotional disorder category' includes children with other types of emotional disorder.
2. The 1999 data covered different types of disability benefit.

Table **5.5**

Region, country and area type by type of emotional disorder, 1999 and 2004 combined

All children   Great Britain

	Type of emotional disorder							
	Separation anxiety	Specific phobia	Social phobia	Generalised anxiety disorder	Depression	Any emotional disorder[1]	No emotional disorder	All
	%	%	%	%	%	%	%	%
Region and country								
London inner	4	3	2	10	4	5	5	5
London outer	7	6	9	6	9	7	7	7
Other met England	35	29	30	30	31	31	31	31
Non-met England	40	47	49	42	45	45	45	44
England	86	85	89	88	90	89	86	86
Scotland	12	12	8	6	6	8	9	8
Wales	2	3	3	6	4	3	5	5
Base (weighted 1999 and 2004 data)	*115*	*164*	*57*	*121*	*161*	*732*	*17683*	*18415*
Area type (ACORN classification)								
Wealthy achievers	14	24	(4)	16	25	17	26	26
Urban prosperity	3	5	(13)	2	1	5	8	8
Comfortably off	24	28	(25)	28	23	24	26	26
Moderate means	14	16	(21)	24	19	20	17	17
Hard pressed	45	27	(37)	31	31	34	23	24
Base (weighted 2004 data)[2]	*32*	*59*	*23*	*57*	*65*	*278*	*7639*	*7916*

1. The 'Any emotional disorder category' includes children with other types of emotional disorder.
2. The 1999 data had a different ACORN classification.

Table **5.6**

Child's general health by type of emotional disorder, 1999 and 2004 combined

All children   Great Britain

	Type of emotional disorder							
	Separation anxiety	Specific phobia	Social phobia	Generalised anxiety disorder	Depression	Any emotional disorder[1]	No emotional disorder	All
	%	%	%	%	%	%	%	%
Child's general health								
Very good	35	47	41	34	34	41	70	69
Good	38	34	41	37	34	37	24	24
Fair	24	14	14	24	24	18	5	6
Bad	3	4	4	5	6	4	0	1
Very bad	-	-	-	-	2	1	0	0
Base (weighted)	*114*	*162*	*57*	*118*	*159*	*724*	*17448*	*18172*

1. The 'Any emotional disorder category' includes children with other types of emotional disorder.

Table **5.7**

Co-occurrence of physical and developmental problems with emotional disorders, 1999 and 2004 combined

All children   Great Britain

	Type of emotional disorder							
	Separation anxiety	Specific phobia	Social phobia	Generalised anxiety disorder	Depression	Any Emotional disorder[1]	No Emotional disorder	All
	Percentage of children with each type of physical complaint							
Asthma	29	24	21	28	22	23	14	15
Eczema	14	18	16	14	17	15	13	13
Hay fever	12	13	14	19	21	14	10	11
Eyesight problems	20	16	16	15	11	16	10	10
Stomach or digestive problems	17	13	9	15	15	14	5	6
Non-food allergy	4	8	7	9	9	8	6	6
Migraine/severe headache	13	8	14	13	21	12	4	5
Bed wetting	21	12	12	8	5	10	4	5
Glue ear/otitis media/grommits	6	7	7	4	5	5	4	4
Hearing problems	4	8	2	5	4	5	4	4
Speech or language problems	17	12	14	8	4	11	4	4
Food allergy	6	7	4	1	3	6	3	4
Difficulty with co-ordination	9	11	5	3	4	7	2	2
Stiffness or deformity of foot	3	6	5	5	6	5	2	2
Heart problems	4	2		3	1	2	1	1
Soiling pants	3	5	2	2	2	3	1	1
Muscle disease or weakness	2	4	3	3	4	3	1	1
Kidney/urinary tract problems	2	3	2	4	2	3	1	1
Obesity	4	2	4	4	2	3	1	1
Congenital abnormality	2	1	2	-	1	1	1	1
Epilepsy	3	2	-	3	2	2	1	1
Any blood disorder	1	2	-	1	1	1	0	0
Diabetes	2	1	-	-	1	1	0	0
Cerebral Palsy	1	-	-	-	-	0	0	0
Cancer	1	-	-	-	1	1	0	0
Any physical or developmental problem[2]	**80**	**72**	**73**	**73**	**73**	**72**	**53**	**54**
No problem	20	28	27	27	27	28	47	46
Base (weighted)	*114*	*162*	*57*	*118*	*159*	*724*	*17448*	*18172*

1. The 'Any emotional disorder category' includes children with other types of emotional disorder.
2. Some physical complaints are not listed in the table above because of their rarity (less than 25 cases): ME (10) Spina bifida (6) Cystic fibrosis (11) Missing digits (20). They are included in the 'Any physical or developmental problem' category.

Table **5.8**

Co-occurrence of other mental disorders with emotional disorders, 1999 and 2004 combined

All children   Great Britain

	Type of emotional disorder							
	Separation anxiety	Specific phobia	Social phobia	Generalised anxiety disorder	Depression	Any emotional disorder[1]	No emotional disorder	All
	Percentage of children with each type of disorder							
Other mental disorders								
Conduct disorders:								
Oppositional defiant disorder	15	12	12	18	8	12	2	3
Other conduct disorders	9	4	4	5	26	11	2	2
All conduct disorders	24	16	16	23	33	23	4	5
Hyperkinetic disorders	8	4	7	5	4	4	1	1
Less common disorders	2	3	3	5	8	5	1	1
Any other disorder	**27**	**20**	**24**	**26**	**38**	**27**	**5**	**6**
No (other) disorders	73	80	76	74	62	73	95	94
Base (weighted)	*115*	*164*	*57*	*121*	*161*	*732*	*17683*	*18415*

1. The 'Any emotional disorder category' includes children with other types of emotional disorder.

Table **5.9**

Parent's view of child's mental health by type of emotional disorder, 1999 and 2004 combined

All children   Great Britain

	Type of emotional disorder							
	Separation anxiety	Specific phobia	Social phobia	Generalised anxiety disorder	Depression	Any emotional disorder[1]	No emotional disorder	All
	Percentage of children with each type of problem							
Parent's view of child's mental health								
Emotional problems	29	21	32	39	40	29	3	5
Behavioural problems	23	18	23	23	33	23	5	6
Hyperactivity	19	9	7	10	9	10	3	4
Any of the above	44	29	40	54	53	40	9	10
Base (weighted)	*114*	*163*	*57*	*119*	*159*	*725*	*17449*	*18174*

1. The 'Any emotional disorder category' includes children with other types of emotional disorder.

Table **5.10**

Whether child is taking any medication by whether has an emotional disorder, 2004

All children   Great Britain

	Any emotional disorder	No emotional disorder	All
	Percentage of children taking each type of medication		
Methylphenidate, Equasym, Ritalin	3	1	1
Dexamphetamine, Dexedrine	-	0	0
Imipramine, Tofranil	-	0	0
Clonidine, Catepres, Dixarit	1	-	0
Fluoxetine, Prozac	1	0	0
Sertraline, Lustral	0	0	0
Fluvoxamine, Faverin	0	-	0
Citalopram, Cimpramil	1	0	0
Amitryptaline, Lentizol, Triptafen	0	0	0
Sulpirade, Dolmatil, Sulparex, Sulpitil	-	0	0
Risperidone, Riperadal	1	0	0
Haloperidol, Dozic, Haldol, Serenace	0	-	0
Any medication	7	1	1
No medication	93	99	99
Base (weighted)	*280*	*7581*	*7862*

Table **5.11**

Help sought in last year for child's mental health problems by type of emotional disorder, 2004

All children   Great Britain

	Separation anxiety	Specific phobia	Social phobia	Generalised anxiety disorder	Depression	Any emotional disorder[1]	No emotional disorder	All

Percentage of children using each service/source

Specialist services								
Child/adult mental health specialist (eg psychiatrist)	27	20	(31)	27	27	24	3	3
Child physical health specialist (eg paediatrician)	6	11	(-)	7	3	8	2	2
Social services (eg social worker)	8	8	(9)	9	12	10	1	2
Education services (eg educational psychologist)	26	12	(23)	17	24	18	3	4
Front line services								
Primary health care (eg GP or practice nurse)	29	17	(26)	31	40	29	5	6
Teachers	52	36	(36)	52	53	47	17	18
All professional services	**67**	**53**	**(52)**	**72**	**72**	**64**	**21**	**22**
Informal sources								
Family member/friends	43	28	(42)	45	46	34	11	12
Internet	8	3	(14)	5	7	5	1	1
Telephone help line	12	3	(5)	5	6	4	0	1
Self-help group	6	6	-	-	2	3	0	0
Other type of help	12	3	(9)	7	11	8	1	2
All sources	**76**	**63**	**(76)**	**85**	**77**	**73**	**26**	**28**
No help sought	24	37	(24)	15	23	27	74	72
Base (weighted)	*33*	*61*	*22*	*56*	*64*	*277*	*7508*	*7784*

1. The 'Any emotional disorder category' includes children with other types of emotional disorder.

Table **5.12**

Teacher's rating of child's basic skills by type of emotional disorder, 1999 and 2004 combined

Children whose teacher completed a questionnaire

	Type of emotional disorder							
	Separation anxiety	Specific phobia	Social phobia	Generalised anxiety disorder	Depression	Any emotional disorder[1]	No emotional disorder	All
	%	%	%	%	%	%	%	%
Reading								
Above average	15	23	24	23	26	23	37	37
Average	29	41	26	41	42	37	40	40
Some difficulty	33	23	37	26	24	25	17	17
Marked difficulty	23	13	13	9	9	15	6	6
Mathematics								
Above average	10	21	14	21	22	18	32	31
Average	35	44	38	36	35	37	44	44
Some difficulty	36	24	29	34	31	29	18	19
Marked difficulty	20	12	19	9	12	16	6	6
Spelling								
Above average	9	17	19	18	20	16	29	28
Average	32	42	26	37	43	38	41	41
Some difficulty	33	22	21	29	23	26	21	21
Marked difficulty	27	19	35	16	14	20	9	9
Base (weighted)	*82*	*131*	*37*	*89*	*114*	*541*	*13633*	*14174*
Overall scholastic ability[2]								
4 or more years behind	9	6	9	8	7	8	2	2
3 years behind	5	3	-	3	5	5	2	2
2 years behind	6	7	17	9	12	10	5	5
1 year behind	24	18	21	21	22	21	15	15
Equivalent	36	39	29	37	29	33	36	35
1 or more years ahead	20	27	24	22	25	23	41	40
Base (weighted)	*76*	*129*	*34*	*81*	*103*	*503*	*12751*	*13254*

1. The 'Any emotional disorder category' includes children with other types of emotional disorder.
2. Functioning age-actual age.

Table **5.13**

Whether child has special educational needs by type of emotional disorder, 1999 and 2004 combined

Children whose teacher completed a questionnaire

Great Britain

	Type of emotional disorder							
	Separation anxiety	Specific phobia	Social phobia	Generalised anxiety disorder	Depression	Any emotional disorder[1]	No emotional disorder	All
	%	%	%	%	%	%	%	%
Whether child has officially recognised special educational needs								
Yes	51	32	34	31	27	35	16	17
No	49	68	66	69	73	65	84	83
Base (weighted)	*81*	*132*	*37*	*89*	*116*	*541*	*13403*	*13944*

1. The 'Any emotional disorder category' includes children with other types of emotional disorder.
2. Functioning age-actual age.

Table **5.14**

Absence from school and truancy (teacher's report) by type of emotional disorder, 1999 and 2004 combined

Children whose teacher completed a questionnaire

Great Britain

	Type of emotional disorder							
	Separation anxiety	Specific phobia	Social phobia	Generalised anxiety disorder	Depression	Any emotional disorder[1]	No emotional disorder	All
	%	%	%	%	%	%	%	%
Number of days absent in last term								
0	24	30	(4)	14	5	19	32	32
1–5	33	35	(50)	31	31	37	46	46
6–10	20	17	(20)	26	24	19	13	13
11–15	10	7	(9)	5	15	7	4	4
16 or more	14	12	(17)	25	26	17	4	5
Any days absent	77	70	(96)	86	95	81	68	68
Base (weighted)	*64*	*105*	*23*	*56*	*68*	*387*	*9998*	*10385*
Any unauthorised days absent								
Yes	(4)	20	(0)	25	44	21	9	9
No	(96)	80	(100)	75	56	79	91	91
Base (weighted) 2004 data[2]	*22*	*37*	*9*	*30*	*33*	*157*	*4533*	*4689*
Whether plays truant								
Not true	95	93	94	75	67	84	97	97
Somewhat true	1	5	6	15	18	9	2	2
Certainly true	4	1	-	11	16	7	1	1
Base (weighted)	*83*	*133*	*36*	*89*	*116*	*545*	*13720*	*14265*

1. The 'Any emotional disorder category' includes children with other types of emotional disorder.
2. This question was not asked in 1999.

Table **5.15**

Absence from school (parent's report) by whether has an emotional disorder, 2004

All children   Great Britain

	Any emotional disorder	No emotional disorder	All
	%	%	%
Whether missed school in last term[1]			
Yes	54	33	34
No	46	67	66
Base (weighted): all children	*263*	*7358*	*7621*
Reasons for absence			
Short-term illness	64	79	78
Long-term illness	9	2	2
Refused to attend	10	2	2
Has a school phobia	5	0	1
Other	23	20	21
Base (weighted): those who missed school	*141*	*2458*	*2599*
Whether child received any educational provision			
Yes	8	10	10
No	92	90	90
Base (weighted): those who missed school (excluding short-term illness)	*61*	*591*	*652*

1. *Excluding exclusions.*

Table **5.16**

Exclusion from school (parent's report) by whether has an emotional disorder, 2004

All children   Great Britain

	Any emotional disorder	No emotional disorder	All
	%	%	%
Number of times child has been excluded from school			
None	88	96	96
Once	4	2	2
Twice	2	1	1
Three or more times	5	1	1
Base (weighted)	*274*	*7496*	*7770*

Table **5.17**

Number of times child has changed schools by whether has an emotional disorder, 2004

All children   Great Britain

	Any emotional disorder	No emotional disorder	All
	%	%	%
Number of times child has changed school[1]			
None	70	81	81
Once	22	14	14
Twice	3	3	3
Three or more times	5	2	2
Base (weighted)	274	7502	7776

1. Apart from normal transitions.

Table **5.18**

Parent's GHQ-12 score by type of emotional disorder, 1999 and 2004 combined

All children   Great Britain

	Type of emotional disorder							
	Separation anxiety	Specific phobia	Social phobia	Generalised anxiety disorder	Depression	Any emotional disorder[1]	No emotional disorder	All
	%	%	%	%	%	%	%	%
Parent's GHQ–12[2]								
0–2	44	56	50	41	39	49	77	76
3–5	17	20	16	23	19	18	13	13
6–8	19	13	14	14	15	15	6	7
9–12	21	11	20	22	26	18	4	4
3 or more	**56**	**44**	**50**	**59**	**61**	**51**	**23**	**24**
Base (weighted)	114	162	56	118	159	714	17269	17983

1. The 'Any emotional disorder category' includes children with other types of emotional disorder.
2. For this survey, scores of 3 or more were taken to indicate a severe emotional problem.

Table **5.19**

Family functioning score by type of emotional disorder, 1999 and 2004 combined

All children   Great Britain

	Type of emotional disorder							
	Separation anxiety	Specific phobia	Social phobia	Generalised anxiety disorder	Depression	Any emotional disorder[1]	No emotional disorder	All
	%	%	%	%	%	%	%	%
Family functioning score[2]								
Up to 1.50	27	33	31	22	18	27	36	36
1.51 – 2.00	37	38	46	41	33	26	15	16
2.51 or more	11	7	7	7	10	7	2	2
Unhealthy functioning (2.01 or more)	**37**	**29**	**23**	**36**	**43**	**33**	**18**	**18**
Base (weighted)	*114*	*162*	*55*	*117*	*154*	*704*	*17204*	*17908*

1. The 'Any emotional disorder category' includes children with other types of emotional disorder.
2. For this survey, scores over 2.0 were taken to indicate unhealthy family functioning.

Table **5.20**

Stressful life events by type of emotional disorder, 2004

All children

Great Britain

	Separation anxiety	Specific phobia	Social phobia	Generalised anxiety disorder	Depression	Any emotional disorder[1]	No emotional disorder	All
					Percentage reporting each event			
Stressful life events								
Since child was born, parent had a separation due to marital difficulties or broken off steady relationship	53	43	54	56	62	55	30	31
Since child was born, parent had a major financial crisis such as losing the equivalent of three months income	17	22	13	26	36	25	13	13
Since child was born, parent had a problem with the police involving a court appearance	15	11	10	18	16	14	6	6
Since child was born, parent has had serious physical illness	3	16	17	12	16	13	7	8
Since child was born, parent has had serious mental illness	24	21	27	42	27	28	7	8
At any stage in child's life, a parent, brother or sister died	11	2	19	3	4	7	3	4
At any stage in child's life, a close friend died	11	10	4	15	13	13	6	6
At some stage in the child's life, s/he had a serious illness which required a stay in hospital	18	25	21	17	19	20	13	13
At any stage in child's life, s/he had been in a serious accident or badly hurt in an accident	18	10	7	6	9	11	5	5
In the past year child has broken off a steady relationship with a boy or girl friend (aged 13 or above)/ a close friendship has ended (any age)	18	8	28	23	26	17	6	7
Base (weighted)	*33*	*61*	*22*	*56*	*64*	*274*	*7496*	*7770*

1. The 'Any emotional disorder category' includes children with other types of emotional disorder.

Table 5.21

Number of stressful life events by type of emotional disorder, 2004

All children   Great Britain

	Type of emotional disorder							
	Separation anxiety	Specific phobia	Social phobia	Generalised anxiety disorder	Depression	Any emotional disorder[1]	No emotional disorder	All
	%	%	%	%	%	%	%	%
Number of stressful life events								
0	17	22	(13)	16	9	16	43	42
1	36	29	(24)	21	23	25	33	32
2	21	22	(32)	23	28	24	14	15
3	15	19	(19)	23	20	19	7	7
4	3	6	(3)	10	12	9	2	3
5 or more	9	3	(8)	8	8	7	1	1
Two or more events	**47**	**49**	**(63)**	**63**	**67**	**59**	**25**	**26**
Base (weighted)	*33*	*61*	*22*	*56*	*64*	*274*	*7496*	*7770*

1. The 'Any emotional disorder category' includes children with other types of emotional disorder.

Table 5.22

Child's strengths (parent's and child's assessment) by whether has an emotional disorder, 2004

Great Britain

	Any emotional disorder	No emotional disorder	All
	%	%	%
ALL CHILDREN			
Strength score – parent assessment			
0–36	58	24	25
37–40	19	25	25
41–43	15	25	25
44–48	8	26	25
Base (weighted)	*268*	*7303*	*7571*
CHILDREN AGED 11–16			
Strength score – child assessment			
0–23	34	23	23
24–27	25	27	27
28–30	24	23	23
31–38	17	28	27
Base (weighted)	*147*	*3191*	*3338*

Table **5.23**

Social aptitude (parent's assessment) by whether has an emotional disorder, 2004

All children   Great Britain

Social aptitude score	Any emotional disorder	No emotional disorder	All
	%	%	%
0–20	48	24	25
21–24	22	28	27
25–28	14	23	22
29–40	16	26	25
Base (weighted)	265	7218	7483

Table **5.24**

Friendships by type of emotional disorder, 2004

All children   Great Britain

	Type of emotional disorder							
	Separation anxiety	Specific phobia	Social phobia	Generalised anxiety disorder	Depression	Any emotional disorder[1]	No emotional disorder	All
	%	%	%	%	%	%	%	%
What is child like at making friends?								
Finds it harder than average	37	28	(61)	41	33	35	9	10
About average	32	40	(26)	20	23	31	36	36
Easier than average	31	32	(13)	38	45	34	55	54
What is child like at keeping friends?								
Finds it harder than average	20	12	(30)	31	23	22	5	5
About average	49	45	(30)	38	36	42	35	35
Easier than average	31	43	(40)	31	41	36	60	59
Number of friends								
0	6	5	(17)	12	8	6	1	2
1	21	6	(17)	14	13	14	4	4
2–4	37	48	(46)	37	42	45	43	43
5–9	26	37	(19)	30	29	29	40	39
10 or more	10	5	(-)	7	8	6	12	11
Base (weighted): all children	*33*	*61*	*(23)*	*56*	*64*	*280*	*7560*	*7840*
Do child and friends have things in common								
No	3	3	(6)	2	5	4	1	1
A little	19	23	(24)	40	19	29	21	21
A lot	78	74	(70)	58	76	66	78	78
Do child and friends do things together								
No	13	18	(26)	6	8	11	3	4
A little	15	27	(30)	28	25	27	21	21
A lot	72	55	(44)	66	67	61	76	75
If worried, can child talk to friends								
No	49	28	(34)	23	15	29	21	21
Perhaps	38	37	(15)	33	33	33	42	42
Definitely	13	35	(51)	44	53	38	37	37
Whether friends get into trouble								
Not at all	54	67	(55)	60	55	57	68	67
A few are like that	40	32	(29)	35	31	36	31	31
Many are like that	6	-	(5)	6	11	5	1	1
All are like that	-	2	(11)	-	3	2	0	0
Whether parent approves of child's friends								
No	-	3	(6)	4	8	5	2	2
A little	28	14	(30)	36	34	30	14	14
A lot	72	83	(65)	60	58	65	85	84
Base (weighted): those who had friends	*31*	*57*	*19*	*50*	*58*	*261*	*7309*	*7570*

1. The 'Any emotional disorder category' includes children with other types of emotional disorder.

Table **5.25**

Child's sources of emotional support by whether has an emotional disorder, 2004

Children aged 11–16   Great Britain

	Any emotional disorder	No emotional disorder	All
	%	%	%
Social support score			
0–17	42	27	28
18	19	16	16
19	23	20	20
20	17	36	35
Base (weighted)	*148*	*3182*	*3331*

Table **5.26**

Views about the neighbourhood by whether has an emotional disorder, 2004

Children aged 11–16   Great Britain

	Any emotional disorder	No emotional disorder	All
	%	%	%
Whether enjoys living in the neighbourhood			
A lot	39	65	64
A little	38	29	29
No	23	7	7
How safe child feels walking alone in the neighbourhood during the daytime			
Very safe	46	62	61
Fairly safe	36	32	32
A bit unsafe	11	5	5
Very unsafe	7	1	1
Never goes out alone	1	1	1
Whether ever goes to the local shops or park alone			
Yes	79	80	80
No	21	20	20
How many people in the neighbourhood can be trusted			
Many	23	38	38
Some	40	45	44
A few	27	16	16
None	10	1	2
Likelihood of someone returning a lost bag			
Very likely	7	12	12
Quite likely	30	46	45
Not very likely	39	30	30
Not at all likely	23	12	13
Base (weighted)	*144*	*3175*	*3319*

Table **5.27**

Help provided to others by whether has an emotional disorder, 2004

Children aged 11–16   Great Britain

	Any emotional disorder	No emotional disorder	All	Any emotional disorder	No emotional disorder	All
	Percentage giving each type of help to relatives			*Percentage giving each type of help to non-relatives*		
Type of help						
Doing shopping for someone	41	36	37	14	9	9
Cooking or helping to prepare family meals	58	52	52	10	5	6
Cleaning, hoovering or gardening	76	69	69	17	10	11
Washing or ironing clothes	51	35	36	6	2	2
Decorating or repairs	23	21	21	5	5	5
Baby sitting or caring for children	48	38	39	30	19	19
Writing letters or filling in forms	15	10	10	1	4	4
Taking care of someone who is sick	42	33	34	12	9	9
Helping out in a family business	13	11	11	..	..	..
Anything else	6	9	9	4	3	3
None of the above	3	7	7	48	61	60
Base (weighted): all aged 11 or over	149	3209	3358	149	3209	3358
Frequency of providing help						
Every day	19	17	17	10	6	6
At least once a week	57	59	59	41	31	32
At least once a month	14	17	17	33	38	38
Less often	9	6	6	15	25	24
Base (weighted): those who helped	145	2989	3134	78	1264	1342

Table **5.28**

Whether child does any paid work by whether has an emotional disorder, 2004

Children aged 11–16   Great Britain

	Any emotional disorder	No emotional disorder	All
	%	%	%
Whether child does any paid work at least once a month			
Yes	19	22	22
No	81	78	78
Base(weighted): all childen aged 11 or over	*150*	*3209*	*3359*
		Percentage doing each type of work	
Type of paid work			
Family business	10	10	10
Newspaper round delivery	20	25	25
Shop or restaurant	24	27	27
Building, decorating or gardening	-	2	2
Household chores	31	18	18
Other	22	23	23
Base (weighted): those doing paid work	*29*	*742*	*740*

Table 5.29

Participation in groups, clubs and organisations by whether has an emotional disorder, 2004

Children aged 11–16   Great Britain

Type of group/club/ organisation	Any emotional disorder	No emotional disorder	All	Any emotional disorder	No emotional disorder	All
	Percentage particpating in clubs at school			*Percentage particpating in clubs outside school*		
Sports	35	52	51	20	38	37
Art, drama, dance or music	31	32	32	20	17	18
Youth	11	11	11	21	21	21
Computers	13	14	14	3	3	3
Political	-	2	2	-	1	1
Debating	3	4	4	1	0	1
Religious	4	3	3	6	4	5
Local community or neighbourhood	3	2	2	4	2	2
Voluntary groups helping people	5	4	4	4	2	2
Safety, First Aid	6	4	4	2	3	3
Environmental	5	5	5	1	2	2
Animal (welfare)	1	1	1	1	1	1
Human rights	1	1	1	1	0	0
School holiday playschemes	7	9	9	4	7	7
After-school clubs	18	28	28	..	..	..
School student councils	12	11	11	..	..	..
Student Union	-	1	1	..	..	..
Extra teaching or special lessons	10	9	9	..	..	..
Other	..	..	..	6	9	9
None of the above	32	21	22	45	33	33
Base (weighted)	*142*	*3147*	*3288*	*142*	*3149*	*3290*

Table 5.30

Unpaid help given to groups, clubs and organisations by whether has an emotional disorder, 2004

Children aged 11–16   Great Britain

Unpaid help given to groups, clubs and organisations in last 12 months	Any emotional disorder	No emotional disorder	All
	Percentage mentioning each type of help		
Collected or raised money	25	33	33
Took part in a sponsored activity	27	32	32
Was part of a committee	6	6	6
Helped to organise or run an event	23	19	19
Other help	12	9	9
None of the above	46	42	42
Base (weighted)	*149*	*3209*	*3358*

Table **5.31**

Barriers to participation in groups, clubs and organisations by whether has an emotional disorder, 2004

Children aged 11–16

Great Britain

Barriers to participation	Any emotional disorder	No emotional disorder	All
	Percentage mentioning each barrier		
Difficulty getting to clubs	11	6	6
No good groups or clubs locally	19	16	16
Cannot afford to join	4	2	2
Would not feel safe travelling to club	7	2	2
No clubs of interest	13	14	14
Too busy	12	15	15
Do not want to participate	28	15	16
Do not have time after homework	14	12	12
Not allowed	8	2	2
Other barrier	6	3	3
None of the above	26	42	42
Base (weighted)	*142*	*3150*	*3291*

Table **5.32**

Smoking behaviour by whether has an emotional disorder, 1999 and 2004 combined

Children aged 11–16

Great Britain

	11- to 13-year-olds			14- to 16-year-olds			All aged 11–16		
	Any emotional disorder	No emotional disorder	All	Any emotional disorder	No emotional disorder	All	Any emotional disorder	No emotional disorder	All
	%	%	%	%	%	%	%	%	%
Smoking behaviour									
Regular smoker	6	1	1	33	11	13	19	5	6
Occasional smoker	3	1	1	4	5	5	3	3	3
All smokers	**8**	**2**	**2**	**37**	**17**	**18**	**23**	**8**	**9**
Used to smoke	5	3	3	11	9	9	8	5	5
Tried smoking once	22	16	16	25	28	28	24	21	21
Never smoked	64	79	78	27	46	45	45	65	64
Base (weighted)	*192*	*4208*	*4400*	*194*	*3075*	*3269*	*387*	*7283*	*7670*

Table **5.33**

Drinking behaviour by whether has an emotional disorder, 1999 and 2004 combined

Children aged 11–16   Great Britain

	11- to 13-year-olds			14- to 16-year-olds			All aged 11–16		
	Any emotional disorder	No emotional disorder	All	Any emotional disorder	No emotional disorder	All	Any emotional disorder	No emotional disorder	All
	%	%	%	%	%	%	%	%	%
Drinking behaviour									
Almost every day	1	0	0	1	1	1	1	0	0
About twice a week	1	1	1	8	6	6	4	3	3
About once a week	1	2	2	15	10	10	8	5	6
All regular drinkers	**3**	**3**	**3**	**23**	**17**	**17**	**13**	**9**	**9**
About once a fortnight	4	3	3	13	12	12	9	7	7
About once a month	7	5	5	16	16	16	12	9	10
Only a few times a year	28	20	21	24	29	29	26	24	24
Never drinks alcohol	4	2	2	1	2	2	3	2	2
Never had a drink	54	67	67	23	24	24	39	49	49
Base (weighted)	*192*	*4205*	*4397*	*195*	*3075*	*3270*	*387*	*7282*	*7669*

Table **5.34**

Drug use by whether has an emotional disorder, 1999 and 2004 combined

Children aged 11–16   Great Britain

	11- to 13-year-olds			14- to 16-year-olds			All aged 11–16		
	Any emotional disorder	No emotional disorder	All	Any emotional disorder	No emotional disorder	All	Any emotional disorder	No emotional disorder	All
	%	%	%	%	%	%	%	%	%
Ever used:									
Cannabis	4	1	1	28	14	15	16	7	7
Inhalants	1	0	0	2	1	1	1	1	1
Ecstasy	1	0	0	1	1	1	1	0	0
Amphetamines	1	0	0	4	1	1	3	1	1
LSD	1	0	0	1	0	0	1	0	0
Tranquilisers	-	0	0	1	0	0	1	0	0
Cocaine	-	0	0	-	1	1	-	0	0
Heroin	-	0	0	1	-	0	0	0	0
Any drugs	**8**	**2**	**3**	**31**	**16**	**16**	**20**	**8**	**9**
Base (weighted)	*192*	*4203*	*4395*	*194*	*3074*	*3268*	*387*	*7278*	*7665*

Table **5.35**

Social context of last drinking occasion by whether has an emotional disorder, 2004

Children aged 11–16 who had had an alcoholic drink in the last 6 months

Great Britain

	Any emotional disorder	No emotional disorder	All
	%	%	%
Where had last drink			
Own home	43	43	42
Other's home	28	28	28
Public house	8	8	8
Restaurant	7	3	3
Nightclub/other club	6	5	5
Outside in public place	3	8	7
Other venue	6	6	6
Number of other people in group			
Alone	2	3	3
1	20	14	14
2–5	44	45	45
6–10	20	19	19
More than 10	14	19	18
Base (weighted)[1]	86	1375	1461
Who was with respondent[2]			
Boyfriend/girlfriend	10	7	7
Other friend(s)	54	53	53
Family	48	44	44
Other	4	3	3
Base (weighted)[1]	84	1328	1411

1. The bases are those who had engaged in the behaviour with others.
2. Percentages may sum to more than 100 because some children were accompanied by more than one group.

Table **5.36**

Deliberate self-harm by whether has an emotional disorder, 1999 and 2004 combined

	Any emotional disorder	No emotional disorder	All
	Percentage who have tried to harm, hurt or kill themselves		
All children			
Parent's report	14	2	2
Base (weighted)	*595*	*17060*	*17655*
Children aged 11–16			
Parent's report	19	2	3
Base (weighted)	*367*	*7872*	*8239*
Child's report	28	6	7
Base (weighted)	*324*	*7080*	*7404*

Conduct disorders

Chapter 6

Introduction

This chapter follows the same structure as Chapter 5. First, we describe the types of behaviour patterns typically found among children and young people who have a conduct disorder. We then go on to describe the characteristics of these children and young people, looking at their:

- demographic characteristics;
- family situation;
- socio-economic characteristics;
- geographic distribution;
- general, physical and mental health;
- use of services;
- scholastic ability and attendance at school;
- family's social functioning;
- own social functioning; and
- lifestyle behaviours.

There was no change between 1999 and 2004 in the prevalence of conduct disorders among children and young people, either overall or within different subgroups. It is therefore possible to combine the two sets of data so as to increase the sample base. This allows us to analyse the larger subcategories of conduct disorders:

- Oppositional defiant disorder.
- Socialised conduct disorder.
- Unsocialised conduct disorder.

The numbers of children with other types of conduct disorder are too small for separate analysis and are not shown as separate categories in the tables. However, they are included in the 'Any conduct disorder' total.

As far as possible, the same questions and classifications were used in both the 1999 and the 2004 surveys. However, some changes were necessary to improve the questions or to cover new topics. In these cases, data are presented for 2004 only and hence the bases in some subgroups are very small. We have not commented on the characteristics of these very small groups.

Within each topic, the text generally follows the same pattern: first, children with any form of conduct disorder are compared with those who have no such disorder; then, any variations from the overall pattern within the subcategories of conduct disorders are reported. The shaded boxes summarise the main features of the group as a whole followed by those for each subgroup including any characteristics on which they differ from the overall pattern. The commentary is descriptive, the

aim being to provide a profile of children who have different types of conduct disorder. It therefore takes no account of the inter-relationships between the characteristics. The analysis at the end of Chapter 4 described the factors which had the largest independent effects on prevalence and this gives an indication of the key variables.

Typical behaviour patterns

This section describes typical symptoms displayed by children with different types of conduct disorder. The symptoms listed are found, to some extent, in most children. To count as a disorder they have to be sufficiently severe to cause distress to the child or an impairment in his/her functioning. In order to illustrate the impact of the disorder on the child's life and that of his or her family, the symptoms are followed by a case vignette of a fictitious child.[1]

Oppositional defiant disorder

This is characterised by: temper outbursts, arguing with adults, disobedience, deliberately annoying others, passing on blame, being easily annoyed, angry, resentful, spiteful and vindictive. The behaviour is likely to have caused complaints from parents and teachers.

He just will not do what he is told. He answers back and throws huge temper tantrums if he cannot get his own way. He has always been like this, but it is getting more of a problem now he has started junior school. He winds others up, particularly his younger brothers, and is glad when he gets other children into trouble because he has provoked them into shouting at him or hitting him. He is just the same at school; he is always in trouble for being rude, doing things that he has been asked not to and upsetting other children. He just will not admit when he is in the wrong. He is so stroppy, it does not take much to set him off and it feels like we all tip toe around him to avoid arguments.

Unsocialised and socialised conduct disorders

Typical behaviour includes: telling lies, fighting, bullying, staying out late, running away from home, playing truant, being cruel to people or animals, criminal behaviour such as robbery, rape, using weapons. This type of behaviour would often have resulted in complaints from school staff or contact with the police.

In *socialised* conduct disorder, the young person has friends (though usually antisocial friends). They may engage in antisocial behaviours such as shoplifting or stealing cars

---

1. *The symptoms and vignettes are based on descriptions of a 'made up' child created by Youthinmind to illustrate the diagnostic classification system.*

together. In *unsocialised* conduct disorder, the young person lacks any real friends and typically engages in solitary antisocial activities. These are the opposite ends of a spectrum, so dividing conduct disorder into these two categories is somewhat arbitrary.

Socialised conduct disorder

She used to bunk off school with her friends to go shop lifting, and they sold what they stole to buy drugs, alcohol and cigarettes. Once she started secondary school, I lost all control over her. She would stay out late with these friends, some of whom were much older than her. When she did go to school she was constantly in trouble because she would swear at teachers and refuse to do any work. She was finally permanently excluded from school because she was caught selling drugs to other pupils. She was first in contact with the police for trespassing when she was 12 years old, but now has several cautions for taking and driving away, shop lifting and the possession of drugs. Social services became involved when she had a baby aged 14.

Unsocialised conduct disorder

He has never had any friends, and he doesn't like school. He walks out if he does not like a lesson and wanders round town on his own. He was horribly bullied when he was younger, and now he gets into trouble for bullying younger children. When his teachers told him off for this, he vandalised the school toilets and ended up being excluded. He has also tried setting fire to a shed in the local park – he was caught and has been cautioned by the police. We have also caught him being really cruel to our cat and he just doesn't seem to understand that this is a bad thing to do.

Demographic, socio-economic and area characteristics

Demographic characteristics

Children with a conduct disorder were more likely to be boys and more likely to be older than children with no such disorder. About two-thirds (69 per cent) of children with a conduct disorder were boys and over a half (55 per cent) were aged 11–16 compared with about a half (50 per cent and 47 per cent) of other children. Boys predominated in all the subgroups of conduct disorder but there were considerable age variations within these groups: the proportion aged 11–16 ranged from 37 per cent among children with oppositional defiant disorder to 61 per cent among those with unsocialised conduct disorder to 86 per cent among those with socialised conduct disorder. The only ethnic variation was that children with unsocialised conduct disorder were more likely to be white than children

Figure 6.1

Age by type of conduct disorder, 1999 and 2004 combined

Great Britain

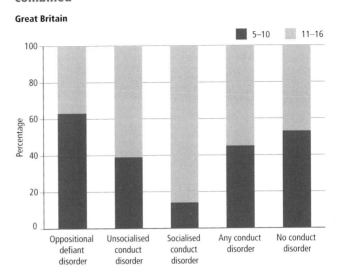

with no conduct disorder (96 per cent compared with 89 per cent). (Figure 6.1 and Table 6.1)

Family characteristics

Fewer than a half (46 per cent) of children with conduct disorders lived with married parents compared with about two-thirds (69 per cent) of children with no such disorder. Among the former, higher proportions lived with cohabiting parents (12 per cent compared with 8 per cent), single lone parents (14 per cent compared with 7 per cent) or previously married lone parents (27 per cent compared with 15 per cent). Among children with unsocialised and socialised conduct disorders,

Figure 6.2

Family type by type of conduct disorder, 1999 and 2004 combined

Great Britain

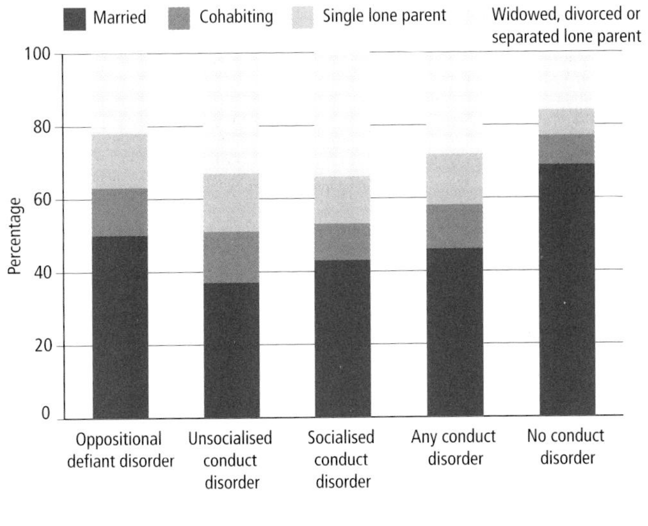

Married   Cohabiting   Single lone parent   Widowed, divorced or separated lone parent

about a third lived with a previously married lone parent (32 per cent and 35 per cent). For those with oppositional defiant disorder, the proportion was about a fifth (22 per cent).

(Figure 6.2 and Table 6.2)

Children with conduct disorders were more likely than other children to live in households containing a large number of children: 17 per cent lived in households containing 4 or more children compared with 10 per cent of children with no conduct disorder. These patterns were evident in all the subgroups but children with unsocialised conduct disorder were particularly likely to have a large number of siblings: 26 per cent lived in households containing 4 or more children. Children with conduct disorders were also almost twice as likely as other children to live in households containing stepchildren (18 per cent compared with 10 per cent). This proportion was relatively high among children with unsocialised and those with socialised conduct disorders (18 per cent and 22 per cent). The difference between those with oppositional defiant disorder and those with no conduct disorder was not quite statistically significant. (Table 6.2)

Parental education and socio-economic characteristics

Children with conduct disorders, like those with emotional disorders, were more likely than other children to have parents with no educational qualifications and to live in low-income families. Those with unsocialised conduct disorder seemed to live in the most economically disadvantaged circumstances, as indicated by a range of measures.

Children with a conduct disorder were twice as likely as those with no such disorder to have parents who had no educational qualifications (39 per cent compared with 20 per cent) The same variation occurred in all the subgroups but was most pronounced among those with unsocialised conduct disorder of whom well over a half (57 per cent) had parents with no educational qualifications. (Table 6.3)

A third of children with conduct disorders lived in households in which neither parent was working (34 per cent compared with 14 per cent of other children). Conversely, only a half (49 per cent) lived in households in which both parents worked compared with two thirds (68 per cent) of children with no such disorder. Similarly, with respect to the socio-economic classification of the household reference person: 51 per cent of the children with a conduct disorder had a parent in the semi-routine or routine occupational group compared with 38 per cent of other children. Again, the differences were evident in all the subgroups but were particularly marked among children with unsocialised conduct disorder: 49 per cent lived in

households in which neither parent was working and 70 per cent had a parent in the semi-routine or routine group.

(Table 6.3)

Housing and income

A half (50 per cent) of children with conduct disorders lived in social rented sector accommodation compared with less than a quarter (23 per cent) of those with no such disorder. Conversely, only 41 per cent compared with 71 per cent lived in owned accommodation. The income measure showed the same kind of differential. Nearly three fifths (58 per cent) of children with a conduct disorder lived in households with a gross weekly income of less that £300 compared with a third (33 per cent) of other children. These housing and income variations occurred in all three subgroups. (Table 6.4)

Table 6.4 also shows the disability benefits received by households containing children with a conduct disorder. One-fifth (20 per cent) were receiving a disability benefit, including 15 per cent who were receiving severe disablement allowance. Households with children who had unsocialised conduct disorders were particularly likely to receive a disability benefit, 31 per cent, and the proportion was also relatively high among children with oppositional defiant disorder, 17 per cent. However, households in which the child had socialised conduct disorder were no more likely to receive a disability benefit than households in which the child had no conduct disorder.

(Table 6.4)

Area characteristics

There were no differences between countries or between metropolitan and other areas within England in the distribution of children with and those with no conduct disorder. There were, however, marked differences in the types of area in which they lived. Households containing children with conduct disorders were almost twice as likely as other households to live in areas classified as 'Hard pressed', 41 per cent compared with 23 per cent. This proportion was relatively high in all the subgroups but, again, was particularly high, 61 per cent, among those with unsocialised conduct disorder. (Table 6.5)

Among children with conduct disorders:

- 69 per cent were boys *(compared with 50 per cent for children with no conduct disorder)*
- 55 per cent were aged 11–16 *(47 per cent)*
- 92 per cent were white *(89 per cent)*
- 27 per cent lived with a widowed, divorced or separated lone parent *(15 per cent)*
- 46 per cent lived in a married couple family *(69 per cent)*
- 17 per cent lived in households containing 4 or more children *(10 per cent)*
- 18 per cent lived in households containing stepchildren *(10 per cent)*
- 39 per cent had parents with no educational qualifications *(20 per cent)*
- 41 per cent lived in owned accommodation *(71 per cent)*
- 58 per cent lived in households with gross incomes under £300 per week *(33 per cent)*
- 20 per cent lived in households in which someone received a disability benefit *(8 per cent)*
- 41 per cent lived in areas classified as 'Hard pressed' *(23 per cent)*

Among children with oppositional defiant disorder:

- 69 per cent were boys
- 37 per cent were aged 11–16
- 91 per cent were white
- 22 per cent lived with a widowed, divorced or separated lone parent
- 14 per cent lived in households containing 4 or more children
- 16 per cent lived in households containing stepchildren
- 53 per cent lived in households with gross incomes under £300 per week

Among children with unsocialised conduct disorder:

- 71 per cent were boys
- 61 per cent were aged 11–16
- 96 per cent were white
- 32 per cent lived with a widowed, divorced or separated lone parent
- 26 per cent lived in households containing 4 or more children
- 18 per cent lived in households containing stepchildren
- 66 per cent lived in households with gross incomes under £300 per week

Among children with socialised conduct disorder:

- 70 per cent were boys
- 86 per cent were aged 11–16
- 90 per cent were white
- 35 per cent lived with a widowed, divorced or separated lone parent
- 19 per cent lived in households containing 4 or more children
- 22 per cent lived in households containing stepchildren
- 61 per cent lived in households with gross incomes under £300 per week

Child's general, physical and mental health

General health

The parents of children with a conduct disorder were more than three times as likely as other parents to say that their child's general health was fair or bad (17 per cent compared with 5 per cent) and less likely to say that it was very good (50 per cent compared with 70 per cent).

(Figure 6.3 and Table 6.6)

Physical and developmental problems

About two-thirds (65 per cent) of children with conduct disorders had some type of physical or developmental problem as well. Among other children the proportion was just over a half (53 per cent). Among both groups, there was no difference in the proportions reporting some of the more common complaints, for example, eczema and hay fever. The parents of children with conduct disorders were, however, the more likely to report bed wetting (12 per cent and 4 per cent), speech or

Figure **6.3**
Child's general health by type of conduct disorder, 1999 and 2004 combined

Great Britain

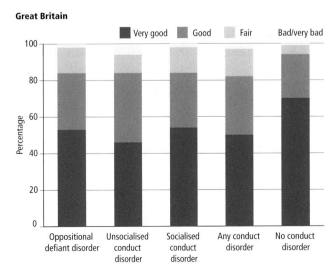

language problems (11 per cent and 3 per cent), co-ordination difficulties (7 per cent and 2 per cent) asthma (19 per cent and 15 per cent) and eyesight problems (14 per cent and 10 per cent). (Table 6.7)

The poorer general and physical health of children with conduct disorders compared with other children was evident in the three subgroups of conduct disorders and there was very little variation between them.

Mental disorders

About one-third (35 per cent) of children with conduct disorders had another clinically recognisable disorder as well: 19 per cent had an emotional disorder, including 15 per cent with anxiety disorders; 17 per cent had a hyperkinetic disorder; and 3 per cent had one of the less common disorders. However, there were marked differences between the subgroups in both the extent and the nature of their co-morbidity. Those with unsocialised conduct disorder were the most likely to have another mental disorder (54 per cent), usually hyperkinesis (34 per cent). About one-fifth (22 per cent) of this group had an emotional disorder, 17 per cent having an anxiety disorder and 12 per cent having depression. Among children with oppositional defiant disorder, one-third (33 per cent) had multiple disorders, evenly split between hyperkinesis (18 per cent) and emotional disorders (18 per cent), usually anxiety disorders (17 per cent). In the third subgroup, children with socialised conduct disorder, 27 per cent had another disorder: 11 per cent had a hyperkinetic disorder and 18 per cent had an emotional disorder, evenly divided between anxiety and depressive disorders. (Figure 6.4 and Table 6.8)

Figure **6.4**
Proportion of children with a conduct disorder who had another type of mental disorder, 1999 and 2004 combined

Great Britain

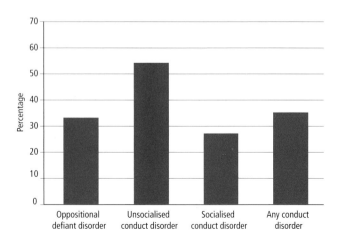

Parents were asked whether their child had any emotional problems, behavioural problems or hyperactivity. Just under two-thirds (64 per cent) of the parents whose children were clinically assessed as having a conduct disorder reported these kinds of problems: 55 per cent reported behavioural problems, 27 per cent emotional problems and 23 per cent hyperactivity. Since these proportions sum to well over 64 per cent, it is clear that many parents reported more than one type of problem – which is consistent with the co-morbidity observed in the clinical classification. As discussed above, children with unsocialised conduct disorders were most likely to suffer from multiple disorders and their parents were most likely to report some kind of problem (78 per cent). While the majority mentioned behavioural problems (72 per cent), high proportions mentioned hyperactivity (39 per cent) and emotional problems (37 per cent). As was the case with the clinical assessments, the parental reports also indicate multiple types of disorder among these children. (Table 6.9)

Medication

Medication would not often be prescribed for behavioural problems per se. Nine per cent of children with a conduct disorder were taking some form of medication, mainly Methylphenidate (7 per cent), which is usually prescribed for hyperactivity. Further investigation showed that all but two of the children with conduct disorders who were taking medication had another disorder as well, usually hyperkinesis. One of the two exceptions was taking citalopram (an anti-depressant) and was reported to have had depressed mood with deliberate self-harm but did not fulfil diagnostic criteria for emotional disorder at the time of assessment. The other child was taking imipramine and had symptoms of overactivity at home following brain injury, but the onset was too late to diagnose hyperkinetic disorder. (Table 6.10)

Among the parents of children with conduct disorders:

- 17 per cent reported that the child's general health was fair or bad *(compared with 5 per cent for children with no conduct disorder)*
- 65 per cent reported that the child had a specific physical or developmental problem *(53 per cent)*
- 64 per cent reported that the child had mental health problems *(7 per cent)*
- 27 per cent reported that the child had emotional problems, 55 per cent reported behavioural problems and 23 per cent reported hyperactivity *(3 per cent, 3 per cent and 3 per cent)*
- 35 per cent of the children had another main type of clinically recognisable disorder *(4 per cent)*

Among the parents of children with oppositional defiant disorder:

- 16 per cent reported that the child's general health was fair or bad
- 66 per cent reported that the child had a specific physical or developmental problem
- 59 per cent reported that the child had mental health problems
- 24 per cent reported that the child had emotional problems, 50 per cent reported behavioural problems and 23 per cent reported hyperactivity
- 33 per cent of the children had another main type of clinically recognisable disorder

Among the parents of children with unsocialised conduct disorder:

- 16 per cent reported that the child's general health was fair or bad
- 66 per cent reported that the child had a specific physical or developmental problem
- 78 per cent reported that the child had mental health problems
- 37 per cent reported that the child had emotional problems, 72 per cent reported behavioural problems and 39 per cent reported hyperactivity
- 54 per cent of the children had another main type of clinically recognisable disorder

Among the parents of children with socialised conduct disorder:

- 16 per cent reported that the child's general health was fair or bad
- 60 per cent reported that the child had a specific physical or developmental problem
- 66 per cent reported that the child had mental health problems
- 27 per cent reported that the child had emotional problems, 57 per cent reported behavioural problems and 15 per cent reported hyperactivity
- 27 per cent of the children had another main type of clinically recognisable disorder

Use of services

In the previous survey, the questioning about service use was directed only at those for whom significant problems had been reported in the interview. The questions in the 2004 survey were asked about all children. Parents were asked whether, in the last year, they had had contact with a range of specialist

and non-professional services because they were worried about their child's emotions, behaviour or concentration.

Over three-quarters (81 per cent) of parents of children with a conduct disorder had sought some form of advice or help in the previous 12 months because of concerns about their child's mental health or behaviour. The majority of these (76 per cent overall) had approached a professional source, most commonly a teacher (60 per cent). Substantial minorities had contacted, or been referred to, a specialist, 28 per cent had contacted a mental health specialist and 24 per cent a special educational service such as an educational psychologist. A third (32 per cent) had approached their GP or a practice nurse and a similar proportion (34 per cent) had talked to family members or friends. Children with unsocialised or socialised conduct disorders were more likely than those with oppositional defiant disorder to have sought help with their child's health or behavioural problems, 90 per cent and 87 per cent compared with 74 per cent. This difference was evident for both professional and informal sources. It may reflect the younger age profile of children with oppositional defiant disorder but further analysis showed that the variation was present for both children aged 5–10 and these aged 11–16. (Table 6.11).

Parents who had mentioned a problem with their child's emotions, attention or behaviour during the course of the interview and who had not seen a specialist were asked whether there was anything that had stopped them seeking such help. Fewer than a half (45 per cent) of the parents of children with conduct disorders mentioned any of the barriers prompted by the interviewer. The most common obstacles mentioned were lack of awareness of the service available (14 per cent), difficulty in getting a referral (14 per cent) and a belief that a specialist would be of no help (10 per cent). Similar barriers were mentioned by parents of children with emotional disorders although, again, the numbers with problems were quite small. (Table not shown)

Among the parents of children with conduct disorders:

- 81 per cent had sought help or advice in the last year because of worries about their child's mental health *(compared with 25 per cent for children with no conduct disorder)*
- 76 per cent had contacted a professional service *(19 per cent)*
- The most commonly used services were: teachers (60 per cent), family members or friends (34 per cent), primary health care (32 per cent) and mental health specialists (28 per cent).

Among the parents of children with oppositional defiant disorder:

- 74 per cent had sought help or advice in the last year because of worries about their child's mental health
- 69 per cent had contacted a professional service

Among the parents of children with unsocialised conduct disorder:

- 90 per cent had sought help or advice in the last year because of worries about their child's mental health
- 85 per cent had contacted a professional service

Among the parents of children with socialised conduct disorder:

- 87 per cent had sought help or advice in the last year because of worries about their child's mental health
- 81 per cent had contacted a professional service

Scholastic ability and attendance at school

Teachers were asked to rate the child's abilities in reading, mathematics and spelling compared with an average child of the same age and to estimate the child's age in terms of their scholastic ability. They were also asked to say whether the child had officially recognised special educational needs.

Basic skills

Over a half (56 per cent – 57 per cent) of children with conduct disorders had difficulty with reading and mathematics and nearly two-thirds (64 per cent) had problems with spelling. Among those with no such disorder these proportions were around a quarter (21 per cent, 23 per cent and 29 per cent). The difficulties of children with conduct disorders are reflected in the teacher's assessment of their overall functioning in relation to what would be expected of a child of that age: 59 per cent were rated as being behind in their overall intellectual development and 36 per cent were 2 or more years behind. For other children, these proportions were 24 per cent and 9 per cent. Children with unsocialised conduct disorders were more likely to be behind than those with oppositional defiant disorder (73 per cent compared with 53 per cent). Those with socialised conduct disorders were in between with 61 per cent being behind. (Figure 6.5 and Table 6.12).

Special educational needs

About a half (52 per cent) of children with conduct disorders were considered by their teachers to have special educational needs. This figure is over three times the proportion among other children, 15 per cent. The proportion with special educational needs ranged from 62 per cent among those with

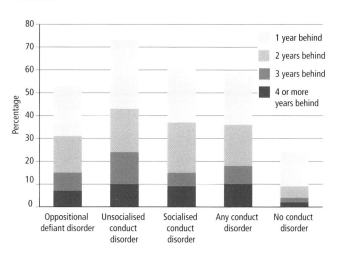

Figure 6.5

Proportion of children who were behind in their overall scholastic ability by type of conduct disorder, 1999 and 2004 combined

Great Britain

unsocialised conduct disorder to 37 per cent among those with socialised conduct disorder. (Table 6.13)

Among the children who had special needs, those with conduct disorders were more likely than other children to have a written statement. (60 per cent compared with 44 per cent.)

(Based on 2004 data, Table not shown)

Absence from school

Teachers reported that two thirds of all children had missed school for some reason in the previous term. However, those with a conduct disorder were more likely to have done so than other children (79 per cent compared with 68 per cent). The former were also away for longer periods – 42 per cent had had more than 5 days absence and 14 per cent had had more than 15 days absence in the previous term. Among those with no such disorder, these proportions were much lower, 21 per cent and 4 per cent. In both groups, the majority of absences were authorised but 28 per cent of children with conduct disorders had had unauthorised absences compared with 8 per cent of other children. Truancy is one of the diagnostic criteria for conduct disorder and teachers reported that nearly one quarter (22 per cent) of children with such disorders had possibly or certainly played truant. The corresponding proportion for other children was just 3 per cent.

(Figure 6.6 and Table 6.14)

Absenteeism and truancy rates were relatively high in all the subgroups with conduct disorders but particularly among those with socialised conduct disorder. In this group: 87 per cent had been absent in the previous term; 55 per cent had had an unauthorised absence; and 55 per cent were considered by their teachers to be definite or possible truants.

(Figure 6.6 and Table 6.14)

Figure **6.6**
Proportion of children whose teacher thought that they played truant by type of conduct disorder, 1999 and 2004 combined

Great Britain

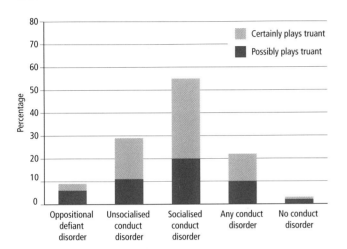

The teachers' questions were asked in both the 1999 and 2004 surveys and the figures quoted above are based on combined data from these studies. In 2004, parents were also asked about their child's absences from school and about any occasions on which they had been excluded. As with the teachers' reports, the parents of children with conduct disorders were more likely than other parents to report absences. Among the former, 41 per cent said that their child had missed school for reasons other than exclusion in the previous term compared with 34 per cent of the latter. Among the children who had been absent, 16 per cent of those with a conduct disorder had missed school because they refused to attend or had a school phobia. For other children this proportion was 2 per cent. One-tenth (10 per cent) of the children who had been absent from school had received some form of educational provision and there were no differences between children with and those with no conduct disorder in this respect. (The absence figures based on the parents' reports are lower than those based on the teachers' reports because the latter include exclusions and truancies; they also relate to a different population.)

(Table 6.15)

A third (33 per cent) of children with conduct disorders had been excluded from school at some time and nearly a quarter (22 per cent) had been excluded more than once. Among children with unsocialised or socialised conduct disorders, nearly a half (46 per cent and 48 per cent) had been excluded

and over a quarter had been excluded more than once (27 per cent and 28 per cent). For children with no conduct disorder, these proportions were 2 per cent and 1 per cent. (Table 6.16)

Overall, 8 per cent of exclusions had been permanent and 14 per cent of children had received some educational provision after exclusion. There were no differences between children with conduct disorders and other children who had been excluded in these respects. (Tables not shown)

Children with conduct disorders were also more likely than other children to have changed schools other than at the usual transition stages, although the differences were much less marked than for exclusions and there were no differences between the three subgroups. Nearly a third (30 per cent) of children with conduct disorders had changed schools compared with just under a fifth (18 per cent) of other children. This variation was not attributable to the higher rate of exclusions among those with a conduct disorder since only 3 per cent of children had changed schools following their exclusion and there was no difference between those with and those with no conduct disorder in this respect. (Table 6.17)

Among children with conduct disorders:
- 59 per cent were behind in their overall intellectual development *(compared with 24 per cent for children with no conduct disorder)*
- 52 per cent had officially recognised special educational needs *(15 per cent)*
- 42 per cent had more than 5 days away from school in the previous term and 14 per cent had had more than 15 days absence *(21 per cent and 4 per cent)*
- 22 per cent were considered by teachers to be definite or possible truants *(3 per cent)*
- 33 per cent had been excluded from school and 30 per cent had changed schools apart from normal transitions *(2 per cent and 19 per cent)*

Among children with oppositional defiant disorder:
- 53 per cent were behind in their overall intellectual development
- 53 per cent had officially recognised special educational needs
- 33 per cent had more than 5 days away from school in the previous term and 9 per cent had had more than 15 days absence
- 9 per cent were considered by teachers to be definite or possible truants
- 22 per cent had been excluded from school

Among children with unsocialised conduct disorder:

- 73 per cent were behind in their overall intellectual development
- 62 per cent had officially recognised special educational needs
- 45 per cent had more than 5 days away from school in the previous term and 19 per cent had had more than 15 days absence
- 29 per cent were considered by teachers to be definite or possible truants
- 46 per cent had been excluded from school

Among children with socialised conduct disorder:

- 61 per cent were behind in their overall intellectual development
- 37 per cent had officially recognised special educational needs
- 62 per cent had more than 5 days away from school in the previous term and 26 per cent had had more than 15 days absence
- 55 per cent were considered by teachers to be definite or possible truants
- 48 per cent had been excluded from school

Social functioning of the family

This section looks at various aspects of parental health, attitudes and behaviour which provide indicators of the social functioning of the family.

Mental health of parent

The parent who was interviewed about the child's behaviour, usually the mother, was asked about her own mental health using the General Health Questionnaire (GHQ-12 –see Chapter 2 for details). Scores range from 0 (no psychological distress) to 12 (severe psychological distress). A score of 3 is generally taken as the threshold with scores at this level or higher being considered indicative of an emotional disorder.

Nearly a half (48 per cent) of the parents of children with conduct disorders had scores of 3 or more, twice the proportion among other parents (23 per cent). Among the parents of children with unsocialised or socialised conduct disorders, the proportion was as high as three-fifths (61 per cent and 58 per cent). (Figure 6.7 and Table 6.18)

Figure 6.7

Proportion of children whose parent scored 3 or more on the GHQ-12, 1999 and 2004 combined

Great Britain

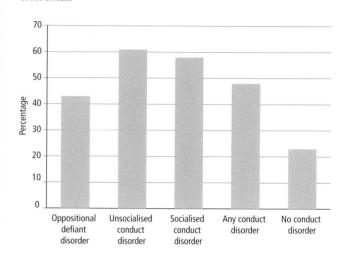

Family functioning

Family functioning was measured using the FAD-GFS scale in which parents rated 12 statements about family relationships (see Chapter 2 for details). For this survey, families which scored over 2.00 on this scale were considered to have unhealthy functioning.

Children with conduct disorders were much more likely than other children to live in families classified as having unhealthy functioning, 42 per cent compared with 17 per cent. This pattern was evident in all three subgroups, the proportion living in families scoring above 2.00 ranging from 36 per cent among those with oppositional defiant disorder to 56 per cent among those with socialised conduct disorder. (Table 6.19)

Stressful life events

Parents were asked whether their child had experienced any of 10 potentially stressful events. The list in the 2004 survey was slightly different to that used in 1999 so the data are presented for 2004 only.

For all but two events, the proportions of children who had experienced the event were higher among those with conduct disorders than among other children. For both groups, the separation of parents was the most common life event. This was reported by over a half (54 per cent) of children with conduct disorders but by less than a third of those with no such disorder (30 per cent). There were also large differences in the proportions whose parents had experienced a major financial crisis (22 per cent and 13 per cent), who had been in trouble with the police (15 per cent and 5 per cent), or who had had a serious mental illness (17 per cent and 7 per cent). Overall, children with conduct disorders were twice as likely as other children to have experienced two or more stressful life events (50 per cent compared with 25 per cent)

(Tables 6.20 and 6.21)

The proportions reporting two or more events were relatively high in all three subgroups with conduct disorder, 45 per cent among those with oppositional defiant disorder, 55 per cent among those with socialised conduct disorder and 60 per cent among those with unsocialised conduct disorder. In the last group, a fifth of parents (21 per cent) had been in trouble with the police and a quarter (24 per cent) had had a serious mental illness.

(Tables 6.20 and 6.21)

Among children with conduct disorders:

- 48 per cent of parents had an emotional disorder *(compared with 23 per cent for the parents of children with no conduct disorder)*
- 42 per cent lived in families with unhealthy functioning *(17 per cent)*
- 50 per cent had had two or more stressful life events *(25 per cent)*

Among children with oppositional defiant disorder:

- 43 per cent of parents had an emotional disorder
- 36 per cent lived in families with unhealthy functioning
- 45 per cent had had two or more stressful life events

Among children with unsocialised conduct disorder:

- 61 per cent of parents had an emotional disorder
- 46 per cent lived in families with unhealthy functioning
- 60 per cent had had two or more stressful life events

Among children with socialised conduct disorders:

- 58 per cent of parents had an emotional disorder
- 56 per cent lived in families with unhealthy functioning
- 55 per cent had had two or more stressful life events

Child's social functioning

In 2004, new questions were introduced to examine the child's strengths, the rationale being that these might provide protection against the onset and course of mental disorder as well as providing parents with the opportunity to describe their child's good points rather than focussing exclusively on their problems. The section also covers other features of social functioning which might affect the child's resilience: their relationships with friends, their social aptitudes and various measures of social capital.

Strengths

Both parents and young people were asked to rate the child on a series of items covering various qualities (see Chapter 2 for details). Scores on the adult scale ranged from 0-48 and those on the children's scale ranged from 0–38. Table 6.22 shows the scores on each scale grouped into quartiles. Looking first at the parent's assessment, three-quarters (77 per cent) of children with conduct disorders had scores in the bottom quartile compared with 23 per cent of other children. The same pattern occurred in all three subcategories of conduct disorder but children with unsocialised or socialised conduct disorder were more likely than those with oppositional defiant disorder to fall into the bottom quartile, 88 per cent and 85 per cent compared with 68 per cent.

(Table 6.22)

The children's own assessments of their strengths showed the same pattern of variation as those of the parents but the differences were not so large. On this measure, nearly a half (46 per cent) of children with conduct disorders had scores in the bottom quartile compared with 22 per cent of other children. The children's scale did not include all the items on the parent's scale and was asked only of young people aged 11–16 so the scores are not directly comparable.

(Table 6.22)

Social aptitudes

The social aptitude scale consisted of 10 questions addressed to parents designed to measure the child's ability to empathise with others (see Chapter 2 for details). Scores ranged from 0–40 and were grouped into quartiles. About two-thirds (69 per cent) of children with conduct disorders had scores in the bottom quartile compared with 22 per cent of other children. Children with unsocialised conduct disorder again had particularly low scores, 82 per cent were in the bottom quartile compared with 64 per cent of those with oppositional defiant or socialised conduct disorders.

(Table 6.23)

Social capital

'Social capital' is a multi-faceted concept which has been defined as 'networks together with shared norms, values and understandings that facilitate co-operation within and among groups' (Cote and Healey, 2001). It is believed that high levels of social capital have a positive effect on health. The aspects of social capital covered in this report are:

- relationships with friends;
- social support;
- views about the neighbourhood;
- help provided to others; and
- participation in clubs and groups.

Many of the questions are taken from the children and young

person modules included in the 2003 Home Office Citizenship Survey The questions on friends were asked of all parents. The remaining topics were asked of young people aged 11 or over only because previous research has shown that younger children were not able to cope with some of the more complex questioning. The analysis of these questions is not presented for the subcategories of conduct disorders because of the small bases.

Relationships with friends

Questions on friendships were asked of the interviewed parent and covered:

- the child's ability to make and keep friends;
- number of friends;
- common interests and shared activities;
- emotional support; and
- parent's approval of child's friends.

On all these measures children with conduct disorders performed less well than other children. For example, among the former, 24 per cent found it harder than average to make friends and 33 per cent found it harder to keep friends. The proportions for children with no conduct disorder were 9 per cent and 4 per cent. Likewise, 35 per cent compared with 20 per cent did not have a friend whom they could talk to if they were worried. The variations in the proportions who shared interests or activities with friends and in the number of friends were similar. (Table 6.24)

As might be expected, children with unsocialised conduct disorders who tended to have solitary behaviour patterns, fared particularly badly on these measures. Thus about a half had difficulty making and keeping friends (47 per cent and 54 per cent) and a similar proportion had no-one to talk to if they were worried (50 per cent). Those with socialised conduct disorders, on the other hand, were similar in many respects to children with no conduct disorder, although they did have more difficulty in keeping friends – 17 per cent compared with 4 per cent found this harder than average. (Table 6.24)

The parents of children with conduct disorders were much more likely than other parents to disapprove of their child's friends, 10 per cent compared with 1 per cent. Similarly, the former were more likely to say that many or all of their child's friends got into trouble, 15 per cent compared with 1 per cent. This last proportion rose to 35 per cent among those with unsocialised conduct disorder. Children with oppositional defiant disorder tend to be rated more positively than the other subgroups at these questions: only 4 per cent of parents disapproved of their friends and 8 per cent thought that many or all of their child's friends got into trouble. Further analysis

showed that this variation was not attributable to their younger age profile. (Table 6.24)

Social support

Young people aged 11–16 were asked about the number of family members and friends to whom they felt close. A scale was constructed from the responses with scores ranging from 0 to 20 which were grouped into rough quartiles. Those with a conduct disorder were twice as likely as other young people to have a score in the lowest quartile (54 per cent compared with 27 per cent). (Table 6.25)

Views about the neighbourhood

Young people aged 11–16 who had conduct disorders were less positive about their neighbourhood than other children. For example, 21 per cent (compared with 7 per cent) did not enjoy living there, 32 per cent (compared with 18 per cent) thought that few or no people could be trusted and 65 per cent (compared with 42 per cent) thought that it was unlikely that a lost bag would be returned. As was shown earlier, children with conduct disorders tended to live in poorer areas than other children. However, the differences in their views persisted within different types of area. (Table not shown) There were no differences, however, between children with and those with no conduct disorder in opinions about safety while walking alone during the daytime or in visiting local shops or the park alone. (Table 6.26)

Help provided to others

Young people were asked separately about types of help that they provided to relatives and non-relatives. In the previous chapter, it was noted that children with an emotional disorder were more likely than other children to give help to family members and other relatives. The reverse was the case for those with a conduct disorder, 84 per cent gave help compared with 94 per cent. There were no differences, however, in the extent to which the two groups provided help to non-relatives, or in the frequency with which either form of help was given. (Table 6.27)

Likewise, there were no differences in the proportions who were paid for the help they gave (Table not shown) or in the proportions who did some form of paid work at least once a month. (Table 6.28)

Participation in groups, clubs and organisations

Young people with conduct disorders were much less likely than those with no such disorder to take part in school-based groups, clubs or organisations, 56 per cent compared with 79 per cent. Looking at the more common types of group, 38 per cent of children with conduct disorders attended sports groups compared with 52 per cent of other children. For art, drama and music clubs, the proportions were 15 per cent and 33 per cent. However, there were no differences in the proportions involved in computer clubs and youth clubs. (Table 6.29)

The same pattern prevailed in relation to groups, clubs or organisations outside school: 55 per cent of children with a conduct disorder attended such groups compared with 67 per cent of other children. Again there were large differences in participation rates for sport clubs (24 per cent and 38 per cent) and arts, drama and music clubs (9 per cent and 18 per cent) but no differences with regard to youth clubs. (Table 6.29)

Children with conduct disorders were also the less likely to have given unpaid help in the last 12 months to a group, club or organisation, 39 per cent compared with 59 per cent.
(Table 6.30)

There were no differences between children with conduct disorders and those with no such disorder in the proportions mentioning any type of barrier to participation, but the former were a little less likely to mention lack of time, either because of homework (5 per cent and 12 per cent) or simply that they were too busy (8 per cent and 15 per cent). Common reasons for non-participation among both groups were that the child thought that there were no suitable groups available locally or that they had no desire to participate (16 per cent overall for both). (Table 6.31)

Among children with conduct disorders:
- 24 per cent found it harder than average to make friends *(compared with 9 per cent for children with no conduct disorder)*
- 46 per cent of parents did not fully approve of their child's friends *(14 per cent)*
- 21 per cent did not enjoy living in the neighbourhood *(7 per cent)*
- 84 per cent had given help to relatives and 43 per cent had helped non-relatives *(94 per cent and 40 per cent)*
- 56 per cent had taken part in a school-based group and 55 per cent had taken part in a group outside school in the last year *(79 per cent and 67 per cent)*

Smoking, drinking and drug use

Questions on smoking, drinking and drug use were included in both the 1999 and 2004 surveys. They were addressed to children aged 11–16 and were based on questions used in the national surveys of smoking, drinking and drug use among schoolchildren. A comparison of the data from the 1999

Children's Mental Health Survey with the 1999 Schools Survey showed that children interviewed at home systematically under-reported their smoking, drinking and drug use compared with those interviewed in school. The rates presented in this report should not therefore be taken as true estimates of prevalence. Their main value is in enabling comparisons to be made between children with a disorder and other children. As these behaviours vary with age, percentages are shown separately for young people aged 11–13 and those aged 14–16.

Young people with conduct disorders were much more likely than other young people to smoke, drink and take drugs. As was the case with emotional disorders, the largest differences were in smoking and drug taking. Thus, looking at smoking behaviour among young people with a conduct disorder and those with no such disorder, 34 per cent compared with 8 per cent were smokers and 30 per cent compared with 5 per cent were regular smokers (smoking at least one cigarette a week). The differences were evident even in the younger age group, 11–13: 13 per cent of those with a conduct disorder smoked compared with only 2 per cent of other children. Among older children, aged 14–16, over a half (54 per cent) of those with a conduct disorder smoked compared with 16 per cent of other young people. (Figure 6.8 and Table 6.32)

Figure **6.8**
Smoking, drinking and drug use by whether has a conduct disorder: children aged 11–16, 1999 and 2004 combined

Great Britain

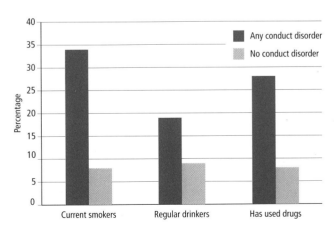

Drinking behaviour showed the same pattern but the differences were less marked and largely confined to the older age group. Among those aged 14–16, young people with conduct disorders were twice as likely as those with no such disorder to be regular drinkers (drinking once a week or more often), 32 per cent compared with 16 per cent. Even in the younger age group, however, there were differences in exposure: nearly a half (46 per cent) of those with a conduct disorder had had an alcoholic drink at some time compared with only a third (33 per cent) of other young people.

(Figure 6.8 and Table 6.33)

Turning to drug use, 28 per cent of young people with a conduct disorder had taken drugs at some time compared with only 8 per cent of other young people. As with smoking, the differences were large even in the youngest age group: 13 per cent of 11- to 13-year-olds with a conduct disorder had taken drugs compared with 2 per cent of other young people. Among 14- to 16-year-olds, the difference was very marked, 43 per cent compared with 15 per cent. Cannabis was the most commonly used drug, taken by 23 per cent of young people with a conduct disorder and 6 per cent of other young people. Among the former, 5 per cent had taken amphetamines and 4 per cent had taken inhalants. These substances had been taken by less than 1 per cent of other young people.

(Figure 6.8 and Table 6.34)

In the 2004 survey, young people were asked about the social context of the last occasions on which they had smoked, drunk alcohol and taken drugs. The only statistically significant variations were in the situations on the last drinking occasion. Young people with conduct disorders were much more likely than other young people to have drunk alcohol outside in a public place (25 per cent compared with 6 per cent) and less likely to have drunk at home (31 per cent compared with 43 per cent). There were no differences between young people with a conduct disorder and those with no such disorder in the size of the group with whom they had been drinking but the former were more likely to have been accompanied by a boyfriend or girlfriend (15 per cent compared with 6 per cent) or other friends (64 per cent compared with 52 per cent) and less likely to have been with family members (32 per cent compared with 45 per cent).

(Table 6.35)

Among children aged 11–16 with conduct disorders:
- 30 per cent were regular smokers *(compared with 5 per cent for children with no conduct disorder)*
- 19 per cent were regular drinkers *(9 per cent)*
- 28 per cent had taken drugs at some time *(8 per cent)*

Self-harm

All parents were asked whether the child had ever tried to hurt, harm or kill themselves and the same question were asked of older children aged 11–16 (see Chapter 2 for details). Looking first at parents' reports for children of all ages, those whose child had a conduct disorder were much more likely to say that the child had tried to harm themselves, 16 per cent compared with 2 per cent. The variations for young people aged 11–16

showed a similar pattern, 18 per cent and 2 per cent based on parents' reports and 21 per cent and 6 per cent based on self-reports.

(Table 6.36)

Results from the six-month follow-up survey

Samples of the parents of children interviewed in the 1999 and 2004 surveys were sent a self-completion questionnaire six months after the interview in order to establish whether there had been any change in their symptoms (see Chapter 3).

The average levels of total and behavioural symptoms among the children with conduct disorders did fall slightly over the six months following the survey. However, as Figures 6.9 and 6.10 show, the gap between children with and those with no conduct disorder only narrowed a little as a result. The symptoms of conduct disorders were typically persistent, at least in the short term. By contrast, the impact of these symptoms fell by about a third over the six months, as shown in Figure 6.11. At first glance, it seems surprising that impact dropped by a third although the level of symptoms was fairly steady. The most likely explanation is that the impact of symptoms depends not just on the symptoms themselves but on everything else in the child's life. Changes at home or at school may make symptoms easier or harder to live with.

(Figures 6.9–6.11)

Since a diagnosis of a conduct disorder is only made when a child experiences both conduct symptoms and resultant impact, children can move in and out of having a diagnosable disorder according to whether or not their symptoms have a substantial impact at any given time. Some of the children who had a diagnosis of a conduct disorder at the time of the main survey would not have warranted a diagnosis six months later because their symptoms were not having a substantial impact. Conversely, some children who did not quite warrant a diagnosis at the time of the main survey would have met the criteria six months later because their symptoms were then having a substantial impact. The frontier between normality and disorder is somewhat arbitrary, so it not surprising that some children cross and re-cross the boundary as a result of the ups and downs of life (not to mention the imprecision of the diagnostic process itself).

Figure **6.9**
Total symptoms[1] at main interview and at six-month follow-up by whether child had a conduct disorder at main interview, 1999 and 2004 combined

Great Britain

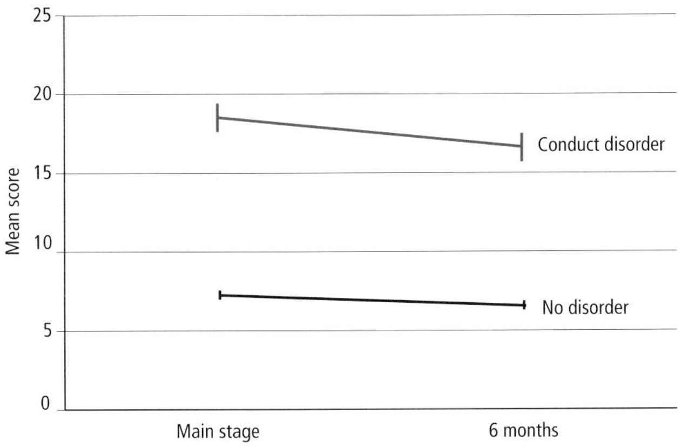

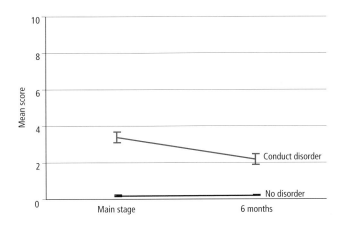

1 Total symptoms is the 'total difficulties score' on the parent-reported SDQ, reflecting the sum of the subscale scores for emotional symptoms, conduct problems, hyperactivity and peer problems.

Figure **6.10**
Conduct symptoms at main interview and at six-month follow-up by whether child had a conduct disorder at main interview, 1999 and 2004 combined

Great Britain

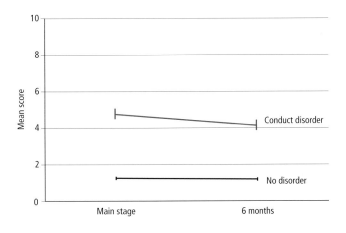

Figure **6.11**
Impact of symptoms at main interview and at six-month follow-up by whether child had a conduct disorder at main interview, 1999 and 2004 combined

Great Britain

References

Goddard E and Higgins V (1999) *Smoking, drinking and drug use among young teenagers in 1998 (Volume I: England)*, TSO: London.

Home Office (December 2004) *2003 Home Office Citizenship Survey*, Home Office Research, Development and Statistics Directorate.

Table **6.1**

Sex, age and ethnicity of child by type of conduct disorder, 1999 and 2004 combined

All children

Great Britain

| | Type of conduct disorder | | | | | |
	Oppositional defiant disorder	Unsocialised conduct disorder	Socialised conduct disorder	Any conduct disorder[1]	No conduct disorder	All
	%	%	%	%	%	%
Sex						
Boys	69	71	70	69	50	51
Girls	31	29	30	31	50	49
Age						
5–10	63	39	14	45	53	53
11–16	37	61	86	55	47	47
Ethnicity						
White	91	96	90	92	89	89
Black[2]	4	3	6	4	3	3
Indian	1	1	1	1	2	2
Pakistani/ Bangladeshi	2	-	1	2	3	3
Other	2	-	2	2	3	3
Base (weighted)	481	102	184	902	17502	18403

1. The 'Any conduct disorder category' includes children with other types of conduct disorder.
2. Includes people of mixed black and white origin.

Table **6.2**

Family characteristics by type of conduct disorder, 1999 and 2004 combined

All children   Great Britain

| | Type of conduct disorder | | | | | |
	Oppositional defiant disorder	Unsocialised conduct disorder	Socialised conduct disorder	Any conduct disorder[1]	No conduct disorder	All
	%	%	%	%	%	%
Family type						
Married	50	37	43	46	69	68
Cohabiting	13	14	10	12	8	8
Lone parent – single	15	16	13	14	7	8
Lone parent – widowed, divorced or separated	22	32	35	27	15	16
Number of children in household						
1	20	24	24	22	23	23
2	41	31	37	38	45	45
3	26	20	20	23	22	22
4	9	19	13	12	7	7
5 or more	5	7	6	5	3	3
Base (weighted 1999 and 2004 data)	*481*	*102*	*184*	*902*	*17514*	*18415*
If stepchildren in family						
Yes	16	18	22	18	10	11
No	84	82	78	82	90	89
Base (weighted 2004 data)[2]	*215*	*57*	*90*	*407*	*7570*	*7977*

1. The 'Any conduct disorder category' includes children with other types of conduct disorder.
2. The 1999 data had a different classification for whether or not a family contained stepchildren.

Table **6.3**

Parent's education and socio-economic characteristics by type of conduct disorder, 1999 and 2004 combined

All children   Great Britain

	Type of conduct disorder					
	Oppositional defiant disorder	Unsocialised conduct disorder	Socialised conduct disorder	Any conduct disorder[1]	No conduct disorder	All
	%	%	%	%	%	%
Parent's highest educational qualification						
Degree level	7	1	6	6	13	13
Teaching/HND/Nursing	7	7	5	7	11	11
A /AS level or equivalent	9	6	8	8	11	11
GCSE Grades A–C or equivalent	25	18	22	23	30	30
GCSE Grades D–F or equivalent	15	12	11	13	11	11
Other qualification	4	-	6	4	3	3
No qualification	34	57	43	39	20	21
Parent's employment status						
Both working/lone parent working	54	33	51	49	68	67
One parent working	18	18	15	17	19	19
Neither working/lone parent not working	28	49	34	34	14	15
Base (weighted 1999 and 2004 data)	478	102	183	894	17217	18111
Family's socio-economic classification						
Large employers and higher managerial	2	-	-	1	2	2
Higher professional	2	-	2	2	3	3
Lower managerial and professional	11	4	13	11	21	20
Intermediate occupations	19	11	18	17	19	19
Small employers and own account	8	2	2	6	7	7
Lower supervisory and technical	1	3	2	1	1	1
Semi-routine	33	46	32	33	26	26
Routine occupations	15	24	23	18	12	12
Never worked/ long-term unemployed	8	12	6	9	5	5
FT student/inadequate description	3	-	1	3	4	4
Base (weighted 2004 data)[2]	215	57	90	407	7570	7977

1. The 'Any conduct disorder category' includes children with other types of conduct disorder.
2. The 1999 data had a different social classification.
3. This is the National Statistics Socio-economic Classification (NS-SEC).

Table **6.4**

Housing and income by type of conduct disorder, 1999 and 2004 combined

All children   Great Britain

	Type of conduct disorder					
	Oppositional defiant disorder	Unsocialised conduct disorder	Socialised conduct disorder	Any conduct disorder[1]	No conduct disorder	All
	%	%	%	%	%	%
Type of accommodation						
Detached	13	8	8	11	26	25
Semi-detached	38	39	39	39	38	38
Terraced house	42	45	45	42	30	30
Flat/maisonette	8	8	8	8	7	7
Tenure						
Owners	46	30	36	41	71	69
Social sector tenants	45	56	58	50	23	24
Private renters	9	14	6	9	7	7
Base (weighted 1999 and 2004 data)	*481*	*102*	*184*	*902*	*17503*	*18404*
Gross weekly household income						
Under £100	8	7	6	7	4	4
£100–£199	26	32	35	30	15	16
£200–£299	19	27	20	21	14	14
£300–£399	14	10	14	13	12	12
£400–£499	11	6	7	8	11	11
£500–£599	6	8	5	6	10	10
£600–£770	5	7	6	5	13	13
Over £770	11	3	8	9	21	20
Base (weighted 1999 and 2004 data)	*443*	*90*	*169*	*821*	*16075*	*16896*
Receipt of disability benefits						
Carers allowance	6	20	3	9	2	3
Severe Disablement allowance	14	18	7	15	5	6
Disability living/attendance allowance	2	3	1	2	0	0
Incapacity allowance	1	5	4	3	2	2
Any disability allowance	**17**	**31**	**10**	**20**	**8**	**8**
No disability allowance	83	69	90	80	92	92
Base (weighted 2004 data)[2]	*215*	*57*	*90*	*407*	*7570*	*7977*

1. The 'Any conduct disorder category' includes children with other types of conduct disorder.
2. The 1999 data covered different types of disability benefit.

Table **6.5**

Region, country and area type by type of conduct disorder, 1999 and 2004 combined

All children   Great Britain

	Type of conduct disorder					
	Oppositional defiant disorder	Unsocialised conduct disorder	Socialised conduct disorder	Any conduct disorder[1]	No conduct disorder	All
	%	%	%	%	%	%
Region and country						
London Inner	4	3	5	4	5	5
London Outer	6	2	7	5	7	7
Other met England	33	28	33	32	31	31
Non-met England	47	54	43	48	44	44
England	90	87	89	89	86	86
Scotland	6	9	8	8	9	8
Wales	4	4	4	4	5	5
Base (weighted 1999 and 2004 data)	481	102	184	902	17513	18415
Area type (ACORN classification)						
Wealthy achievers	10	10	12	11	26	26
Urban prosperity	6	2	6	5	8	8
Comfortably off	26	7	18	22	26	26
Moderate means	22	21	19	21	17	17
Hard pressed	36	61	45	41	23	24
Base (weighted 2004 data)[2]	214	57	90	406	7510	7917

1. The 'Any conduct disorder category' includes children with other types of conduct disorder.
2. The 1999 data had a different ACORN classification.

Table **6.6**

Child's general health by type of conduct disorder, 1999 and 2004 combined

All children   Great Britain

	Type of conduct disorder					
	Oppositional defiant disorder	Unsocialised conduct disorder	Socialised conduct disorder	Any conduct disorder[1]	No conduct disorder	All
	%	%	%	%	%	%
Child's general health						
Very good	53	46	54	50	70	69
Good	31	38	30	32	24	24
Fair	14	10	14	15	5	6
Bad	2	5	2	2	0	1
Very bad	0	1	-	0	0	0
Base (weighted)	479	102	183	897	17276	18172

1. The 'Any conduct disorder category' includes children with other types of conduct disorder.

Table **6.7**

Co-occurrence of physical and developmental problems with conduct disorders, 1999 and 2004 combined

All children   Great Britain

	Type of conduct disorder					
	Oppositional defiant disorder	Unsocialised conduct disorder	Socialised conduct disorder	Any conduct disorder[1]	No conduct disorder	All
	Percentage of children with each type of physical complaint					
Asthma	19	21	15	19	15	15
Eczema	13	11	11	13	13	13
Hay fever	12	11	14	12	10	11
Eyesight problems	13	19	14	14	10	10
Stomach or digestive problems	8	7	7	7	6	6
Non-food allergy	5	9	9	6	6	6
Migraine/severe headache	5	9	10	8	5	5
Bed wetting	14	11	7	12	4	5
Glue ear/otitis media/grommits	6	5	2	5	4	4
Hearing problems	8	6	3	6	4	4
Speech or language problems	13	7	3	11	3	4
Food allergy	6	4	3	6	3	4
Difficulty with co-ordination	9	7	1	7	2	2
Stiffness or deformity of foot	4	4	5	4	2	2
Heart problems	2	2	0	2	1	1
Soiling pants	4	3	2	4	1	1
Muscle disease or weakness	2	2	3	2	1	1
Kidney/urinary tract problems	2	1	2	2	1	1
Obesity	2	2	1	2	1	1
Congenital abnormality	0	-	-	0	1	1
Epilepsy	2	1	0	3	1	1
Any blood disorder	1	-	1	1	0	0
Diabetes	0	1	2	1	0	0
Cerebral Palsy	1	-	-	1	0	0
Cancer	-	1	-	0	0	0
Any physical or developmental problem[2]	**66**	**66**	**60**	**65**	**53**	**54**
No problem	34	34	40	35	47	46
Base (weighted)	*479*	*102*	*183*	*897*	*17276*	*18172*

1. The 'Any conduct disorder category' includes children with other types of conduct disorder.
2. Some physical complaints are not listed in the table above because of their rarity (less than 25 cases): ME (10), Spina bifida (6), Cystic fibrosis (11), Missing digits (20) They are included in the 'Any physical or developmental problem' category.

Table 6.8

Co-occurrence of other mental disorders with conduct disorders, 1999 and 2004 combined

All children   Great Britain

	Type of conduct disorder					
	Oppositional defiant disorder	Unsocialised conduct disorder	Socialised conduct disorder	Any conduct disorder[1]	No conduct disorder	All
	Percentage of children with each type of disorder					
Other mental disorders						
Emotional disorders:						
Anxiety disorders	17	17	10	15	3	4
Depression	3	12	11	6	1	1
All emotional disorders	18	22	18	19	3	4
Hyperkinetic disorders	18	34	11	17	1	1
Less common disorders	1	3	0	3	1	1
Any other disorder	**33**	**54**	**27**	**35**	**4**	**6**
No (other) disorders	67	46	73	65	96	94
Base (weighted)	*481*	*102*	*184*	*902*	*17513*	*18415*

1. The 'Any conduct disorder category' includes children with other types of conduct disorder.

Table 6.9

Parent's view of child's mental health by type of conduct disorder, 1999 and 2004 combined

All children   Great Britain

	Type of conduct disorder					
	Oppositional defiant disorder	Unsocialised conduct disorder	Socialised conduct disorder	Any conduct disorder[1]	No conduct disorder	All
	Percentage of children with each type of problem					
Parent's view of child's mental health						
Emotional problems	24	37	27	27	3	5
Behavioural problems	50	72	57	55	3	6
Hyperactivity	23	39	15	23	3	4
Any of the above	**59**	**78**	**66**	**64**	**7**	**10**
Base (weighted)	*479*	*102*	*183*	*897*	*17277*	*18174*

1. The 'Any conduct disorder category' includes children with other types of conduct disorder.

Table **6.10**

Whether child is taking any medication by whether has a conduct disorder, 2004

All children

	Any conduct disorder	No conduct disorder	All
	Percentage of children taking each type of medication		
Methylphenidate, Equasym, Ritalin	7	0	1
Dexamphetamine, Dexedrine	1	-	0
Imipramine, Tofranil	0	0	0
Clonidine, Catepres, Dixarit	0	0	0
Fluoxetine, Prozac	-	0	0
Sertraline, Lustral	0	0	0
Fluvoxamine, Faverin	-	0	0
Citalopram, Cimpramil	1	0	0
Amitryptaline, Lentizol, Triptafen	-	0	0
Sulpirade, Dolmatil, Sulparex, Sulpitil	-	0	0
Risperidone, Riperadal	1	0	0
Haloperidol, Dozic, Haldol, Serenace	0	-	0
Any medication	**9**	**1**	**1**
No medication	91	99	99
Base (weighted)	*404*	*7458*	*7862*

Table **6.11**

Help sought in last year for child's mental health problems by type of conduct disorder, 2004

All children   Great Britain

	Type of conduct disorder					
	Oppositional defiant disorder	Unsocialised conduct disorder	Socialised conduct disorder	Any conduct disorder[1]	No conduct disorder	All
	Percentage of children using each service/source					
Specialist services						
Child/adult mental health specialist (eg psychiatrist)	26	43	19	28	2	3
Child physical health specialist (eg paediatrician)	5	6	2	7	2	2
Social services (eg social worker)	10	32	15	16	1	2
Education services (eg educational psychologist)	23	30	19	24	3	4
Front line services						
Primary health care (eg GP or practice nurse)	30	34	34	32	5	6
Teachers	54	63	64	60	16	18
All professional services	**69**	**85**	**81**	**76**	**19**	**22**
Informal sources						
Family member/friends	29	44	47	34	11	12
Internet	6	5	5	6	1	1
Telephone help line	2	10	5	4	0	1
Self-help group	5	-	1	3	0	0
Other type of help	7	10	6	7	1	2
All sources	**74**	**90**	**87**	**81**	**25**	**28**
No help sought	26	10	13	19	75	72
Base (weighted)	*213*	*57*	*89*	*402*	*7383*	*7784*

1. The 'Any conduct disorder category' includes children with other types of conduct disorder.

Table **6.12**

Teacher's rating of child's basic skills by type of conduct disorder, 199 and 2004 combined

All children   Great Britain

	Type of conduct disorder					
	Oppositional defiant disorder	Unsocialised conduct disorder	Socialised conduct disorder	Any conduct disorder[1]	No conduct disorder	All
	%	%	%	%	%	%
Reading						
Above average	14	6	13	13	38	37
Average	30	29	38	31	41	40
Some difficulty	33	38	37	34	16	17
Marked difficulty	23	27	13	22	5	6
Mathematics						
Above average	15	6	11	13	32	31
Average	30	29	38	30	45	44
Some difficulty	34	42	38	36	18	19
Marked difficulty	21	23	13	21	5	6
Spelling						
Above average	12	4	10	10	29	28
Average	26	24	31	27	42	41
Some difficulty	32	41	45	36	21	21
Marked difficulty	30	31	13	28	8	9
Base (weighted)	*408*	*77*	*126*	*708*	*13466*	*14174*
Overall scholastic ability[2]						
4 or more years behind	7	10	9	10	2	2
3 years behind	8	14	6	8	2	2
2 years behind	16	19	22	18	5	5
1 year behind	22	30	24	23	15	15
Equivalent	30	22	24	27	36	35
1 or more years ahead	16	5	15	15	41	40
Base (weighted)	*375*	*64*	*111*	*638*	*12616*	*13254*

1. The 'Any conduct disorder category' includes children with other types of conduct disorder.
2. Functioning age-actual age.

Table **6.13**

Whether child has special educational needs by type of conduct disorder, 1999 and 2004 combined

All children   Great Britain

	Type of conduct disorder					
	Oppositional defiant disorder	Unsocialised conduct disorder	Socialised conduct disorder	Any conduct disorder[1]	No conduct disorder	All
	%	%	%	%	%	%
If child has officially recognised special educational needs						
Yes	53	62	37	52	15	17
No	47	38	63	48	85	83
Base (weighted)	*404*	*76*	*125*	*701*	*13242*	*13943*

1. The 'Any conduct disorder category' includes children with other types of conduct disorder.

Table **6.14**

Absence from school and truancy (teacher's report) by type of conduct disorder, 1999 and 2004 combined

All children   Great Britain

	Type of conduct disorder					
	Oppositional defiant disorder	Unsocialised conduct disorder	Socialised conduct disorder	Any conduct disorder[1]	No conduct disorder	All
	%	%	%	%	%	%
Number of days absent in last term						
0	26	19	13	21	32	32
1–5	42	36	26	38	46	46
6–10	18	19	18	18	13	13
11–15	6	7	18	10	4	4
16 or more	9	19	26	14	4	5
Any days absent	74	81	87	79	68	68
Base (weighted)	*282*	*57*	*89*	*495*	*9890*	*10385*
Any unauthorised days absent						
Yes	18	26	55	28	8	9
No	82	74	45	72	92	91
Base (weighted 2004 data)[2]	*127*	*29*	*47*	*222*	*4467*	*4689*
Whether plays truant						
Not true	91	71	44	78	98	97
Somewhat true	6	11	20	10	2	2
Certainly true	3	18	35	12	1	1
Base (weighted)	*410*	*77*	*125*	*712*	*13553*	*14265*

1. The 'Any conduct disorder category' includes children with other types of conduct disorder.
2. This question was not asked in 1999.

Table **6.15**

Absence from school (parent's report) by whether has a conduct disorder, 2004

All children   Great Britain

	Any conduct disorder	No conduct disorder	All
	%	%	%
Whether missed school in last term[1]			
Yes	41	34	34
No	59	66	66
Base (weighted): all children	*377*	*7244*	*7621*
Reasons for absence			
Short-term illness	67	79	78
Long-term illness	5	2	2
Refused to attend	13	1	2
Has a school phobia	3	0	0
Other	25	20	20
Base (weighted): those who missed school	*155*	*2445*	*2599*
Whether child received any educational provision			
Yes	9	10	10
No	91	90	90
Base (weighted): those who missed school (excluding short-term illness)	*65*	*587*	*652*

1. Excluding exclusions.

Table **6.16**

Exclusions from school (parent's report) by type of conduct disorder, 2004

All children   Great Britain

	Type of conduct disorder					All
	Oppositional defiant disorder	Unsocialised conduct disorder	Socialised conduct disorder	Any conduct disorder[1]	No conduct disorder	
	%	%	%	%	%	%
Number of times child has been excluded from school						
None	78	54	52	67	98	96
Once	7	19	20	12	1	2
Twice	6	3	8	7	0	1
Three or more times	8	24	20	15	0	1
Base (weighted)	*212*	*57*	*88*	*398*	*7372*	*7770*

1. The 'Any conduct disorder category' includes children with other types of conduct disorder.

Table **6.17**

Number of times child has changed schools by whether has a conduct disorder, 2004

All children   Great Britain

	Any conduct disorder	No conduct disorder	All
	%	%	%
Number of times child has changed school[1]			
None	70	82	81
Once	19	14	14
Twice	4	3	3
Three or more times	7	2	2
Base (weighted)	*401*	*7376*	*7776*

1. Apart from normal transitions.

Table **6.18**

Parent's GHQ–12 score by type of conduct disorder, 1999 and 2004 combined

All children   Great Britain

	Type of conduct disorder					
	Oppositional defiant disorder	Unsocialised conduct disorder	Socialised conduct disorder	Any conduct disorder[1]	No conduct disorder	All
	%	%	%	%	%	%
Parent's GHQ–12[2]						
0–2	57	39	42	52	77	76
3–5	20	24	21	20	13	13
6–8	13	18	14	14	6	7
9–12	10	19	22	14	4	4
3 or more	**43**	**61**	**58**	**48**	**23**	**24**
Base (weighted)	*474*	*101*	*182*	*886*	*17097*	*17983*

1. The 'Any conduct disorder category' includes children with other types of conduct disorder.
2. For this survey, scores of 3 or more were taken to indicate a severe emotional problem.

Table **6.19**

Family functioning score by type of conduct disorder, 1999 and 2004 combined

All children   Great Britain

	Type of conduct disorder					
	Oppositional defiant disorder	Unsocialised conduct disorder	Socialised conduct disorder	Any conduct disorder[1]	No conduct disorder	All
	%	%	%	%	%	%
Family functioning score[2]						
Up to 1.50	22	18	12	18	37	36
1.51–2.00	42	36	32	40	46	46
2.01–2.50	28	23	41	30	15	16
2.51 or more	8	22	15	12	2	3
Unhealthy functioning (2.01 or more)	**36**	**46**	**56**	**42**	**17**	**18**
Base (weighted)	*472*	*101*	*180*	*878*	*17030*	*17908*

1. The 'Any conduct disorder category' includes children with other types of conduct disorder.
2. For this survey, scores over 2.0 were taken to indicate unhealthy family functioning.

Table **6.20**

Stressful life events by type of conduct disorder, 2004

All children   Great Britain

Stressful life events	Type of conduct disorder					
	Oppositional defiant disorder	Unsocialised conduct disorder	Socialised conduct disorder	Any conduct disorder[1]	No conduct disorder	All
	Percentage reporting each event					
Since child was born, parent had a separation due to marital difficulties or broken off steady relationship	52	57	62	54	30	31
Since child was born, parent had a major financial crisis such as losing the equivalent of three months income	21	30	25	22	13	13
Since child was born, parent had a problem with the police involving a court appearance	12	21	14	15	5	6
Since child was born, parent has had serious physical illness	9	15	14	11	7	8
Since child was born, parent has had serious mental illness	18	24	14	17	7	8
At any stage in child's life, a parent, brother or sister died	6	3	5	6	3	4
At any stage in child's life, a close friend died	9	13	15	11	6	6
At some stage in the child's life, s/he had a serious illness which required a stay in hospital	20	22	18	21	13	13
At any stage in child's life, s/he had been in a serious accident or badly hurt in an accident	9	13	6	10	5	5
In the past year child has broken off a steady relationship with a boy or girl friend (aged 13 or above)/ a close friendship has ended (any age)	12	16	17	13	6	7
Base (weighted)	*213*	*56*	*89*	*401*	*7369*	*7770*

1. The 'Any conduct disorder category' includes children with other types of conduct disorder.

Table 6.21

Number of stressful life events by type of conduct disorder, 1999 and 2004 combined

All children   Great Britain

	Type of conduct disorder					
	Oppositional defiant disorder	Unsocialised conduct disorder	Socialised conduct disorder	Any conduct disorder[1]	No conduct disorder	All
	%	%	%	%	%	%
Number of stressful life events						
0	18	24	16	18	43	42
1	36	16	29	32	32	32
2	20	21	21	20	15	15
3	17	17	20	18	7	7
4	5	10	11	7	2	3
5 or more	3	12	3	5	1	1
Two or more events	**45**	**60**	**55**	**50**	**25**	**26**
Base (weighted)	*213*	*56*	*89*	*401*	*7369*	*7770*

1. The 'Any conduct disorder category' includes children with other types of conduct disorder.

Table 6.22

Child's strengths (parent's and child's assessment) by type of conduct disorder, 2004

All children   Great Britain

	Type of conduct disorder					
	Oppositional defiant disorder	Unsocialised conduct disorder	Socialised conduct disorder	Any conduct disorder[1]	No conduct disorder	All
	%	%	%	%	%	%
ALL CHILDREN						
Strength score – parent assessment						
0–36	68	88	85	77	23	25
37–40	17	5	8	13	25	25
41–43	7	3	5	6	26	25
44–48	7	4	1	5	26	25
Base (weighted)	*205*	*54*	*87*	*386*	*7185*	*7571*
CHILDREN AGED 11–16						
Strength score – child assessment						
0–23	41	(42)	53	46	22	23
24–27	24	(34)	32	28	27	27
28–30	26	(15)	6	16	23	23
31–38	10	(9)	9	10	28	27
Base (weighted)	*68*	*20*	*63*	*162*	*3176*	*3338*

1. The 'Any conduct disorder category' includes children with other types of conduct disorder.

Table **6.23**

Social aptitude (parent's assessment) by type of conduct disorder, 2004

All children   Great Britain

	Type of conduct disorder					
	Oppositional defiant disorder	Unsocialised conduct disorder	Socialised conduct disorder	Any conduct disorder[1]	No conduct disorder	All
	%	%	%	%	%	%
Social aptitude score						
0–20	64	82	64	69	22	25
21–24	19	12	22	17	28	27
25–28	10	3	7	8	23	22
29–40	7	2	7	6	26	25
Base (weighted)	*202*	*55*	*87*	*385*	*7098*	*7483*

1. The 'Any conduct disorder category' includes children with other types of conduct disorder.

Table **6.24**

Friendships by type of conduct disorder, 2004

All children

	Type of conduct disorder					
	Oppositional defiant disorder	Unsocialised conduct disorder	Socialised conduct disorder	Any conduct disorder[1]	No conduct disorder	All
	%	%	%	%	%	%
What is child like at making friends?						
Finds it harder than average	23	47	6	24	9	10
About average	36	27	42	36	36	36
Easier than average	41	26	53	40	55	54
What is child like at keeping friends?						
Finds it harder than average	31	54	17	33	4	5
About average	38	30	43	37	35	35
Easier than average	31	16	40	30	61	59
Number of friends						
None	7	10	-	8	1	2
1	12	24	4	12	4	4
2–4	44	42	43	43	43	43
5–9	25	24	42	28	40	39
10 or more	12	-	11	9	12	11
Base (weighted): all children	*212*	*57*	*88*	*401*	*7439*	*7840*
Do child and friends have things in common						
No	6	6	2	5	1	1
A little	30	43	29	32	20	21
A lot	64	51	69	63	79	78
Do child and friends do things together						
No	9	13	2	7	3	4
A little	29	37	19	28	21	21
A lot	62	51	79	65	76	75
If worried, can child talk to friends						
No	41	50	17	35	20	21
Perhaps	30	28	35	33	42	42
Definitely	28	22	48	32	38	37
Whether friends get into trouble						
Not at all	40	28	23	34	69	67
A few are like that	52	36	58	51	30	31
Many are like that	7	24	12	11	1	1
All are like that	1	11	6	4	0	0
Whether parent approves of child's friends						
No	4	21	17	10	1	2
A little	32	42	41	36	13	14
A lot	64	37	42	54	86	84
Base (weighted): those who had friends	*195*	*49*	*86*	*362*	*7208*	*7570*

1. The 'Any conduct disorder category' includes children with other types of conduct disorder.

Table 6.25

Child's sources of emotional support by whether has a conduct disorder, 2004

Children aged 11–16

Great Britain

	Any conduct disorder	No conduct disorder	All
	%	%	%
Social support score			
0–17	54	27	28
18	16	16	16
19	15	21	20
20	16	36	35
Base (weighted)	162	3168	3330

Table 6.26

Views about the neighbourhood by whether has a conduct disorder, 2004

Children aged 11–16

Great Britain

	Any conduct disorder	No conduct disorder	All
	%	%	%
Whether enjoys living in the neighbourhood			
A lot	44	65	64
A little	35	29	29
No	21	7	7
How safe child feels walking alone in the neighbourhood during the daytime			
Very safe	62	61	61
Fairly safe	26	32	32
A bit unsafe	8	5	5
Very unsafe	4	1	1
Never goes out alone	1	1	1
Whether ever goes to the local shops or park alone			
Yes	82	80	80
No	18	20	20
How many people in the neighbourhood can be trusted			
Many	20	39	38
Some	48	44	44
A few	26	16	16
None	6	2	2
Likelihood of someone returning a lost bag			
Very likely	10	12	12
Quite likely	26	46	45
Not very likely	38	30	30
Not at all likely	27	12	13
Base (weighted)	162	3169	3331

Table **6.27**

Help provided to others by whether has a conduct disorder, 2004

Children aged 11–16   Great Britain

Type of help	Any conduct disorder	No conduct disorder	All	Any conduct disorder	No conduct disorder	All
	Percentage giving each type of help to relatives			Percentage giving each type of help to non-relatives		
Type of help						
Doing shopping for someone	34	37	37	12	9	9
Cooking or helping to prepare family meals	48	52	52	7	6	6
Cleaning, hoovering or gardening	60	69	69	16	10	11
Washing or ironing clothes	35	36	36	2	2	2
Decorating or repairs	18	21	21	5	5	5
Baby sitting or caring for children	35	39	39	24	19	19
Writing letters or filling in forms	9	10	10	2	4	4
Taking care of someone who is sick	29	34	34	9	9	9
Helping out in a family business	10	11	11	..	..	..
Anything else	6	9	9	4	3	3
None of the above	16	6	7	57	60	60
Base (weighted): all aged 11 or over	*163*	*3195*	*3358*	*163*	*3195*	*3358*
Frequency of providing help						
Every day	15	18	17	7	6	6
At least once a week	58	59	59	30	32	32
At least once a month	20	17	17	36	38	38
Less often	6	6	6	27	24	24
Base (weighted): those who helped	*138*	*2996*	*3134*	*71*	*1270*	*1341*

Table **6.28**

Whether child does any paid work by whether has a conduct disorder, 2004

Children aged 11–16

	Any conduct disorder	No conduct disorder	All
	%	%	%
Whether child does any paid work at least once a month			
Yes	23	22	22
No	77	78	78
Base(weighted): all childen aged 11 or over	*163*	*3195*	*3359*
		Percentage doing each type of work	
Type of paid work			
Family business	10	10	10
Newspaper round delivery	13	26	25
Shop or restaurant	27	27	27
Building, decorating or gardening	5	2	2
Household chores	21	18	18
Other	29	23	23
Base (weighted): those doing paid work	*37*	*703*	*740*

Table 6.29

Participation in groups, clubs and organisations by whether has a conduct disorder, 2004

Children aged 11–16   Great Britain

Type of group/club/ organisation	Any conduct disorder	No conduct disorder	All	Any conduct disorder	No conduct disorder	All
	Percentage particpating in clubs at school			*Percentage particpating in clubs outside school*		
Sports	38	52	51	24	38	37
Art, drama, dance or music	15	33	32	9	18	18
Youth	10	11	11	24	21	21
Computers	14	14	14	3	3	3
Political	1	2	2	1	1	1
Debating	1	4	4	-	0	0
Religious	1	3	3	2	5	5
Local community or neighbourhood	-	2	2	3	2	2
Voluntary groups helping people	4	4	4	1	3	2
Safety, First Aid	3	4	4	1	3	3
Environmental	3	5	5	3	2	2
Animal (welfare)	1	1	1	1	1	1
Human rights	1	1	1	-	0	0
School holiday playschemes	7	9	9	6	7	7
After-school clubs	18	28	28	..	..	..
School student councils	5	11	11	..	..	..
Student Union	-	1	1	..	..	..
Extra teaching or special lessons	7	9	9	..	..	..
Other	..	..	..	7	9	9
None of the above	44	21	22	45	33	33
Base (weighted)	*151*	*3138*	*3288*	*151*	*3139*	*3290*

Table 6.30

Unpaid help given to groups, clubs and organisations by whether has a conduct disorder, 2004

Children aged 11–16   Great Britain

Unpaid help given to groups, clubs and organisations in the last 12 months	Any conduct disorder	No conduct disorder	All
	Percentage mentioning each type of help		
Collected or raised money	21	34	33
Took part in a sponsored activity	18	32	32
Was part of a committee	1	7	6
Helped to organise or run an event	13	20	19
Other help	6	9	9
None of the above	61	41	42
Base (weighted)	*163*	*3195*	*3358*

Table **6.31**

Barriers to participation in groups, clubs and organisations by whether has a conduct disorder, 2004

Children aged 11–16   Great Britain

	Any conduct disorder	No conduct disorder	All
	Percentage mentioning each barrier		
Barriers to participation			
Difficulty getting to clubs	9	6	6
No good groups or clubs locally	17	16	16
Cannot afford to join	4	2	2
Would not feel safe travelling to club	3	2	2
No clubs of interest	13	14	14
Too busy	8	15	15
Do not want to participate	22	15	16
Do not have time after homework	5	12	12
Not allowed	2	2	2
Other barrier	4	3	3
None of the above	42	42	42
Base (weighted)	*151*	*3140*	*3291*

Table **6.32**

Smoking behaviour by whether has a conduct disorder, 1999 and 2004 combined

Children aged 11–16   Great Britain

	11- to 13-year-olds			14- to 16-year-olds			All aged 11–16		
	Any conduct disorder	No conduct disorder	All	Any conduct disorder	No conduct disorder	All	Any conduct disorder	No conduct disorder	All
	%	%	%	%	%	%	%	%	%
Smoking behaviour									
Regular smoker	10	1	1	50	10	13	30	5	6
Occasional smoker	3	1	1	4	5	5	3	3	3
All smokers	**13**	**2**	**2**	**54**	**16**	**18**	**34**	**8**	**9**
Used to smoke	7	3	3	13	9	9	10	5	5
Tried smoking once	34	15	16	17	29	28	25	21	21
Never smoked	46	80	79	17	47	45	31	66	64
Base (weighted)	*193*	*4208*	*4400*	*193*	*3077*	*3269*	*385*	*7285*	*7670*

Table **6.33**

Drinking behaviour by whether has a conduct disorder, 1999 and 2004 combined

Children aged 11–16

	11- to 13-year-olds			14- to 16-year-olds			All aged 11–16		
	Any conduct disorder	No conduct disorder	All	Any conduct disorder	No conduct disorder	All	Any conduct disorder	No conduct disorder	All
	%	%	%	%	%	%	%	%	%
Drinking behaviour									
Almost every day	2	0	0	2	0	1	2	0	0
About twice a week	3	1	1	17	6	6	10	3	3
About once a week	1	2	2	14	10	10	7	5	6
All regular drinkers	**6**	**3**	**3**	**32**	**16**	**17**	**19**	**9**	**9**
About once a fortnight	4	3	3	11	12	12	8	7	7
About once a month	6	5	5	16	16	16	11	10	10
Only a few times a year	26	20	21	24	29	29	25	24	24
Never drinks alcohol	4	2	2	1	2	2	2	2	2
Never had a drink	54	67	67	16	25	24	35	49	49
Base (weighted)	*193*	*4205*	*4397*	*193*	*3078*	*3270*	*386*	*7282*	*7669*

Table **6.34**

Drug use by whether has a conduct disorder, 1999 and 2004 combined

Children aged 11–16

	11- to 13-year-olds			14- to 16-year-olds			All aged 11–16		
	Any conduct disorder	No conduct disorder	All	Any conduct disorder	No conduct disorder	All	Any conduct disorder	No conduct disorder	All
	%	%	%	%	%	%	%	%	%
Ever used:									
Cannabis	7	1	2	40	14	15	23	6	7
Inhalants	2	0	0	6	1	1	4	0	1
Ecstasy	2	0	0	3	1	1	2	0	0
Amphetamines	2	0	0	8	1	1	5	1	1
LSD	-	0	0	4	0	1	2	0	0
Tranqulisers	-	0	0	2	0	0	1	0	0
Cocaine	-	0	0	3	1	1	1	0	0
Heroin	1	0	0	1	-	0	1	0	0
Any drugs	**13**	**2**	**3**	**43**	**15**	**16**	**28**	**8**	**9**
Base (weighted)	*191*	*4204*	*4395*	*191*	*3077*	*3268*	*383*	*7281*	*7665*

Table **6.35**

Social context of last smoking, drinking and drug taking occasions by whether has a conduct disorder, 2004

Children aged 11–16 who had engaged in each behaviour   Great Britain

	Last smoking occasion			Last drinking occasion			Last occasion took cannabis		
	Any conduct disorder	No conduct disorder	All	Any conduct disorder	No conduct disorder	All	Any conduct disorder	No conduct disorder	All
	%	%	%	%	%	%	%	%	%
Where had last drink									
Own home	37	30	32	31	43	42	4	11	10
Other's home	8	10	9	21	29	28	33	40	39
Public house	-	3	2	10	7	8	2	0	1
Restaurant	-	-	-	3	3	3	-	-	-
Nightclub/other club	2	3	3	4	5	5	-	2	2
Outside in public place	44	39	40	25	6	7	49	38	40
Other venue	8	15	14	5	6	6	11	8	9
Number of other people in group									
Alone	20	21	21	7	3	3	-	2	2
1	29	26	27	19	14	14	16	15	15
2–5	27	33	31	36	46	45	51	55	54
6–10	19	8	11	19	19	19	20	15	16
More than 10	5	12	11	18	19	18	13	13	13
Base (weighted)[1]	*59*	*178*	*237*	*98*	*1362*	*1461*	*45*	*213*	*258*
Who was with respondent[2]									
Boyfriend/girlfriend	10	12	11	15	6	7	2	8	7
Other friend(s)	80	81	81	64	52	53	90	91	91
Family	14	10	11	32	45	44	2	5	4
Other	6	3	4	2	3	3	8	4	5
Base (weighted)[3]	*47*	*139*	*186*	*91*	*1321*	*1411*	*44*	*207*	*252*

1. The bases are: regular smokers; those who had had an alcoholic drink in the last 6 months; those who had used cannabis in the last year.
2. Percentages may sum to more than 100 because some children were accompanied by more than one group.
3. The bases are those who had engaged in the behaviour with others.

Table **6.36**

Deliberate self-harm by whether has a conduct disorder, 1999 and 2004 combined

	Any conduct disorder	No conduct disorder	All
	Percentage who have tried to harm, hurt or kill themselves		
All children			
Parent's report	16	2	2
Base (weighted)	*805*	*16851*	*17655*
Children aged 11–16			
Parent's report	18	2	3
Base (weighted)	*438*	*7800*	*8239*
Child's report	21	6	7
Base (weighted)	*355*	*7050*	*7404*

Mental health of children and young people in Great Britain, 2004

Hyperkinetic disorders

Chapter 7

Introduction

This chapter begins with a description of the typical behaviour patterns displayed by children and young people who have a hyperkinetic disorder. This is followed by an overview of their characteristics looking at their:

- demographic characteristics;
- family situation;
- socio-economic characteristics;
- geographic distribution;
- general, physical and mental health;
- use of services;
- scholastic ability and attendance at school;
- family's social functioning;
- own social functioning; and
- lifestyle behaviours.

As noted in Chapter 4, there was no change in the prevalence of hyperkinetic disorders between 1999 and 2004. The two datasets have therefore been combined, so as to increase the sample base.

In 1999 hyperkinetic disorders were subdivided into two categories: *hyperkinesis* and *other hyperkinetic disorders*. As there were very few cases in the latter category in 2004, all types of hyperkinetic disorder were classified into a single category of *hyperkinetic disorders*. This type of disorder is sometimes referred to as Attention Deficit Hyperactivity Disorder (ADHD), which is the name for a broader (and therefore commoner but milder) disorder defined by the American Psychiatric Association.

The tables compare the children with any form of hyperkinetic disorder with those who have no such disorder. The commentary is descriptive, the aim being to provide a profile of children who have a hyperkinetic disorder. It therefore takes no account of the inter-relationships between the characteristics. The analysis at the end of Chapter 4 described the factors which had the largest independent effects on prevalence and this gives an indication of the key variables.

Typical behaviour patterns

This section describes the typical behavioural symptoms displayed by children with hyperkinetic disorders. The symptoms described below can be observed, to some degree, in most children but for a child to be diagnosed as having a hyperkinetic disorder the symptoms have to be sufficiently severe so as to cause the child distress or impairment in his/her social functioning. As an illustration of the possible impact of

such a disorder on the child's life and that of his/her family, the description of symptoms is followed by a case vignette of a fictitious child.[1]

Hyperkinetic disorders

The child is *hyperactive* (for example, fidgeting, running around, climbing on furniture, always making a lot of noise), *impulsive* (for example, blurts out answers, cannot wait his/her turn, butts into conversations or games, cannot stop talking) and *inattentive* (for example, cannot concentrate on a task, makes careless mistakes, loses interest, does not listen, is disorganised, forgetful and easily distracted). The child's teachers are likely to have complained about his/her overactivity, impulsiveness and poor attention.

> *He is all over the place – always on the move. He won't sit still at the table while we are eating – it's fidgeting the whole time, getting up between courses. He'd get up between mouthfuls if I let him. If there's a task that needs doing, whether it's homework or tidying his room, he'll start willingly but within a few minutes he's been distracted and begun doing something else instead. Sometimes, it is just an excuse and he never really wanted to do it anyway, but there are many times when I'm sure he couldn't help it. The teachers complain too, but I think they agree that it's the way he is made. Outside the family he is quite shy, and this keeps him a bit under control. But within the family, he has no inhibitions. He's forever interrupting, poking his nose in, acting without thinking of the consequences. At home, we try to make allowances, but there are still times when it leads to family rows – when he has yet again broken a pen or a remote control as a result of his ceaseless fidgeting, or when it's bedtime and he still hasn't finished homework that anyone else could have finished ages ago. At school, they can't make as many allowances as we can, and I think it has been stopping him doing as well as he should in his lessons.*

Demographic, socio-economic and area characteristics

Demographic characteristics

Children with hyperkinetic disorders were predominantly boys, 86 per cent compared with 50 per cent of those with no such disorder. Almost all were white, 97 per cent compared with 89 per cent of other children. There were no differences in the age profile of children with a hyperkinetic disorder and those with no such disorder.   (Figure 7.1 and Table 7.1)

---

1. *The symptoms and vignettes are based on descriptions of a 'made up' child created by Youthinmind to illustrate the diagnostic classificatory system.*

Figure **7.1**
Sex by whether has a hyperkinetic disorder, 1999 and 2004 combined

Great Britain

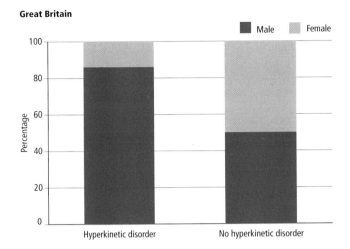

Family characteristics

Children with hyperkinetic disorders were more likely than other children to live with single or previously married lone parents (15 and 23 per cent compared with 8 and 16 per cent). Conversely, just over half (53 per cent) of children with hyperkinetic disorders lived with parents who were married compared with about two-thirds (69 per cent) of children with no such disorder. (Figure 7.2 and Table 7.2)

Figure **7.2**
Family type by whether has a hyperkinetic disorder, 1999 and 2004 combined

Great Britain

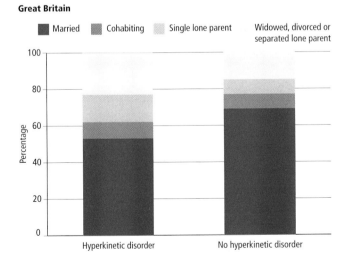

Unlike children with emotional and conduct disorders who tended to live in relatively large families, there were no differences between children with and those with no hyperkinetic disorder in relation to the number of children in the household and whether or not there were stepchildren in the family. (Table 7.2)

Parental education and socio-economic characteristics

Children with hyperkinetic disorders were more likely than other children to live in low income households and to have parents who had no educational qualifications.

Over a third (36 per cent) of children with hyperkinetic disorders had parents with no educational qualifications compared with a fifth (21 per cent) of those with no such disorder. (Table 7.3)

Children with hyperkinetic disorders were more than twice as likely as children with no such disorder to live in a household in which neither parent was working (31 per cent compared with 14 per cent). Similarly, children with hyperkinetic disorders were twice as likely as other children to have parents in the routine occupational group (25 per cent compared with 12 per cent). (Table 7.3)

Housing and income

More than half (54 per cent) of children with hyperkinetic disorders lived in rented property compared with less than a third (31 per cent) of other children. Most of these lived in the social rented sector (41 per cent compared with 24 per cent of other children). (Table 7.4)

About a half (52 per cent) of children with hyperkinetic disorders lived in households with a gross weekly income of less than £300 compared with a third (34 per cent) of other children. Conversely, children with hyperkinetic disorders were much less likely than other children to live in households with a gross weekly income of over £600 (17 per cent compared with 33 per cent). (Table 7.4)

Over a quarter of children with hyperkinetic disorders were living in households in which someone received a disability benefit (27 per cent compared with 8 per cent of other children). (Table 7.4)

Area characteristics

There were no significant differences between countries in the distribution of children with and those with no hyperkinetic disorder. The only regional differences were that the former were more likely than other children to live in a non-metropolitan areas of England (53 per cent compared with 44 per cent). (Table 7.5)

Households containing children with hyperkinetic disorders were more likely than other households to live in areas classified as 'Hard Pressed' (36 per cent compared with 24 per cent) and less likely to live in areas classified as 'Wealthy Achievers' (18 per cent compared with 26 per cent). (Table 7.5)

Among children with hyperkinetic disorders:

- 86 per cent were boys *(compared with 50 per cent for children with no hyperkinetic disorder)*
- 55 per cent were aged 5–10 *(53 per cent)*
- 97 per cent were white *(89 per cent)*
- 23 per cent lived with a widowed, divorced or separated lone parent *(16 per cent)*
- 15 per cent lived with a single lone parent *(8 per cent)*
- 53 per cent lived in a married couple family *(69 per cent)*
- 36 per cent had parents with no educational qualifications *(21 per cent)*
- 46 per cent lived in owned accommodation (69 per cent)
- 52 per cent lived in households with gross incomes under £300 per week *(34 per cent)*
- 27 per cent lived in households in which someone received a disability benefit *(8 per cent)*
- 36 per cent lived in areas classified as 'Hard pressed' *(24 per cent)*

Child's general, physical and mental health

General health

Parents of children with hyperkinetic disorders were more than twice as likely as other parents to report that their child's general health was fair or bad (18 per cent compared with 7 per cent). (Figure 7.3 and Table 7.6)

Figure 7.3
Child's general health by whether has a hyperkinetic disorder, 1999 and 2004 combined

Great Britain

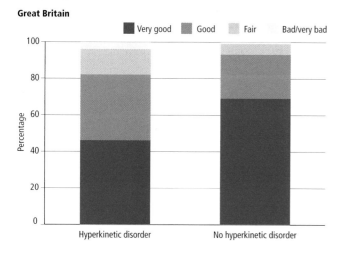

Physical or developmental problems

Just over two-thirds (70 per cent) of children with hyperkinetic disorders had a specific physical or developmental problem compared with just over a half (54 per cent) of other children. The largest differences were for difficulty with co-ordination (14 per cent compared with 2 per cent), bed wetting (17 per cent compared with 4 per cent) and speech or language difficulties (15 per cent compared with 4 per cent). (Table 7.7)

Mental disorders

Two-thirds (66 per cent) of children with a hyperkinetic disorder also suffered from another of the main types of clinically recognisable mental disorder, most commonly conduct disorder (62 per cent). One in eight (12 per cent) also had an emotional disorder. (Table 7.8)

The parents of those with hyperkinetic disorders mentioned a range of mental health problems among their children. Two-thirds (66 per cent) reported that their child had behavioural problems, over a half (56 per cent) said that their child was hyperactive and nearly a third (29 per cent) mentioned emotional problems. (Table 7.9)

Medication

About 2 in 5 (43 per cent) children with a hyperkinetic disorder were taking some kind of medication. The majority of these children were taking Methylphenidate (41 per cent) while the others were taking other medications that are recognised for use with hyperkinetic disorders (3 per cent Risperidone, 2 per cent Dexamphetamine, 1 per cent Clonidine and 1 per cent Amitriptyline). There have been some concerns about the over-prescription of stimulant medication. However, while we would expect the majority of children with a hyperkinetic disorder to respond to stimulant medication, less than half the children with this disorder were taking such medication. Moreover, we did not find children taking stimulant medication who did not have evidence of pervasive hyperactivity. This suggests that, despite a large increase in the numbers of children prescribed stimulant medication in recent years, concerns about over-prescription are unfounded, and that there is still a large proportion of children with hyperkinetic disorders who are not gaining access to an evidence-based treatment. (Table 7.10)

Among the parents of children with hyperkinetic disorders:

- 18 per cent reported that the child's general health was fair or bad *(compared with 7 per cent for children with no hyperkinetic disorder)*
- 70 per cent reported that the child had a specific physical complaint *(54 per cent)*
- 77 per cent reported that the child had mental health or developmental problems *(9 per cent)*
- 29 per cent reported that the child had emotional problems, 66 per cent reported behavioural problems and 56 per cent reported hyperactivity *(4 per cent, 5 per cent and 3 per cent)*
- 66 per cent of the children had another main type of clinically recognisable disorder *(8 per cent)*

Use of services

Parents were asked if they had had contact with any services in the past year because they were concerned about their child's emotions, behaviour or concentration. In the 1999 survey these questions were asked only of children who had been identified as having some significant problem in the interview whereas, in the 2004 survey, the questions were asked of all children. Data is presented for the 2004 survey only.

Almost all (95 per cent) parents of children with hyperkinetic disorders had sought some form of help in the previous 12 months because of concerns about their child's mental health.

Most (93 per cent) had accessed some professional service. The most commonly used source of professional help were teachers (70 per cent) but parents also sought help from, or were referred to, other professional sources such as mental health services (52 per cent), primary health care (46 per cent) and specialist education services, such as educational psychologists (37 per cent).

The parents of children with hyperkinetic disorders had also sought advice from informal sources such as family and friends (35 per cent), self help groups (7 per cent) and the internet (11 per cent). (Table 7.11)

Parents of children with hyperkinetic disorders who had not accessed any services were asked if there was anything that prevented them from doing so. They were shown a list of potential obstacles to service use and asked to identify any that they had encountered. Almost a half (49 per cent) had

Among the parents of children with hyperkinetic disorders:

- 95 per cent had sought help or advice in the last year because of worries about their child's mental health *(compared with 27 per cent for children with no hyperkinetic disorder)*
- 93 per cent had contacted a professional service *(21 per cent)*
- The most commonly used services were: Teachers (70 per cent), mental health services (52 per cent), primary health care (46 per cent), specialist educational services (37 per cent) and family members or friends (35 per cent)

experienced one or more of the obstacles listed. The most common were that parents found it difficult to get a referral (23 per cent), that they often did not know such services existed (15 per cent) or did not believe that the specialist help would be of any use (10 per cent). (Table not shown)

Scholastic ability and attendance at school

Teachers were asked to rate the child's abilities in reading, mathematics and spelling compared with an average child of the same age and to estimate the child's age in terms of scholastic ability. They were also asked whether or not the child had officially recognised special educational needs.

Basic skills

Almost two-thirds (64 per cent and 63 per cent) of children with hyperkinetic disorders had difficulties with reading and mathematics while three-quarters (75 per cent) had difficulties with spelling. The corresponding figures for children with no such disorder were 23 per cent, 25 per cent and 30 per cent. These difficulties were also reflected in the teacher's assessment of the child's overall scholastic ability. About two-thirds (65 per cent) of children with hyperkinetic disorders were rated as being behind on their overall intellectual development compared with about a quarter (24 per cent) of children with no such disorder. Teachers' ratings indicated that 18 per cent of children with hyperkinetic disorders were three or more years behind in their schooling (compared with 4 per cent of other children). (Figure 7.4 and Table 7.12)

Figure **7.4**
Proportion of children who were behind in their overall scholastic ability by whether they had a hyperkinetic disorder, 1999 and 2004 combined

Great Britain

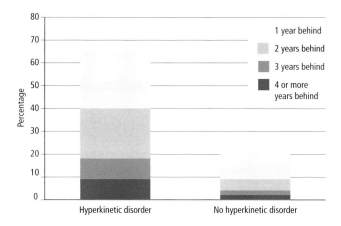

Figure **7.5**
Proportion of children whose teacher thought that they played truant by whether has a hyperkinetic disorder, 1999 and 2004 combined

Great Britain

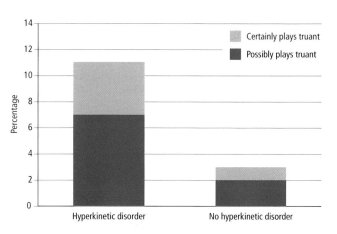

Special educational needs

Almost three-quarters (71 per cent) of children with hyperkinetic disorders had officially recognised special educational needs (compared with 16 per cent of other children). (Table 7.13)

Over a half (56 per cent) of those with recognised needs had a written statement of special educational needs but there was no difference between the two groups in this respect. (Table not shown)

Absence from school

Unlike children with emotional and conduct disorders, children with hyperkinetic disorders were no more likely to have been absent from school than other children. They were, however, more likely than other children to have been absent for long periods: 11 per cent had missed more than fifteen days, compared with 5 per cent of other children. (Table 7.14)

There were no differences between children with hyperkinetic disorders and other children in relation to the proportions who had had an unauthorised absence from school for any reason but teachers were more likely to consider that the former definitely or possibly played truant (11 per cent compared with 3 per cent of other children). (Figure 7.5 and Table 7.14)

In the 2004 survey, parents were asked about absence and exclusions from school. As with the teachers' reports, there were no differences between children with a hyperkinetic disorder and other children in terms of the proportions who had been absent but there were differences in relation to the

reasons: 15 per cent of children with a hyperkinetic disorder refused to attend school compared with 2 per cent of other children. (Table 7.15)

Overall, 10 per cent of children had received some form of educational provision when they were absent from school but there were no differences in this respect between children with hyperkinetic disorders and those with no such disorder. (Table 7.15)

Nearly one-third (29 per cent) of children with hyperkinetic disorders had been excluded from school and 12 per cent had been excluded three or more times. Among other children, these proportions were very low, 4 per cent and 1 per cent. (Table 7.16)

As previously mentioned, 62 per cent of children with hyperkinetic disorders also had a clinically recognisable conduct disorder. Further investigation showed that over four-fifths (84 per cent) of the children with a hyperkinetic disorder who had been excluded from school also had a conduct disorder. Among those children who had a hyperkinetic disorder but no conduct disorder, only 14 per cent had ever been excluded from school. (Table not shown)

Children with a hyperkinetic disorder were also more likely than other children to have changed schools other than at the usual transition stages (35 per cent compared with 19 per cent). This variation was not attributable to the higher rate of exclusions among those with a hyperkinetic disorder since hardly any of these children had changed schools following their exclusion. (Table 7.17)

Among children with hyperkinetic disorders:

- 65 per cent were behind in their overall scholastic ability *(compared with 24 per cent of children with no hyperkinetic disorder)*
- 71 per cent had officially recognised special educational needs *(16 per cent)*
- 11 per cent had had more than 15 days away from school in the previous term *(5 per cent)*
- 11 per cent were considered by teachers to be definite or possible truants *(3 per cent)*
- 29 per cent had been excluded from school and 35 per cent had changed schools apart from the normal transitions *(4 per cent and 19 per cent)*

Social functioning of the family

This section looks at various aspects of parental health, attitudes and behaviour which provide indicators of the social functioning of the family.

Mental health of parent

The parent who was interviewed about the child, usually the mother, was asked about her own mental health using the General Health Questionnaire (GHQ-12 – see Chapter 2 for details). Scores range from 0 (no psychological distress) to 12 (severe psychological distress). A score of 3 is generally taken as the threshold, with scores at this level or higher being considered suggestive of an emotional disorder.

Over two-fifths (43 per cent) of parents of children with hyperkinetic disorders had scores of 3 or more on the GHQ-12 (compared with 24 per cent of other parents) and 10 per cent had a score of 9 or more (compared with 4 per cent).

(Figure 7.6 and Table 7.18)

Figure 7.6
Proportion of children whose parent scored 3 or more on the GHQ-12, 1999 and 2004 combined

Great Britain

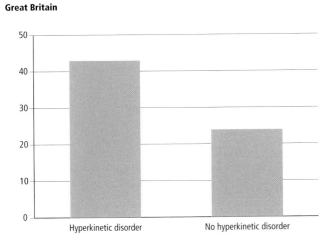

Family functioning

Family functioning was measured using the FAD-GFS scale in which parents rated 12 statements about family relationships (see Chapter 2 for details). For this survey, families that scored over 2.00 on this scale were considered to have unhealthy functioning.

Children with hyperkinetic disorders were twice as likely as other children to live in families classified as having unhealthy functioning (36 per cent compared with 18 per cent).

(Table 7.19)

Stressful life events

Parents were asked whether their child had experienced any of 10 potentially stressful events. The list in the 2004 survey differed slightly to that used in the 1999 survey so data are presented for 2004 only.

For 6 out of the 10 events the proportions of children who had experienced the event were higher among children with hyperkinetic disorders than other children. The separation of a parent was the most common stressful life event for both groups of children. Almost half (49 per cent) of children with a hyperkinetic disorder had experienced this compared with just under a third (31 per cent) of other children. Children with hyperkinetic disorders were also more likely to have had a serious illness which required a stay in hospital (23 per cent compared with 13 per cent), to have parents who had had a major financial crisis (21 per cent compared with 13 per cent), had experienced a problem with the police involving a court appearance (18 per cent compared with 6 per cent) or had had a serious mental illness (17 per cent compared with 8 per cent). Overall, children with hyperkinetic disorders were almost twice as likely as other children to have experienced two or more stressful life events (47 per cent compared with 26 per cent).

(Table 7.20 and Table 7.21)

Among children with hyperkinetic disorders:

- 43 per cent of parents had an emotional disorder *(compared with 24 per cent of children with no hyperkinetic disorder)*
- 36 per cent lived in families with unhealthy functioning *(18 per cent)*
- 47 per cent had two or more stressful life events *(26 per cent)*

Child's social functioning

This section covers features of social functioning which might affect the child's resilience against the onset and course of mental disorder. These include their strengths, relationships with friends, social aptitudes and various measures of social capital. The questions on strengths were introduced in the 2004 survey as an added measure of resilience and to give parents the opportunity to describe their child's good points. For all scales, a low score indicates negative social functioning on that measure.

Strengths

Parents were asked to rate their child and young people aged 11–16 were asked to rate themselves on a series of items covering various qualities (see Chapter 2 for details). Scores on the adult's scale ranged from 0–48 and those on the children's scale ranged from 0–38. Table 7.22 shows the scores on each scale grouped into quartiles.

Looking first at the adult's assessment, 84 per cent of children with hyperkinetic disorders had scores in the lowest quartile compared with 25 per cent of children with no such disorder. Conversely, none of the children with hyperkinetic disorders had a score in the highest quartile compared with 26 per cent of other children.

(Table 7.22)

The young people's own assessment of their strengths showed a similar pattern of variation as the parents' assessments although there was less difference between the groups. Nearly half (48 per cent) of children with hyperkinetic disorders had a score of 23 or less on this measure compared with about a quarter (23 per cent) of other children.

(Table 7.22)

Social aptitudes

Parents were asked to rate their children on 10 questions designed to measure the child's ability to empathise with others. Scores ranged from 0–40 and were grouped into quartiles. Over four-fifths (83 per cent) of children with hyperkinetic disorders had scores in the lowest quartile compared with 24 per cent of other children. Conversely, only 2 per cent of the former had scores in the highest quartile compared with 26 per cent of other children.

(Table 7.23)

Social capital

'Social capital' is a multi-faceted concept which has been defined as 'networks together with shared norms, values and understandings that facilitate co-operation within and among groups' (Cote and Healey, 2001). It is believed that high levels of social capital have a positive effect on health. The aspects of social capital covered in this report are:

- relationships with friends;
- social support;
- views about neighbourhood;
- help provided to others; and
- participation in clubs and groups.

Many of the questions are taken from the children and young person modules included in the 2003 Home Office Citizenship Survey. The questions on friends were asked of all parents. The remaining topics were asked of young people aged 11 or over only because previous research has shown that younger children are not able to cope with some of the more complex questioning.

Relationships with friends

Questions on friendships were asked of parents and covered:

- the child's ability to make and keep friends;
- number of friends;
- common interests and shared activities;
- emotional support; and
- parent's approval of child's friends.

Children with hyperkinetic disorders performed less well than other children on all the above measures. For example, 32 per cent found it harder than average to make friends and 44 per cent found it harder to keep friends (compared with 10 per cent and 5 per cent for other children). Likewise, 10 per cent had no friends and 50 per cent had no friend they could confide in if they were worried. The proportions for children with no hyperkinetic disorder were 2 per cent and 21 per cent.

(Table 7.24)

The parents of children with hyperkinetic disorders were more likely than other parents to express some reservations about their child's friends (43 per cent compared with 16 per cent). The former were also more likely to say that many or all of their child's friends got into trouble (19 per cent compared with 1 per cent).

(Table 7.24)

Social support

As a measure of social support, young people aged 11–16 were asked about the number of family members and friends to whom they felt close. Scores ranged from 0–20 and were grouped into rough quartiles. Young people with a hyperkinetic disorder were almost twice as likely as other children to have a social support score in the lowest quartile (54 per cent compared with 28 per cent).

Views about the neighbourhood

Unlike young people with emotional and conduct disorders, those with hyperkinetic disorders were, in general, no more likely than other young people to have negative views about their neighbourhood. The only difference was that the former were more likely to think that nobody in their neighbourhood could be trusted (8 per cent compared with 2 per cent).

(Table 7.26)

Help provided to others

There were no differences between young people with a hyperkinetic disorder and other young people in relation to the amount or frequency of help given to relatives and non-relatives and very few differences in the proportions giving specific forms of help. (Table 7.27)

There were also no differences between the two groups in the proportions who were paid for the help they gave (Table not shown) or in the proportions that did some paid work at least once a month. (Table 7.28)

Participation in groups, clubs and organisations

Young people with hyperkinetic disorders were less likely than other young people to participate in school-based groups, clubs and organisations (59 per cent compared with 78 per cent) but there were no differences between the two groups in the proportions who participated in such clubs outside of school. (Table 7.29)

Among children with hyperkinetic disorders:
- 32 per cent found it harder than average to make friends and 44 per cent found it harder than average to keep friends *(compared with 10 per cent and 5 per cent for children with no hyperkinetic disorder)*
- 43 per cent of parents did not fully approve of their child's friends *(16 per cent)*
- 59 per cent had taken part in a school-based group in the last year *(78 per cent)*

Smoking, drinking and drug use

Questions on smoking, drinking and drug use were addressed to children aged 11–16 and were based on questions used in the national surveys of smoking, drinking and drug use among schoolchildren. A comparison of the data from the 1999 Children's Mental Health Survey with the 1999 Schools Survey showed that children interviewed at home systematically under-reported their smoking, drinking and drug use compared with those interviewed in school. The rates presented in this report should not therefore be taken as true estimates of prevalence. Their main value is in enabling comparisons to be made between children with a disorder and other children. As

these behaviours vary with age, percentages are shown separately for young people aged 11–13 and those aged 14–16.

Young people with hyperkinetic disorders were more likely than other young people to smoke and take drugs. Unlike young people with emotional and conduct disorders, however, those with hyperkinetic disorders were no more likely than other young people to drink alcohol.

(Figure 7.7 and Tables 7.30– 7.32)

Figure **7.7**
Smoking, drinking and drug use by whether has a hyperkinetic disorder: children aged 11–16, 1999 and 2004 combined

Great Britain

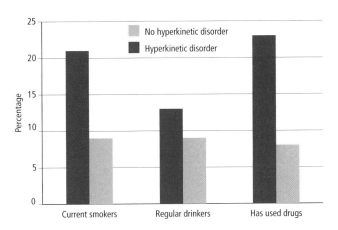

Among all young people with a hyperkinetic disorder, 21 per cent were smokers and most of these (15 per cent) were classified as 'regular smokers' (smokes at least one cigarette per week). For other young people the proportions were 9 per cent and 6 per cent. This pattern of variation was also evident among the younger age group, 11–13: 8 per cent of those with a hyperkinetic disorder smoked compared with only 2 per cent of other children. Among the older group, aged 14–16, 41 per cent of those with a hyperkinetic disorder smoked, compared with 18 per cent of other young people.

(Figure 7.7 and Table 7.30)

Drug use showed a similar pattern to smoking behaviour, although the differences were more pronounced for the older age group: 45 per cent of young people aged 14–16 who had a hyperkinetic disorder had used drugs compared with 16 per cent of other young people. Among the younger age group, 11–13, 8 per cent of those with hyperkinetic disorders had used drugs compared with 3 per cent of those with no such disorder. Cannabis was the most commonly used drug, taken by 18 per cent of young people with a hyperkinetic disorder and 7 per cent of other young people. Among the former, 4 per cent had taken amphetamines and 3 per cent had taken inhalants. These substances were taken by only 1 per cent of other young people. (Figure 7.7 and Table 7.32)

All but one of the children with a hyperkinetic disorder who were regular smokers also had a conduct disorder. Among those children who had a hyperkinetic disorder but no conduct disorder the percentages of regular smokers were very similar to those among children with no such disorder. However, there were no differences between children who had both a conduct and hyperkinetic disorder and other children with hyperkinetic disorders in terms of the percentages who were regular drinkers or who had taken drugs.

In the 2004 survey, young people were asked about the social context of the last time they had smoked, drank alcohol and taken drugs but there were too few cases of young people with hyperkinetic disorders to analyse the data.

Among children aged 11–16 with hyperkinetic disorders:

- 15 per cent were regular smokers (compared with 6 per cent for children with no hyperkinetic disorder)
- 13 per cent were regular drinkers (9 per cent)
- 23 per cent had taken drugs at some time (8 per cent)

Self-harm

Both parents and children were asked if the child had ever tried to hurt, harm or kill themselves. Looking first at parents' reports for children of all ages, those who had a child with a hyperkinetic disorder were much more likely to say that their child had tried to harm themselves (14 per cent compared with 2 per cent). The variations for children aged 11–16 showed a similar pattern, 18 per cent and 7 per cent based on self-reports and 14 per cent and 3 per cent based on parents' reports. (Table 7.33)

Among children with a hyperkinetic disorder whose parents had reported that they had tried to harm themselves, over three-quarters also had a conduct disorder.

Results from the six-month follow-up survey

Samples of the parents of children interviewed in the 1999 and 2004 surveys were sent a self-completion questionnaire six months after the interview in order to establish whether there had been any change in their symptoms (see Chapter 3).

The average levels of total and hyperactive symptoms among the children with hyperkinetic disorders did fall slightly over the six months following the survey. However, as Figures 7.8 and 7.9 show, the gap between children with and those with no hyperkinetic disorder only narrowed a little as a result. The symptoms of hyperkinetic disorder were typically persistent, at least in the short term. The impact of these symptoms changed rather more, falling by about a quarter over the six months, as shown in Figure 7.10. It is important to remember that the impact of symptoms depends not just on the symptoms themselves but on everything else in the child's life. Changes at home or at school may make hyperkinetic symptoms easier or harder to live with.

Figure **7.8**

Total symptoms[1] at main interview and at six-month follow-up by whether child had a hyperkinetic disorder at main interview, 1999 and 2004 combined

Great Britain

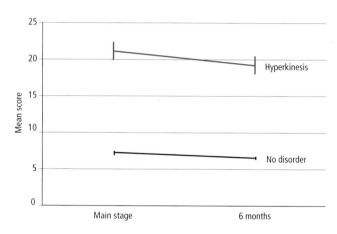

1 Total symptoms is the 'total difficulties score' on the parent-reported SDQ, reflecting the sum of the subscale scores for emotional symptoms, conduct problems, hyperactivity and peer problems.

Figure **7.9**

Hyperactivity symptoms at main interview and at six-month follow-up by whether child had a hyperkinetic disorder at main interview, 1999 and 2004 combined

Great Britain

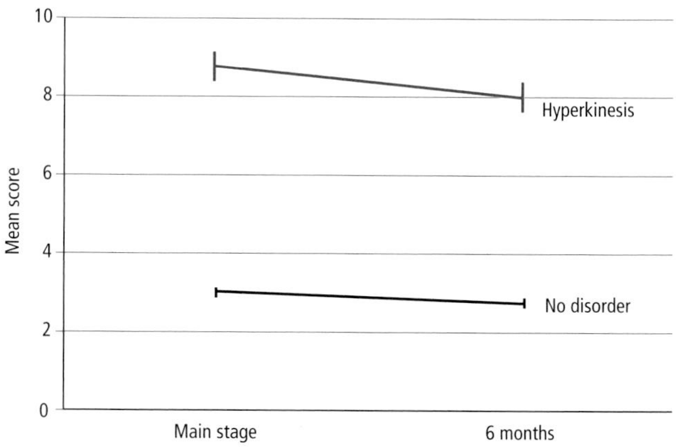

Figure **7.10**

Impact of symptoms at main interview and at six-month follow-up by whether child had a hyperkinetic disorder at main interview, 1999 and 2004 combined

Great Britain

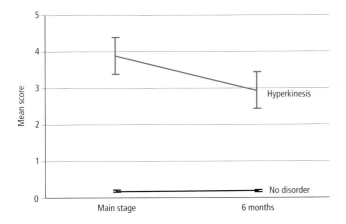

(Figures 7.8–7.10)

References

Goddard E and Higgins V (1999) *Smoking, drinking and drug use among young teenagers in 1998 , Volume 1: England,* TSO: London.

Home Office (December 2004) *2003 Home Office Citizenship Survey,* Home Office Research, Development and Statistics Directorate.

Table **7.1**

Sex, age and ethnicity of child by whether has a hyperkinetic disorder, 1999 and 2004 combined

All children   Great Britain

	Hyperkinetic disorder	No hyperkinetic disorder	All
	%	%	%
Sex			
Boys	86	50	51
Girls	14	50	49
Age			
5–10	55	53	53
11–16	45	47	47
Ethnicity			
White	97	89	89
Black[1]	1	3	3
Indian	-	2	2
Pakistani/ Bangladeshi	-	3	3
Other	2	3	3
Base (weighted)	*246*	*18157*	*18403*

1. Includes people of mixed black and white origin.

Table **7.2**

Family characteristics by whether has a hyperkinetic disorder, 1999 and 2004 combined

All children   Great Britain

	Hyperkinetic disorder	No hyperkinetic disorder	All
	%	%	%
Family type			
Married	53	69	68
Cohabiting	9	8	8
Lone parent – single	15	8	8
Lone parent – widowed, divorced or separated	23	16	16
Number of children in household			
1	28	23	23
2	42	45	45
3	21	22	22
4	6	7	7
5 or more	3	3	3
Base (weighted 1999 and 2004 data)	*246*	*18169*	*18415*
If stepchildren in family			
Yes	15	11	11
No	85	89	89
Base (weighted 2004 data)[1]	*108*	*7869*	*7977*

1. The 1999 data had a different classification for whether or not a family contained stepchildren.

Table **7.3**

Parent's education and socio-economic characteristics by whether has a hyperkinetic disorder, 1999 and 2004 combined

All children   Great Britain

	Hyperkinetic disorder	No hyperkinetic disorder	All
	%	%	%
Parent's highest educational qualification			
Degree level	7	13	13
Teaching/HND/Nursing	6	11	11
A /AS level or equivalent	9	11	11
GCSE Grades A–C or equivalent	21	30	30
GCSE Grades D–F or equivalent	16	11	11
Other qualification	6	3	3
No qualification	36	21	21
Parents' employment status			
Both working/lone parent working	52	67	67
One parent working	18	19	19
Neither working/lone parent not working	31	14	15
Base (weighted 1999 and 2004 data)	*245*	*17866*	*18111*
Family's socio-economic classification[1]			
Large employers and higher managerial	4	2	2
Higher professional	3	3	3
Lower managerial and professional	8	21	20
Intermediate occupations	19	19	19
Small employers and own account	5	7	7
Lower supervisory and technical	1	1	1
Semi-routine	26	26	26
Routine occupations	25	12	13
Never worked/ long-term unemployed	8	5	5
FT student/inadequate description	2	4	4
Base (weighted 2004 data)[2]	*108*	*7869*	*7977*

1. *This is the National Statistics Socio-economic Classification (NS-SEC).*
2. *The 1999 data had a different social classification.*

Table **7.4**

Housing and income by whether has a hyperkinetic disorder, 1999 and 2004 combined

All children   Great Britain

	Hyperkinetic disorder	No hyperkinetic disorder	All
	%	%	%
Type of accommodation			
Detached	16	25	25
Semi-detached	38	38	38
Terraced house	38	30	30
Flat/maisonette	9	7	7
Tenure			
Owners	46	69	69
Social sector tenants	41	24	24
Private renters	13	7	7
Base (weighted 1999 and 2004 data)	*246*	*18158*	*18404*
Gross weekly household income			
Under £100	8	4	4
£100–£199	25	16	16
£200–£299	19	14	14
£300–£399	12	12	12
£400–£499	8	11	11
£500–£599	10	10	10
£600–£770	7	13	13
Over £770	10	20	20
Base (weighted 1999 and 2004 data)	*226*	*16670*	*16896*
Receipt of disability benefits			
Carers allowance	11	3	3
Severe Disablement allowance	23	6	6
Disability living/attendance allowance	3	0	0
Incapacity allowance	1	2	2
Any disability allowance	**27**	**8**	**8**
No disability allowance	73	92	92
Base (weighted 2004 data)[1]	*108*	*7869*	*7977*

1. The 1999 data covered different types of disability benefit.

Table 7.5

Region, country and area type by whether has a hyperkinetic disorder, 1999 and 2004 combined

All children   Great Britain

	Hyperkinetic disorder	No hyperkinetic disorder	All
	%	%	%
Region and country			
London Inner	6	5	5
London Outer	5	7	7
Other met England	24	31	31
Non-met England	53	44	44
England	88	86	86
Scotland	7	9	8
Wales	5	5	5
Base (weighted 1999 and 2004 data)	*246*	*18169*	*18415*
Area type (ACORN classification)			
Wealthy achievers	18	26	26
Urban prosperity	7	8	8
Comfortably off	21	26	26
Moderate means	19	17	17
Hard pressed	36	24	24
Base (weighted 2004 data)[1]	*108*	*7809*	*7916*

1. The 1999 data had a different ACORN classification.

Table 7.6

Child's general health by whether has a hyperkinetic disorder, 1999 and 2004 combined

All children   Great Britain

	Hyperkinetic disorder	No hyperkinetic disorder	All
	%	%	%
Child's general health			
Very good	46	69	69
Good	36	24	24
Fair	14	6	6
Bad	4	1	1
Very bad	0	0	0
Base (weighted)	*246*	*17926*	*18172*

Table **7.7**

Co-occurrence of physical and developmental problems with hyperkinetic disorders, 1999 and 2004 combined

All children   Great Britain

	Hyperkinetic disorder	No hyperkinetic disorder	All
	Percentage of children with each type of complaint		
Asthma	23	15	15
Eczema	14	13	13
Hay fever	12	11	11
Eyesight problems	15	10	10
Stomach or digestive problems	7	6	6
Non-food allergy	7	6	6
Migraine/severe headache	5	5	5
Bed wetting	17	4	5
Glue ear/otitis media/grommits	7	4	4
Hearing problems	7	4	4
Speech or language problems	15	4	4
Food allergy	8	3	4
Difficulty with co-ordination	14	2	2
Stiffness or deformity of foot	5	2	2
Heart problems	2	1	1
Soiling pants	6	1	1
Muscle disease or weakness	4	1	1
Kidney/urinary tract problems	2	1	1
Obesity	2	1	1
Congenital abnormality	2	1	1
Epilepsy	1	1	1
Any blood disorder	0	0	0
Diabetes	1	0	0
Cerebral Palsy	1	0	0
Cancer	0	-	0
Any physical or developmental problems[1]	**70**	**54**	**54**
No problem	30	46	46
Base (weighted)	*246*	*17926*	*18172*

1. *Some physical complaints are not listed in the table above because of their rarity (less than 25 cases): ME (10), Spina bifida (6), Cystic fibrosis (11), Missing digits (23). They are included in the 'Any physical or developmental problem' category.*

Table **7.8**

Co-occurrence of other mental disorders with hyperkinetic disorders, 1999 and 2004 combined

All children   Great Britain

	Hyperkinetic disorder	No hyperkinetic disorder	All
	Percentage of children with each type of disorder		
Other mental disorders			
Emotional disorders:			
Anxiety disorders	10	3	4
Depression	2	1	1
All emotional disorders	12	4	4
Conduct disorders:			
Oppositional defiant disorder	34	2	3
Other conduct disorders	28	2	2
All conduct disorders	62	4	5
Less common disorders	2	1	1
Any other disorder	**66**	**8**	**9**
No (other) disorders	34	92	91
Base (weighted)	*246*	*18169*	*18415*

Table **7.9**

Parent's view of child's mental health by whether child has a hyperkinetic disorder, 1999 and 2004 combined

All children   Great Britain

	Hyperkinetic disorder	No hyperkinetic disorder	All
	Percentage of children with each type of problem		
Parent's view of child's mental health			
Emotional problems	29	4	5
Behavioural problems	66	5	6
Hyperactivity	56	3	4
Any of the above	77	9	10
Base (weighted)	*246*	*17927*	*18174*

Table **7.10**

Whether child is taking any medication by whether has a hyperkinetic disorder, 2004

All children | | | Great Britain

	Hyperkinetic disorder	No hyperkinetic disorder	All
	Percentage of children taking each type of medication		
Methylphenidate, Equasym, Ritalin	41	0	1
Dexamphetamine, Dexedrine	2	-	0
Imipramine, Tofranil	-	0	0
Clonidine, Catepres, Dixarit	1	0	0
Fluoxetine, Prozac	-	0	0
Sertraline, Lustral	-	0	0
Fluvoxamine, Faverin	-	0	0
Citalopram, Cimpramil	-	0	0
Amitryptaline, Lentizol, Triptafen	1	0	0
Sulpirade, Dolmatil, Sulparex, Sulpitil	-	0	0
Risperidone, Riperadal	3	0	0
Haloperidol, Dozic, Haldol, Serenace	-	0	0
Any medication	**43**	**0**	**1**
No medication	57	100	99
Base (weighted)	*107*	*7755*	*7862*

Table **7.11**

Help sought in last year for child's mental health problems by whether has a hyperkinetic disorder, 2004

All children   Great Britain

	Hyperkinetic disorder	No hyperkinetic disorder	All
	Percentage of children using each service		
Specialist services			
Child/adult mental health specialist (eg psychiatrist)	52	3	3
Child physical health specialist (eg paediatrician)	15	2	2
Social services (eg social worker)	15	2	2
Education services (eg educational psychologist)	37	3	4
Front line services			
Primary health care (eg GP or practice nurse)	46	5	6
Teachers	70	17	18
All professional services	**93**	**21**	**22**
Informal sources			
Family member/friends	35	11	12
Internet	11	1	1
Telephone help line	6	1	1
Self-help group	7	0	0
Other type of help	4	2	2
All sources	**95**	**27**	**28**
No help sought	5	73	73
Base (weighted)	*107*	*7678*	*7784*

Table **7.12**

Teacher's rating of child's basic skills by whether has a hyperkinetic disorder, 1999 and 2004 combined

All children   Great Britain

	Hyperkinetic disorder	No hyperkinetic disorder	All
	%	%	%
Reading			
Above average	8	37	37
Average	28	40	40
Some difficulty	31	17	17
Marked difficulty	33	6	6
Mathematics			
Above average	11	32	31
Average	26	44	44
Some difficulty	34	19	19
Marked difficulty	29	6	6
Spelling			
Above average	5	28	28
Average	19	42	41
Some difficulty	35	21	21
Marked difficulty	40	9	9
Base (weighted)	*197*	*13977*	*14174*
Overall scholastic ability[1]			
4 or more years behind	9	2	2
3 years behind	9	2	2
2 years behind	22	5	6
1 year behind	25	15	15
Equivalent	25	36	35
1 or more years ahead	10	40	40
Base (weighted)	*179*	*13075*	*13254*

1. Functioning age-actual age.

Table **7.13**

Whether child has special educational needs by whether has a hyperkinetic disorder, 1999 and 2004 combined

All children   Great Britain

	Hyperkinetic disorder	No hyperkinetic disorder	All
	%	%	%
If child has officially recognised special educational needs			
Yes	71	16	17
No	29	84	83
Base (weighted)	*193*	*13750*	*13943*

Table **7.14**

Absence from school and truancy (teacher's report) by whether has a hyperkinetic disorder, 1999 and 2004 combined

All children

Great Britain

	Hyperkinetic disorder	No hyperkinetic disorder	All
	%	%	%
Number of days absent in last term			
0	29	32	32
1–5	41	46	46
6–10	14	13	13
11–15	5	4	4
16 or more	11	5	5
Any days absent	71	68	68
Base (weighted)	*131*	*10254*	*10385*
Any unauthorised days absent			
Yes	13	9	9
No	87	91	91
Base (weighted 2004 data)[1]	*58*	*4632*	*4689*
Whether plays truant			
Not true	89	97	97
Somewhat true	7	2	2
Certainly true	5	1	1
Base (weighted)	*195*	*14070*	*14265*

1. This question was not asked in 1999.

Table **7.15**

Absence from school (parent's report) by whether has a hyperkinetic disorder, 2004

All children   Great Britain

	Hyperkinetic disorder	No hyperkinetic disorder	All
	%	%	%
Whether missed school in last term[1]			
Yes	37	34	34
No	63	66	66
Base (weighted): all children	*103*	*7518*	*7621*
Reasons for absence			
Short-term illness	73	78	78
Long-term illness	2	2	2
Refused to attend	15	2	2
Has a school phobia	-	0	0
Other	18	21	20
Base (weighted): those who missed school	*38*	*2561*	*2599*
Whether child received any educational provision			
Yes	(7)	10	10
No	(93)	90	90
Base (weighted): those who missed school (excluding short term illness)	*13*	*639*	*652*

1. Excluding exclusions.

Table **7.16**

Exclusions from school (parent's report) by whether has a hyperkinetic disorder, 1999 and 2004 combined

All children   Great Britain

	Hyperkinetic disorder	No hyperkinetic disorder	All
	%	%	%
Number of times child has been excluded from school			
None	71	97	96
Once	13	2	2
Twice	4	1	1
Three or more times	12	1	1
Base (weighted)	*107*	*7664*	*7770*

Table **7.17**

Number of times child has changed schools by whether has a hyperkinetic disorder, 2004

All children   Great Britain

	Hyperkinetic disorder	No hyperkinetic disorder	All
	%	%	%
Number of times child has changed school[1]			
None	64	81	81
Once	23	14	14
Twice	8	3	3
Three or more times	4	2	2
Base (weighted)	*107*	*7670*	*7776*

1. Apart from normal transitions.

Table **7.18**

Parent's GHQ–12 score by whether has a hyperkinetic disorder, 1999 and 2004 combined

All children   Great Britain

	Hyperkinetic disorder	No hyperkinetic disorder	All
	%	%	%
Parent's GHQ–12[1]			
0–2	57	76	76
3–5	19	13	13
6–8	14	7	7
9–12	10	4	4
3 or more	**43**	**24**	**24**
Base (weighted)	*244*	*17738*	*17983*

1 For this survey, scores of 3 or more were taken to indicate a severe emotional problem.

Table **7.19**

Family functioning score by whether has a hyperkinetic disorder, 1999 and 2004 combined

All children   Great Britain

	Hyperkinetic disorder	No hyperkinetic disorder	All
	%	%	%
Family functioning score[1]			
Up to 1.50	22	36	36
1.51–2.00	43	46	46
2.01 –2.50	27	16	16
2.51 or more	9	2	2
Unhealthy functioning (2.01 or more)	**36**	**18**	**18**
Base (weighted)	*243*	*17665*	*17908*

1. For this survey, scores over 2.0 were taken to suggest unhealthy family functioning.

Table **7.20**

Stressful life events by whether has a hyperkinetic disorder, 2004

All children
Great Britain

Stressful life events	Hyperkinetic disorder	No hyperkinetic disorder	All
		Percentage reporting each event	
Since child was born, parent had a separation due to marital difficulties or broken off steady relationship	49	31	31
Since child was born, parent had a major financial crisis such as losing the equivalent of three months income	21	13	13
Since child was born, parent had a problem with the police involving a court appearance	18	6	6
Since child was born, parent has had serious physical illness	8	8	8
Since child was born, parent has had serious mental illness	17	8	8
At any stage in child's life, a parent, brother or sister died	4	3	4
At any stage in child's life, a close friend died	6	6	6
At some stage in the child's life, s/he had a serious illness which required a stay in hospital	23	13	13
At any stage in child's life, s/he had been in a serious accident or badly hurt in an accident	9	5	5
In the past year child has broken off a steady relationship with a boy or girl friend (aged 13 or above)/ a close friendship has ended (any age)	14	7	7
Base (weighted)	*107*	*7663*	*7770*

Table **7.21**

Number of stressful life events by whether has a hyperkinetic disorder, 1999 and 2004 combined

All children
Great Britain

	Hyperkinetic disorder	No hyperkinetic disorder	All
	%	%	%
Number of stressful life events			
0	22	42	42
1	31	32	32
2	19	15	15
3	17	7	7
4	6	2	3
5 or more	5	1	1
Two or more events	**47**	**26**	**26**
Base (weighted)	*107*	*7663*	*7770*

Table **7.22**

Child's strengths (parent's and child's assessment) by whether has a hyperkinetic disorder, 2004

All children   Great Britain

	Hyperkinetic disorder	No hyperkinetic disorder	All
	%	%	%
ALL CHILDREN			
Strength score – parent assessment			
0–36	84	25	25
37–40	14	25	25
41–43	2	25	25
44–48	-	26	25
Base (weighted)	*103*	*7468*	*7571*
CHILDREN AGED 11–16			
Strength score – child assessment			
0–23	48	23	23
24–27	20	27	27
28–30	20	23	23
31–38	12	27	27
Base (weighted)	*34*	*3304*	*3338*

Table **7.23**

Social aptitude (parent's assessment) by whether has a hyperkinetic disorder, 2004

All children   Great Britain

	Hyperkinetic disorder	No hyperkinetic disorder	All
	%	%	%
Social aptitude score			
0–20	83	24	25
21–24	11	28	27
25–28	5	23	22
29–40	2	26	25
Base (weighted)	*104*	*7378*	*7483*

Table **7.24**

Friendships by whether has a hyperkinetic disorder, 2004

All children

	Hyperkinetic disorder	No hyperkinetic disorder	All
	%	%	%
What is child like at making friends?			
Finds it harder than average	32	10	10
About average	31	36	36
Easier than average	36	55	54
What is child like at keeping friends?			
Finds it harder than average	44	5	5
About average	32	35	35
Easier than average	24	60	59
Number of friends			
None	10	2	2
1	15	4	4
2–4	47	43	43
5–9	19	40	39
10 or more	9	12	11
Base (weighted): all children	*108*	*7732*	*7840*
Do child and friends have things in common			
No	7	1	1
A little	32	21	21
A lot	61	78	78
Do child and friends do things together			
No	6	3	4
A little	34	21	21
A lot	60	75	75
If worried, can child talk to friends			
No	50	21	21
Perhaps	30	42	42
Definitely	20	38	37
Whether friends get into trouble			
Not at all	31	68	67
A few are like that	50	31	31
Many are like that	14	1	1
All are like that	5	0	0
Whether parent approves of child's friends			
No	6	2	2
A little	37	14	14
A lot	57	84	84
Base (weighted): those who had friends	*93*	*7477*	*7570*

Table **7.25**

Child's sources of emotional support by whether has a hyperkinetic disorder, 2004

Children aged 11–16   Great Britain

	Hyperkinetic disorder	No hyperkinetic disorder	All
	%	%	%
Social support score			
0–17	54	28	28
18	21	16	16
19	3	20	20
20	21	35	35
Base (weighted)	*32*	*3298*	*3330*

Table **7.26**

Views about the neighbourhood by whether has a hyperkinetic disorder, 2004

Children aged 11–16   Great Britain

	Hyperkinetic disorder	No hyperkinetic disorder	All
	%	%	%
Whether enjoys living in the neighbourhood			
A lot	50	64	64
A little	37	29	29
No	13	7	7
How safe child feels walking alone in the neighbourhood during the daytime			
Very safe	66	61	61
Fairly safe	26	32	32
A bit unsafe	6	5	5
Very unsafe	-	1	1
Never goes out alone	2	1	1
Whether ever goes to the local shops or park alone			
Yes	89	80	80
No	11	20	20
How many people in the neighbourhood can be trusted			
Many	25	38	38
Some	51	44	44
A few	15	16	16
None	8	2	2
Likelihood of someone returning a lost bag			
Very likely	14	12	12
Quite likely	49	45	45
Not very likely	19	30	30
Not at all likely	17	13	13
Base (weighted)	*34*	*3297*	*3331*

Table 7.27

Help provided to others by whether has a hyperkinetic disorder, 2004

Children aged 11–16   Great Britain

Type of help	Hyperkinetic disorder	No hyperkinetic disorder	All	Hyperkinetic disorder	No hyperkinetic disorder	All
	Percentage giving each type of help to relatives			*Percentage giving each type of help to non-relatives*		
Doing shopping for someone	41	36	37	18	9	9
Cooking or helping to prepare family meals	46	52	52	6	6	6
Cleaning, hoovering or gardening	66	69	69	29	10	11
Washing or ironing clothes	29	36	36	3	2	2
Decorating or repairs	22	21	21	8	5	5
Baby sitting or caring for children	25	39	39	17	19	19
Writing letters or filling in forms	11	10	10	-	4	4
Taking care of someone who is sick	35	34	34	-	9	9
Helping out in a family business	10	11	11	..	..	..
Anything else	14	8	9	8	3	3
None of the above	12	7	7	58	60	60
Base (weighted): all aged 11 or over	*34*	*3324*	*3358*	*34*	*3324*	*3358*
Frequency of providing help						
Every day	26	17	17	(14)	6	6
At least once a week	48	59	59	(21)	32	32
At least once a month	13	17	17	(52)	38	38
Less often	10	6	6	(13)	24	24
Base (weighted): those who helped	*30*	*3103*	*3133*	*14*	*1327*	*1341*

Table 7.28

Whether child does any paid work by whether has a hyperkinetic disorder, 2004

Children aged 11–16   Great Britain

	Hyperkinetic disorder	No hyperkinetic disorder	All
	%	%	%
Whether child does any paid work at least once a month			
Yes	18	22	22
No	82	78	78
Base (weighted)	*34*	*3325*	*3359*

Table **7.29**

Participation in groups, clubs and organisations by whether has a hyperkinetic disorder, 2004

Children aged 11–16 Great Britain

Type of group/club/ organisation	Hyperkinetic disorder	No hyperkinetic disorder	All	Hyperkinetic disorder	No hyperkinetic disorder	All
	Percentage particpating in clubs at school			*Percentage particpating in clubs outside school*		
Sports	35	51	51	33	37	37
Art, drama, dance or music	17	32	32	8	18	18
Youth	18	11	11	34	21	21
Computers	28	13	14	12	3	3
Political	3	2	2	3	1	1
Debating	3	4	4	3	0	0
Religious	..	3	3	..	5	5
Local community or neighbourhood	..	2	2	..	2	2
Voluntary groups helping people	6	4	4	3	2	2
Safety, First Aid	3	4	4	..	3	3
Environmental	12	5	5	3	2	2
Animal (welfare)	..	1	1	..	1	1
Human rights	..	1	1	..	0	0
School holiday playschemes	12	9	9	3	7	7
After-school clubs	23	28	28	..	..	..
School student councils	6	11	11	..	..	..
Student Union	3	1	1	..	..	..
Extra teaching or special lessons	3	9	9	..	..	..
Other	..	..	..	3	9	9
None of the above	41	22	22	39	33	33
Base (weighted)	*33*	*3255*	*3288*	*33*	*3257*	*3290*

Table **7.30**

Smoking behaviour by whether has a hyperkinetic disorder, 1999 and 2004 combined

Children aged 11–16   Great Britain

	11- to 13-year-olds			14- to 16-year-olds			All aged 11–16		
	Hyperkinetic disorder	No hyperkinetic disorder	All	Hyperkinetic disorder	No hyperkinetic disorder	All	Hyperkinetic disorder	No hyperkinetic disorder	All
	%	%	%	%	%	%	%	%	%
Smoking behaviour									
Regular smoker	4	1	1	32	13	13	15	6	6
Occasional smoker	4	1	1	9	5	5	6	3	3
All smokers	**8**	**2**	**2**	**41**	**18**	**18**	**21**	**9**	**9**
Used to smoke	10	3	3	22	9	9	15	5	5
Tried smoking once	37	16	16	13	28	28	28	21	21
Never smoked	45	79	78	23	45	45	36	65	64
Base (weighted)	*50*	*4350*	*4400*	*34*	*3235*	*3269*	*84*	*7586*	*7670*

Table **7.31**

Drinking behaviour by whether has a hyperkinetic disorder, 1999 and 2004 combined

Children aged 11–16   Great Britain

	11- to 13-year-olds			14- to 16-year-olds			All aged 11–16		
	Hyperkinetic disorder	No hyperkinetic disorder	All	Hyperkinetic disorder	No hyperkinetic disorder	All	Hyperkinetic disorder	No hyperkinetic disorder	All
	%	%	%	%	%	%	%	%	%
Drinking behaviour									
Almost every day	2	0	0	-	1	1	1	0	0
About twice a week	2	1	1	13	6	6	6	3	3
About once a week	-	2	2	15	10	10	6	6	6
All regular drinkers	**4**	**3**	**3**	**28**	**17**	**17**	**13**	**9**	**9**
About once a fortnight	2	3	3	10	12	12	5	7	7
About once a month	8	5	5	9	16	16	8	10	10
Only a few times a year	25	20	21	32	29	29	28	24	24
Never drinks alcohol	4	2	2	-	2	2	2	2	2
Never had a drink	57	67	67	21	24	24	43	49	49
Base (weighted)	*51*	*4346*	*4397*	*33*	*3237*	*3270*	*84*	*7585*	*7669*

Table **7.32**

Drug use by whether has a hyperkinetic disorder, 1999 and 2004 combined

Children aged 11–16   Great Britain

	11- to 13-year-olds			14- to 16-year-olds			All aged 11–16		
	Hyperkinetic disorder	No hyperkinetic disorder	All	Hyperkinetic disorder	No hyperkinetic disorder	All	Hyperkinetic disorder	No hyperkinetic disorder	All
	%	%	%	%	%	%	%	%	%
Ever used:									
Cannabis	4	1	1	39	15	15	18	7	7
Inhalants	-	0	0	8	1	1	3	1	1
Ecstasy	-	0	0	-	1	1	-	0	0
Amphetamines	-	0	0	9	1	1	4	1	1
LSD	-	0	0	-	0	0	-	0	0
Tranquilisers	-	0	0	-	0	0	-	0	0
Cocaine	-	0	0	-	1	1	-	0	0
Heroin	-	0	0	-	0	0	-	0	0
Any drugs	**8**	**3**	**3**	**45**	**16**	**16**	**23**	**8**	**9**
Base (weighted)	*50*	*4345*	*4395*	*34*	*3234*	*3268*	*83*	*7581*	*7665*

Table **7.33**

Deliberate self-harm by whether has a hyperkinetic disorder, 1999 and 2004 combined

Great Britain

	Hyperkinetic disorder	No hyperkinetic disorder	All
	Percentage who have tried to harm, hurt or kill themselves		
All children			
Parent's report	14	2	2
Base (weighted)	*223*	*17432*	*17655*
Children aged 11–16			
Parent's report	14	3	3
Base (weighted)	*100*	*8138*	*8238*
Child's report	18	7	7
Base (weighted)	*79*	*7325*	*7404*

Autistic spectrum disorder and other less common disorders

Chapter 8

Introduction

This chapter focuses on less common disorders – autistic spectrum disorder, tics, eating disorders and selective mutism. As in previous chapters, we describe the types of behaviour patterns typically found among children and young people with these disorders. We then go on to describe the characteristics of children and young people with autistic spectrum disorder, looking at their:

- demographic characteristics;
- family situation;
- socio-economic characteristics;
- geographic distribution;
- general, physical and mental health;
- use of services;
- scholastic ability and attendance at school;
- family's social functioning;
- own social functioning; and
- lifestyle behaviours.

The tables compare children with autistic spectrum disorder with those who have no such disorder. Where possible, data from the 1999 and 2004 surveys have been combined to increase the sample base. The numbers of children with tics (33), eating disorders (24) and selective mutism (3) are too small for analysis, even when data from two survey years are combined.

Typical behaviour patterns

This section describes typical symptoms displayed by children with these less common disorders. The symptoms listed are found, to some extent, in most children. To count as a disorder they have to be sufficiently severe to cause distress to the child or impair his/her functioning. In order to illustrate the impact of the disorder on the child's life and that of his or her family, the symptoms are followed by a case vignette of a fictitious child.[1]

Autistic spectrum disorder

Typical symptoms include: impaired social interaction (e.g. abnormal eye contact, inability to pick up non-verbal cues, difficulty making friends), lack of social or emotional reciprocity (e.g. difficulty sharing or co-operating with others), delayed or absent speech, repetitive language, impoverished play, inflexible routines and rituals, repetitive mannerisms and preoccupation with unusual parts of objects.

He was late learning to talk and he still speaks in a slightly odd way now – he can understand and people understand him, but his voice and the words he chooses are a bit strange. He insists on doing everything his way and is really cross if he can't have his way. When he was little, he just liked lining up his toy cars or bricks into rows or other patterns. The other thing he'd do was sniff everything or hold it to his cheek. His eye contact was never very good, but it has got better over the years, perhaps because I reminded him about it all the time. Now it's gone too much to the opposite extreme and he makes so much eye contact that people think he is staring. He used to flap his arms whenever he was excited, but that has mostly gone now. He still likes fiddling with a favourite bit of string that he has had for ages, but he knows not to do that too much in public. He never took part in any sort of pretend play when he was younger, and his interests still focus on facts and objects rather than people or stories.

He has a lot of fixed routines in his life. He has to go the same way to school everyday – if the traffic is bad the normal way and I try to take a short cut, he gets very upset and I don't hear the end of it for days. Every day he gets up at the same time, even when it is the weekend or a holiday. He wants to wear the same clothes every day. When they have holes in them and can't be repaired any more, it leads to a massive tantrum when I finally throw clothes away even if I have bought him a replacement as close to the original as possible.

He collects old packets that used to have food in them and he stores them in the spare room (it's full of them!) and catalogues them. There are hundreds of old packets but he knows every one of them and can talk for hours on the differences between packets that look pretty much the same to anyone else.

He's never really made proper friends. Now he does want to have friends, but he can't make and keep ordinary friends. The people he now describes as his friends put up with him for as long as he is useful to them. I think this lack of friends is the worst thing about his life. In addition, his interests are so different from everybody else's that he doesn't get to do many leisure activities. His fixed routines make him hard to live with – and there is often friction at home as a result.

Eating disorders

Children with eating disorders are excessively concerned with their eating habits, weight and shape. For example, they may perceive themselves as being too fat even though they are thin, they may be ashamed of, or feel guilty about eating or engage in binge eating followed by fasting. Measures to control eating may involve excessive dieting, hiding food, vomiting, taking pills to aid weight loss.

---

1. *The symptoms and vignettes are based on descriptions of a 'made up' child created by Youthinmind to illustrate the diagnostic classification system.*

She will eat all the chocolate in the house. This might be a whole packet of chocolate biscuits, and any chocolate cake she can find, and one or more bars of chocolate. It really depends what is around – we try to keep as little chocolate in the house as possible or hide it. But sometimes she finds our hidden chocolate and that goes all at once.

She has got more concerned about her appearance lately. I think she's getting interested in boys. She's lost a lot of weight and is now painfully thin, but she still insists that she is fat. She says she isn't hungry, but I'm sure that's not true, because of the times when she eats loads of chocolate and biscuits. She once got hold of some diuretics that her grandmother was on, but we found out and she hasn't got any more since.

Tic disorders including Tourette's syndrome

This disorder covers motor and vocal tics. The former include: eye blinking, squinting, eye rolling, nose twitching, head nodding, screwing up face, shoulder shrugging, jerking of arm or leg. Vocal tics include: throat clearing, excessive sniffing, coughing, squeaking, sucking noises, word repetition.

He went through a time when his hand kept on coming up to his head – if there was anyone about, he'd pretend that he was smoothing his hair into place. When he went through a phase of squinting his eyes, we took him for an eye test and they gave him glasses because he was a bit short sighted. The squinting did get better after that. About a year ago, he made barking noises as if he were a dog. Fortunately, those have stopped now. The sniffing is a bit worse in the summer when there is pollen about, so I have wondered if it is hay fever – but it happens at other times of the year too.

At present he blinks a lot and keeps on wrinkling up his nose – the bigger tics are not there at the moment. He also sniffs all the time, and has been through phases of barking, coughing and squeaking. He's usually at his worst after coming back from school – he'll sit down in front of the TV and he has lots of tics. When he knows people are watching him, he has less. They come in bouts, being bad for several weeks, and then having good periods when he hardly has any. They began when he was 7, initially with a lot of eye blinking, but then with various other motor tics coming in too. The sounds didn't start until he was about 10. They make it very hard for him to keep and make friends. This is the main problem – we are used to it at home and try not to let it interfere with his life. We try going out, but it is hard sometimes with people staring. The doctor prescribed him some medicine, and it did reduce the number of tics – but

the side effects included weight gain and some drowsiness. So he doesn't take anything regularly now – medicine is just for when he has a particularly nasty upsurge of tics.

Selective mutism

This disorder is characterised by a failure to speak in certain circumstances although the child is able to converse normally in other situations.

She has always been a shy child, but the main thing is that she won't speak when she is at school. She has been at school for over a year now, and she still won't talk to the teacher or to her classmates. That doesn't stop her doing her work in class, or playing chase with her friends during break. At home, she chats away happily to us, but she'll go completely silent if we have a visitor.

As explained in earlier in this chapter, the numbers of children with tics, eating disorders and selective mutism are too small for analysis and therefore no data have been shown for these groups. The following sections focus on children with autistic spectrum disorder.

Demographic, socio-economic and area characteristics

Demographic and family characteristics

Children with autistic spectrum disorder were predominantly boys, 82 per cent. There were no differences between autistic and other children in their age and ethnic profiles or in any of the measures of family size or composition.

(Tables 8.1 and 8.2)

Parental education and socio-economic characteristics

Unlike children with the more common disorders discussed in previous chapters, autistic children tended to have more highly qualified parents than other children: 46 per cent had parents with qualifications above GCSE compared with 35 per cent of other children. The same proportions, 21 per cent, had parents with no qualifications. Likewise, autistic children were no more likely than other children to have a parent in a routine or semi-routine occupational group. Autistic children were, however, similar to children with other types of disorder in that a relatively high proportion lived in families in which neither parent worked (30 per cent compared with 14 per cent of other children). The unusual combination of high educational status and low economic activity rate among the parents of autistic children probably reflects their heavy caring responsibilities, as discussed in the following section.

(Table 8.3)

Housing and income

Housing and income followed the same pattern as education. Autistic children were no less likely than other children to live in owned accommodation and they were less likely to live in low income families: only 9 per cent compared with 20 per cent of other children lived in households with a gross weekly income of less than £200 per week. (Table 8.4)

Over a half (56 per cent) of families containing autistic children were receiving a disability benefit; 54 per cent received Severe Disablement Allowance and 23 per cent received Carers Allowance. Whilst we do not know for certain that the benefits were awarded on behalf of the child, this would have been the case for the majority. The proportion of these families receiving such benefits is much higher than for the families of children with conduct or emotional disorder (20 per cent in each case). This reflects the particularly heavy burden of caring for autistic children partly because of their behaviour patterns but also, as is discussed later in the chapter, because they often have learning and physical disabilities as well. (Table 8.4)

Area characteristics

There were no differences between families containing autistic children and other families with respect to the country and region in which they lived or in the type of area. Again, this is consistent with the other measures of affluence described above. Children with other types of disorder tended to live in poorer areas than other children but there was no such relationship for autistic children. (Table 8.5)

Among children with autistic spectrum disorder:

- 82 per cent were boys *(compared with 50 per cent for children with no autistic spectrum disorder)*
- 62 per cent were aged 5–10 *(53 per cent)*
- 92 per cent were white *(89 per cent)*
- 66 per cent lived in a married couple family *(68 per cent)*
- 46 per cent had parents with qualifications above GCSE level *(35 per cent)*
- 30 per cent lived in households in which neither parent worked *(14 per cent)*
- 56 per cent lived in households in which someone received a disability benefit *(8 per cent)*

Child's general, physical and mental health

General health

The parents of children with autistic spectrum disorder were much more likely than the parents of other children to say that their child's health was fair or bad (24 per cent compared with

---

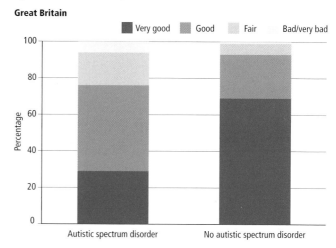

Figure 8.1

Child's general health by whether they had autistic spectrum disorder, 1999 and 2004 combined

Great Britain

Legend: Very good | Good | Fair | Bad/very bad

(Y-axis: Percentage, 0 to 100)

(Categories: Autistic spectrum disorder | No autistic spectrum disorder)

---

7 per cent). Conversely, less than one-third of the former described their child's health as very good compared with about two-thirds of the latter (29 per cent compared with 69 per cent) (Figure 8.1 and Table 8.6)

Physical and developmental problems

Consistent with their reported poor general health, the great majority of autistic children had a physical or developmental problem (89 per cent compared with 54 per cent of other children). The most common complaints were: speech or language problems (67 per cent), difficulty with co-ordination (47 per cent), bed wetting (29 per cent) and eyesight problems (23 per cent). These were reported for 10 per cent or fewer of other children. Autistic children were also much more likely than other children to have stomach and digestive problems (19 per cent), epilepsy (19 per cent) and to soil their pants (19 per cent). These problems were very rare among other children. (Table 8.7)

Mental disorders

Just under one-third (30 per cent) of autistic children had another clinically recognisable mental disorder: 16 per cent had an emotional disorder, usually an anxiety disorder; and 19 per cent had an additional diagnosis of conduct disorder, often made on the basis of severely challenging behaviour. (Table 8.8)

The parents of autistic children reported multiple types of mental health problem: 71 per cent reported behavioural problems, 51 per cent emotional problems and 42 per cent hyperactivity. Overall, about three-quarters (78 per cent) of parents reported some form of mental health problem.

(Table 8.9)

Medication

Thirteen per cent of children with autistic spectrum disorder were taking some form of medication. Overactivity and inattention are common symptoms of autism and all those on medication were taking drugs that were likely to have been prescribed for hyperkinesis: Methylphenidate (12 per cent), Clonidine (1 per cent) and Risperidone (1 per cent). (Table 8.10)

Among the parents of children with autistic spectrum disorder:

- 24 per cent reported that the child's general health was fair or bad (compared with 7 per cent for children with no autistic spectrum disorder)
- 89 per cent reported that the child had a specific physical or developmental problem (54 per cent)
- 78 per cent reported that the child had mental health problems (10 per cent)
- 51 per cent reported that the child had emotional problems, 71 per cent reported behavioural problems and 42 per cent reported hyperactivity (4 per cent, 6 per cent and 3 per cent)
- 30 per cent of the children had another main type of clinically recognisable disorder (9 per cent)

Use of services

Nine out of ten parents (89 per cent) of children with autistic spectrum disorder had sought help in the previous 12 months for their child's mental help problem and almost all of these had approached, or been referred to a professional source for advice (86 per cent). As with other groups, teachers were the most commonly used source (69 per cent) followed by specialist educational services, such as educational psychologists (51 per cent), mental health specialists (43 per cent) and child physical health specialists, such as paediatricians (36 per cent). About a quarter (22 per cent) had asked family members or friends for help or advice.   (Table 8.11)

Scholastic ability and attendance at school

Teachers were asked to rate the child's abilities in reading, mathematics and spelling compared with an average child of the same age and to estimate the child's age in terms of their scholastic ability. They were also asked to say whether the child had officially recognised special educational needs.

Basic skills

In general, autistic children had much lower levels of educational attainment than other children and they had more difficulty with basic skills than children with other types of

Among the parents of children with autistic spectrum disorder:

- 89 per cent had sought help or advice in the last year because of worries about their child's mental health (compared with 27 per cent for children with no conduct disorder)
- 86 per cent had contacted a professional service (22 per cent)
- The most commonly used services were: teachers (69 per cent), specialist educational services (51 per cent), mental health specialists (43 per cent) and child physical health specialists (36 per cent)

disorder. About a half were reported as having marked difficulty with reading and mathematics (48 per cent compared with 6 per cent of other children) and over a half were behind with spelling (58 per cent compared with 9 per cent). Overall, they were three times as likely as other children to be behind in their overall intellectual development (72 per cent compared with 24 per cent). Two-fifths (39 per cent) were more than two years behind.   (Figure 8.2 and Table 8.12)

Figure **8.2**
Proportion of children who were behind in their overall scholastic ability by whether they had autistic spectrum disorder, 1999 and 2004 combined

Great Britain

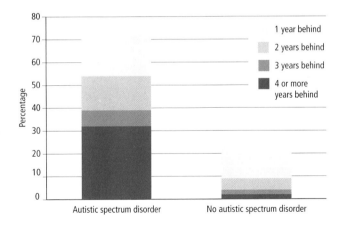

Special educational needs

Almost all children with autistic spectrum disorder were reported to have special educational needs (97 per cent compared with 16 per cent of other children) and the majority of these had a written statement of their needs (84 per cent compared with 45 per cent).   (Table 8.13)

Absence from school

The lower level of educational attainment among autistic children was not attributable to poor attendance at school. As Tables 8.14 and 8.15 show, they were no more likely than other children to have missed school nor was their truancy rate any higher. There is, however, evidence of interrupted schooling. Over a quarter (27 per cent) had been excluded from school at some point and most of these (23 per cent overall) had been excluded on more than one occasion. Just over a half of the autistic children who had been excluded also had a conduct disorder. Exclusion was very rare among other children (4 per cent). Similarly, a half (50 per cent) of autistic children had changed schools other than at normal transition stages, including 17 per cent who had experienced more than one change. None of these changes followed exclusion from school. Among other children, 19 per cent had changed schools and only 5 per cent had changed more than once.

(Tables 8.14–8.17)

> **Among children with autistic spectrum disorder:**
> - 72 per cent were behind in their overall intellectual development *(compared with 24 per cent for children with no autistic spectrum disorder)*
> - 97 per cent had officially recognised special educational needs *(16 per cent)*
> - 27 per cent had been excluded from school and 50 per cent had changed schools apart from normal transitions *(4 per cent and 19 per cent)*

Social functioning of the family

This section looks at various aspects of parental health, attitudes and behaviour which provide indicators of the social functioning of the family.

Mental health of parent

The parent who was interviewed about the child's behaviour, usually the mother, was asked about her own mental health using the General Health Questionnaire (GHQ-12 – see Chapter 2 for details). Scores range from 0 (no psychological distress) to 12 (severe psychological distress). A score of 3 is generally taken as the threshold with scores at this level or higher being considered indicative of an emotional disorder.

The parents of autistic children were almost twice as likely as other parents to have scores at or above the threshold (44 per cent compared with 24 per cent).   (Figure 8.3 and Table 8.18)

Figure 8.3
Proportion of children whose parent scored 3 or more on the GHQ-12, 1999 and 2004 combined

Great Britain

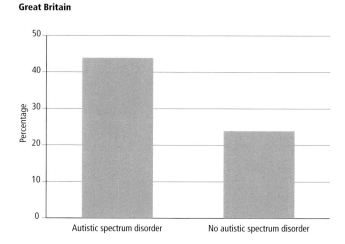

Family functioning

Family functioning was measured using the FAD-GFS scale in which parents rated 12 statements about family relationships (see Chapter 2 for details). For this survey, families which scored over 2.00 on this scale were considered to have unhealthy functioning.

Family functioning scores showed the same pattern as parental mental health. Autistic children were twice as likely as other children to live in families classified as having unhealthy functioning on this scale (37 per cent compared with 18 per cent). (Table 8.19)

Stressful life events

Autistic children were more likely than other children to have experienced two or more stressful life events (42 per cent compared with 26 per cent). There was also a general pattern across several events for the proportions experiencing the event to be higher among autistic children but none of the differences was large enough to be statistically significant. Since autism is present from infancy onwards, there is no reason to believe that exposure to stressful life events in childhood cause the autism. The link in this study may be a coincidence or, more likely, autism may trigger life events by placing extra stress on the family. (Tables 8.20 and 8.21)

> **Among children with autistic spectrum disorder:**
> - 44 per cent of parents had an emotional disorder *(compared with 24 per cent for the parents of children with no autistic spectrum disorder)*
> - 37 per cent lived in families with unhealthy functioning *(18 per cent)*

Child's social functioning

This section covers features of the child's social functioning which might provide protection against the onset and course of mental disorder: their strengths, their relationships with friends and their social aptitudes. In previous chapters, this section has also described various measures of social capital, such as children's views about their neighbourhood and the extent to which they participated in group activities. These questions were addressed to children aged 11–16 who were interviewed in the 2004 survey. However, it was often not possible to conduct an interview with an autistic child. Of the 28 children with autistic spectrum disorder who were potentially eligible for the questions, interviews were achieved with only 10 and some of these did not provide full information. Data have therefore not been presented for these topics or for the child's assessment of their strengths.

Strengths

Parents were asked to rate the child on 24 items covering various qualities (see Chapter 2 for details). The scores ranged from 0–48 and were divided into quartiles. Almost all of the children with autistic spectrum disorder fell into the bottom quartile (96 per cent compared with 25 per cent of other children). (Table 8.22)

Social aptitudes

The social aptitude scale consisted of 10 questions addressed to parents designed to measure the child's ability to empathise with others (see Chapter 2 for details). Scores ranged from 0–40 and were grouped into quartiles. The results showed the same pattern as the strengths scores with almost all children with autistic spectrum disorder falling into the bottom quartile (96 per cent compared with 24 per cent of other children). (Table 8.23)

Friendships

As discussed at the beginning of the chapter, impaired social interaction is a common feature of autistic spectrum disorder and the responses to the questions on friendships illustrate this problem. Thus, well over two-thirds of autistic children found it harder than average to make and keep friends, 71 and 73 per cent compared with 10 and 5 per cent of other children. Two-fifths (42 per cent) had no friends whereas hardly any other

Among children with autistic spectrum disorder:
- 71 per cent found it harder than average to make friends *(compared with 10 per cent for children with no autistic spectrum disorder)*
- 42 per cent had no friends *(1 per cent)*

children (1 per cent) were in this position. Among those who had friends, autistic children were less likely to share interests and activities with friends and a high proportion, 59 per cent did not have a friend to whom they could talk if they were worried. However, there were no differences between autistic and other children in the likelihood of their parents disapproving of their friends. (Table 8.24)

Smoking, drinking and drug use

Questions about smoking, drinking and drug use were asked of 11- to 16-year-olds who were interviewed in the 1999 and 2004 surveys. The information was collected by self-completion. As with the social capital questions, the number of children with autistic spectrum disorder who were able to complete the questionnaire was too small for analysis.

Self-harm

All parents were asked whether their child had ever tried to hurt, harm or kill themselves (see Chapter 2 for details). A quarter (25 per cent) of parents of autistic children reported such instances of self-harm. Among other parents, the proportion was 2 per cent. Again, there were too few interviews with autistic children aged 11–16 for the equivalent analysis based on the child's report. (Table 8.25)

Results from the six-month follow-up survey

Samples of the parents of children interviewed in the 1999 and 2004 surveys were sent a self-completion questionnaire six months after the interview in order to establish whether there had been any change in their symptoms (see Chapter 3).

The average levels of total symptoms and problems with peer relationships among the children with autistic spectrum disorders did fall slightly over the 6 months following the survey. However, as Figures 8.4 and 8.5 show, the gap between children with and those with no autistic spectrum disorders only narrowed a little as a result. Nor did the impact of symptoms change much (Figure 8.6). Both the symptoms and the impact of autistic spectrum disorders were typically very persistent, at least in the short term. (Figures 8.4–8.6)

Figure **8.4**

Total symptoms[1] at main interview and at six-month follow-up by whether child had autistic spectrum disorder at main interview, 1999 and 2004 combined

Great Britain

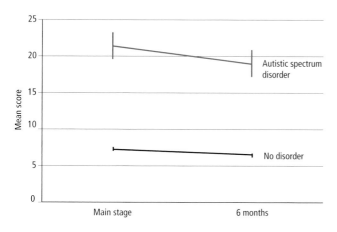

1. Total symptoms is the 'total difficulties score' on the parent-reported SDQ, reflecting the sum of the subscale scores for emotional symptoms, conduct problems, hyperactivity and peer problems.

Figure **8.5**

Peer problems at main interview and at six-month follow-up by whether child had an autistic spectrum disorder at main interview, 1999 and 2004 combined

Great Britain

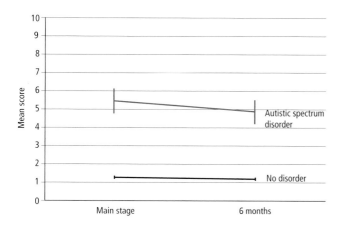

Figure **8.6**

Impact of symptoms at main interview and at six-month follow-up by whether child had an autistic spectrum disorder at main interview, 1999 and 2004 combined

Great Britain

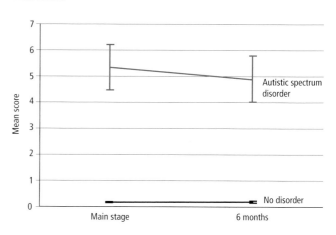

Table 8.1

Sex, age and ethnicity of child by whether has autistic spectrum disorder, 1999 and 2004 combined

All children   Great Britain

	Autistic spectrum disorder	No autistic spectrum disorder	All
	%	%	%
Sex			
Boys	82	50	51
Girls	18	50	49
Age			
5–10	62	53	53
11–16	38	47	47
Ethnicity			
White	92	89	89
Black[1]	3	3	3
Indian	1	2	2
Pakistani/ Bangladeshi	1	3	3
Other	3	3	3
Base (weighted)	98	18306	18403

1. Includes people of mixed black and white origin.

Table 8.2

Family characteristics by whether has autistic spectrum disorder, 1999 and 2004 combined

All children   Great Britain

	Autistic spectrum disorder	No autistic spectrum disorder	All
	%	%	%
Family type			
Married	66	68	68
Cohabiting	6	8	8
Lone parent – single	8	8	8
Lone parent – widowed, divorced or separated	19	16	16
Number of children in household			
1	21	23	23
2	48	45	45
3	22	22	22
4	9	7	7
5 or more	1	3	3
Base (weighted 1999 and 2004 data)	98	18318	18415
If stepchildren in family			
Yes	14	11	11
No	86	89	89
Base (weighted 2004 data)[1]	66	7911	7977

1. The 1999 data had a different classification for whether or not a family contained stepchildren.

Table **8.3**

Parent's education and socio-economic characteristics by whether has autistic spectrum disorder, 1999 and 2004 combined

All children   Great Britain

	Autistic spectrum disorder	No autistic spectrum disorder	All
	%	%	%
Parent's highest educational qualification			
Degree level	19	13	13
Teaching/HND/Nursing	10	11	11
A /AS level or equivalent	17	11	11
GCSE Grades A–C or equivalent	18	30	30
GCSE Grades D–F or equivalent	14	11	11
Other qualification	1	3	3
No qualification	21	21	21
Parent's employment status			
Both working/lone parent working	47	67	67
One parent working	23	19	19
Neither working/lone parent not working	30	14	15
Base (weighted 1999 and 2004 data)	*91*	*18020*	*18111*
Family's socio-economic classification[1]			
Large employers and higher managerial	2	2	2
Higher professional	2	3	3
Lower managerial and professional	19	20	20
Intermediate occupations	10	19	19
Small employers and own account	4	7	7
Lower supervisory and technical	-	1	1
Semi-routine	20	26	26
Routine occupations	14	12	12
Never worked/ long-term unemployed	7	5	5
FT student/inadequate description	21	4	4
Base (weighted 2004 data)[2]	*66*	*7911*	*7977*

1. *This is the National Statistics Socio-economic Classification (NS-SEC).*
2. *The 1999 data had a different social classification.*

Table **8.4**

Housing and income by whether has autistic spectrum disorder, 1999 and 2004 combined

All children   Great Britain

	Autistic spectrum disorder	No autistic spectrum disorder	All
	%	%	%
Type of accommodation			
Detached	26	25	25
Semi-detached	38	38	38
Terraced house	30	30	30
Flat/maisonette	5	7	7
Tenure			
Owners	63	69	69
Social sector tenants	26	24	24
Private renters	11	7	7
Base (weighted 1999 and 2004 data)	*98*	*18307*	*18404*
Gross weekly household income			
Under £100	1	4	4
£100–£199	8	16	16
£200–£299	22	14	14
£300–£399	18	12	12
£400–£499	12	11	11
£500–£599	10	10	10
£600–£770	7	13	13
Over £770	22	20	20
Base (weighted 1999 and 2004 data)	*79*	*16817*	*16896*
Receipt of disability benefits			
Carers allowance	23	3	3
Severe Disablement allowance	54	5	6
Disability living/attendance allowance	-	0	0
Incapacity allowance	-	2	2
Any disability allowance	**56**	**8**	**8**
No disability allowance	44	92	92
Base (weighted 2004 data[1])	*66*	*7911*	*7977*

1. The 1999 data covered different types of disability benefit.

Table **8.5**

Region, country and area type by whether has autistic spectrum disorder, 1999 and 2004 combined

All children   Great Britain

	Autistic spectrum disorder	No autistic spectrum disorder	All
	%	%	%
Region and country			
London Inner	2	5	5
London Outer	11	7	7
Other met England	29	31	31
Non-met England	49	44	44
England	92	86	86
Scotland	6	9	8
Wales	2	5	5
Base (weighted 1999 and 2004 data)	*98*	*18318*	*18415*
Area type (ACORN classification)			
Wealthy achievers	20	26	26
Urban prosperity	6	8	8
Comfortably off	34	26	26
Moderate means	20	17	17
Hard pressed	19	24	24
Base (weighted 2004 data)[1]	*65*	*7852*	*7917*

1. *The 1999 data had a different ACORN classification.*

Table **8.6**

Child's general health by whether has autistic spectrum disorder, 1999 and 2004 combined

All children   Great Britain

	Autistic spectrum disorder	No autistic spectrum disorder	All
	%	%	%
Child's general health			
Very good	29	69	69
Good	47	24	24
Fair	18	6	6
Bad	3	1	1
Very bad	3	0	0
Base (weighted)	*98*	*18075*	*18172*

Table **8.7**

Co-occurrence of physical and developmental problems, and autistic spectrum disorder, 1999 and 2004 combined

All children   Great Britain

	Autistic spectrum disorder	No autistic spectrum disorder	All
	Percentage of children with each type of physical complaint		
Asthma	20	15	15
Eczema	18	13	13
Hay fever	10	11	11
Eyesight problems	23	10	10
Stomach or digestive problems	19	6	6
Non-food allergy	10	6	6
Migraine/severe headache	6	5	5
Bed wetting	29	4	5
Glue ear/otitis media/grommits	10	4	4
Hearing problems	6	4	4
Speech or language problems	67	4	4
Food allergy	18	3	4
Difficulty with co-ordination	47	2	2
Stiffness or deformity of foot	8	2	2
Heart problems	5	1	1
Soiling pants	19	1	1
Muscle disease or weakness	7	1	1
Kidney/urinary tract problems	1	1	1
Obesity	3	1	1
Congenital abnormality	6	1	1
Epilepsy	19	1	1
Any blood disorder	1	0	0
Diabetes	-	0	0
Cerebral Palsy	3	0	0
Cancer	-	0	0
Any physical or developmental problem[1]	**89**	**54**	**54**
No problem	11	46	46
Base (weighted)	*96*	*18076*	*18172*

1. *Some physical complaints are not listed in the table above because of their rarity(less than 25 cases): ME (10), Spina bifida (6), Cystic fibrosis (11), Missing digits (20). They are included in the 'Any physical or developmental problems' category.*

Table **8.8**

Co-occurrence of other mental disorders and autistic spectrum disorder, 1999 and 2004 combined

All children   Great Britain

	Autistic spectrum disorder	No autistic spectrum disorder	All
	Percentage of children with each type of disorder		
Other mental disorders			
Emotional disorders:			
Anxiety disorders	16	3	4
Depression	1	1	1
All emotional disorders	16	4	4
Conduct disorders:			
Oppositional defiant disorder	-	3	3
Other conduct disorders	19	2	2
All conduct disorders	19	5	5
Hyperkinetic disorders	-	1	1
Less common disorders (excluding ASD)	-	0	0
Any other disorder	30	9	9
No (other) disorders	70	91	91
Base (weighted)	*98*	*18318*	*18415*

Table **8.9**

Parent's view of child's mental health by whether has autistic spectrum disorder, 1999 and 2004 combined

All children   Great Britain

	Autistic spectrum disorder	No autistic spectrum disorder	All
	Percentage of children with each type of problem		
Parent's view of child's mental health			
Emotional problems	51	4	5
Behavioural problems	71	6	6
Hyperactivity	42	3	4
Any of the above	78	10	10
Base (weighted)	*98*	*18076*	*18174*

Table **8.10**

Whether child is taking any medication by whether has autistic spectrum disorder, 2004

All children   Great Britain

	Autistic spectrum disorder	No autistic spectrum disorder	All
	Percentage of children taking each type of medication		
Methylphenidate, Equasym, Ritalin	12	1	1
Dexamphetamine, Dexedrine	-	0	0
Imipramine, Tofranil	-	0	0
Clonidine, Catepres, Dixarit	1	0	0
Fluoxetine, Prozac	-	0	0
Sertraline, Lustral	-	0	0
Fluvoxamine, Faverin	-	0	0
Citalopram, Cimpramil	-	0	0
Amitryptaline, Lentizol, Triptafen	-	0	0
Sulpirade, Dolmatil, Sulparex, Sulpitil	-	0	0
Risperidone, Riperadal	1	0	0
Haloperidol, Dozic, Haldol, Serenace	-	0	0
Any medication	**13**	**1**	**1**
No medication	87	99	99
Base (weighted)	*66*	*7795*	*7862*

Table **8.11**

Help sought in last year for child's mental health problems by whether has autistic spectrum disorder, 2004

All children   Great Britain

	Autistic spectrum disorder	No autistic spectrum disorder	All
	Percentage of children using each service/source		
Specialist services			
Child/adult mental health specialist (eg psychiatrist)	43	3	3
Child physical health specialist (eg paediatrician)	36	2	2
Social services (eg social worker)	23	2	2
Education services (eg educational psychologist)	51	4	4
Front line services			
Primary health care (eg GP or practice nurse)	33	6	6
Teachers	69	17	18
All professional services	**86**	**22**	**22**
Informal sources			
Family member/friends	22	12	12
Internet	10	1	1
Telephone help line	3	1	1
Self-help group	10	0	0
Other type of help	8	2	2
All sources	**89**	**27**	**28**
No help sought	11	73	72
Base (weighted)	*58*	*7726*	*7784*

Table **8.12**

Teacher's rating of child's basic skills by whether has autistic spectrum disorder, 1999 and 2004 combined

All children   Great Britain

	Autistic spectrum disorder	No autistic spectrum disorder	All
	%	%	%
Reading			
Above average	16	37	37
Average	14	40	40
Some difficulty	22	17	17
Marked difficulty	48	6	6
Mathematics			
Above average	17	32	31
Average	9	44	44
Some difficulty	25	19	19
Marked difficulty	48	6	6
Spelling			
Above average	5	28	28
Average	21	41	41
Some difficulty	16	21	21
Marked difficulty	58	9	9
Base (weighted)	75	14100	14174
Overall scholastic ability[1]			
4 or more years behind	32	2	2
3 years behind	7	2	2
2 years behind	15	5	5
1 year behind	18	15	15
Equivalent	11	36	35
1 or more years ahead	17	40	40
Base (weighted)	66	13188	13254

1. Functioning age-actual age.

Table **8.13**

Whether child has special educational needs by whether has autistic spectrum disorder, 1999 and 2004 combined

All children   Great Britain

	Autistic spectrum disorder	No autistic spectrum disorder	All
	%	%	%
If child has officially recognised special educational needs			
Yes	97	16	17
No	3	84	83
Base (weighted)	75	13869	13944

Table **8.14**

Absence from school and truancy (teacher's report) by whether has autistic spectrum disorder, 1999 and 2004 combined

All children   Great Britain

	Autistic spectrum disorder	No autistic spectrum disorder	All
	%	%	%
Number of days absent in last term			
0	32	32	32
1–5	38	46	46
6–10	17	13	13
11–15	7	4	4
16 or more	6	5	5
Any days absent	68	68	68
Base (weighted)	*57*	*10328*	*10385*
Any unauthorised days absent			
Yes	13	9	9
No	87	91	91
Base (weighted): 2004 data[1]	*38*	*4651*	*4689*
Whether plays truant			
Not true	93	97	97
Somewhat true	1	2	2
Certainly true	6	1	1
Base (weighted)	*74*	*14191*	*14265*

1. This question was not asked in 1999.

Table **8.15**

Absence from school (parent's report) by whether has autistic spectrum disorder, 2004

All children   Great Britain

	Autistic spectrum disorder	No autistic spectrum disorder	All
	%	%	%
Whether missed school in last term[1]			
Yes	37	34	34
No	63	66	66
Base (weighted): all children	*56*	*7566*	*7621*
Reasons for absence			
Short-term illness	(71)	78	78
Long-term illness	(10)	2	2
Refused to attend	-	2	2
Has a school phobia	(4)	0	0
Other	(23)	20	20
Base (weighted): those who missed school	*20*	*2579*	*2599*

1. Excluding exclusions.

Table **8.16**

Exclusions from school (parent's report) by whether has autistic spectrum disorder, 2004

All children   Great Britain

	Autistic spectrum disorder	No autistic spectrum disorder	All
	%	%	%
Number of times child has been excluded from school			
None	73	96	96
Once	3	2	2
Twice	8	1	1
Three or more times	15	1	1
Base (weighted)	*57*	*7713*	*7770*

Table **8.17**

Number of times child has changed schools by whether has autistic spectrum disorder, 2004

All children   Great Britain

	Autistic spectrum disorder	No autistic spectrum disorder	All
	%	%	%
Number of times child has changed school[1]			
None	50	81	81
Once	33	14	14
Twice	3	3	3
Three or more times	14	2	2
Base (weighted)	*57*	*7719*	*7776*

1. Apart from normal transitions.

Table **8.18**

Parent's GHQ–12 score by whether has autistic spectrum disorder, 1999 and 2004 combined

All children   Great Britain

	Autistic spectrum disorder	No autistic spectrum disorder	All
	%	%	%
Parent's GHQ–12[1]			
0–2	56	76	76
3–5	15	13	13
6–8	17	7	7
9–12	12	4	4
3 or more	**44**	**24**	**24**
Base (weighted)	*83*	*17899*	*17983*

1. For this survey, scores of 3 or more were taken to indicate a severe emotional problem.

Table **8.19**

Family functioning score by whether has autistic spectrum disorder, 1999 and 2004 combined

All children   Great Britain

	Autistic spectrum disorder	No autistic spectrum disorder	All
	%	%	%
Family functioning score[1]			
Up to 1.50	21	36	36
1.51–2.00	42	46	46
2.01–2.50	29	16	16
2.51 or more	9	2	2
Unhealthy functioning (2.01 or more)	**37**	**18**	**18**
Base (weighted)	*82*	*17826*	*17908*

1. For this survey, scores over 20 were taken to suggest unhealthy family functioning.

Table **8.20**

Stressful life events by whether has autistic spectrum disorder, 2004

All children   Great Britain

	Autistic spectrum disorder	No autistic spectrum disorder	All
		Percentage reporting each event	
Stressful life events			
Since child was born, parent had a separation due to marital difficulties or broken off steady relationship	38	31	31
Since child was born, parent had a major financial crisis such as losing the equivalent of three months income	19	13	13
Since child was born, parent had a problem with the police involving a court appearance	8	6	6
Since child was born, parent has had serious physical illness	7	8	8
Since child was born, parent has had serious mental illness	15	8	8
At any stage in child's life, a parent, brother or sister died	7	3	4
At any stage in child's life, a close friend died	11	6	6
At some stage in the child's life, s/he had a serious illness which required a stay in hospital	22	13	13
At any stage in child's life, s/he had been in a serious accident or badly hurt in an accident	7	5	5
In the past year child has broken off a steady relationship with a boy or girl friend (aged 13 or above)/ a close friendship has ended (any age)	4	7	7
Base (weighted)	*57*	*7713*	*7770*

Table **8.21**

Number of stressful life events by whether has autistic spectrum disorder, 2004

All children   Great Britain

	Autistic spectrum disorder	No autistic spectrum disorder	All
	%	%	%
Number of stressful life events			
0	34	42	42
1	24	32	32
2	20	15	15
3	16	7	7
4	2	3	3
5 or more	4	1	1
Two or more events	**42**	**26**	**26**
Base (weighted)	*57*	*7713*	*7770*

Table **8.22**

Child's strengths (parent's assessment) by whether has autistic spectrum disorder, 2004

All children   **Great Britain**

	Autistic spectrum disorder	No autistic spectrum disorder	All
	%	%	%
Strength score – parent assessment			
0–36	96	25	25
37–40	4	25	25
41–43	-	25	25
44–48	-	25	25
Base (weighted)	*51*	*7520*	*7571*

Table **8.23**

Social aptitude (parent's assessment) by whether has autistic spectrum disorder, 2004

All children   **Great Britain**

	Autistic spectrum disorder	No autistic spectrum disorder	All
	%	%	%
Social aptitude score			
0–20	96	24	25
21–24	4	28	27
25–28	-	23	22
29–40	-	26	25
Base (weighted)	*56*	*7426*	*7483*

Table **8.24**

Friendships by whether has autistic spectrum disorder, 2004

All children

Great Britain

	Autistic spectrum disorder	No autistic spectrum disorder	All
	%	%	%
What is child like at making friends?			
Finds it harder than average	71	10	10
About average	21	36	36
Easier than average	7	55	54
What is child like at keeping friends?			
Finds it harder than average	73	5	5
About average	21	35	35
Easier than average	6	60	59
Number of friends			
0	42	1	2
1	18	4	4
2–4	34	43	43
5–9	4	40	39
10 or more	1	12	11
Base (weighted): All children	*65*	*7775*	*7840*
Do child and friends have things in common			
No	9	1	1
A little	59	21	21
A lot	33	78	78
Do child and friends do things together			
No	30	3	4
A little	29	21	21
A lot	41	75	75
If worried, can child talk to friends			
No	59	21	21
Perhaps	30	42	42
Definitely	11	38	37
Whether friends get into trouble			
Not at all	67	67	67
A few are like that	21	31	31
Many are like that	5	1	1
All are like that	6	0	0
Whether parent approves of child's friends			
No	6	2	2
A little	16	14	14
A lot	78	84	84
Base (weighted): those who had friends	*36*	*7534*	*7570*

Table **8.25**

Deliberate self-harm (parent's report) by whether has autistic spectrum disorder, 1999 and 2004 combined

All children   Great Britain

	Autistic spectrum disorder	No autistic spectrum disorder	All
Percentage who have tried to harm, hurt or kill themselves	25	2	2
Base (weighted)	84	17571	17655

Children with multiple disorders

Chapter 9

Introduction

The previous chapters focused on each of the main broad categories of mental disorder. However, some children were diagnosed with more than one of these disorders. While this subgroup is relatively small, it is likely to include children with the most serious problems. This short chapter first examines the prevalence of co-morbidity and then explores whether children with multiple disorders have poorer health, educational and behavioural characteristics and make greater use of services than those with a single disorder.

Prevalence of multiple disorders

One in five of the children with a disorder were diagnosed with more than one of the main categories of mental disorder (emotional, conduct, hyperkinetic or less common disorders). This figure represents 1.9 per cent of all children. The most common combinations were conduct and emotional disorder and conduct and hyperkinetic disorder (0.7 per cent in each case). (Table 9.1)

The tables in the next section compare children who had multiple disorders with those who had a single disorder. As the former include a higher proportion of children with conduct disorders (90 per cent compared with 45 per cent), who tend to have more problems than children with emotional disorders, we would expect the multiple disorder group to fare worse quite apart from the effects of their co-morbidity. However, the aim of this analysis is simply to describe key features of the subgroup rather than to determine the independent effects of factors such as the type or extent of comorbidity.

Characteristics and behaviour of children with multiple disorders

Demographic characteristics

Nearly three-quarters (72 per cent) of children with multiple disorders were boys reflecting the high proportion of children with conduct disorder in this group. Among those with a single disorder, boys were also in the majority but by a smaller margin (58 per cent). There were no differences by number of disorders with regard to age profiles. (Table 9.2)

Physical and developmental problems and general health

About three-quarters (76 per cent) of children with multiple disorders had a physical or developmental problem as well compared with two-thirds (66 per cent) of those with a single disorder. The former were the more likely to report asthma (26 per cent and 18 per cent), bed wetting (17 per cent and 10 per cent), speech or language problems (21 per cent and 10 per

cent) and difficulty with co-ordination (15 per cent and 7 per cent). (Table 9.3)

Similarly, parents whose child had multiple disorders were more likely than those whose child had a single disorder to report that the child's general health was fair or bad (26 per cent compared with 17 per cent) and much less likely to say that their child's health was very good (37 per cent compared with 50 per cent). (Table not shown)

Use of services

Almost all parents of children with multiple disorders had sought help with their child's mental health problems in the previous 12 months (96 per cent) and most had sought, or been referred to, some form of professional advice (93 per cent). Nearly three quarters (73 per cent) had approached a teacher and about a half had approached specialist mental health services (51 per cent) or GP services (46 per cent). These proportions are much higher than the corresponding figures for parents of children with a single disorder: 71 per cent had sought help of some kind and 64 per cent had sought professional advice. (Table 9.4)

There is particular interest among clinicians in the diagnostic make-up of children who present at specialist mental health clinics. Overall 3 per cent of children had attended such clinics in the previous year. This group consisted of roughly equal proportions of children with 2 or more disorders (32 per cent), children with single disorders (37 per cent) and those with no diagnosed disorder (31 per cent). Thus, while children with multiple disorders represent only 2 per cent of all children, they account for about one-third of the cases using specialist mental health services. It may seem surprising that children with no diagnosed disorder should have had contact with specialist mental health services. However, these children may have had a disorder at the time that they were referred which may have been some months before the assessment carried out for this survey. (Table not shown)

Scholastic ability

Teachers' ratings of children's progress at school showed that nearly two thirds (63 per cent) of children with multiple disorders were behind with their overall intellectual development and 40 per cent were more than a year behind. Among children with a single disorder, these proportions were 49 per cent and 27 per cent. (Table 9.5)

Child's strengths and social aptitudes

Both parents and young people were asked to rate the child on a series of items covering various qualities (see Chapter 2 for details). Scores on the adult scale ranged from 0-48 and those on the children's scale ranged from 0–38. Table 9.6 shows the scores on each scale grouped into quartiles. Looking first at the parent's assessment, 88 per cent of children with multiple disorders had scores in the bottom quartile compared with 61 per cent of those with a single disorder. There was no such difference between the young people's assessments probably because those with multiple disorders tend to have less insight into their problems. (Table 9.6)

Parents were also asked to rate their child's social aptitude using a scale of 10 questions designed to measure the child's ability to empathise with others (see Chapter 2 for details). Scores ranged from 0–40 and were grouped into quartiles. These scores showed the same pattern as the strengths scores. About three-quarters (78 per cent) of children with multiple disorders had scores in the bottom quartile compared with just over a half (56 per cent) of children with a single disorder. (Table 9.7)

Smoking, drinking and drug use

There were no differences between children with multiple and those with single disorders in terms of the proportions who were smokers, regular drinkers or who had ever taken cannabis. The apparent difference between the proportions of smokers was not statistically significant. (Table 9.8)

Results from the six-month follow-up survey

Samples of the parents of children interviewed in the 1999 and 2004 surveys were sent a self-completion questionnaire six months after the interview in order to establish whether there had been any change in their symptoms (see Chapter 3).

The average level of total symptoms among the children with two or more disorders did fall slightly over the six months following the survey. However, as Figure 9.1 shows, the gap between children with multiple disorders and their comparison groups only narrowed a little as a result. The impact attributable to these symptoms was less persistent, falling by around a third (Figure 9.2). At first glance, it seems surprising that impact dropped by a third although the level of symptoms was fairly steady. The most likely explanation is that the impact of symptoms depends not just on the symptoms themselves but on everything else in the child's life. Changes at home or at school may make symptoms easier or harder to live with. (Figures 9.1 and 9.2)

Figure **9.1**

Total symptoms[1] at main interview and at six-month follow-up by number of disorders at main interview, 1999 and 2004 combined

Great Britain

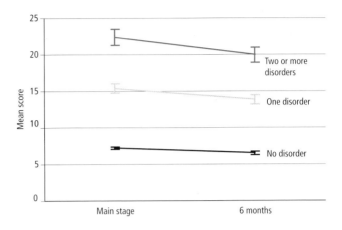

1 Total symptoms is the 'total difficulties score' on the parent-reported SDQ, reflecting the sum of the subscale scores for emotional symptoms, conduct problems, hyperactivity and peer problems.

Figure **9.2**

Impact of symptoms at main interview and at six-month follow-up by number of disorders at main interview, 1999 and 2004 combined

Great Britain

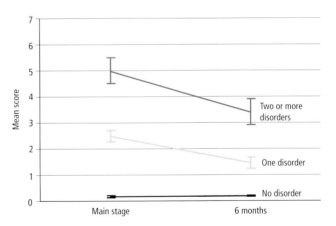

Table **9.1**

Number and combinations of main disorder categories, 1999 and 2004 combined

All children   Great Britain

	Percentage of children
Three or more disorders:	**0.2**
Emotional, conduct and hyperkinetic disorders	0.1
Emotional, conduct and less common disorders	0.1
Other combinations	0.0
Two disorders:	**1.7**
Emotional and conduct disorders	0.7
Conduct and hyperkinetic disorders	0.7
Emotional and less common disorders	0.1
Other combinations	0.1
One disorder:	**7.1**
Emotional disorder	2.9
Conduct disorder	3.2
Hyperkinetic disorder	0.5
Less common disorder	0.6
Base (weighted)	18415

Table **9.2**

Sex and age by number of mental disorders, 1999 and 2004 combined

All children   Great Britain

	Number of mental disorders[1]			
	Two or more	One	None	All
	%	%	%	%
Sex				
Boys	72	58	50	51
Girls	28	42	50	49
Age				
5–10	45	44	54	53
11–16	55	56	46	47
Base (weighted)	349	1306	16760	18415

1. Based on broad categories of emotional, conduct, hyperkinetic and less common disorders.

Table **9.3**

Occurrence of physical or developmental problems by number of mental disorders, 1999 and 2004 combined

All children   Great Britain

	Number of mental disorders[1]			
	Two or more	One	None	All
	Percentage of children with each type of physical complaint			
Asthma	26	18	14	15
Eczema	13	15	12	13
Hay fever	13	13	10	11
Eyesight problems	18	14	10	10
Stomach or digestive problems	11	10	5	6
Non-food allergy	9	6	6	6
Migraine/severe headache	11	8	4	5
Bed wetting	17	10	4	5
Glue ear/otitis media/grommits	7	5	4	4
Hearing problems	5	6	3	4
Speech or language problems	21	10	3	4
Food allergy	8	6	3	4
Difficulty with co-ordination	15	7	2	2
Stiffness or deformity of foot	5	4	2	2
Heart problems	3	2	1	1
Soiling pants	7	3	1	1
Muscle disease or weakness	3	3	1	1
Kidney/urinary tract problems	3	2	1	1
Obesity	3	2	1	1
Congenital abnormality	1	1	1	1
Epilepsy	4	2	0	1
Any blood disorder	1	0	0	0
Diabetes	1	0	0	0
Cerebral Palsy	0	1	0	0
Cancer	1	0	0	0
Any physical or developmental problem[2]	**76**	**66**	**53**	**54**
No physical problem	24	34	47	46
Base (weighted)	*349*	*1294*	*16531*	*18172*

1. *Based on broad categories of emotional, conduct, hyperkinetic and less common disorders.*
2. *Some physical complaints are not listed in the table above because of their rarity(less than 25 cases): ME (10), Spina bifida (6), Cystic fibrosis (11), Missing digits (20) They are included in the 'Any physical or developmental problem' category.*

Table **9.4**

Help sought in last year for child's mental health problems by number of mental disorders, 2004

All children   Great Britain

	Number of mental disorders[1]			
	Two or more	One	None	All
	Percentage of children using each service/source			
Specialist services				
Child/adult mental health specialist (eg psychiatrist)	51	17	1	3
Child physical health specialist (eg paediatrician)	14	8	1	2
Social services (eg social worker)	23	8	1	2
Education services (eg educational psychologist)	38	18	2	4
Front line services				
Primary health care (eg GP or practice nurse)	46	26	4	6
Teachers	73	48	14	18
All professional services	**93**	**64**	**17**	**22**
Informal sources				
Family member/friends	43	29	10	12
Internet	10	4	1	1
Telephone help line	5	4	0	1
Self-help group	7	2	0	0
Other type of help	9	5	1	2
All sources	**96**	**71**	**23**	**28**
No help sought	4	29	77	72
Base (weighted)	*158*	*542*	*7084*	*7784*

1. *Based on broad categories of emotional, conduct, hyperkinetic and less common disorders.*

Table **9.5**

Overall scholastic ability by number of mental disorders, 1999 and 2004 combined

All children   Great Britain

	Number of mental disorders[1]			
	Two or more	One	None	All
	%	%	%	%
Overall scholastic ability[2]				
4 or more years behind	12	9	2	2
3 years behind	8	6	2	2
2 years behind	20	12	5	6
1 year behind	23	22	14	15
Equivalent	25	30	36	35
1 or more years ahead	12	21	42	40
Base (weighted)	*238*	*933*	*12083*	*13254*

1. *Based on broad categories of emotional, conduct, hyperkinetic and less common disorders.*
2. *Functioning age-actual age.*

Table 9.6

Child's strengths (parent's and child's assessment) by number of mental disorders, 2004

All children   Great Britain

	Number of mental disorders[1]			
	Two or more	One	None	All
	%	%	%	%
ALL CHILDREN				
Strength score–parent assessment				
0–36	88	61	21	25
37–40	7	19	26	25
41–43	3	13	26	25
44–48	1	8	27	25
Base (weighted)	*150*	*523*	*6899*	*7571*
CHILDREN AGED 11–16				
Strength score–child assessment				
0–23	43	40	21	23
24–27	23	27	27	27
28–30	20	19	23	23
31–38	13	14	29	27
Base (weighted)	*57*	*252*	*3030*	*3338*

1. Based on broad categories of emotional, conduct, hyperkinetic and less common disorders.

Table 9.7

Social aptitude (parent's assessment) by number of mental disorders, 2004

All children   Great Britain

	Number of mental disorders[1]			
	Two or more	One	None	All
	%	%	%	%
Social aptitude score				
0–20	78	56	21	25
21–24	11	21	28	27
25–28	6	12	24	22
29–40	6	11	27	25
Base (weighted)	*152*	*519*	*6811*	*7483*

1. Based on broad categories of emotional, conduct, hyperkinetic and less common disorders.

Table **9.8**

Smoking, drinking and drug use by number of mental disorders, 1999 and 2004 combined

Children aged 11–16   Great Britain

	11- to 13-year-olds				14- to 16-year-olds				All aged 11–16			
	Two or more	One	None	All	Two or more	One	None	All	Two or more	One	None	All
	%	%	%	%	%	%	%	%	%	%	%	%
All smokers	16	7	2	2	51	41	15	18	32	24	7	9
All regular drinkers	4	5	3	3	24	28	16	17	13	16	8	9
Ever used cannabis	6	5	1	1	41	30	13	15	22	18	6	7
Base (weighted)	*81*	*287*	*4029*	*4397*	*70*	*300*	*2899*	*3269*	*150*	*587*	*6928*	*7665*

1. *Based on broad categories of emotional, conduct, hyperkinetic and less common disorders.*

Mental disorders
in Scotland

Chapter 10

Introduction

This chapter describes the characteristics and behaviour of children and young people with emotional and conduct disorders living in Scotland. The characteristics covered are:

- demographic characteristics;
- family situation;
- socio-economic characteristics;
- general, physical and mental health;
- scholastic ability and attendance at school;
- family's social functioning; and
- lifestyle behaviours.

The tables compare children with any form of emotional and conduct disorder with those who have no such disorders. Because of the relatively small numbers of children sampled in Scotland, it has only been possible to analyse those characteristics for which data for 1999 and 2004 could be combined. There were too few cases to show hyperkinetic and less common disorders or to show tables based only on 2004 data.

The commentary is descriptive, the aim being to provide profiles of children in Scotland who have emotional or conduct disorders. It therefore takes no account of the inter-relationships between the characteristics. The analysis at the end of Chapter 4 described the factors which had the largest independent effects on prevalence and this gives an indication of the key variables.

On the whole, the patterns of variation in Scotland were very similar to those in Great Britain as a whole. Where large differences did occur they have been noted in the text.

Descriptions of typical symptoms displayed by children with different types of emotional and conduct disorders are provided in Chapters 5 and 6 of this report.

Demographic, socio-economic and area characteristics

Demographic characteristics

There were no differences between children with an emotional disorder and those with no such disorder in relation to their sex, age and ethnic profile. In Great Britain as a whole, children with an emotional disorder were more likely than other children to be girls. The same pattern was evident in Scotland but the difference was not large enough to reach statistical significance at the 95 per cent confidence level. (Figure 10.1 and Table 10.1)

Children with conduct disorders were predominantly boys, 69 per cent compared with 51 per cent of those with no such disorder. Otherwise, there were no differences between

children with and those with no conduct disorder with regard to the other demographic characteristics, age and ethnic group. (Figure 10.1 and Table 10.1)

Figure **10.1**
Sex by type of mental disorder, 1999 and 2004 combined

Scotland

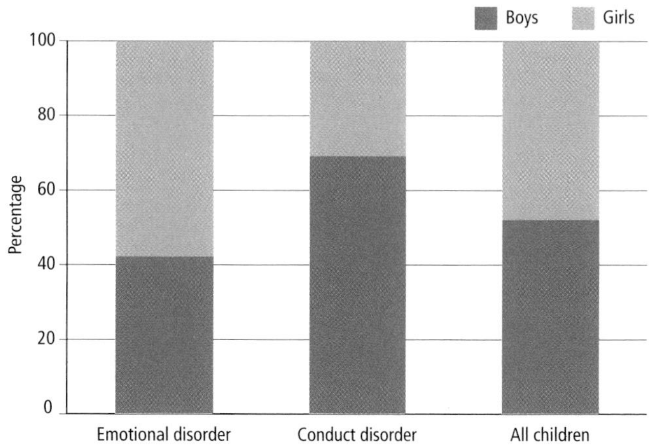

Family characteristics

Children with an emotional disorder were more likely than other children to live with a single lone parent (14 per cent compared with 6 per cent) and less likely to live with parents who were married (57 per cent compared with 73 per cent of other children). (Figure 10.2 and Table 10.2)

Almost a third (31 per cent) of children with conduct disorders lived with a previously married lone parent compared with under a fifth (15 per cent) of children with no such disorder.

Figure **10.2**
Family type by type of mental disorder, 1999 and 2004 combined

Scotland

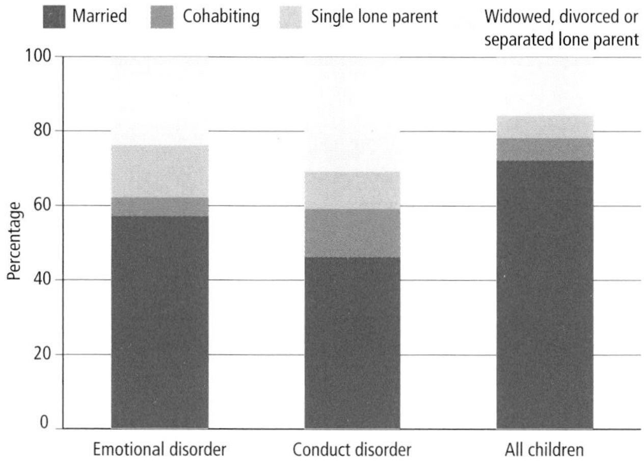

The former were more likely than the latter to live with cohabiting parents (13 per cent compared with 6 per cent) and less likely to live with parents who were married (46 per cent compared with 73 per cent). (Figure 10.2 and Table 10.2)

There was no consistent pattern of variation between children with emotional or conduct disorders and other children in relation to the number of children in the household. This was different to the findings for children in Great Britain as a whole. As noted in Chapters 5 and 6 children with emotional disorders and those with conduct disorders were more likely than other children to live in large families. (Table 10.2)

Parental education and employment status

Children with emotional disorders were more than twice as likely as other children to live with parents who had no educational qualifications (52 per cent compared with 21 per cent of other children). Conversely, the former were less likely to live with parents who had been educated to degree level (4 per cent compared with 17 per cent of other children).

(Table 10.3)

In Great Britain as a whole, there was a smaller differential between the parents of children with and those with no emotional disorder in the proportions who had no educational qualifications (35 per cent compared with 20 per cent).

Children with emotional disorders were about three times as likely as other children to live in households in which neither parent was working (37 per cent compared with 12 per cent). Conversely, they were much less likely than other children to live in households in which both parents were working (45 per cent compared with 70 per cent). (Table 10.3)

Like children with emotional disorders, those with conduct disorders were more likely than other children to live with parents who had no educational qualifications (42 per cent compared with 21 per cent) and less likely to have parents who had been educated to degree level (4 per cent compared with 17 per cent). Almost a half (44 per cent) of children with conduct disorders lived in households in which neither parent was working compared with just over one-tenth (12 per cent) of other children. The former were much less likely than other children to live in households in which both parents were working (38 per cent compared with 70 per cent). (Table 10.3)

Housing and Income

Housing and income followed the same pattern as education. Almost two-thirds (72 per cent) of children with emotional disorders lived in rented property compared with around one-third (32 per cent) of other children. Most of these lived in the social rented sector (64 per cent compared with 27 per cent of other children). An almost identical pattern emerged for children with conduct disorders with 69 per cent of such children living the social rented sector compared with 27 per cent of other children. (Table 10.4)

The findings for Great Britain were similar but the concentrations of children with emotional and conduct disorders in the social rented sector were much less pronounced (41 per cent for children with emotional disorders and 50 per cent for those with conduct disorders).

Children with emotional disorders were about twice as likely as other children to have a household income of less than £200 (37 per cent compared with 18 per cent). Again, the pattern was similar for children with conduct disorders. Over a third (37 per cent) had a household income of less than £200 compared with about a sixth (17 per cent) of other children. (Table 10.4)

Among children with emotional disorders in Scotland:
- 58 per cent were girls *(compared with 48 per cent for children with no emotional disorder)*
- 51 per cent were aged 5-10 *(52 per cent)*
- 100 per cent were white *(98 per cent)*
- 14 per cent lived with a single lone parent *(6 per cent)*
- 57 per cent lived in a married couple family *(73 per cent)*
- 52 per cent had parents with no educational qualifications *(21 per cent)*
- 72 per cent lived in rented accommodation *(32 per cent)*
- 37 per cent lived in households with gross incomes under £200 per week *(18 per cent)*

Among children with conduct disorders in Scotland:
- 69 per cent were boys *(compared with 51 per cent for children with no conduct disorder)*
- 57 per cent were aged 11-16 *(48 per cent)*
- 100 per cent were white *(98 per cent)*
- 31 per cent lived with a previously married lone parent *(15 per cent)*
- 46 per cent lived in a married couple family *(73 per cent)*
- 42 per cent had parents with no educational qualifications *(21 per cent)*
- 72 per cent lived in rented accommodation *(32 per cent)*
- 37 per cent lived in households with gross incomes under £200 per week *(17 per cent)*

Child's general health and mental health

General health

The parents of children with emotional disorders were much more likely than other parents to say that their child's health was fair or bad (28 per cent compared with 5 per cent). Conversely, less than half (45 per cent) of the former described their child's health as very good, compared with almost three-quarters (71 per cent) of the latter. (Figure 10.3 and Table 10.5)

Likewise, the parents of children with conduct disorders were three times as likely as other parents to say that their child's health was fair or bad (20 per cent compared with 6 per cent) and less likely to say that there child's health was very good (38 per cent compared with 72 per cent).

(Figure 10.3 and Table 10.5)

Figure 10.3
Child's general health by type of mental disorder, 1999 and 2004 combined

Scotland

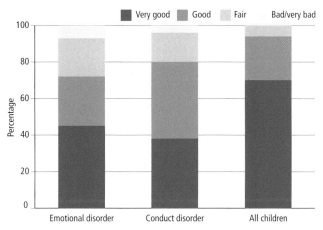

Physical and developmental problems

There were no differences between children with an emotional disorder and those with no such disorder in relation to the overall proportions who had a physical or developmental problem. There were some differences, however, in relation to certain physical and developmental problems. Children with emotional disorders were more likely than other children to have bed wetting and urinary tract problems and to have difficulty with co-ordination (10, 6 and 6 per cent). The proportions for children with no emotional disorder were 3, 1 and 1 per cent. (Table 10.6)

As with children with emotional disorders, there were no differences between children with conduct disorders and other children in relation to the occurrence of physical or developmental problems overall. Again, however, there were some differences between the groups for certain complaints. For example, children with conduct disorders were more likely than other children to have hearing, speech and muscle problems. (6, 8 and 6 per cent compared with 2, 3, and 1 per cent).

(Table 10.6)

In Great Britain as a whole those with emotional and conduct disorders were more likely than other children to report physical complaints. In the case of emotional disorders, the differential in Scotland was somewhat smaller than in Great Britain, while, for conduct disorders, the proportions in Scotland were similar to those in Great Britain. However, the Scotland data is based on a much smaller sample and the differences need to be correspondingly larger in order to reach statistical significance.

Mental disorders

A quarter (25 per cent) of children with an emotional disorder had another clinically diagnosed mental disorder: 20 per cent had a conduct disorder, 8 per cent had a hyperkinetic disorder and 3 per cent had a less common disorder.

(Table 10.7)

The parents of children with emotional disorders reported multiple types of mental health problems: 23 per cent reported emotional problems, 29 per cent reported behavioural problems and 8 per cent reported hyperactivity. (Table 10.8)

A third (34 per cent) of children with conduct disorders had another clinically diagnosed mental disorder: 18 per cent had an emotional disorder, 17 per cent had a hyperkinetic disorder and 6 per cent had a less common disorder.

(Table 10.7)

Two-thirds of the parents of children with conduct disorders reported that their child had some form of mental health problem: 31 per cent reported emotional problems, 57 per cent reported behavioural problems and 21 per cent reported hyperactivity. (Table 10.8)

Among the parents of children with emotional disorders:

- 28 per cent reported that the child's general health was fair or bad *(compared with 5 per cent for children with no emotional disorder)*
- 65 per cent reported that the child had a specific physical or developmental problem *(52 per cent)*
- 36 per cent reported that the child had mental health problems *(7 per cent)*
- 23 per cent reported that the child had emotional problems, 29 per cent reported behavioural problems and 8 per cent reported hyperactivity *(3 per cent, 4 per cent and 3 per cent)*
- 25 per cent of the children had another main type of clinically recognisable disorder *(4 per cent)*

Among the parents of children with conduct disorders:

- 20 per cent reported that the child's general health was fair or bad *(compared with 6 per cent for children with no conduct disorder)*
- 63 per cent reported that the child had a specific physical or developmental problem *(52 per cent)*
- 65 per cent reported that the child had mental health problems *(5 per cent)*
- 31 per cent reported that the child had emotional problems, 57 per cent reported behavioural problems and 21 per cent reported hyperactivity *(2 per cent, 3 per cent and 2 per cent)*
- 34 per cent of the children had another main type of clinically recognisable disorder *(4 per cent)*

Scholastic ability and attendance at school

Teachers were asked to rate their child's abilities in reading, mathematics and spelling compared with an average child of the same age and to estimate the child's age in terms of scholastic ability. They were also asked whether or not the child had officially recognised special educational needs.

Basic skills

Children with emotional disorders had more difficulty with basic skills than other children. Around two-fifths had problems with reading (44 per cent), mathematics (37 per cent) and spelling (41 per cent). The corresponding proportions for children with no emotional disorders were 19 per cent for reading and mathematics and 25 per cent for spelling. Children with emotional disorders were more than twice as likely as other children to be behind in terms of their overall scholastic ability (47 per cent compared with 18 per cent).

(Figure 10.4 and Table 10.9)

Figure 10.4

Proportion of children who were behind in their overall scholastic ability by type of mental disorder, 1999 and 2004 combined

Scotland

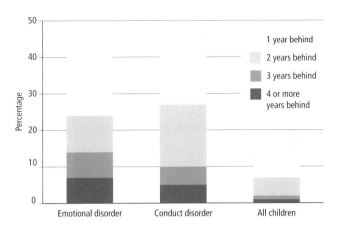

There was a similar pattern for children with conduct disorders but the differential was larger. Almost a half (46 per cent) had problems with reading and mathematics and almost two-thirds (61 per cent) had problems with spelling. The proportions for children with no such disorder were 18 per cent for reading and mathematics and 24 per cent for spelling. Children with conduct disorders were about three times as likely as other children to be behind in terms of their overall scholastic ability (48 per cent compared with 18 per cent).

(Figure 10.4 and Table 10.9)

The overall proportion of children who were behind in their scholastic ability was higher among children in Great Britain as a whole but the difference between those with and those with no conduct disorder was about the same.

Special educational needs

Almost a fifth (17 per cent) of children with emotional disorders and nearly a quarter (22 per cent) of those with conduct disorders had officially recognised special educational needs compared with under a tenth (7 per cent and 6 per cent) of their comparison groups.

(Table 10.10)

Truancy and Exclusions

Teachers reported that 10 per cent of children with emotional disorders had possibly or definitely played truant. The corresponding proportion for other children was just 3 per cent.

(Figure 10.5 and Table 10.11)

Figure **10.5**

Proportion of children whose teacher thought that they played truant by type of mental disorder, 1999 and 2004 combined

Scotland

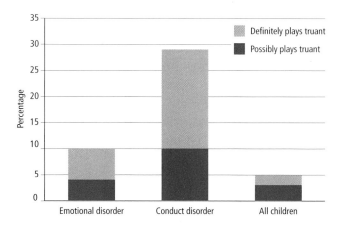

Among children with emotional disorders:

- 47 per cent were behind in their overall scholastic ability *(compared with 18 per cent of children with no emotional disorder)*
- 17 per cent had officially recognised special educational needs *(7 per cent)*
- 10 per cent were considered by teachers to be definite or possible truants *(3 per cent)*

Among children with conduct disorders:

- 48 per cent were behind in their overall scholastic ability *(compared with 18 per cent of children with no conduct disorder)*
- 22 per cent had officially recognised special educational needs *(6 per cent)*
- 29 per cent were considered by teachers to be definite or possible truants *(3 per cent)*
- 36 per cent had been excluded from school *(2 per cent)*

The findings were much more pronounced for children with conduct disorders: 29 per cent were considered to be possible or definite truants compared with 3 per cent of other children.

(Figure 10.5 and Table 10.11)

Over a third (36 per cent) of children with conduct disorders had been excluded from school and almost a fifth (18 per cent) had been excluded three or more times. Among other children these proportions were very low, 2 per cent and 0 per cent.

(Table 10.12)

Social functioning of the family

This section looks at various aspects of parental health, attitudes and behaviour which provide indicators of the social functioning of the family.

Mental health of parent

The parent who was interviewed about the child, usually the mother, was asked about her own mental health using the General Health Questionnaire (GHQ-12 – see Chapter 2 for details). Scores range from 0 (no psychological distress) to 12 (severe psychological distress). A score of 3 is generally taken as the threshold, with scores at this level or higher being considered indicative of an emotional disorder.

Over half (53 per cent) of parents of children with an emotional disorder had scores of 3 or more on the GHQ-12 (compared with 22 per cent of other parents) and 21 per cent had a score of 9 or more (compared with 4 per cent of other parents).

(Figure 10.6 and Table 10.13)

The results were similar for children with conduct disorders: 56 per cent of parents had a score of 3 or more on the GHQ-12 (compared with 22 per cent of other parents) and 18 per cent had a score of 9 or more (compared with 4 per cent of other parents).

(Figure 10.6 and Table 10.13)

Figure **10.6**

Proportion of children whose parent scored 3 or more on the GHQ-12, 1999 and 2004 combined

Scotland

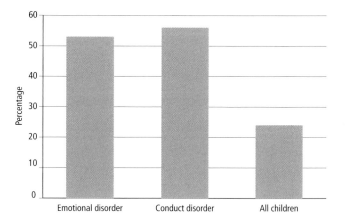

Family functioning

Family functioning was measured using the FAD-GFS scale in which parents rated 12 statements about family relationships (see Chapter 2 for details). For this survey, families that scored over 2.00 on this scale were considered to have unhealthy functioning.

Children with emotional disorders were more than twice as likely as other children to live in families classified as having unhealthy functioning (38 per cent compared with 17 per cent). (Table 10.14)

A half (50 per cent) of children with conduct disorders lived in families classified as having unhealthy functioning (compared with 16 per cent of other children). (Table 10.14)

Stressful life events

Parents were asked whether their child had experienced any of 10 potentially stressful events.

Three-fifths (60 per cent) of children with conduct disorders had experienced two or more stressful life events compared with around a quarter (24 per cent) of other children. The former were much more likely than other children to have experienced four or more stressful life events (19 per cent compared with 3 per cent). (The number of children with emotional disorders for whom we have information about life events was too small for analysis.) (Table 10.15)

Among children with emotional disorders:
- 53 per cent of parents had an emotional disorder *(compared with 22 per cent of children with no emotional disorder)*
- 38 per cent lived in families with unhealthy functioning *(17 per cent)*

Among children with conduct disorders:
- 56 per cent of parents had an emotional disorder *(compared with 22 per cent of children with no conduct disorder)*
- 50 per cent lived in families with unhealthy functioning *(16 per cent)*
- 60 per cent had had two or more stressful life events *(24 per cent)*

Self-harm

Both parents and children were asked if the child had ever tried to hurt, harm or kill themselves. Table 10.16 shows the data based on parents' reports only as the sample base for the children's reports was too small for analysis.

The parents of children with an emotional disorder and those who had children with conduct disorders were more likely than other parents to say that their child had tried to harm themselves (6 per cent and 11 per cent compared with 1 per cent of their comparison groups). (Table 10.16)

Table **10.1**

Age, sex and ethnicity of child by whether has an emotional or conduct disorder, 1999 and 2004 combined

All children

Scotland

	Emotional disorder	No emotional disorder	Conduct disorder	No conduct disorder	All
	%	%	%	%	%
Sex					
Boys	42	52	69	51	52
Girls	58	48	31	49	48
Age					
5–10	51	52	43	52	52
11–16	49	48	57	48	48
Ethnicity					
White	100	98	100	98	98
Black[1]	-	0	-	0	0
Indian	-	0	-	0	0
Pakistani/Bangladeshi	-	1	-	1	1
Other	-	1	-	1	1
Base (weighted)	*59*	*1505*	*68*	*1496*	*1564*

1. Includes people of mixed black and white origin.

Table **10.2**

Family characteristics by whether has an emotional or conduct disorder, 1999 and 2004 combined

All children

Scotland

	Emotional disorder	No emotional disorder	Conduct disorder	No conduct disorder	All
	%	%	%	%	%
Family type					
Married	57	73	46	73	72
Cohabiting	5	6	13	6	6
Lone parent – single	14	6	10	6	6
Lone parent – widowed, divorced or separated	24	15	31	15	16
Number of children in household					
1	24	25	27	25	25
2	39	46	32	47	46
3	26	20	28	20	20
4	6	7	8	7	7
5 or more	5	2	4	2	2
Base (weighted)	*59*	*1505*	*68*	*1496*	*1564*

Table **10.3**

Parent's education and employment status by whether has an emotional or conduct disorder, 1999 and 2004 combined

All children

Scotland

	Emotional disorder	No emotional disorder	Conduct disorder	No conduct disorder	All
	%	%	%	%	%
Parent's highest educational qualification					
Degree level	4	17	4	17	16
Teaching/HND/Nursing	17	15	12	15	15
A /AS level or equivalent	5	13	11	13	13
GCSE Grades A–C or equivalent	13	26	21	26	25
GCSE Grades D–F or equivalent	5	4	4	4	4
Other qualification	4	5	6	5	5
No qualification	52	21	42	21	22
Parent's employment status					
Both working/lone parent working	45	70	38	70	69
One parent working	19	18	18	18	18
Neither working/lone parent not working	37	12	44	12	13
Base (weighted)	57	1495	68	1484	1552

Table **10.4**

Housing and income by whether has an emotional or conduct disorder, 1999 and 2004 combined

All children   Scotland

	Emotional disorder	No emotional disorder	Conduct disorder	No conduct disorder	All
	%	%	%	%	%
Type of accommodation					
Detached	11	29	10	29	28
Semi-detached	30	28	27	29	29
Terraced house	20	24	38	24	24
Flat/maisonette	39	18	25	19	19
Tenure					
Owners	28	68	28	68	67
Social sector tenants	64	27	69	27	28
Private renters	8	5	3	5	5
Base (weighted)	*59*	*1504*	*68*	*1495*	*1563*
Gross weekly household income					
Under £100	7	3	5	3	4
£100–£199	30	15	32	14	15
£200–£299	20	14	27	13	14
£300–£399	13	11	17	10	11
£400–£499	12	12	6	13	12
£500–£599	7	10	5	10	10
£600–£770	5	13	3	14	13
Over £770	5	22	5	22	21
Base (weighted)	*53*	*1387*	*59*	*1381*	*1439*

Table **10.5**

Child's general health by whether has an emotional or conduct disorder, 1999 and 2004 combined

All children   Scotland

	Emotional disorder	No emotional disorder	Conduct disorder	No conduct disorder	All
	%	%	%	%	%
Child's general health					
Very good	45	71	38	72	70
Good	27	23	42	23	24
Fair	21	5	16	5	6
Bad	7	0	4	1	1
Very bad	-	0	-	0	0
Base (weighted)	*57*	*1498*	*68*	*1488*	*1556*

Table **10.6**

Co-occurrence of physical and developmental problems with emotional and conduct disorders, 1999 and 2004 combined

All children   Scotland

	Emotional disorder	No emotional disorder	Conduct disorder	No conduct disorder	All
	Percentage of children with each type of physical complaint				
Asthma	16	13	16	13	13
Eczema	6	12	9	12	12
Hay fever	6	9	10	9	9
Eyesight problems	17	11	10	11	11
Stomach or digestive problems	11	5	7	5	5
Non-food allergy	8	7	3	8	7
Migraine/severe headache	10	5	6	5	5
Bed wetting	10	3	9	3	3
Glue ear/otitis media/grommits	-	2	6	2	2
Hearing problems	3	2	6	2	2
Speech or language problems	8	3	8	3	3
Food allergy	7	4	4	4	4
Difficulty with co-ordination	6	1	4	1	1
Stiffness or deformity of foot	1	1	1	1	1
Heart problems	-	1	-	1	1
Soiling pants	3	1	3	1	1
Muscle disease or weakness	-	1	6	1	1
Kidney/urinary tract problems	6	1	1	1	1
Obesity	2	0	-	1	1
Congenital abnormality	2	0	-	0	0
Epilepsy	2	0	3	0	0
Any blood disorder	2	0	1	0	0
Diabetes	2	1	1	1	1
Cerebral Palsy	-	0	1	0	0
Cancer	2	0	-	0	0
Any physical or developmental problem[1]	**65**	**52**	**63**	**52**	**53**
No problem	35	48	37	48	47
Base (weighted)	*57*	*1498*	*68*	*1488*	*1556*

1. *Some physical complaints are not listed in the table above because of their rarity. They are included in the 'Any physical or developmental problem' category.*

Table **10.7**

Co-occurrence of other mental disorders with emotional and conduct disorders, 1999 and 2004 combined

All children   Scotland

	Emotional disorder	No emotional disorder	Conduct disorder	No conduct disorder	All
		Percentage of children with each type of disorder			
Other mental disorders					
Emotional disorders:					
Anxiety disorders	..	..	13	3	3
Depression	..	..	6	0	1
All emotional disorders	..	..	18	3	4
Conduct disorders:					
Oppositional defiant disorder	11	2	..	..	2
Other conduct disorders	10	2	..	..	3
All conduct disorders	20	4	..	..	4
Hyperkinetic disorders	8	1	17	0	1
Less common disorders	3	1	6	0	1
Any other disorder	**25**	**4**	**34**	**4**	**5**
No (other) disorders	75	96	66	96	95
Base (weighted)	*59*	*1505*	*68*	*1496*	*1564*

Table **10.8**

Parent's view of child's mental health by whether child has an emotional or conduct disorder, 1999 and 2004 combined

All children   Scotland

	Emotional disorder	No emotional disorder	Conduct disorder	No conduct disorder	All
		Percentage of children with each type of problem			
Parent's view of child's mental health					
Emotional problems	23	3	31	2	4
Behavioural problems	29	4	57	3	5
Hyperactivity	8	3	21	2	3
Any of the above	36	7	65	5	8
Base (weighted)	*57*	*1498*	*68*	*1488*	*1556*

Table **10.9**

Teacher's rating of child's basic skills by whether has an emotional or conduct disorder, 1999 and 2004 combined

All children   Scotland

	Emotional disorder	No emotional disorder	Conduct disorder	No conduct disorder	All
	%	%	%	%	%
Reading					
Above average	19	37	16	37	36
Average	37	45	38	45	45
Some difficulty	29	15	31	15	15
Marked difficulty	15	4	15	3	4
Mathematics					
Above average	17	32	11	32	31
Average	46	49	43	50	49
Some difficulty	21	15	35	14	15
Marked difficulty	16	4	11	4	5
Spelling					
Above average	19	28	11	28	27
Average	39	47	28	48	47
Some difficulty	25	19	42	18	19
Marked difficulty	16	6	19	6	6
Base (weighted)	*43*	*1218*	*55*	*1206*	*1259*
Overall scholastic ability[1]					
4 or more years behind	7	1	5	1	1
3 years behind	7	1	5	1	1
2 years behind	10	4	17	4	5
1 year behind	23	12	21	12	12
Equivalent	31	41	40	41	41
1 or more years ahead	23	41	13	41	40
Base (weighted)	*40*	*1143*	*50*	*1132*	*1183*

1. Functioning age-actual age.

Table **10.10**

Whether child has special educational needs by whether has an emotional or conduct disorder, 1999 and 2004 combined

All children   Scotland

	Emotional disorder	No emotional disorder	Conduct disorder	No conduct disorder	All
	%	%	%	%	%
If child has officially recognised special educational needs					
Yes	17	7	22	6	7
No	83	93	78	94	93
Base (weighted)	*43*	*1193*	*54*	*1182*	*1235*

Table **10.11**

Truancy (teacher's report) by whether has an emotional or conduct disorder, 1999 and 2004 combined

All children   Scotland

	Emotional disorder	No emotional disorder	Conduct disorder	No conduct disorder	All
	%	%	%	%	%
Whether plays truant					
Not true	90	96	71	97	96
Somewhat true	4	2	10	2	3
Certainly true	6	1	19	1	2
Base (weighted)	*45*	*1238*	*58*	*1225*	*1283*

Table **10.12**

Exclusions from school (parent's report) by whether has an emotional or conduct disorder, 1999 and 2004 combined

All children   Scotland

	Emotional disorder	No emotional disorder	Conduct disorder	No conduct disorder	All
	%	%	%	%	%
Number of times child has been excluded from school					
None	(92)	96	63	98	96
Once	(4)	2	15	2	2
Twice		0	3	0	0
Three or more times	(4)	1	18	0	1
Base (weighted)	*18*	*648*	*31*	*635*	*666*

Table **10.13**

Parent's GHQ–12 score by whether has an emotional or conduct disorder, 1999 and 2004 combined

All children   Scotland

	Emotional disorder	No emotional disorder	Conduct disorder	No conduct disorder	All
	%	%	%	%	%
Parent's GHQ–12[1]					
0–2	47	78	44	78	76
3–5	23	12	29	12	13
6–8	10	6	10	6	6
9–12	21	4	18	4	5
3 or more	**53**	**22**	**56**	**22**	**24**
Base (weighted)	*57*	*1494*	*68*	*1483*	*1551*

1. For this survey, scores of 3 or more were taken to suggest a severe emotional problem.

Table **10.14**

Family functioning score by whether has an emotional or conduct disorder, 1999 and 2004 combined

All children   Scotland

	Emotional disorder	No emotional disorder	Conduct disorder	No conduct disorder	All
	%	%	%	%	%
Family functioning score[1]					
Up to 1.50	27	35	11	36	35
1.51–2.00	36	48	39	48	47
2.01 –2.50	25	15	39	14	15
2.51 or more	13	2	11	2	2
Unhealthy functioning (2.01 or more)	**38**	**17**	**50**	**16**	**18**
Base (weighted)	*57*	*1492*	*68*	*1481*	*1549*

1. For this survey, scores over 2.0 were taken to suggest unhealthy family functioning.

Table **10.15**

Number of stressful life events by whether has an emotional or conduct disorder, 1999 and 2004 combined

All children   Scotland

	Emotional disorder	No emotional disorder	Conduct disorder	No conduct disorder	All
	%	%	%	%	%
Number of stressful life events					
0	(20)	43	9	44	42
1	(42)	32	31	33	32
2	(5)	16	31	15	16
3	(4)	6	10	6	6
4	(19)	2	10	2	2
5 or more	(9)	1	9	1	2
Two or more events	**(38)**	**25**	**60**	**24**	**25**
Base (weighted)	*18*	*649*	*30*	*637*	*667*

Table **10.16**

Deliberate self-harm by whether has an emotional or conduct disorder, 1999 and 2004 combined

Scotland

	Emotional disorder	No emotional disorder	Conduct disorder	No conduct disorder	All
	Percentage of children who have tried to harm, hurt or kill themselves				
All children					
Parent's report	6	1	11	1	2
Base (weighted)	*46*	*1469*	*61*	*1454*	*1514*

Sampling, weighting and adjustment procedures

Sampling procedures

The sampling frame

The sample was drawn from the Child Benefit Register (CBR) held by the Department for Work and Pensions' Child Benefit Centre (CBC). The principal advantage of this frame over alternatives is that the CBR lists children and their date of birth, so the sample can be identified directly. This means that response can be maximised by avoiding an initial sifting step, and survey costs can be contained by avoiding the collection of the information needed to establish the eligibility of different addresses. A second advantage of the CBR sample, compared with that of a PAF-based sift, is that it is possible to select the children with equal probabilities and so avoid weights that are required when one child is selected per household, with the consequent reduction in effective sample size.

The Department for Work and Pensions believe that Child Benefit is claimed by virtually all the eligible population in Britain, though there is some delay in claiming for new babies. The register should therefore provide almost complete coverage of children in the required age group (5–16) in Britain, although it excludes children in foster care and those living in non-private households.

Of the 8,040,445 eligible records on the CBR 98 per cent had a valid postcode sector. The remaining 2 per cent of addresses that did not have a valid postcode sector were excluded from the sample, as was a further 0.25 per cent in sectors that were considered too small to be viable (i.e. had fewer than 100 children). In addition, some children were not accessible for sampling because they were considered sensitive cases by CBC. It is assumed that these represent a random sub-sample that will not create any coverage bias.

Stratification and selection of sectors

The sampling design for the survey involved a two-stage process: the selection of 426 postal sectors and then 29 children within each sector.

The CBC provided ONS with a list of postcode sectors with counts of eligible children whose parents were in receipt of Child Benefit. These postcode sectors were linked to the current version of the Postcode Address File (PAF) to establish their validity, as mentioned above. Any sectors which contained fewer than 100 children were excluded from the sampling frame.

The frame was then stratified by government office region (GOR) and within that by socio-economic group (SEG). In England and Scotland the sectors were selected with probability proportional to the number of eligible children: 378 sectors in England and 37 sectors in Scotland. In Wales, for

financial reasons, a half sample of 11 sectors was selected. The data have been weighted to take account of any imbalance in the distribution of sectors by geographical area.

CBC were supplied with the list of 426 postal sectors and asked to select a random sample of 29 children from each area, using date of birth to establish age eligibility. Five sectors contained fewer than 29 children resulting in a shortfall of 60 families. The set sample therefore consisted of 12,294 families.

The sampling design results in a self-weighting sample in which each child should have the same probability of selection. However, there was some delay between sampling the areas and sampling the children within the areas so that the size measure used to select the children sample was inaccurate in some areas. Also, as noted above, a small number of children were withdrawn by the Agency prior to drawing the sample of children. As a result, the final sampling probabilities for the children were not exactly equal. The weighting procedure corrects for this.

Response

As discussed in Chapter 3, interviews were achieved with 76 per cent of the parents approached, representing 65 per cent of the original set sample. Table A1 shows that there was considerable regional variation in response, the rate ranging from 69 per cent in London to 81 per cent in the South West. The weighting procedure described in the following section corrects for this variation.

Weighting procedures

Weighting was carried out in two stages. First, weights were applied to correct for the unequal sampling probabilities of the children which arose because of the delay between selecting the area and children samples (see above). Respondents were then weighted to represent the age/sex/region structure of the total population of children and young people aged 5–16 in Great Britain, using ONS population figures for April–June 2004. The weights were calculated separately for boys and girls aged 5–9, 10–15 and 16. Tables A2–A4 show both unscaled and scaled weights. The former allow the data to be grossed to population figures. The latter scale the weights so that the number of respondents in each age/sex group matches the total number of interviews carried out in that group. The tables in the report show weighted bases using the scaled weights.

Adjustment procedures for teacher non-response

The assessments of mental disorders among children and young people by psychiatrists were based on data obtained from the parent, the child (aged 11–16), and the teacher. In most cases, data were available from both the parent and child where appropriate, but for a substantial number of cases (17 per cent), the teacher did not provide any information.

We can assume that, given a complete set of data from both home and school, the psychiatrists would on average, make the right assessment. Therefore, if they were able to use both home and school information to assess all children in the population and we were able to average the results of this census over a large number of repeats under identical circumstances, they would arrive at the prevalence level in the population. Therefore if this complete information were available for all sampled children in the survey, the estimated prevalence level would be unbiased for the actual prevalence level, differing only through sampling error and response error.

On the other hand, if repeated censuses were taken but collecting only the home information, another average prevalence would be measured. The question is: would the prevalence level measured with the school and home information taken together be the same as with just the home information? If the measures were the same, then we would not need to carry out adjustments for the missing teacher data. If the measures were different, some adjustment factor would need to be incorporated into the reported data.

Estimating and measuring the difference in the two measures

The evidence for the need to carry out this readjustment comes from looking at the ratio of parent-based to clinical-based diagnoses in no teacher information (t=0) and with teacher information (t=1) groups. If the ratio is the same, it suggests that having the teacher report doesn't make a significant contribution. If the ratio is higher for the t=1 group, it suggests that clinical diagnoses underestimate prevalence in the absence of teacher reports.

Estimating and measuring the difference in the two measures

Table A5 shows the prevalence rates for the three types of disorder and for any disorder under the conditions of no teacher information (t=0) and with teacher (t=1) information. Table A6 shows the ratio of clinical-parent assessments under these two conditions. The ratios were higher when the teacher information was available for all disorders but particularly for conduct and hyperkinetic disorders. Thus, the clinical diagnoses under-estimate prevalence in the absence of teacher reports. A similar pattern was observed in 1999.

These findings fit in with clinical experience, namely, that teacher reports contribute relatively little to the diagnosis of

emotional disorders but make a substantial difference to the diagnosis of conduct and hyperkinetic disorders, though for rather different reasons. As far as conduct disorder is concerned, the key issue is that there are a lot of children who are oppositional, aggressive and antisocial at school but not at home. Psychiatrists rarely get to know about these children unless they have a teacher report. As far as hyperkinetic disorders are concerned, there are many children where the parental evidence is inconclusive and where the teacher report tips the balance, (Ford et al 2005).

The adjustment factors shown in Table A7 were applied to the prevalence rates of mental disorders incorporated in all the tables in Chapter 4. They were calculated on the raw number according to the following rules.

(a) Calculate revised number of children with each clinically-assessed type of mental disorder with no teacher data:

$$N(clin)_{revised} = \frac{N(clin)_{t=1} \times N(parent)_{t=0}}{N(parent)t=1}$$

$N(clin)_{t=1}$ = Number of children with disorder from a clinical assessment with teacher data.

$N(parent)_{t=1}$ = Number of children with disorder from a parent only assessment with teacher data.

$N(parent)_{t=0}$ = Number of children with disorder from a parent only assessment with no teacher data.

(b) Calculate adjustment factor:

$$\text{Adjustment factor} = \frac{N(clin)_{revised} + N(clin)_{t=1}}{N(clin)_{t=0} + N(clin)_{t=1}}$$

The adjustment factors used in the 1999 and 2004 surveys were very similar. For presenting joint estimates of prevalence the adjusted numbers from the two datasets were added together.

References

Ford T, Goodman R and Melter H (2003) The British Child and Adolescent Mental Health Survey 1999. The prevalence of DSM-IV disorder. *Journal of the American Academy of Child and Adolescent Psychiatry* **42**, 1203–12110.

Table A1

Response by Government Office Region

Region	Response rate	Number interviewed	Number approached
1. North East	70	328	468
2. North West and Merseyside	75	1,000	1,339
3. Yorkshire and Humberside	79	763	968
4. East Midlands	79	635	804
5. West Midlands	73	787	1,079
6. Eastern	78	783	1,005
7. London	69	881	1,268
8. South East	77	1,144	1,481
9. South West	81	723	894
10. Wales	79	212	269
11. Scotland	78	721	920
Total	**76**	**7,977**	**10,495**

Table A2

Boys and girls age 5–9 by Government Office Region

Region	Boys aged 5–9				Girls aged 5–9			
	Unweighted numbers in survey	ONS population estimates	Grossed weight	Scaled weight	Unweighted numbers in survey	ONS population estimates	Grossed weight	Scaled weight
1 North East	69	74,907	1085.60	1.009	64	71,775	1121.48	1.041
2 North West and Merseyside	208	209,490	1007.16	0.936	193	200,004	1036.29	0.962
4 Yorkshire and Humberside	158	155,014	981.01	0.912	130	148,380	1141.38	1.059
5 East Midlands	113	130,619	1155.92	1.074	115	123,850	1076.96	1.000
6 West Midlands	162	169,219	1044.56	0.971	164	161,158	982.67	0.912
7 Eastern	162	173,113	1068.60	0.993	164	164,963	1005.87	0.934
8 London	193	231,854	1201.32	1.116	159	222,706	1400.67	1.300
9 South East	261	253,082	969.66	0.901	236	240,001	1016.95	0.944
10 South West	149	146,795	985.20	0.916	155	139,699	901.28	0.837
11 Wales	39	90,955	2332.17	2.167	44	86,641	1969.12	1.828
12 Scotland	143	148,019	1035.01	0.962	154	140,834	914.51	0.849
Total	**1657**	**1783,065**			**1578**	**1700,011**		

Table A3

Boys and girls age 10 –15 by Government Office Region

Region	Boys aged 10–15				Girls aged 10–15			
	Unweighted numbers in survey	ONS population estimates	Grossed weight	Scaled weight	Unweighted numbers in survey	ONS population estimates	Grossed weight	Scaled weight
1 North East	95	100,581	1058.74	0.986	79	96,135	1216.89	1.108
2 North West and Merseyside	276	281,906	1021.40	0.951	235	267,555	1138.53	1.037
4 Yorkshire and Humberside	212	203,636	960.55	0.895	201	194,894	969.62	0.883
5 East Midlands	183	171,048	934.69	0.870	171	161,650	945.32	0.861
6 West Midlands	198	219,251	1107.33	1.031	195	208,622	1069.85	0.974
7 Eastern	197	216,224	1097.58	1.022	199	207,634	1043.39	0.950
8 London	240	270,219	1125.91	1.049	231	261,054	1130.10	1.029
9 South East	297	323,000	1087.54	1.013	278	305,029	1097.23	0.999
10 South West	197	193,420	981.83	0.914	162	184,983	1141.87	1.040
11 Wales	58	120,159	2071.71	1.929	56	113,847	2032.97	1.851
12 Scotland	183	194,181	1061.01	0.988	185	185,929	1005.02	0.915
Total	**2,136**	**2293,624**			**1,992**	**2187,331**		

Table A4

Boys and girls age 16 by Government Office Region

Region	Boys aged 16				Girls aged 16			
	Unweighted numbers in survey	ONS population estimates	Grossed weight	Scaled weight	Unweighted numbers in survey	ONS population estimates	Grossed weight	Scaled weight
1 North East	13	17,524	1,348.00	1.106	8	16,669	2083.63	1.669
2 North West and Merseyside	44	47,869	1,087.93	0.892	44	45,721	1039.11	0.832
4 Yorkshire and Humberside	32	34,001	1,062.53	0.872	30	33,113	1103.77	0.884
5 East Midlands	26	29,029	1,116.50	0.916	27	27,302	1011.19	0.810
6 West Midlands	26	36,885	1,418.65	1.164	42	35,009	833.55	0.668
7 Eastern	35	36,118	1,031.94	0.847	26	34,740	1336.15	1.070
8 London	34	44,737	1,315.79	1.079	24	42,377	1765.71	1.414
9 South East	34	54,462	1,601.82	1.314	38	51,895	1365.66	1.094
10 South West	29	33,094	1,141.17	0.936	31	31,826	1026.65	0.822
11 Wales	10	20,378	2,037.80	1.672	5	19,473	3894.60	3.119
12 Scotland	35	33,549	958.54	0.786	21	31,506	1500.29	1.201
Total	**318**	**387,646**			**296**	**369,631**		

Table **A5**

Prevalence of mental disorders with and without teacher data by type of assessment

	Clinical diagnoses			Parental assessments		
	T=0	T=1	All	T=0	T=1	All
Emotional disorders	4.0	3.4	3.5	3.8	2.7	3.0
Conduct disorders	5.1	5.2	5.1	4.1	2.7	3.1
Hyperkinesis	1.7	1.3	1.4	1.1	0.6	0.7
Other	1.4	1.2	1.3	1.7	1.1	1.3
Any disorder	9.2	9.0	9.0	7.1	5.4	5.9

Table **A6**

Ratio of parent-based to clinical-based diagnoses by whether teacher data obtained

	No teacher data	With teacher data
	T=0	T=1
Emotional disorders	1.05	1.26
Conduct disorders	1.25	1.89
Hyperkinesis	1.50	2.08
Other	0.85	1.07
Any disorder	1.29	1.66

Table **A7**

Final adjustment factors

Disorder	Adjustment factor
Emotional disorders	1.05
Conduct disorders	1.13
Hyperkinesis	1.12
Other disorders	1.07
Any disorder	1.07

Statistical terms and their interpretation

Confidence interval

The percentages quoted in the text of this report represent summary information about a variable (e.g. presence of a mental disorder) based on the sample of people interviewed in this study. However, extrapolation from these sample statistics is required in order to make inferences about the distribution of that particular variable in the population. This is done by calculating confidence intervals around the statistic in question. These confidence intervals indicate the range within which the 'true' (or population) percentage is likely to lie. Where 95 per cent confidence intervals are calculated, this simply indicates that one is '95 per cent confident' that the population percentage lies within this range. (More accurately, it indicates that if repeated samples were drawn from the population, the true percentage would lie within this range in 95 per cent of the samples).

Confidence intervals are calculated on the basis of the sampling error (q.v.). The upper 95 per cent confidence intervals are calculated by adding the sampling error multiplied by 1.96 to the sample percentage or mean. The lower confidence interval is derived by subtracting the same value. Ninety-nine per cent confidence intervals can also be calculated, by replacing the value 1.96 by the value 2.58.

Sampling errors

The sampling error is a measure of the degree to which a percentage (or other summary statistic) would vary if repeatedly calculated in a series of samples. For example, if the prevalence rate of a mental disorder was calculated for a random sample of children and young people drawn from the population at large, then another sample drawn and the rate calculated again, its value would be unlikely to be identical to the first. If this process were continued, the rate would continue to vary from sample to sample. Thus, the sampling error provides a measure of this variability, and is used in the calculation of confidence intervals and statistical significance tests. In this survey a multi-stage stratified sampling design was used instead of simple random sampling. To take account of this design, sampling errors were calculated using STATA. However, this does not affect the interpretation of the sampling errors or their use in the calculation of confidence intervals.

Tables C1 – C7 in Appendix C show the sampling errors and confidence intervals for a range of variables.

Multiple logistic regression and Odds Ratios

Logistic regression analysis has been used in the analysis of the survey data to provide a measure of the effect of various sociodemographic variables on the prevalence of mental disorders among children. Unlike the cross-tabulations presented elsewhere in the report, multiple logistic regression estimates the effect of any sociodemographic variable while controlling for the confounding effects of other variables in the analysis.

Logistic regression produces an estimate of the probability of an event occurring when an individual is in a particular sociodemographic category compared to a reference category. This effect is measured in terms of odds. For example, Table 4.15 shows that being in a family in which parents are classified as having 'no educational qualifications' increases the odds of having an emotional disorder compared to the reference category of 'any educational qualifications'. The amount by which the odds of this disorder actually increases is shown by the Adjusted Odds Ratio (OR). In this case, the OR is 1.52 indicating that being a child of parents with no educational qualifications increases the odds of having an emotional disorder by about one half, controlling for the possible confounding effects of the other variables in the statistical model, for example, age, sex, family type and family employment.

Confidence intervals around an Odds Ratio

The confidence intervals around odds ratios can be interpreted in the manner described earlier in this section. For example, Table 4.20, shows an odds ratio of 6.10 for the association between sex and hyperkinetic disorders, with a confidence interval from 3.39 to 10.99, indicating that the 'true' (i.e., population) OR is likely to lie between these two values. If the confidence interval does not include 1.00 then the OR is likely to be significant - that is, the association between the variable and the odds of a particular disorder is unlikely to be due to chance. If the interval includes 1.00, then it is possible that the 'true' OR is actually 1.00, that is, no increase in odds can be attributed to the variable.

Odds ratios and how to use them multiplicatively

The odds ratios presented in the tables show the adjusted odds due solely to membership of one particularly category – for example, being a boy rather than a girl. However, odds for more than one category can be combined by multiplying them together. This provides an estimate of the increased odds of a disorder or symptom due to being a member of more than one category at once – for example, being a boy and aged 11–15. For example, in Table 4.20 being a boy rather than a girl increases the odds of any mental disorder (OR=1.52), while being aged 11–15 (compared with 5-10 year olds) also independently increases the odds (OR=1.73). The increased odds for 11- to 15-year-old boys compared with 5- to 10-year-old girls is therefore the product of the two independent odds ratios, 2.63.

Sampling errors

Appendix C

This survey involved a multi-stage sampling design with both clustering and stratification. Clustering can lead to a substantial increase in standard error if the households or individuals within the primary sampling units (postal sectors) are relatively homogenous but the primary sampling units differ from one another. Stratification tends to reduce standard error and is of most advantage where the stratification factor is related to the characteristics of interest on the survey.

The effect of a complex sampling design on the precision of survey estimates is usually quantified by means of the design factor (deft). For any survey estimate, the deft is calculated as the ratio of the standard error allowing for the full complexity of the survey design to the standard error assuming a simple random sample. The standard error based on a simple random sample (se_{srs}) multiplied by the deft gives the standard error of a complex design (se):

$$se(p) = deft \times se_{srs}(p)$$

where:

$$se_{srs}(p) = \sqrt{p(1-p)/N}$$

The formula to measure whether the differences between the percentages is likely to be due entirely to sampling error for a complex design is:

$$se(p_1-p_2) = \sqrt{(deft^2_1 \; p1(100-p_1)/n_1 + deft^2_2 \; p_2(100-p_2)/n_2)}$$

where p_1 and p_2 are observed percentages for the two subsamples and n_1 and n_2 are the subsample sizes.

The 95 per cent confidence interval for the difference between two percentages is then given by:

$$(p_1-p_2) +/- 1.96 \times se(p_1-p_2)$$

If this confidence interval includes zero then the observed difference is considered to be a result of chance variation in the sample. If the interval does not include zero then it is unlikely (less than 5 per cent probability) that the observed differences could have occurred by chance.

Tables C1 to C7 show standard errors for selected variables for children in each of the main disorder categories. The standard errors of survey measures which are not presented in these tables, or for other subgroups, may be estimated by applying an appropriate value of deft to the standard error for a simple random sample. The choice of an appropriate value of deft will vary according to whether the basic survey measure is included in the tables. Since most deft values are relatively small (1.2 or less) the absolute effect of adjusting sampling errors to take account of the survey's complex design will be small.

Table C1

Standard errors and 95% confidence intervals for prevalence of mental disorders by sex, age and ethnicity

Base	Characteristic	%(p) adj	Sample size	True standard error of p	Deft	95% confidence interval	
All children	Emotional disorders	3.71	7,977	0.25	1.13	3.23	4.20
	Conduct disorders	5.77	7,977	0.32	1.16	5.13	6.40
	Hyperkinetic disorders	1.51	7,977	0.15	1.07	1.21	1.82
	Any mental disorder	9.64	7,977	0.42	1.22	8.82	10.47
Boys	Emotional disorders	3.13	4,111	0.28	1.00	2.58	3.67
	Conduct disorders	7.49	4,111	0.48	1.09	6.56	8.43
	Hyperkinetic disorders	2.58	4,111	0.28	1.08	2.03	3.14
	Any mental disorder	11.42	4,111	0.57	1.11	10.30	12.54
Girls	Emotional disorders	4.34	3,866	0.38	1.12	3.60	5.08
	Conduct disorders	3.93	3,866	0.36	1.07	3.23	4.63
	Hyperkinetic disorders	0.38	3,866	0.09	0.88	0.20	0.55
	Any mental disorder	7.75	3,866	0.50	1.12	6.77	8.73
5- to 10-year-olds	Emotional disorders	2.36	3,925	0.27	1.01	1.83	2.89
	Conduct disorders	4.88	3,925	0.38	1.03	4.14	5.62
	Hyperkinetic disorders	1.59	3,925	0.20	0.97	1.19	1.99
	Any mental disorder	7.70	3,925	0.47	1.07	6.77	8.63
11- to 16-year-olds	Emotional disorders	5.03	4,052	0.37	1.04	4.31	5.74
	Conduct disorders	6.62	4,052	0.49	1.17	5.66	7.58
	Hyperkinetic disorders	1.44	4,052	0.21	1.08	1.02	1.86
	Any mental disorder	11.53	4,052	0.62	1.20	10.30	12.75
5- to 10-year-olds: boys	Emotional disorders	2.20	2,008	0.34	1.02	1.53	2.88
	Conduct disorders	6.89	2,008	0.57	0.95	5.77	8.02
	Hyperkinetic disorders	2.74	2,008	0.38	0.98	2.00	3.48
	Any mental disorder	10.16	2,008	0.70	1.01	8.78	11.54
11- to 16-year-olds: boys	Emotional disorders	4.01	2,103	0.40	0.92	3.22	4.80
	Conduct disorders	8.07	2,103	0.72	1.13	6.67	9.48
	Hyperkinetic disorders	2.43	2,103	0.38	1.07	1.68	3.18
	Any mental disorder	12.63	2,103	0.84	1.12	10.98	14.28
5- to 10-year-olds: girls	Emotional disorders	2.53	1,917	0.40	1.09	1.74	3.31
	Conduct disorders	2.78	1,917	0.43	1.07	1.94	3.61
	Hyperkinetic disorders	0.39	1,917	0.12	0.81	0.15	0.63
	Any mental disorder	5.12	1,917	0.54	1.03	4.06	6.17
11- 16-year-olds: girls	Emotional disorders	6.12	1,949	0.61	1.10	4.92	7.32
	Conduct disorders	5.06	1,949	0.58	1.10	3.92	6.20
	Hyperkinetic disorders	0.36	1,949	0.14	0.95	0.01	0.63
	Any mental disorder	10.34	1,949	0.80	1.12	8.77	11.91

The standard errors are slight under–estimates because they take account of adjustment factors which are estimated from the same sample.

Table **C1** (contd)

Standard errors and 95% confidence intervals for prevalence of mental disorders by sex, age and ethnicity

Base	Characteristic	%(p) adj	Sample size	True standard error of p	Deft	95% confidence interval	
All 5- to 10-year-olds	Separation anxiety	0.55	3,925	0.11	0.92	0.33	0.77
	Specific phobia	0.73	3,925	0.14	1.01	0.46	1.01
	Social phobia	0.06	3,925	0.04	1.02	−0.02	0.13
	Generalised anxiety	0.25	3,925	0.08	0.97	0.09	0.41
	Depression	0.25	3,925	0.08	0.96	0.09	0.40
	Oppositional defiant disorder	3.46	3,925	0.34	1.08	2.81	4.12
	Unsocialised conduct disorder	0.60	3,925	0.13	0.98	0.35	0.86
	Socialised conduct disorder	0.29	3,925	0.09	1.00	0.11	0.47
	Autistic Spectrum Disorder	1.02	3,925	0.19	1.13	0.65	1.39
All 11- to 16-year-olds	Separation anxiety	0.32	4,052	0.01	1.06	0.13	0.51
	Specific phobia	0.88	4,052	0.16	1.08	0.56	1.19
	Social phobia	0.55	4,052	0.12	1.00	0.32	0.78
	Generalised anxiety	1.24	4,052	0.17	0.94	0.91	1.57
	Depression	1.44	4,052	0.20	1.05	1.05	1.84
	Oppositional defiant disorder	2.63	4,052	0.27	1.02	2.09	3.16
	Unsocialised conduct disorder	1.00	4,052	0.18	1.10	0.65	1.37
	Socialised conduct disorder	2.23	4,052	0.27	1.09	1.70	2.76
	Autistic Spectrum Disorder	0.76	4,052	0.15	1.05	0.47	1.06
White	Emotional disorders	3.81	6,920	0.26	1.01	3.31	4.32
	Conduct disorders	6.09	6,920	0.35	1.15	5.40	6.79
	Hyperkinetic disorders	1.67	6,920	0.17	1.07	1.33	2.02
	Any mental disorder	10.05	6,920	0.45	1.19	9.18	10.93
Black	Emotional disorders	3.26	325	1.05	1.09	1.20	5.31
	Conduct disorders	5.86	325	1.41	1.06	3.01	8.62
	Hyperkinetic disorders	0.61	325	0.43	0.99	−0.24	1.46
	Any mental disorder	9.18	325	2.03	1.28	5.20	13.15
Indian	Emotional disorders	1.44	199	0.97	1.12	−0.45	3.34
	Conduct disorders	0.63	199	0.62	1.04	−0.58	1.84
	Hyperkinetic disorders	0.00	199	0.00	–	0.00	0.00
	Any mental disorder	2.61	199	1.20	1.03	0.25	4.96
Pakistani and Bangladeshi	Emotional disorders	4.27	307	1.60	1.35	1.14	7.40
	Conduct disorders	3.98	307	1.03	0.86	1.97	5.99
	Hyperkinetic disorders	0.00	307	0.00	–	0.00	0.00
	Any mental disorder	7.81	307	1.76	1.11	4.36	11.26
Other	Emotional disorders	2.79	222	1.14	1.04	0.55	5.03
	Conduct disorders	2.86	222	1.15	1.00	0.59	5.12
	Hyperkinetic disorders	1.44	222	0.83	1.01	−0.19	3.08
	Any mental disorder	6.94	222	1.88	1.01	3.25	10.63

The standard errors are slight under–estimates because they take account of adjustment factors which are estimated from the same sample.

Table C2

Standard errors and 95% confidence intervals for prevalence of mental disorders by family and household characteristics

Base	Characteristic	%(p) adj	Sample size	True standard error of p	Deft	95% confidence interval	
Married/cohabiting parents	Emotional disorders	2.64	6,039	0.22	1.02	2.22	3.06
	Conduct disorders	4.45	6,039	0.30	1.05	3.86	5.03
	Hyperkinetic disorders	1.21	6,039	0.15	0.99	0.92	1.50
	Any mental disorder	7.70	6,039	0.38	1.08	6.95	8.45
Single lone parent	Emotional disorders	4.92	684	0.89	1.06	3.18	6.66
	Conduct disorders	9.57	684	1.20	1.01	7.21	11.92
	Hyperkinetic disorders	2.57	684	0.64	1.02	1.31	3.83
	Any mental disorder	13.41	684	1.39	1.04	10.69	16.14
Previously married lone parent	Emotional disorders	8.21	1,254	0.88	1.10	6.49	9.93
	Conduct disorders	9.97	1,254	0.98	1.08	8.04	11.89
	Hyperkinetic disorders	2.38	1,254	0.49	1.07	1.42	3.33
	Any mental disorder	16.86	1,254	1.22	1.11	14.46	19.25
Both parents/lone parent working	Emotional disorders	2.76	5,200	0.25	1.07	2.27	3.26
	Conduct disorders	4.01	5,200	0.32	1.12	3.37	4.64
	Hyperkinetic disorders	1.22	5,200	0.18	1.13	0.86	1.57
	Any mental disorder	7.48	5,200	0.43	1.13	6.64	8.32
One parent working	Emotional disorders	3.44	1,401	0.53	1.05	2.41	4.47
	Conduct disorders	6.02	1,401	0.66	0.97	4.74	7.30
	Hyperkinetic disorders	1.14	1,401	0.27	0.89	0.62	1.66
	Any mental disorder	9.30	1,401	0.81	1.00	7.72	10.89
No parent working	Emotional disorders	8.46	1,203	0.89	1.08	6.72	10.20
	Conduct disorders	13.30	1,203	1.07	1.02	11.21	15.40
	Hyperkinetic disorders	3.33	1,203	0.56	1.02	2.24	4.42
	Any mental disorder	19.52	1,203	1.25	1.06	17.06	21.98
Owner occupiers	Emotional disorders	2.61	5,667	0.23	1.04	2.17	3.06
	Conduct disorders	3.81	5,667	0.28	1.02	3.27	4.35
	Hyperkinetic disorders	1.06	5,667	0.14	0.97	0.79	1.34
	Any mental disorder	7.02	5,667	0.36	1.03	6.30	7.73
Social sector tenants	Emotional disorders	6.30	1,718	0.66	1.01	5.01	7.59
	Conduct disorders	11.80	1,718	0.85	1.02	10.14	13.46
	Hyperkinetic disorders	2.35	1,718	0.39	1.01	1.59	3.12
	Any mental disorder	16.70	1,718	1.05	1.12	14.65	18.75
Private renters	Emotional disorders	6.67	587	1.06	1.01	4.60	8.75
	Conduct disorders	6.85	587	1.10	1.00	4.70	9.01
	Hyperkinetic disorders	3.33	587	0.82	1.06	1.72	4.95
	Any mental disorder	14.12	587	1.55	1.05	11.09	17.16

The standard errors are slight under-estimates because they take account of adjustment factors which are estimated from the same sample.

Table **C3**

Standard errors and 95% confidence intervals for prevalence of mental disorders by area characteristics

Base	Characteristic	%(p) adj	Sample size	True standard error of p	Deft	95% confidence interval	
Wealthy achievers[1]	Emotional disorders	2.44	2,041	0.37	1.04	1.72	3.15
	Conduct disorders	2.51	2,041	0.39	1.05	1.74	3.27
	Hyperkinetic disorders	1.07	2,041	0.23	0.96	0.61	1.53
	Any mental disorder	5.84	2,041	0.55	1.02	4.76	6.92
Urban Prosperity[1]	Emotional disorders	2.59	600	0.78	1.19	1.07	4.11
	Conduct disorders	3.97	600	0.89	1.07	2.22	5.72
	Hyperkinetic disorders	1.29	600	0.53	1.11	0.25	2.33
	Any mental disorder	7.44	600	1.16	1.06	5.16	9.71
Comfortably off[1]	Emotional disorders	3.37	2,057	0.44	1.06	2.52	4.23
	Conduct disorders	4.87	2,057	0.45	0.89	3.98	5.76
	Hyperkinetic disorders	1.21	2,057	0.25	0.97	0.72	1.69
	Any mental disorder	8.16	2,057	0.61	0.98	6.96	9.36
Moderate means[1]	Emotional disorders	4.23	1,335	0.62	1.01	3.02	5.44
	Conduct disorders	7.20	1,335	0.79	1.06	5.65	8.76
	Hyperkinetic disorders	1.72	1,335	0.47	1.25	0.80	2.64
	Any mental disorder	11.66	1,335	1.06	1.17	9.58	13.74
Hard pressed[1]	Emotional disorders	5.32	1,882	0.59	1.12	4.16	6.48
	Conduct disorders	9.93	1,882	0.73	0.99	8.50	11.36
	Hyperkinetic disorders	2.29	1,882	0.36	0.98	1.59	2.99
	Any mental disorder	14.61	1,882	0.95	1.12	12.74	16.47
England	Emotional disorders	4.02	7,044	0.28	1.14	3.48	4.56
	Conduct disorders	6.03	7,044	0.35	1.14	5.35	6.72
	Hyperkinetic disorders	1.51	7,044	0.16	1.00	1.21	1.82
	Any mental disorder	10.16	7,044	0.45	1.20	9.27	11.04
Scotland	Emotional disorders	2.88	721	0.67	1.01	1.57	4.19
	Conduct disorders	5.22	721	1.23	1.34	2.81	7.63
	Hyperkinetic disorders	1.44	721	0.49	1.01	0.48	2.41
	Any mental disorder	8.35	721	1.67	1.51	5.08	11.63

1. Acorn classification.
The standard errors are slight under-estimates because they take account of adjustment factors which are estimated from the same sample.

Table C4

Standard errors and 95% confidence intervals for key characteristics of children with emotional disorders

Base	Characteristic	%(p) adj	Sample size	True standard error of p	Deft	95% confidence interval	
Children with	Parental GHQ score 3–12	51.45	293	2.88	0.97	45.78	57.13
emotional	2 or more stressful life events	57.58	293	2.90	0.99	51.87	63.29
disorders	Unhealthy family functioning (2.01 or more)	31.46	276	2.83	0.99	25.89	37.04
	Strengths score in lowest quartile (<37)[1]	58.11	278	2.65	0.88	52.88	63.33
	Social aptitude score in lowest quartile (<21)[1]	47.79	275	2.83	0.92	42.22	53.37
	Social support score in lowest quartile (<18)[1]	41.98	154	4.30	1.08	33.51	50.45
	Enjoys living in neighbourhood 'a lot'	38.47	155	3.93	1.00	30.72	46.21
	Participates in groups, clubs or organisations	57.13	201	3.73	1.07	49.78	64.48
	Smoker (regular or occasional)	23.57	153	3.30	0.96	17.07	30.07
	Regular drinker (once a week or more)	9.91	153	2.24	0.93	5.49	14.33
	Ever used cannabis	17.20	153	3.27	1.07	10.75	23.65

Some of the proportions are different from those shown in the main tables because they are based on 2004 data only.
1. Based on parent's report.

Table C5

Standard errors and 95% confidence intervals for key characteristics of children with conduct disorders

Base	Characteristic	%(p) adj	Sample size	True standard error of p	Deft	95% confidence interval	
Children with	Parental GHQ score 3–12	46.73	420	2.50	1.00	41.81	51.65
conduct	2 or more stressful life events	48.86	420	2.39	0.96	44.14	53.57
disorders	Unhealthy family functioning (2.01 or more)	41.50	406	2.51	1.01	36.55	46.45
	Strengths score in lowest quartile (<37)[1]	76.69	399	2.24	1.04	72.27	81.11
	Social aptitude score in lowest quartile (<21)[1]	68.77	398	2.34	0.99	64.16	73.38
	Social support score in lowest quartile (<18)[1]	53.72	170	3.92	1.02	46.00	61.45
	Enjoys living in neighbourhood 'a lot'	43.08	171	3.88	1.02	35.43	50.73
	Participates in groups, clubs or organisations	47.41	246	3.14	0.98	41.22	53.59
	Smoker (regular or occasional)	39.83	170	3.85	1.02	32.25	47.41
	Regular drinker (once a week or more)	26.62	170	3.20	0.94	20.31	32.93
	Ever used cannabis	28.70	169	3.46	0.99	21.88	35.52

Some of the proportions are different from those shown in the main tables because they are based on 2004 data only.
1. Based on parent's report.

Table **C6**

Standard errors and 95% confidence intervals for key characteristics of children with hyperkinetic disorders

Base	Characteristic	%(p) adj	Sample size	True standard error of p	Deft	95% confidence interval	
Children with	Parental GHQ score 3–12	43.65	109	4.83	1.01	34.13	53.17
hyperkinetic	2 or more stressful life events	46.68	109	4.52	0.94	37.77	55.59
disorders	Unhealthy family functioning (2.01 or more)	34.71	106	4.40	0.95	26.05	43.37
	Strengths score in lowest quartile (<37)[1]	84.41	104	3.46	0.97	77.59	91.23
	Social aptitude score in lowest quartile (<21)[1]	82.54	105	3.72	1.00	75.20	89.88
	Social support score in lowest quartile (<18)[1]	54.38	33	8.18	0.93	38.25	70.51
	Enjoys living in neighbourhood 'a lot'	49.58	35	8.93	1.04	31.99	67.18
	Participates in groups, clubs or organisations	52.71	52	6.97	1.00	38.96	66.46
	Smoker (regular or occasional)	25.54	35	7.51	1.01	10.73	40.35
	Regular drinker (once a week or more)	11.52	35	5.31	0.97	1.06	21.98
	Ever used cannabis	13.50	35	5.70	0.97	2.26	24.73

Some of the proportions are different from those shown in the main tables because they are based on 2004 data only.
1. Based on parent's report.

Table **C7**

Standard errors and 95% confidence intervals for key characteristics of children with autistic spectrum disorder

Base	Characteristic	%(p) adj	Sample size	True standard error of p	Deft	95% confidence interval	
Children with	Parental GHQ score 3-12	30.88	67	5.75	1.01	19.54	42.22
autistic	2 or more stressful life events	36.30	67	5.40	0.92	25.66	46.95
spectrum	Unhealthy family functioning						
disorder	(2.01 or more)	39.45	54	7.30	1.08	25.06	53.84
	Strengths score in lowest quartile (<37)[1]	96.48	52	2.45	0.95	91.66	101.31
	Social aptitude score in lowest quartile (<21)[1]	96.40	58	2.46	0.99	91.55	101.25

Some of the proportions are different from those shown in the main tables because they are based on 2004 data only.
1. Based on parent's report.

Recent research on the Strengths and Difficulties Questionnaire

Appendix D

Appendix D gives a brief description of research on the Strengths and Difficulties Questionnaire (SDQ) over the past five years. The published papers are summarised below in terms of their focus on (a) psychometric properties of the SDQ, (b) comparisons of the performance of the SDQ with the Rutter Scales and the Child Behaviour Checklist (CBCL), and (c) the relationship between the SDQ and subsequent clinical assessments.

Psychometric properties of the SDQ

The first national survey of childhood mental disorders in Great Britain included SDQ data on a representative sample of 10,438, 5- to 15-year-olds. Analysis by Goodman (2001) confirmed the predicted five-factor structure: emotional, conduct, hyperactivity-inattention, peer and prosocial. Reliability was generally satisfactory, whether judged by internal consistency, cross-informant correlation, or retest stability after four to six months.

Muris P et al (2003) examined the psychometric properties of the SDQ in a sample of Dutch young people. A sample of 562 children and young people and their parents completed the SDQ along with a number of other psychopathology measures. Factor analysis of the SDQ yielded the five factors that were consistent with the five hypothesised subscales. They concluded that the internal consistency, test-retest stability and parent-youth agreement of the various SDQ scales were acceptable and that the concurrent validity of the SDQ was good in that its scores correlated in a theoretically meaningful way with other measures of psychopathology.

Muris et al (2004) also looked at the psychometric properties (reliability and validity) of the self-report version of SDQ for younger children: 8- to 13-year-olds. The SDQ was administered to 1,111 non-clinical children. In a subsample, self-report SDQ scores of 439 children with and without behaviour problems were compared, and related inter alia to the teacher version of the SDQ. Although they found the reliability of the self-report SDQ somewhat less satisfactory in the younger children, most other psychometric properties were acceptable and comparable to those obtained in the older children. They concluded that although the self-report SDQ was designed for young people aged 11 years and above, their study suggested that the scale may provide useful information about psychopathological symptoms in children as young as 8 years old.

Woerner, Becker and Rothenberger (2004) carried out a study with the SDQ in Germany. They gathered information from parents, teachers and older children. To allow comparisons with SDQ findings in other countries, they collected data using the German parent-rated form as well as evaluating the scale in both community and clinical samples. Parent ratings were collected for a community-based sample of 930, 6- to 16-year-olds. Statistical evaluation of psychometric properties included a factor analysis verifying the proposed scale structure, assessment of scale homogeneities, and determination of age, gender and social class effects. Based on the distributions of SDQ scores observed in this normative sample, recommended bandings identifying normal, borderline, and clinical ranges were defined for each scale. They reported exact replication of the original scale structure, satisfactory internal reliabilities, and observation of the expected associations with age and gender confirmed the equivalence of the German SDQ parent questionnaire with the English original. Differences between community-based results and clinical groups provided descriptive evidence of a dramatic impact of clinically defined psychiatric status on SDQ scores.

Koskelainen, Sourander and Vauras M (2001) examined the psychometric properties of the self-report version of the SDQ among 1,458 Finnish 13- to 17-year-olds. Their results confirmed the postulated structure of the SDQ self-report. The correlations of the items to their respective subscales ranged from moderate to high. The internal consistency was acceptable on three and somewhat lower on two of the five subscales. In addition, the factor analysis sufficiently confirmed the postulated structure of the SDQ for girls and boys, except for the conduct problem scale of boys, which was fused with emotional symptoms and with hyperactivity. The means of the SDQ self-report total difficulties scores were very similar to those found in the 1999 Great Britain survey.

A study by Malmberg, Rydell and Smedje (2003) investigated the adequacy of the Swedish adaptation of the SDQ (SDQ-Swe). They compared SDQ parent reports on 263, 5- to 15-year-old children drawn from a community sample and a clinical sample of 230 children. They found that the Swedish adaptation of the SDQ differentiated well between the community and the psychiatric samples, the latter displaying more symptoms, fewer strengths and more social impairment. ROC analyses showed satisfactory sensitivity and specificity of the principal scales of the SDQ-Swe at proposed cut-offs.

A study by Ronning et al (2004) used the Norwegian, self-report version of the Strengths and Difficulties Questionnaire (SDQ-S). The survey included 4,167 young people aged 11 to 16 years, attending 66 primary and secondary schools in Northern Norway. Structural analysis of the instrument, including confirmatory factor analysis, internal consistency and intra- and cross-scale correlations revealed somewhat variable psychometric properties. Norwegian cut-off points were similar to those found in other Scandinavian studies. About one-third of the subjects reported at least minor perceived difficulties, while about 5 per cent reported definite or severe difficulties. These difficulties were strongly associated with all symptom scales. Girls reported a significantly higher level of emotional problems and better prosocial functioning. Boys reported significantly higher scores on the externalising scales and on peer problems.

Comparison of the SDQ with Rutter scales and the Child Behaviour Checklist (CBCL)

Goodman (1997) administered the Strengths and Difficulties Questionnaire (SDQ) along with Rutter questionnaires (Rutter *et al*, 1970) to parents and teachers of 403 children drawn from dental and psychiatric clinics. Scores derived from the SDQ and Rutter questionnaires were highly correlated; parent-teacher correlations for the two sets of measures were comparable or favoured the SDQ. The two sets of measures did not differ in their ability to discriminate between psychiatric and dental clinic attenders. Goodman suggests that the SDQ functions as well as the Rutter questionnaires while offering several advantages: a focus on strengths as well as difficulties, better coverage of inattention, peer relationships and prosocial behaviour, a shorter format, and a single form suitable for both parents and teachers. (Achenbach and Edelbrock, 1983).

Goodman R and Scott S (1999) asked parents to complete the SDQ and the CBCL (Achenbach and Edelbrock, 1983) on 132 children aged 4–7 and drawn from psychiatric and dental clinics. They found that scores from the SDQ and CBCL were highly correlated and equally able to discriminate psychiatric from dental cases. As judged against a semi-structured interview, the SDQ was significantly better than the CBCL at detecting inattention and hyperactivity, and at least as good at detecting internalising and externalising problems.

In a Finnish study Koskelainen, Sourander and Kaljonen, 2000, the emotional and behavioural problems of 735, 7- to 15-year-olds were assessed in a community population by the parent-, teacher- and self-reports of the SDQ and with the CBCL and the Youth Self Report. The correlation of the parental SDQ total scores and the Child Behaviour Checklist total scores was 0.75 and the correlation of the self-report SDQ total scores with the Youth Self Report total scores was 0.71.

Klasen *et al* (2000) compared the German versions of the SDQ with the CBCL. Both instruments were completed by the parents of 273 children drawn from psychiatric clinics (163) and from a community sample (110). The children from the community sample also filled in the SDQ self-report and the Youth Self Report (YSR). Scores from the parent and self-rated SDQ and CBCL/YSR were highly correlated and equally able to distinguish between the community and clinic samples, with

the SDQ showing significantly better results regarding the total scores. They were also equally able to distinguish between disorders within the clinic sample, the only significant difference being that the SDQ was better able to differentiate between children with and without hyperactivity-inattention.

Klasen *et al* (2003) reviewed the validation studies carried out on the German version of the Strengths and Difficulties Questionnaire (SDQ-Deu). They reported that it correlated well with the considerably longer German versions of the CBCL and respective teacher and self-report derivatives (TRF, YSR). Both parent-rated instruments were equally able to distinguish between a community and a clinic sample, and between subgroups with and without specified categories of disorders within a clinic sample.

Bettge *et al* (2002) were able to compare the SDQ and the CBCL in the context of a pre-test to a Health Survey for Children and Adolescents in terms of their psychometric properties, their diagnostic power, and the study participants' acceptance of the instruments. With this comparison, the question addressed was which of the two questionnaires was more reliable, valid and acceptable to the participants in describing mental health problems and psychiatric disorders in a population-based survey intended for a target age group of 6- to 17-year-olds. They concluded both instruments detected mental disorders that were established in a clinical interview with equal probability. The self-report tended to be superior to the parents' report in the age group from 11–17 years. The SDQ also had a higher acceptance rate than the CBCL.

Comparisons of the SDQ with subsequent diagnosis

In a study by Goodman *et al* (2000), SDQ predictions were compared with independent psychiatric diagnoses in a community sample of 7,984 5- to 15-year-olds from the 1999 survey in Great Britain. Multi-informant (parents, teachers, older children) SDQs identified young people with a psychiatric diagnosis with a specificity of 94.6 per cent (95 per cent CI 94.1–95.1 per cent) and a sensitivity of 63.3 per cent (59.7–66.9 per cent). The questionnaires identified over 70 per cent of individuals with conduct, hyperactivity, depressive and some anxiety disorders, but under 50 per cent of individuals with specific phobias, separation anxiety and eating disorders. Sensitivity was substantially poorer with single-informant rather than multi-informant SDQs.

Goodman, Renfrew and Mullick (2000) used a computerised algorithm to predict child psychiatric diagnoses on the basis of the symptom and impact scores derived from SDQs completed by parents, teachers and young people. The predictive algorithm generated 'unlikely', 'possible' or 'probable' ratings for four broad categories of disorder: conduct disorders, emotional disorders, hyperactivity disorders, and any psychiatric disorder. The algorithm was applied to 101 patients attending child mental health clinics in Britain and 89 in Bangladesh. The level of chance-corrected agreement between SDQ prediction and an independent clinical diagnosis was substantial and highly significant (Kendall's tau b between 0.49 and 0.73; p < 0.001). A 'probable' SDQ prediction for any given disorder correctly identified 81–91 per cent of the children who definitely had that clinical diagnosis. There were more false positives than false negatives, i.e. the SDQ categories were over-inclusive.

The same computerised algorithm developed by Goodman et al, was used by Mathai, Anderson and Bourne (2004) to examine the level of agreement between clinical diagnoses by a community child and adolescent mental health service (CAMHS) and diagnoses generated by the SDQ. The algorithm was used at a community CAMHS in Australia to predict child psychiatric diagnoses on the basis of the symptom and impact scores derived from the SDQ completed by 130 parents, 101 teachers and 38 young people. These diagnoses were compared with those made by clinicians in a multidisciplinary community outpatient team and an independent clinician that examined the case notes and was blind to the SDQ scores. The level of agreement between SDQ generated diagnoses and clinical team diagnoses was moderate to high, ranging from 0.39 to 0.56. Correlations between the SDQ and an independent clinician ranged from 0.26 to 0.43.

Becker et al (2004) aimed to evaluate the German self-reported SDQ in a clinical setting. SDQ self-reports were collected from 214 in- and out-patients (81 girls and 133 boys) aged 11 to 17 years who were seen at the department of child and adolescent psychiatry of the University of Gottingen. Results obtained with the self-rated questionnaire were compared with the parent and teacher SDQs, corresponding CBCL/YSR scores, and the clinical diagnostic classification. The self-rated version of the SDQ demonstrated good validity with respect to the differentiation between clinically defined cases and non-cases and in detecting various subcategories of psychiatric disorders within the clinic sample.

With the exception of the Goodman, Renfrew and Mullick study which was carried out in Britain and Bangladesh, all of the studies described above regarding the SDQ have been carried out in Europe. Relatively few reports have published SDQ results obtained in other parts of the world Woerner et al (2004) carried out a review of some of the non-European experiences with the SDQ. They presented a selection of projects that have either psychometrically evaluated the

questionnaire, applied it to screen for behaviour disorders, or employed its parent-, teacher- or self-rated versions as research tools. Many of these studies are still in progress or have yet to be published. However, the general conclusions seem to be that experience gained with the SDQ in other continents has supported European evidence of good psychometric properties and its clinical utility.

References

Achenbach T M and Edelbrock C S (1983) *Manual for the Child Behaviour Checklist and Revised Child Behaviour Profile,* Burlington, Vermont, University of Vermont, Department of Psychiatry.

Becker A, Hagenberg N, Roessner V, Woerner W and Rothenberger A (2004) Evaluation of the self-reported SDQ in a clinical setting: do self-reports tell us more than ratings by adult informants? *Eur Child Adolesc Psychiatry* **13 Suppl 2: II,** 17–24.

Bettge S, Ravens-Sieberer U, Wietzker A and Holling H (2002) Methodological comparison between the Child Behavior Checklist and the Strengths and Difficulties Questionnaires. *Gesundheitswesen* **64 Suppl 1,** S 119–124.

Goodman, R (1997) The Strengths and Difficulties Questionnaire: A research note. *Journal of Child Psychology and Psychiatry* **38,** 581–586.

Goodman R (2001) Psychometric properties of the strengths and difficulties questionnaire. *J Am Acad Child Adolesc Psychiatry* **40(11),** 1337–1345

Goodman R, Ford T, Simmons H, Gatward R and Meltzer H (2000) Using the Strengths and Difficulties Questionnaire (SDQ) to screen for child psychiatric disorders in a community sample. *Br J Psychiatry* **Dec:177,** 534–539.

Goodman R, Renfrew D and Mullick M (2000) Predicting type of psychiatric disorder from Strengths and Difficulties Questionnaire (SDQ) scores in child mental health clinics in London and Dhaka. *Eur Child Adolesc Psychiatry* **9(2),** 129–134.

Goodman R and Scott S (1999) Comparing the Strengths and Difficulties Questionnaire and the Child Behavior Checklist: is small beautiful? *J Abnorm Child Psychol.* **27(1),** 17–24.

Klasen H, Woerner W, Wolke D, Meyer R, Overmeyer S, Kaschnitz W, Rothenberger A and Goodman R (2000) Comparing the German versions of the Strengths and Difficulties Questionnaire (SDQ-Deu) and the Child Behavior Checklist. *Eur Child Adolesc Psychiatry.* **9(4),** 271–276

Klasen H, Woerner W, Rothenberger A and Goodman R (2003) German version of the Strength and Difficulties Questionnaire (SDQ-German) – overview and evaluation of initial validation and normative results. *Prax Kinderpsychol Kinderpsychiatr.* **52** **(7)**, 491–502.

Koskelainen M, Sourander A and Vauras M (2001) Self-reported strengths and difficulties in a community sample of Finnish adolescents. *Eur Child Adolesc Psychiatry.* **10(3)**, 180–185.

Koskelainen M, Sourander A and Kaljonen A (2000) The Strengths and Difficulties Questionnaire among Finnish school-aged children and adolescents. *Eur Child Adolesc Psychiatry.* **9(4)**, 277–284.

Malmberg M, Rydell A M and Smedje H (2003) Validity of the Swedish version of the Strengths and Difficulties Questionnaire (SDQ-Swe). *Nord J Psychiatry.* **57 (5)**, 357–363.

Mathai J, Anderson P and Bourne A (2004) Comparing psychiatric diagnoses generated by the Strengths and Difficulties Questionnaire with diagnoses made by clinicians. *Aust N Z J Psychiatry.* **38 (8)**, 639–643.

Muris P, Meesters C and van den Berg F (2003) The Strengths and Difficulties Questionnaire (SDQ) – further evidence for its reliability and validity in a community sample of Dutch children and adolescents. *Eur Child Adolesc Psychiatry.* **12 (1)**, 1–8.

Muris P, Meesters C, Eijkelenboom A and Vincken M (2004) The self-report version of the Strengths and Difficulties Questionnaire: Its psychometric properties in 8- to 13-year-old non-clinical children. *Br J Clin Psychol.* **43(Pt 4)**, 437–448.

Ronning J A, Handegaard B H, Sourander A and Morch W T (2004) The Strengths and Difficulties Self-Report Questionnaire as a screening instrument in Norwegian community samples. *Eur Child Adolesc Psychiatry.* **13(2)**, 73–82.

Rutter M, Tizard J and Whitmore K (1970) *Education, health and behaviour*, Longmans: London.

Woerner W, Becker A and Rothenberger A (2004) Normative data and scale properties of the German parent SDQ. *Eur Child Adolesc Psychiatry.* **13 Suppl 2**, II 3–10.

Woerner W, Fleitlich-Bilyk B, Martinussen R, Fletcher J, Cucchiaro G, Dalgalarrondo P, Lui M and Tannock R (2004) The Strengths and Difficulties Questionnaire overseas: evaluations and applications of the SDQ beyond Europe. *Eur Child Adolesc Psychiatry.* **13 Suppl 2**, II 47–54.

Survey Documents

Appendix E

Note

The Strengths and Difficulties Questionnaire

- Section D in parent questionnaire
- Section CB in young person questionnaire
- Section B in teacher questionnaire

and the Social Aptitude Scale

- Section SAS in the parent questionnaire

HOUSEHOLD DETAILS

FOR ALL ADDRESSES

Area   Information already entered

Address   Information already entered

INFORMATION COLLECTED FOR ALL PERSONS IN THE HOUSEHOLD

WhoHere

Who normally lives at this address?

NAMEA

PLEASE RECORD THE NAME OF THE PARENT YOU WILL BE INTERVIEWING
INTERVIEWER: If necessary copy the parent's name from the information sheet

Asex

PLEASE RECORD THE SEX OF THE PARENT YOU WILL BE INTERVIEWING
INTERVIEWER: If necessary copy the parent's sex from the information sheet

(1)   Male
(2)   female

NameC

PARENT AND CHILD INFORMATION

PLEASE ENTER THE NAME OF YOUNG PERSON

ChldAg

PARENT AND CHILD SELECTION
Selected child's age

ChldDB

PARENT AND CHILD SELECTION
Selected child's DOB

ChldSx

PARENT AND CHILD SELECTION
Selected child's sex

(1)   Male
(2)   female

Name

RECORD THE NAME (OR A UNIQUE IDENTIFIER) FOR RESPONDING PARENT, THEN A NAME/IDENTIFIEER FOR EACH MEMBER OF THE HOUSEHOLD
IF THE YOUNG PERSON IS NOT LIVING AT HOME PLEASE INCLUDE THEM IN THE GRID AS IF THEY WERE

Sex

(1)   Male
(2)   Female

Age

What was your age last birthday?

ASK IF: Age < 20

Birth

(As you are under 20, may I just check) What is your date of birth?

ASK IF: Age >= 16

MarStat

Are you

(1)   Single, that is, never married
(2)   Married and living with your husband/wife
(3)   Married and separated from your husband/wife
(4)   Divorced
(5)   Or widowed?

ASK IF: MarStat = 1, 3, 4, 5

LiveWith

May I just check, are you living with someone in the household as a couple?

(1)   Yes
(2)   No
(3)   SPONTANEOUS ONLY – same sex couple

Hhldr

In whose name is the accommodation owned or rented?

(1)   This person alone
(3)   This person jointly
(5)   NOT owner/renter

Ethnic

To which of these ethnic groups do you consider NAME belongs?

(1)   White British
(2)   Any other White background
(3)   Mixed – White and Black Caribbean
(4)   Mixed – White and Black African
(5)   Mixed – White and Asian
(6)   Any other Mixed background
(7)   Asian or Asian British – Indian
(8)   Asian or Asian British – Pakistani
(9)   Asian or Asian British – Bangladeshi
(10)   Asian or Asian British – Any other Asian background
(11)   Black or Black British – Black Caribbean
(12)   Black or Black British – Black African
(13)   Black or Black British – Any other Black background
(14)   Chinese
(15)   Other ethnic group – Any other

Ask if: ethnic = other

EthDes

Please can you describe the other ethnic group

Accommodation and Tenure

Accom

IS THE HOUSEHOLD'S ACCOMMODATION:

(1)   A house or bungalow
(2)   A flat or maisonette
(3)   A room/rooms
(4)   Or something else?

Ask if: Accom = 1

HseType

IS THE HOUSE/BUNGALOW

(1)   Detached
(2)   Semi-detached
(3)   Or terraced/end of terrace?

Ask if: Accom = 2

FltTyp

IS THE FLAT/MAISONETTE:

(1)   A purpose-built block
(2)   A converted house/some other kind of building?

Ask if: Accom = 4

AccOth

IS THE ACCOMMODATION A:

(1)   Caravan, mobile home or houseboat
(2)   Or some other kind of accommodation?

Ten1

In which of these ways do you occupy this accommodation?

(1)   Own outright
(2)   Buying it with the help of a mortgage or loan
(3)   Pay part rent and part mortgage (shared ownership)
(4)   Rent it
(5)   Live here rent-free (including rent-free in relative's/friend's property; excluding squatting)
(6)   Squatting

Ask if: Ten1 = 4, 5

Tied

Does the accommodation go with the job of anyone in the household?

(1)   Yes
(2)   No

Ask if: Ten1 = 4,5

LLord

Who is your landlord

(1)   The local authority/council/New Town Development/ Scottish Homes
(2)   A housing association or co-operative or charitable trust
(3)   Employer (organisation) of a household member
(4)   Another organisation
(5)   Relative/friend (before you lived here) of a household member
(6)   Employer (individual) of a household member
(7)   Another individual private landlord?

Ask if: Ten1 = 4,5

Furn

Is the accommodation provided: ...

(1)   Furnished
(2)   Partly furnished (eg carpets and curtains only)
(3)   Or unfurnished?

TranSDQ

INTERVIEWER: Code 'YES' if the parent will only be completing a translated version of the strengths and difficulties questionnaire
If you will be proceeding with a full interview with the parent code 'NO'

(1)   Yes, translation only
(2)   No, full interview

PARENT QUESTIONNAIRE

General Health

GenHlth

How is NAME CHILD's health in general?
Would you say it was ...

(1)   Very good
(2)   Good
(3)   Fair
(4)   Bad
(5)   Or is it very bad?

Ask IF: (QSelect.TranSDQ = No) AND (QSelect.AdltInt = YesNow)

B2

GENERAL HEALTH SECTION – PARENT INTERVIEW
Is NAME CHILD registered with a GP?

(1)   Yes
(2)   No

Ask IF: (QSelect.TranSDQ = No) AND (QSelect.AdltInt = YesNow)

B4

GENERAL HEALTH SECTION – PARENT INTERVIEW
Here is a list of health problems or conditions
which some children or young people may have.

Please can you tell me whether NAME CHILD has...

SHOW CARD 3
PRESS <ENTER> TO CONTINUE

SET [12] OF
(1)   Asthma
(2)   Eczema
(3)   Hay fever
(4)   Glue ear or otitis media, or having grommits
(5)   Bed wetting
(6)   Soiling pants
(7)   Stomach/digestive problems or abdominal/tummy pains
(8)   A heart problem
(9)   Any blood disorder
(10) Epilepsy
(11) Food allergy
(12) Some other allergy
(13) None of these

Ask IF: (QSelect.TranSDQ = No) AND (QSelect.AdltInt = YesNow)

B4a

GENERAL HEALTH SECTION – PARENT INTERVIEW
Here is another list of health problems or
conditions which some children or young people may have.

Please can you tell me whether NAME CHILD has...

SHOW CARD 4
PRESS <ENTER> TO CONTINUE

SET [11] OF
(1)   Hyperactivity
(2)   Behavioural problems
(3)   Emotional problems
(4)   Learning difficulties
(5)   Dyslexia
(6)   Cerebral palsy
(7)   Migraine or severe headaches
(8)   The Chronic Fatigue Syndrome or M.E
(9)   Eye/Sight problems
(10) Speech/or language problems
(11) Hearing problems
(12) None of these

Ask if: (QSelect.TranSDQ = No) AND (QSelect.AdltInt = YesNow)

B5

GENERAL HEALTH SECTION – PARENT INTERVIEW
And finally, another list of health problems or
conditions which some children or young people may have.

Please can you tell me whether NAME CHILD has...

(1)   Diabetes
(2)   Obesity
(3)   Cystic fibrosis
(4)   Spina Bifida
(5)   Kidney, urinary tract problems
(6)   Missing fingers, hands, arms, toes, feet or legs
(7)   Any stiffness or deformity of the foot,leg, fingers, arms or back
(8)   Any muscle disease or weakness
(9)   Any difficulty with co-ordination
(10) A condition present since birth such as club foot or cleft palate
(11) Cancer
(12) None of these

AnyElse

Does NAME CHILD have any other health problems?

(1)   Yes
(2)   No

Ask if: AnyElse = 1

ElseSpec

What are these other health problems?

B12

May I just check, is NAME CHILD taking any pills or tablets listed here?

(1)   Yes
(2)   No

Ask if: B12 = Yes

B12a

CODE ALL THAT APPLY

(1)   Methylphenidate, Equasym, Ritalin
(2)   Dexamphetamine, Dexedrine
(3)   Imipramine, Tofranil
(4)   Clonidine, Catepres, Dixarit
(5)   Fluoxetine, Prozac
(6)   Sertraline, Lustral
(7)   Paroxetine, Seroxat
(8)   Fluvoxamine, Faverin
(9)   Citalopram, Cimpramil
(10) Amitryptaline, Lentizol, Triptafen
(11) Clomipramine, Anafranil
(12) Sulpirade, Dolmatil, Sulparex, Sulpitil
(13) Risperidone, Riperadal
(14) Haloperidol, Dozic, Haldol, Serenace

B12b

Who prescribed this medication?

B12c

How long has NAME CHILD been taking it?

Strengths and Difficulties

IntrSDQ

I would now like to ask you about NAME CHILD's personality and behaviour. This is to give us an overall view of his/her strengths and difficulties – we will be coming back to specific areas in more detail later in the interview.

SectnD[1]

For each item that I am going to read out can you please tell me whether it is 'not true', 'partly true' or 'certainly true' for NAME CHILD – over the past six months

D4

Considerate of other people's feelings

D5

Restless, overactive, cannot stay still for long

---

1. Questions D4–D31 are copyrighted © to Professor Robert Goodman, Department of Child and Adolescent Psychiatry, De Crespigny Park, London SE5 8AF.

D6

Often complains of headaches, stomach aches or sickness

D7

Shares readily with other children (treats, toys, pencils etc)

D8

Often has temper tantrums or hot tempers

D9

Rather solitary, tends to play alone

D10

Generally obedient, usually does what adults request

D11

Many worries, often seems worried

D12

Helpful if someone is hurt, upset or feeling ill

D13

Constantly fidgeting or squirming

D14

Has at least one good friend

D15

Often fights with other children or bullies them

D16

Often unhappy, down-hearted or tearful

D17

Generally liked by other children

D18

Easily distracted, concentration wanders

D19

Nervous or clingy in new situations, easily loses confidence

D20

Kind to younger children

D21

Often lies or cheats

D22

Picked on or bullied by other children

D23

Often volunteers to help others (parents, teachers, other children)

D24

Thinks things out before acting

D25

Steals from home, school or elsewhere

1. Questions D4–D31 are copyrighted © to Professor Robert Goodman, Department of Child and Adolescent Psychiatry, De Crespigny Park, London SE5 8AF.

D26

Gets on better with adults than with other children

D27

Many fears, easily scared

D28

Sees tasks through to the end, good attention span?

D29

Overall, do you think that NAME CHILD has difficulties in one or more of the following areas: emotions, concentration, behaviour or getting on with other people?

(5)   No
(6)   Yes: minor difficulties
(7)   Yes: definite difficulties
(8)   Yes: severe difficulties

ASK IF: *D29 = 6, 7, 8*

D29a

How long have these difficulties been present?

(1)   Less than a month
(2)   One to five months
(3)   Six to eleven months
(4)   A year or more

ASK IF: *D29 = 6, 7, 8*

D29b

Do you the difficulties upset or distress NAME CHILD..

(5)   not at all
(6)   only a little
(7)   quite a lot
(8)   or a great deal?

ASK IF: *D29 = 6, 7, 8*

D30

Do the difficulties interfere with NAME CHILD's everyday life in terms of his or her...
...home life?

(5)   Not at all
(6)   Only a little
(7)   Quite a lot
(8)   A great deal

ASK IF: *D29 = 6, 7, 8*

D30a

(Do the difficulties interfere with NAME CHILD's everyday life in terms of his or her)
... friendships?

(5)   Not at all
(6)   Only a little
(7)   Quite a lot
(8)   A great deal

ASK IF: *D29 = 6, 7, 8*

D30b

(Do the difficulties interfere with NAME CHILD's everyday life in terms of his or her)
... classroom learning?

(5)   Not at all
(6)   Only a little
(7)   Quite a lot
(8)   A great deal

ASK IF: *D29 = 6, 7, 8*

D30c

(Do the difficulties interfere with NAME CHILD's everyday life in terms of his or her)
... or leisure activities?

(5)   Not at all
(6)   Only a little
(7)   Quite a lot
(8)   A great deal

ASK IF: *D29 = 6, 7, 8*

D31

Do the difficulties put a burden on you or the family as a whole?

(5)   Not at all
(6)   Only a little
(7)   Quite a lot
(8)   A great deal

1. Questions D4–D31 are copyrighted © to Professor Robert Goodman, Department of Child and Adolescent Psychiatry, De Crespigny Park, London SE5 8AF.

SAS1[2]

(How does NAME CHILD compare with other young people of his/her age in the following abilities:)

Able to laugh around with others, for example accepting light-hearted teasing and responding appropriately?

(1)   A lot worse than average
(2)   A bit worse than average
(3)   About average
(4)   A bit better than average
(5)   A lot better than average

SAS2

Easy to chat with, even if it isn't on a topic that specially interests him/her?

(1)   A lot worse than average
(2)   A bit worse than average
(3)   About average
(4)   A bit better than average
(5)   A lot better than average

SAS3

Able to compromise and be flexible?

(1)   A lot worse than average
(2)   A bit worse than average
(3)   About average
(4)   A bit better than average
(5)   A lot better than average

SAS4

Finds the right thing to say or do in order to calm a tense or embarrassing situation?

(1)   A lot worse than average
(2)   A bit worse than average
(3)   About average
(4)   A bit better than average
(5)   A lot better than average

SAS5

Gracious when s/he doesn't win or get his/her own way. A good loser?

(1)   A lot worse than average
(2)   A bit worse than average
(3)   About average
(4)   A bit better than average
(5)   A lot better than average

SAS6

Other people feel at ease around him/her?

(1)   A lot worse than average
(2)   A bit worse than average
(3)   About average
(4)   A bit better than average
(5)   A lot better than average

SAS7

By reading between the lines of what people say, s/he can work out what they are really thinking and feeling?

(1)   A lot worse than average
(2)   A bit worse than average
(3)   About average
(4)   A bit better than average
(5)   A lot better than average

SAS8

After doing something wrong, s/he's able to say sorry and sort it out so that there are no hard feelings?

(1)   A lot worse than average
(2)   A bit worse than average
(3)   About average
(4)   A bit better than average
(5)   A lot better than average

SAS9

Can take the lead without others feeling they are being bossed about?

(1)   A lot worse than average
(2)   A bit worse than average
(3)   About average
(4)   A bit better than average
(5)   A lot better than average

SAS10

Aware of what is and isn't appropriate in different social situations?

(1)   A lot worse than average
(2)   A bit worse than average
(3)   About average
(4)   A bit better than average
(5)   A lot better than average

2. The Social Aptitudes Scale (Questions SAS1 – SAS10) are copyrighted © to Professor Robert Goodman, Department of Child and Adolescent Psychiatry, De Crespigny Park, London SE5 8AF.

Friendship

FrIntr

This section is about friendship. I'm going to ask separately about making and keeping friends because sometimes young people are good at making friends but not at keeping them, or vice versa

Fr1

What is NAME CHILD like at making friends...

(1)   Finds it harder than average
(2)   About average
(3)   Or finds it easier than average?

Fr2

What is NAME CHILD like at keeping the friends s/he has made...

(1)   Finds it harder than average
(2)   About average
(3)   Or finds it easier than average?

Fr3

At present, how many friends does s/he have that s/he fairly often spends time with, for example chatting, or doing things together, or going out with as part of a group? Does s/he have...

(1)   None
(2)   One
(3)   Two to four
(4)   Five to nine
(5)   Or ten or more?

Ask if: Fr3 is not equal to 1

Fr4

How many of these would you say were close friends?

(1)   None
(2)   One
(3)   Two to four
(4)   Or five or more

Ask if: Fr3 is not equal to 1

Fr5

Do NAME CHILD and his/her friends have interests in common?

(5)   No
(6)   A little
(7)   A Lot

Ask if: Fr3 is not equal to 1

Fr6

Do NAME CHILD and his/her friends do things together such as playing sport or shopping?

(5)   No
(6)   A little
(7)   A Lot

Ask if: Fr3 is not equal to 1

Fr7

If NAME CHILD was very stressed or had some secret worry, do you think s/he'd be able to talk about this with a friend and tell the friend how s/he was feeling?

(5)   No
(6)   Perhaps
(7)   Definitely

Ask if: Fr3 is not equal to 1

Fr8

How about the opposite way round? Do you think friends could easily talk to NAME CHILD about the way they were feeling?

(5)   No
(6)   Perhaps
(7)   Definitely

Ask if: Fr3 is not equal to 1

Fr9

By and large, do you approve of NAME CHILD's friends?

(5)   No
(6)   A little
(7)   A Lot

Ask if: Fr3 is not equal to 1

Fr10

Are many of NAME CHILD's friends the sorts of children/ young people who often get into trouble for bad behaviour...

(1)   Not at all
(2)   A few are like that
(3)   Many are like that
(4)   Or all are like that?

Development

AutIntr

This section is about NAME CHILD's development, starting from when s/he was very little, and continuing to the present moment.

R1Intr

DEVELOPMENT (GENERAL) – PARENT INTERVIEW

In his/her first 3 years of life, was there anything that seriously worried you or anyone else about...

R1a

...the way his/her speech developed?

(1)   Yes
(2)   No

R1b

...how s/he got on with other people?

(1)   Yes
(2)   No

R1c

...the way his/her pretend or make-believe play developed?

(1)   Yes
(2)   No

R1d

...any odd rituals or unusual habits that were very hard to interrupt?

(1)   Yes
(2)   No

R1e

...his/her general mental development, for example his/her ability to figure things out, do puzzles, know about videos, help with getting dressed, and so on?

(1)   Yes
(2)   No

Ask if: R1a, R1b, R1c OR R1d = 1

R2

Have all these early delays or difficulties now cleared up completely?

(1)   Completely cleared up
(2)   Some continuing problems

Ask if: R1a = 1

R3

Could s/he use any real words, other than 'mama' or 'dada' before the age of 2?

(1)   Yes
(2)   No

Ask if: R1a = 1

R4

Did NAME CHILD join words together into phrases or short sentences before the age of 3?

(1)   Yes
(2)   No

R5

Thinking about NAME CHILD's school work and about his/her ability to reason things out, is s/he about average, ahead of his/her age or behind his/her age?

(1)   Ahead
(2)   Average
(3)   Behind

Ask if: R5 = 3

R6

At present, roughly what sort of age level is s/he at in his/her school work and ability to reason things out? For example, like an average AGE year old?

0..16

R7

Thinking now about NAME CHILD's ability to use language – to say what s/he means and to understand what other people are saying – is s/he about average, ahead of his/her age or behind his/her age?

(1)   Ahead
(2)   Average
(3)   Behind

Ask if: R7 = 3

R8

At present, roughly what sort of age level is s/he at in his/her use and understanding of language? For example, like an average AGE year old?

0..16

Ask if: R7 = 3

R9

Is s/he good at getting round his/her speech or language difficulties by using gestures, signs, facial expressions or acting things out?

(5)   No
(6)   A little
(7)   A Lot

R10Intr

My next questions are about NAME CHILD's play, hobbies and special interests. Some of the questions are about how s/he was when s/he was younger, and some of them are about how s/he is now. I'll start by asking about the early years.

R10

When children are little, they usually have the chance to play simple social games like Ring a Ring of Roses, Round and Round the Garden, Peekaboo or Peepo. Some children really take to these games, being keen to join in, copying what the other person is doing and wanting to do it back again.

Did NAME CHILD really take to these games?

(5)   No
(6)   A little
(7)   A Lot

R11

From an early age, some children spend a lot of time arranging things. For example, they may regularly spend ages lining up toy cars into lines or patterns or ordering all their toys by colour.

Has this ever been true of NAME CHILD?

(5)   No
(6)   A little
(7)   A Lot

R12

When they are playing, some children spend most of their time repeating the same action over and over again, for example spinning the wheels on a toy car, turning taps or light switches on and off, or opening and shutting doors.

Has this ever been true of NAME CHILD?

(5)   No
(6)   A little
(7)   A Lot

R13

Children are sometimes very interested in unusual aspects of toys or other things. For example, rather than playing with a toy, they may spend their time sniffing it, or running their fingers over its surface, or listening to any noise or vibration that it makes.

Has this ever been true of NAME CHILD?

(5)   No
(6)   A little
(7)   A Lot

R14

Make-believe play is important to some children. This can include pretend games with other children such as cops and robbers, shop, pirates, or mummies and daddies. Even when they are by themselves, children may act out stories with dolls, action men or animals. Pretending can involve, for example, using a piece of wood as a phone at one moment and as a gun at another.

Has NAME CHILD been through a phase when s/he regularly took part in this sort of make-believe or pretend play?

(1)   Yes
(2)   No

Ask if: R14 = 1

R15

Was the story line of NAME CHILD's make-believe play typically simple or complicated?

(1)   Simple
(2)   Complicated

Ask if: R14 = 1

R16

Would the pretend play typically repeat the same scene over and over again, or did the story line vary a lot from time to time. Was it...

(1)   Repetitve
(2)   half and half
(3)   or it varied?

Ask if: R14 = 1

R17

Would NAME CHILD usually only take part in pretend play if other children started it and then roped him/her in, or would s/he quite often take the initiative in starting pretend play? Was it...

(1)   Mostly started by others
(2)   Half and half
(3)   Or did s/he often take the initiative

Ask if: child is under age 11

R18Intr

> Those questions were about when NAME CHILD was younger. I now want you to think about how s/he is now.

Ask if: child is under age 11

R18

> Will NAME CHILD only join in a game with other children on his/her own terms?

> (1)　　Yes
> (2)　　No

Ask if: child is under age 11

R19

> Do NAME CHILD's games often break down because s/he insists
> on playing it his/her own way?

> (1)　　Yes
> (2)　　No

Ask if: child is under age 11

R20

> Is NAME CHILD often too rigid about rules when playing a game, insisting on following the letter of the law even when that clearly isn't appropriate?

> (1)　　Yes
> (2)　　No

Ask if: child is under age 11

R21

> When playing, does s/he have difficulty taking turns, sharing or co-operating?

> (1)　　Yes
> (2)　　No

Ask if: child is under age 11

R22

> It is sometimes important for children to play differently according to who they are playing with. For example, not being too rough when playing with younger children, or not being too bossy when playing with older children.

> Can NAME CHILD make the right sort of allowances according to who s/he is playing with?

> (1)　　Yes
> (2)　　No

Ask if: child is over age 11

R18BIntr

> For the next few questions, I would like you to think back to when NAME CHILD was younger. Please answer the questions for when NAME CHILD was up to the age of about 11.

Ask if: child is over age 11

R18B

> Would NAME CHILD only join in a game with other children on his/her own terms?

> (1)　　Yes
> (2)　　No

Ask if: child is over age 11

R19B

> Would NAME CHILD's games often break down because s/he insisted on playing it his/her own way?

> (1)　　Yes
> (2)　　No

Ask if: child is over age 11

R20B

> Was NAME CHILD often too rigid about rules when playing a game, insisting on following the letter of the law even when that clearly wasn't appropriate?

> (1)　　Yes
> (2)　　No

Ask if: child is over age 11

R21B

> When playing, did s/he have difficulty taking turns, sharing or co-operating?

> (1)　　Yes
> (2)　　No

Ask if: child is over age 11

R22B

> It is sometimes important for children to play differently according to who they are playing with. For example, not being too rough when playing with younger children, or not being too bossy when playing with older children.
> Could NAME CHILD make the right sort of allowances according to who s/he was playing with?

> (1)　　Yes
> (2)　　No

R23

Children vary a lot in terms of how much they focus down on particular interests or hobbies. For example, some children enjoy putting a lot of time into collecting things, or get a lot of pleasure out of focusing on just one topic, such as sport, cars or a particular pop group. In everyday language, we often say that these children are 'obsessed' by their interest, but this is not an unpleasant obsession – this is something they like. Often they also like talking about their interest – sometime they hardly talk about anything else.

Does NAME CHILD have any obsessions of this sort?

(1) Yes
(2) No

Ask if:: R23 = 1

R24

Sometimes children's obsessions may be about common or unusual topics. For example, it is fairly common for an 8 year old to be obsessed by dinosaurs, but it is unusual for an 8 year old to be obsessed by Victorian fireplaces, bar codes or street lamps.

Are any of NAME CHILD's obsessions about an unusual topic?

(1) Yes
(2) No

Ask if:: R23 = 1

R25

Obsessions can also be unusual in terms of how much time they take up. So even if the topic is an ordinary one, such as dinosaurs or cars, it is unusual if the obsession is so strong that the child spends hours and hours studying books and websites on the subject, neglects friends and won't even come down for an ice-cream.

Are any of NAME CHILD's obsessions unusually strong?

(1) Yes
(2) No

Ask if:: R23 = 1

R26

Does the obsession dominate his/her life?

(5) No
(6) A little
(7) A Lot

Ask if:: R23 = 1

R27

Do any of NAME CHILD's obsessions tend to dominate his/her conversation with other people?

(5) No
(6) A little
(7) A Lot

Ask if:: R23 = 1

R28

Do any of NAME CHILD's obessions stop him/her doing other important
things in his/her life, such as playing, studying or going out?

(5) No
(6) A little
(7) A Lot

Ask if:: R23 = 1

R29

When s/he's caught up in his/her obsession(s), does s/he get really cross or upset if you call him/her away to eat or to go out, or to do his/her homework?

(5) No
(6) A little
(7) A Lot

Ask if:: R23 = 1

R30

Please describe the obsession(s).

R31

When we're talking with someone face-to-face, eye contact is very important. It generally makes us feel uneasy, or as if there's something wrong, if the other person makes too little eye contact, or too much, or makes it at the wrong time.

Has NAME CHILD ever been through a phase of making too little or too much eye contact, or making it in the wrong sort of way?

(5) No
(6) A little
(7) A Lot

Ask if: R31 = 7

R32

Has this been true over the last 12 months?

(1) Yes
(2) No

R33

From an early age, many children spontaneously try to share their enjoyment or interests or achievements. For example, pointing to something that they think another person will enjoy seeing or find interesting. Or bringing a picture home from school to show you.

When s/he was little, say about 4 years old, did NAME CHILD want to share his/her enjoyment, interests or achievements with other people?

(5)   No
(6)   A little
(7)   A Lot

Ask if: R33 = 5 or 6

R34

Over the last 12 months, has NAME CHILD wanted to share his/her enjoyment, interests or achievements with other people?

(5)   No
(6)   A little
(7)   A Lot

R35

Can NAME CHILD change his/her behaviour to fit in with where s/he is, for example knowing that behaviour that is OK at home may not be appropriate in grandma's house or at school or in church?

(1)   Yes
(2)   No

R36

Children respond in different ways to other people's emotions. For example, if their mother is upset because she has cut her finger badly with a knife, children can be sympathetic, or not pay much attention, or respond in unusual ways such as laughing.

What would NAME CHILD typically do in this sort of situation...

(1)   Be sympathetic
(2)   not pay much attention
(3)   or respond in an unusual way?

R37

Does NAME CHILD start conversations with other people?

(5)   No
(6)   A little
(7)   A Lot

R38

If other people start conversations with him/her, can NAME CHILD keep the conversation going?

(5)   No
(6)   A little
(7)   A Lot

R39

Is NAME CHILD genuinely interested in chatting with other people in order to hear what they have to say about their experiences and interests – even if those interests are different from his/her own interests?

(5)   No
(6)   A little
(7)   A Lot

R40

Does NAME CHILD adjust what s/he's saying according to whether s/he is talking to children, teenagers or adults?

(5)   No
(6)   A little
(7)   A Lot

R41

Children also have to adjust their language according to whether it's a formal or informal occasion. For example, using casual, informal speech with family or on the playground, but using more formal speech when meeting new adults or having to write something for school. Some children have trouble with this, for example speaking too casually to the headteacher or speaking too formally to other children like a little Professor.

Does NAME CHILD switch appropriately between formal and informal language according to the situation?

(1)   Yes
(2)   No

R42

Some children's conversation can be hard to follow because they start in the middle of a story, jumping straight into what most concerns them without setting the scene and giving you relevant background details. For example, they may come out with something like 'He didn't give it back' without first explaining who he was or what he didn't give back.

Has NAME CHILD ever been like that?

(5)   No
(6)   A little
(7)   A Lot

Ask if: R42 = 7

R43

Has s/he often been like that over the last 12 months?

(1)   Yes
(2)   No

R44

Those questions were about conversations that don't go well because the child gives too few details. The opposite can also happen, with children's conversations containing far too many details that aren't really relevant or that you already know. They're not just precise about details such as times and dates – they're over-precise.

Has NAME CHILD ever been like that?

(5)   No
(6)   A little
(7)   A Lot

Ask if: R44 = 7

R45

Has s/he often been like that over the last 12 months?

(1)   Yes
(2)   No

R46

Some children have a lot of problems with taking the things you and other people say too literally. For example, if you say 'Dad's stuck on the train', they imagine that he's been glued to the train. Or if you say 'Do you know what the time is?' they say 'Yes' but don't realise that you had wanted them to tell you what time it is.

Has NAME CHILD ever been like that?

(5)   No
(6)   A little
(7)   A Lot

Ask if: R46 = 7

R47

Has s/he often been like that over the last 12 months?

(1)   Yes
(2)   No

R48

Many young children go through a phase of repeating what someone has just said to them. For example, if you said, 'We'll be going home in a few minutes', they might parrot back 'We'll be going home in a few minutes'. Or they might echo back the last word, 'minutes', in your tone of voice. Some children do this a lot.

Has NAME CHILD ever echoed or parroted a lot of speech in this way?

(1)   Yes
(2)   No

R49

Some children spend a lot of time asking the same questions over and over again. For example, 'When are we going to the park?' or 'What's for dinner?' or 'Are we going swimming this weekend?' They keep on and on with these questions even though they've already been told the answers many times. The questions may not be exactly the same from week to week, but as one question goes, another question takes its place and it too is asked many, many times.

Has NAME CHILD ever gone through a long phase of repetitive questioning?

(1)   Yes
(2)   No

Ask if: R49 = 1

R50

Has that been happening a lot over the last 12 months?

(1)   Yes
(2)   No

R51

Another way in which children repeat themselves is by using the same phrase or cliché, over and over again. For example, almost every sentence may begin 'If you want my opinion' or 'Logically speaking' Occasionally the phrase is appropriate, but it is used far more than is really needed.

Has NAME CHILD ever filled his/her speech with a lot of these fairly empty phrases or clichés?

(1)   Yes
(2)   No

Ask if: R51 = 1

R52

Has that been true over the last 12 months?

(1)   Yes
(2)   No

R53

We communicate with one another not just through words but also through physical gestures – waving goodbye, pointing to things, blowing a kiss, clapping, bringing our finger to our mouth and saying Shh! – that sort of thing.

As a toddler and young child, did NAME CHILD use these sorts of gestures as much as other children of the same age? Did s/he use them...

(1)   About the same
(2)   a little less
(3)   or a lot less than other children the same age?

R54

Some children develop unusual gestures. For example, a young child may want the door to be opened or to be given a biscuit, but instead of saying something or pointing, he or she may just grab the parent's hand and pull it to the door handle or the biscuit tin.

Has NAME CHILD ever had unusual gestures?

(1)   Yes
(2)   No

Ask if: R54 = 1

R55

Please describe the unusual gesture(s).

R56Intr

Sometimes, it is not what we say that is important but the way we say it. For example, someone may say something polite to us but in a cold tone of voice that makes it obvious that they don't really like us. What people really mean can also be shown on their faces, through smiles, frowns, looks of surprise, and so on.

R56

Children vary a lot in how easily they can read the clues in other people's tone of voice and facial expressions. Some children find it almost impossible. Others can recognise very obvious clues, such as when a person is very happy or very cross. Yet other children have a talent for recognising subtle as well as obvious clues – for example, immediately knowing when their mother is starting to get a little cross, or when their brother is feeling a bit embarrassed.

What is NAME CHILD like at reading the clues in other people's tone of voice and facial expression?
Does s/he...

(1)   recognise subtle as well as obvious clues
(2)   recognise obvious clues only
(3)   or does s/he find it very difficult?

R57

Children also vary in how much their own thoughts and feelings show in their faces and in their tone of voice. Some children are easy to read in this sort of way, and others are hard to read, except perhaps for their parents or other people who know them very well.

Do most people find it difficult to read what NAME CHILD is thinking or feeling just by looking at his/her face or by listening to his/her tone of voice?

(1)   No
(2)   A little difficult
(3)   Very difficult

R58

Some children find it hard to adapt to any change in their lives. Ever since they were very little, they have really enjoyed routines and tried to insist on things being the same every day. For example, they may want to eat the same food off the same plate while sitting in the same chair every single day. Or their food may need to be arranged in a particular way on the plate, without different foods touching. Or there may be very fixed routines for dressing or undressing. Or their mother may have to kiss all 30 teddies goodnight in a particular order. As long as they can get on with them, these children typically enjoy their routines.

Has NAME CHILD ever had any particularly strong or unusual routines that s/he goes through because s/he enjoys doing it that way?

(1)   Yes
(2)   No

Ask if: R58 = 1

R59

Please describe these routines.

Ask if: R58 = 1

R60

Have these routines continued over the last 12 months?

(1) Yes
(2) No

Ask if: R58 = 1

R61

When children want things to be the same every day, they may get very upset when adults insist on change, even if it is only a small change. For example, they may be very upset by the furniture being moved around, by being taken to school a different way, or by a small change in bath times.

Has NAME CHILD ever gone through a phase of being very upset by changes in routine?

(1) Yes
(2) No

Ask if: R58 = 1 And: R61 = 1

R62

Has s/he been very upset by changes in routine over the last 12 months?

(1) Yes
(2) No

R63

Many young children briefly go through a phase of flapping their hands or arms up and down when they are excited or upset. This doesn't usually last long. Some children, however, continue to do a lot of this 'flapping' as they grow up, particularly when they are excited or upset.

Has NAME CHILD ever done a lot of flapping?

(1) Yes
(2) No

Ask if: R63 = 1

R64

Has s/he gone on flapping over the last 12 months?

(1) Yes
(2) No

R65

Children sometimes get into the habit of moving in unusual ways, for example walking on tiptoe, running around in circles, spinning themselves round and round, or flicking their fingers. Usually, they do these things because they enjoy them, but they can become completely automatic things that they do without thinking. These habits may take up a lot of the child's time, and the child may become upset if adults try to stop them doing it.

Has NAME CHILD ever had unusual habits of this sort?

(1) Yes
(2) No

Ask if: R65 = 1

R66

Please describe the habits.

Ask if: R65 = 1

R67

Have these habits continued over the last 12 months?

(1) Yes
(2) No

R68

You have answered a lot of questions about NAME CHILD's pattern of development – focusing particularly on his/her use of language, his/her ability to be flexible, the development of imaginative play, and his/her ability to get along with other people.

Are you concerned at present about any of these aspects of NAME CHILD's development?

(5) No
(6) A little
(7) A Lot

Ask if: R68 = 7

R69

Thinking about the last 12 months, have difficulties in any of the areas that we have covered resulted in him/her becoming upset or distressed?

(5) Not at all
(6) A little
(7) A medium amount
(8) A great deal

Ask if: R68 = 7

R70Intr

Have difficulties with language, flexibility, play, or social ability interfered with...

Ask if: R68 = 7

R70a

...how well she gets on with you and the rest of the family?

(5)   Not at all
(6)   A little
(7)   A medium amount
(8)   A great deal

Ask if: R68 = 7

R70b

...making and keeping friends?

(5)   Not at all
(6)   A little
(7)   A medium amount
(8)   A great deal

Ask if: R68 = 7

R70c

...learning or class work?

(5)   Not at all
(6)   A little
(7)   A medium amount
(8)   A great deal

Ask if: R68 = 7

R70d

...playing, hobbies, sports or other leisure activities?

(5)   Not at all
(6)   A little
(7)   A medium amount
(8)   A great deal

Ask if: R68 = 7

R71

Have these difficulties put a burden on you or the family as a whole?

(5)   Not at all
(6)   A little
(7)   A medium amount
(8)   A great deal

Ask if: R68 = 7

R72

Some children's development is unusual from birth onwards. With hindsight, their parents realise that development was never quite normal. That's not always the case, though. Sometimes parents are sure that development was completely normal for a while and that there was a relatively sudden change.

Which was true for NAME CHILD?

(1)   Always there to some extent
(2)   Sudden change

Ask if: R68 = 7 And: R72 = 2

R73

How old was NAME CHILD when this change happened?

0..17

Ask if: R68 = 7

R74

We have asked you a lot of questions about the development of NAME CHILD's language, play, social skills and adaptability. But sometimes the answers to these fixed questions don't give a clear picture of what a child is really like. It would help us a lot if you would describe in your own words what you see as the main difficulties in these areas.

Separation Anxiety

A1

Which adults is NAME CHILD specially attached to?
CODE ALL THAT APPLY

(1) Mother (biological or adoptive)
(2) Father (biological or adoptive)
(3) Another mother figure (stepmother, foster mother, father's partner)
(4) Another father figure (stepfather, foster father, mother's partner)
(5) One or more grandparents
(6) One or more adult relatives (e.g. aunt, uncle, grown-up brother or sister)
(7) Childminder, nanny, au pair
(8) One or more teachers
(9) One or more other adult non-relatives (e.g. Social/Key worker, family friend or neighbour)
(10) Not specially attached to any adult

Ask if: A1 = 1

A1a

Is NAME CHILD specially attached to the following children or young people?

(1) One or more brothers, sisters or other young relatives
(2) One or more friends
(3) Not specially attached to anyone

Ask if: A1a = 1 or 2

Livewth

Do any of these people live with NAME CHILD?

(1) Yes
(2) No

Ask if: A1a = 1 or 2

AInt2

What I'd like to know next is how much NAME CHILD worries about being separated from his/her 'attachment figures'. Most young people have worries of this sort, but I'd like to know how NAME CHILD compares with others of his/her age. I am interested in how s/he is usually – not on the occasional 'off day'

Ask if: A1a = 1 or 2

F2

Overall, in the last 4 weeks, has NAME CHILD been particularly worried about being separated from his/her 'attachment figures'?

(1) Yes
(2) No

Ask if: A1a = 1 or 2

F2a

Over the last 4 weeks, and compared with other young people of the same age...
has s/he been worried either about something unpleasant happening to his/her attachment figures or about losing you/them?

(5) No more than others of the same age
(6) A little more than others of the same age
(7) A lot more than others of the same age

Ask if: A1a = 1 or 2

F2b

(Over the last 4 weeks, and compared with other young people of the same age...)
... has s/he worried unrealistically that s/he might be taken away from his/her attachment figures, for example by being kidnapped, taken to hospital or killed?

(5) No more than others of the same age
(6) A little more than others of the same age
(7) A lot more than others of the same age

Ask if: A1a = 1 or 2 AND Livewth = 1

F2c

(Over the last 4 weeks, and compared with other young people of the same age...)
... has s/he not wanted to go to school in case something nasty happened to (his/her attachment figures who live with the child) while s/he was away at school?
(DO NOT INCLUDE RELUCTANCE TO GO TO SCHOOL FOR OTHER REASONS, EG. FEAR OF BULLYING OR EXAMS)

(5) No more than other young people of the same age
(6) A little more than other young people of the same age
(7) A lot more than other young people of the same age
(8) SPONTANEOUS: Not at school

Ask if: A1a = 1 or 2

F2d

(Over the last 4 weeks, and compared with other children of the same age...)
... has s/he worried about sleeping alone?

(5) No more than others of the same age
(6) A little more than others of the same age
(7) A lot more than others of the same age

Ask if: A1a = 1 or 2 AND Livewth = 1

F2e

(Over the last 4 weeks, and compared with other children of the same age...)
... has s/he come out of his/her bedroom at night to check on, or to sleep near (his/her attachment figures who live with child)?

(5)   No more than others of the same age
(6)   A little more than others of the same age
(7)   A lot more than others of the same age

Ask if: A1a = 1 or 2

F2f

(Over the last 4 weeks, and compared with other young people of the same age...)
... has s/he worried about sleeping in a strange place?

(5)   No more than others of the same age
(6)   A little more than others of the same age
(7)   A lot more than others of the same age

Ask if: A1a = 1 or 2 **And:** Livewth = 1 **AND** child is under age 11

F2g

(Over the last 4 weeks, and compared with other children of the same age...)
... has s/he been particularly afraid of being alone in a room/alone at home without (his/her attachment figures who live with child)even if you or they are close by?

(5)   No more than others of the same age
(6)   A little more than others of the same age
(7)   A lot more than others of the same age

Ask if: A1a = 1 or 2 **And:** Livewth = 1 **AND** child is over age 11

F2h

(Over the last 4 weeks, and compared with other young people of the same age...)
...has s/he been afraid of being alone at home if (his/her attachment figures who live with child) pop out for a moment?

(5)   No more than others of the same age
(6)   A little more than others of the same age
(7)   A lot more than others of the same age

Ask if: A1a = 1 or 2

F2i

(Over the last 4 weeks, and compared with other young people of the same age...)
... has s/he had repeated nightmares or bad dreams about being separated from his/her attachment figures?

(5)   No more than others of the same age
(6)   A little more than others of the same age
(7)   A lot more than others of the same age

Ask if: A1a = 1 or 2

F2j

(Over the last 4 weeks, and compared with other young people of the same age...)
... has s/he had headaches, stomach aches or felt sick when s/he had to leave his/her attachment figures or when s/he knew it was about to happen?

(5)   No more than others of the same age
(6)   A little more than others of the same age
(7)   A lot more than others of the same age

Ask if: A1a = 1 or 2

F2k

(Over the last 4 weeks, and compared with other young people of the same age...)
... has being apart or the thought of being apart from his/her attachment
figures led to worry, crying, tantrums, clinginess or misery?

(5)   No more than others of the same age
(6)   A little more than others of the same age
(7)   A lot more than others of the same age

F3

Have NAME CHILD's worries about separations been there for at least a month?

(1)   Yes
(2)   No

Ask if: F3 = Yes

F3a

How old was s/he when his/her worries about separation began?

F4

How much have these worries upset or distressed him/her...

(5)   Not at all
(6)   Only a little
(7)   Quite a lot
(8)   Or a great deal?

F5a

How much have these worries interfered with...

... How well s/he gets on with you and the rest of the family?

(5)   Not at all
(6)   Only a little
(7)   Quite a lot
(8)   A great deal

F5b

(How much have these worries interfered with...)

....Making and keeping friends?

- (5) Not at all
- (6) Only a little
- (7) Quite a lot
- (8) A great deal

F5c

(Have they interfered with...)

...learning new things (or class work)?

- (5) Not at all
- (6) Only a little
- (7) Quite a lot
- (8) A great deal

F5d

(Have they interfered with...)

...playing, hobbies, sports or other leisure activities?

- (5) Not at all
- (6) Only a little
- (7) Quite a lot
- (8) A great deal

F5e

Have these worries put a burden on you or the family as a whole?

- (5) Not at all
- (6) Only a little
- (7) Quite a lot
- (8) A great deal

A6

Thinking of NAME CHILD's attachment behaviour, how much do you think it has upset or distressed him/her?

- (5) Not at all
- (6) Only a little
- (7) Quite a lot
- (8) A great deal

A7a

I also want to ask you about the extent to which this behaviour has interfered with his/her day to day life.
Has it interfered with.....
how well s/he gets on with you and the rest of the family?

- (5) Not at all
- (6) Only a little
- (7) Quite a lot
- (8) A great deal

A7b

(I also want to ask you about the extent to which this behaviour has interfered with his/her day to day life.)
Has it interfered with.....
making and keeping friends?

- (5) Not at all
- (6) Only a little
- (7) Quite a lot
- (8) A great deal

A7c

(I also want to ask you about the extent to which this behaviour has interfered with his/her day to day life.)

Has it interfered with.....

learning new things (or class work)?

- (5) Not at all
- (6) Only a little
- (7) Quite a lot
- (8) A great deal

A7d

(I also want to ask you about the extent to which this behaviour has interfered with his/her day to day life.)

Has it interfered with.....

playing, hobbies, sports or other leisure activities?

- (5) Not at all
- (6) Only a little
- (7) Quite a lot
- (8) A great deal

A8

Has this behaviour put a burden on you or the family as a whole?

- (5) Not at all
- (6) Only a little
- (7) Quite a lot
- (8) A great deal

Specific Phobias

F7

Is NAME CHILD PARTICULARLY scared about any of the things or situations on this list?

(1)   Animals: dogs, spiders, bees and wasps, mice and rats, snakes, or any other bird, animal or insect
(2)   Some aspect of the natural environment, e.g. Storms, thunder, heights or water
(3)   The dark
(4)   Loud noises, e.g. fire alarms, fireworks
(5)   Blood/Injection/Injury: Set off by the sight of blood or injury or by an injection or some other medical procedure
(6)   Dentists or Doctors
(7)   Vomiting, choking or getting particular diseases, e.g. Cancer or AIDS
(8)   Using particular types of transport, e.g. cars, buses, boats, planes, ordinary trains, underground trains, bridges
(9)   Small enclosed spaces, e.g. lifts, tunnels
(10)   Using the toilet, e.g. at school or in someone else's house
(11)   Specific types of people, e.g. clowns, people with beards, with crash helmets, in fancy dress, dressed as Santa Claus
(12)   Imaginary or Supernatural beings, e.g. monsters, ghosts, aliens, witches
(13)   Any other specific fear(specify)
(99)   Not particularly scared of anything

Ask if: F7 = 13

F7Oth

What is this other fear?
 ENTER A SHORT DESRIPTION

Ask if: F7 is not = 99

F7a

Are these fears a real nuisance to him/her, to you, or to anyone else?

(5)   No
(6)   Perhaps
(7)   Definitely

Ask if: F7 is not = 99And: (F7a = Yes) OR (QSDQ2. PEmotion >= 4)

F8

How long has this fear (or the most severe of these fears) been present?

(1)   Less than 1 month
(2)   At least one month but less than 6 months
(3)   Six months or more

Ask if: F7 is not = 99 And: F7a = 1

F9

When NAME CHILD comes up against the things s/he is afraid of, or when s/he thinks
 s/he is about to come up against them, does s/he become anxious or upset?

(5)   No
(6)   A little
(7)   A Lot

Ask if: F7 is not = 99 And: F7a = 1 And: F9 = 7

F9a

Does s/he become anxious or upset every time, or almost every time, s/he comes up against the things s/he is afraid of?

(1)   Yes
(2)   No

Ask if: F7 is not = 99 And: F7a = 1 And: F9 = 7

F10

How often do his/her fears result in his/her becoming upset like this?
 IF THE CHILD IS AFRAID OF SOMETHING THAT IS ONLY THERE FOR PART OF THE YEAR (E.G. WASPS), THIS QUESTION IS ABOUT THAT PARTICULAR SEASON.

(1)   Every now and then
(2)   Most weeks
(3)   Most days
(4)   Many times a day?

Ask if: F7 is not = 99 And: F7a = 1

F11

Do NAME CHILD's fears lead to him/her avoiding the things s/he is afraid of?

(5)   No
(6)   A little
(7)   or a lot ?

Ask if: F7 is not = 99 And: F7a = 1 And: F11 = 7

F11a

Does this avoidance interfere with his/her daily life?

(5)   Not at all
(6)   a little
(7)   or a lot?

Ask if: F7 is not = 99 And: F7a = 1

F11b

Do you think that his/her fears are over the top or unreasonable?

(5)   No
(6)   Perhaps
(7)   Definitely

Ask if: F7 is not = 99 And: F7a = 1

F11c

And what about him/her? Does s/he think that his/her fears are over the top or unreasonable?

(5)   No
(6)   Perhaps
(7)   Definitely

Ask if: F7 is not = 99 And: F7a = 1

F12

Have NAME CHILD's fears put a burden on you or the family as a whole

(5)   Not at all
(6)   Only a little
(7)   Quite a lot
(8)   Or a great deal?

Social Phobias

F13

Overall, does NAME CHILD particularly fear or avoid social situations which involve a lot of people or meeting new people, or doing things in front of other people?

(1)   Yes
(2)   No

F14Intr

Has s/he been particularly afraid of any of the following social situations over the last 4 weeks?

F14a

(Has s/he been particularly afraid of)
. . . meeting new people?

(5)   No
(6)   A little
(7)   A Lot

F14b

(Has s/he been particularly afraid of)
. . .meeting a lot of people, such as at a party?

(5)   No
(6)   A little
(7)   A Lot

F14c

(Has s/he been particularly afraid of)
...eating in front of others?

(5)   No
(6)   A little
(7)   A Lot

F14d

(Has s/he been particularly afraid of)
. . .speaking with other young people around, or in class?

(5)   No
(6)   A little
(7)   A Lot

F14e

(Has s/he been particularly afraid of)
. . .reading out loud in front of others?

(5)   No
(6)   A little
(7)   A Lot

F14f

(Has s/he been particularly afraid of)
. . .writing in front of others?

(5)   No
(6)   A little
(7)   A Lot

F15

Most young people are attached to a few key adults, feeling more secure when they are around. Some young people are only afraid of social situations if they don't have one of these key adults around. Other young people are afraid of social situations even when they are with one of these key adults. Which is true for NAME CHILD?

(1)   mostly fine in social situations as long as key adults are around
(2)   social fears are marked even when key adults are around

Ask if: F15 = 2

F16

Is NAME CHILD just afraid with adults, or is s/he also afraid in situations that involve a lot of children, or meeting new children?

(1)   Just with adults
(2)   Just with children
(3)   with adults and children

Ask if: F15 = 2

F17

Outside of these social situations, is NAME CHILD able to get on well enough with the adults and children s/he knows best?

(1)   Yes
(2)   No

Ask if: F15 = 2

F18

Do you think his/her dislike of social situations is because s/he is afraid s/he will act in a way that will be embarrassing or show him/her up?

(5)   No
(6)   Perhaps
(7)   Definitely

Ask if: F15 = 2 AND F14d = A Lot OR F14d = A Little OR F14e = A Lot OR F14e = A Little OR F14f = A Lot OR F14f = A Little

F18a

Is his/her dislike of social situations related to specific problems with speech, reading or writing?

(5)   No
(6)   Perhaps
(7)   Definitely

Ask if: F15 = 2

F19

How long has this fear of social situations been present?

(1)   Less than a month
(2)   At least one month but less than six months
(3)   Six months or more

Ask if: F15 = 2

F20

How old was s/he when this fear of social situations began?

Ask if: F15 = 2

F21

When NAME CHILD is in one of the social situations s/he fears, or thinks s/he is about to come up against one of these situations does s/he become anxious or upset?

(5)   No
(6)   A little
(7)   Or a lot

Ask if: F15 = 2 AND: F21 = A Lot

F22

How often does his/her fear of social situations result in his/her becoming upset like this

(1)   Many times a day
(2)   Most days
(3)   Most weeks
(4)   Or every now and then?

Ask if: F15 = 2

F23

Does his/her fear lead to NAME CHILD avoiding social situations...

(5)   No
(6)   A little
(7)   or a lot

Ask if: F15 = 2 AND: F23 = A Lot

F23a

How much does this avoidance interfere with his/her daily life?

(5)   No
(6)   A little
(7)   A Lot

Ask if: F15 = 2

F23b

Does s/he think that this fear of social situations is over the top or unreasonable?

(5)   No
(6)   Perhaps
(7)   Definitely

Ask if: F15 = 2

F23c

Is s/he upset about having this fear?

(5)   No
(6)   Perhaps
(7)   Definitely

Ask if: F15 = 2

F24

Have NAME CHILD's fears put a burden on you or the family as a whole?

(5)   not at all
(6)   only a little
(7)   quite a lot
(8)   or a great deal?

Panic Attacks and Agoraphobia

F25Intr

Many children have times when they get very anxious or worked up about silly little things, but some young people get severe panics that come out of the blue – they just don't seem to have any trigger at all.

F25

Over the last 4 weeks has NAME CHILD had a panic attack when s/he suddenly became very panicky for no reason at all, without even a little thing to set him/her off?

(1)   Yes
(2)   No

F26

Over the last 4 weeks has NAME CHILD been very afraid of, or tried to avoid, the things on this card?
CODE ALL THAT APPLY

(1)   Crowds
(2)   Public places
(3)   Travelling alone (if s/he ever does)
(4)   Being far from home
(9)   None of the above

ASK IF: F26 = 1, 2, 3 or 4

F27

Do you think this fear or avoidance is because s/he is afraid that if s/he had a panic attack or something like that, s/he would find it difficult or embarrassing to get away, or would not be able to get the help s/he needs?

(1)   Yes
(2)   No

Post Traumatic Stress Disorder

E1

The next section is about events or situations that are exceptionally stressful, and that would really upset almost anyone. For example being caught in a burning house, being abused, being in a serious car crash or seeing a member of his/her family or friends being mugged at gunpoint.
During NAME CHILD's lifetime has anything like this happened to him/her?

(1)   Yes
(2)   No

ASK IF: E1 = Yes

E2a

(May I just check,)
Has NAME CHILD ever experienced any of the following?

(1)   A serious and frightening accident, e.g. being run over by a car, being in a bad car or train crash etc
(2)   A bad fire, e.g. trapped in a burning building
(3)   Other disasters, e.g. kidnapping, earthquake, war
(4)   A severe attack or threat, e.g. by a mugger or gang
(5)   Severe physical abuse that he/she still remembers
(6)   Sexual abuse
(7)   Rape
(8)   Witnessed severe domestic violence, e.g. saw mother badly beaten up at home
(9)   Saw family member or friend severely attacked or threatened, e.g. by a mugger or a gang
(10)   Witnessed a sudden death, a suicide, an overdose, a serious accident, a heart attack etc..
(11)   Some other severe trauma (Please describe)

ASK IF: E1 = Yes AND E2a = 11

Othtrma

Please describe this other trauma

ASK IF: E1 = Yes AND: response in E2a

E3Intr

I am now going to ask you how this event(s) has affected NAME CHILD's behaviour and feelings.

If there is more than one event, I would like you to think about all of these.

ASK IF: E1 = Yes AND: response in E2a

E3

At the time, was NAME CHILD very distressed or did his/her behaviour change dramatically?

(1)   Yes
(2)   No
(3)   Don't know

Ask if: E1 = Yes And: response in E2a

E5

At present, is it affecting NAME CHILD's behaviour, feelings or concentration?

(1)　Yes
(2)　No

Ask if: E1 = Yes And: response in E2a And: E5 = Yes

E21a

(Over the last 4 weeks, has NAME CHILD. .)

. . 'relived' the event with vivid memories (flashbacks) of it?

(5)　No
(6)　A little
(7)　A Lot

Ask if: E1 = Yes And: response in E2a And: E5 = Yes

E21b

(Over the last 4 weeks, has NAME CHILD. .)

.. had repeated distressing dreams of the event?

(5)　No
(6)　A little
(7)　A Lot

Ask if: E1 = Yes And: response in E2a And: E5 = Yes

E21c

(Over the last 4 weeks, has NAME CHILD. .)

.. got upset if anything happened which reminded him/her of it?

(5)　No
(6)　A little
(7)　A Lot

Ask if: E1 = Yes And: response in E2a And: E5 = Yes

E21d

(Over the last 4 weeks, has NAME CHILD. .)

.. tried to avoid thinking or talking about anything to do with the event?

(5)　No
(6)　A little
(7)　A Lot

Ask if: E1 = Yes And: response in E2a And: E5 = Yes

E21e

(Over the last 4 weeks, has NAME CHILD. .)

.. tried to avoid activities places or people that remind him/her of the event?

(5)　No
(6)　A little
(7)　A Lot

Ask if: E1 = Yes And: response in E2a And: E5 = Yes

E21f

(Over the last 4 weeks, has NAME CHILD. .)

.. blocked out important details of the event from his/her memory?

(5)　No
(6)　A little
(7)　A Lot

Ask if: E1 = Yes And: response in E2a And: E5 = Yes

E21g

(Over the last 4 weeks, has NAME CHILD. .)

.. shown much less interest in activities s/he used to enjoy?

(5)　No
(6)　A little
(7)　A Lot

Ask if: E1 = Yes And: response in E2a And: E5 = Yes

E21h

(Over the last 4 weeks, has NAME CHILD. .)

.. felt cut off or distant from others?

(5)　No
(6)　A little
(7)　A Lot

Ask if: E1 = Yes And: response in E2a And: E5 = Yes

E21i

(Over the last 4 weeks, has NAME CHILD. .)

.. expressed a smaller range of feelings than in the past?
(e.g. no longer able to express loving feelings)

(5)　No
(6)　A little
(7)　A Lot

Ask if: E1 = Yes And: response in E2a And: E5 = Yes

E21j

(Over the last 4 weeks, has NAME CHILD . .)

.. felt less confidence in the future?

(5)　No
(6)　A little
(7)　A Lot

Ask if: E1 = Yes *And:* response in E2a *And:* E5 = Yes

E21k

(Over the last 4 weeks, has NAME CHILD. .)

.. had problems sleeping?

(5)   No
(6)   A little
(7)   A Lot

Ask if: E1 = Yes *And:* response in E2a *And:* E5 = Yes

E21l

(Over the last 4 weeks, has NAME CHILD. .)

.. felt irritable or angry?

(5)   No
(6)   A little
(7)   A Lot

Ask if: E1 = Yes *And:* response in E2a *And:* E5 = Yes

E21m

(Over the last 4 weeks, has NAME CHILD. .)

.. had difficulty concentrating?

(5)   No
(6)   A little
(7)   A Lot

Ask if: E1 = Yes *And:* response in E2a *And:* E5 = Yes

E21n

(Over the last 4 weeks, has NAME CHILD. .)

.. always been on the alert for possible dangers?

(5)   No
(6)   A little
(7)   A Lot

Ask if: E1 = Yes *And:* response in E2a *And:* E5 = Yes

E21o

(Over the last 4 weeks, has NAME CHILD. .)

.. jumped at little noises or easily startled in other ways?

(5)   No
(6)   A little
(7)   A Lot

E22

You have told me about how... (STRESSFUL EVENT)

How long after the stressful event did these other problems begin?

(1)   Within six months
(2)   More than six months after the event

E23

POST TRAUMATIC STRESS-DISORDER SECTION – ADULT INTERVIEW
How long has s/he been having these problems?

(1)   Less than a month
(2)   At least one month but less than three months
(3)   Three months or more

E24

How upset or distressed is s/he by the problems that the stressful events triggered off...

(5)   Not at all
(6)   Only a little
(7)   Quite a lot
(8)   Or a great deal?

E25a

Have these problems interfered with...

... how well s/he gets on with you and the rest of the family?

(5)   Not at all
(6)   Only a little
(7)   Quite a lot
(8)   Or a great deal

E25b

(Have they interfered with...)

....making and keeping friends?

(5)   Not at all
(6)   Only a little
(7)   Quite a lot
(8)   Or a great deal

E25c

(Have they interfered with...)

...learning or class work?

(5)   Not at all
(6)   Only a little
(7)   Quite a lot
(8)   Or a great deal

E25d

(Have they interfered with...)

...playing, hobbies, sports or other leisure activities?

(5)   Not at all
(6)   Only a little
(7)   Quite a lot
(8)   Or a great deal

E26

Have these problems put a burden on you or the family as a whole?

(5)   Not at all
(6)   Only a little
(7)   Quite a lot
(8)   Or a great deal?

Compulsions and Obsessions

F28Intr

Many young people have some rituals or superstitions, e.g. not stepping on the cracks in the pavement, having to go through a special goodnight ritual, having to wear lucky clothes for exams or needing a lucky mascot for school sports matches. It is also common for young people to go through phases when they seem obsessed by one particular subject or activity, e.g. cars, a pop group, a football team. But what I want to know is whether NAME CHILD has any rituals or obsessions that go beyond this.

F28

Does NAME CHILD have rituals or obsessions that upset him/ her, waste a lot of his/her time or interfere with his/her ability to get on with everyday life?

(1)   Yes
(2)   No

F29Intr

Over the last 4 weeks, has s/he had any of the following rituals (doing any of the following things over and over again, even though s/he has already done them or doesn't need to do them at all?)

F29a

Excessive cleaning; handwashing, baths, showers, toothbrushing etc. ?

(5)   No
(6)   A little
(7)   A Lot

F29b

Other special measures to avoid dirt, germs or poisons?

(5)   No
(6)   A little
(7)   A Lot

F29c

Checking: doors, locks, oven, gas taps, electric switches?

(5)   No
(6)   A little
(7)   A Lot

F29d

Repeating the same simple activity many times in a row for no reason, e.g. repeatedly standing up and sitting down or going backwards and forwards through a doorway?

(5)   No
(6)   A little
(7)   A Lot

F29e

Touching things or people in particular ways?

(5)   No
(6)   A little
(7)   A Lot

F29f

Arranging things so they are just so, or exactly symmetrical?

(5)   No
(6)   A little
(7)   A Lot

F29g

Counting to particular lucky numbers or avoiding unlucky numbers?

(5)   No
(6)   A little
(7)   A Lot

F31a

Over the last 4 weeks, has NAME CHILD been obsessively worrying about dirt, germs or poisons, not being able to get thoughts of them out of his/her mind?

(5)   No
(6)   A little
(7)   A Lot

F31b

Over the last 4 weeks, has NAME CHILD been obsessed by the worry that...

... something terrible happening to him/her or to others, e.g. illnesses, accidents, fires?

(5)   No
(6)   A little
(7)   A Lot

ASK IF: F31b = A Lot

F32

Is this obsession about something terrible happening to him/ herself or others just one part of a general concern about being separated from
his/her key attachment figures, or is it a problem in its own right?

(1)   Part of separation anxiety
(2)   a problem in it's own right

F33

Have NAME CHILD's rituals or obsessions been present on most days for a period of at least two weeks?

(1)   Yes
(2)   No

F34

Does s/he think that his/her rituals or obsessions are over the top or unreasonable?

(5)   No
(6)   Perhaps
(7)   Definitely

F35

Does s/he try to resist the rituals or obsessions?

(5)   No
(6)   Perhaps
(7)   Definitely

F36

Do the rituals or obsessions upset him/her...

(5)   No, s/he enjoys them
(6)   Neutral, s/he neither enjoys them nor becomes upset
(7)   They upset him/her a little
(8)   They upset him/her a lot?

F37

Do the rituals or obsessions use up at least an hour a day on average?

(1)   Yes
(2)   No

F38a

Have the rituals or obsessions interfered with...
... How well s/he gets on with you and the rest of the family?

(5)   Not at all
(6)   Only a little
(7)   Quite a lot
(8)   Or a great deal

F38b

(Have they interfered with...)

....Making and keeping friends?

(5)   Not at all
(6)   Only a little
(7)   Quite a lot
(8)   Or a great deal

F38c

(Have they interfered with...)

...learning new things (or class work)?

(5)   Not at all
(6)   Only a little
(7)   Quite a lot
(8)   Or a great deal

F38d

(Have they interfered with...)

...playing, hobbies, sports or other leisure activities?

(5)   Not at all
(6)   Only a little
(7)   Quite a lot
(8)   Or a great deal

F38e

Have the rituals or obsessions put a burden on you or the family as a whole?

(5)   Not at all
(6)   Only a little
(7)   Quite a lot
(8)   Or a great deal

Generalised Anxiety

F39

Does NAME CHILD ever worry?

(1) Yes
(2) No

Ask if: F39 = Yes

F39aIntr

Some young people worry about just a few things, some related to specific fears, obsessions or separation anxieties. Other young people worry about many different aspects of their lives. They may have specific fears, obsessions or separation anxieties, but they may also have a wide range of worries about many things.

Ask if: F39 = Yes

F39a

Is NAME CHILD a worrier in general?

(1) Yes, s/he worries in general
(2) No, s/he just has a few specific worries

Ask if: F39 = Yes And: F39a = Yes

F39aa

Over the last 6 months has NAME CHILD worried so much about so many things that it has really upset him/her or interfered with his/her life?

(5) No
(6) Perhaps
(7) Definitely

Ask if: F39 = Yes

F40a

Over the last 6 months, and by comparison with others of the same age, has NAME CHILD worried about:

Past behaviour: for example, Did I do that wrong? Have I upset someone? Have they forgiven me?

(5) No more than others of the same age
(6) A little more than others of the same age
(7) A lot more than others of the same age

Ask if: F39 = Yes

F40b

(Over the last 6 months, and by comparison with other young people of the same age, has NAME CHILD worried about:)

School work, homework or examinations

(5) No more than other young people of the same age
(6) A little more than other young people of the same age
(7) A lot more than other young people of the same age
(8) SPONTANEOUS: Not at school

Ask if: F39 = Yes

F40c

(Over the last 6 months, and by comparison with other young people of the same age, has NAME CHILD worried about:)

Disasters: Burglaries, muggings, fires, bombs etc.

(5) No more than others of the same age
(6) A little more than others of the same age
(7) A lot more than others of the same age

Ask if: F39 = Yes

F40d

(Over the last 6 months, and by comparison with other young people of the same age, has NAME CHILD worried about:)

His/her own health

(5) No more than others of the same age
(6) A little more than others of the same age
(7) A lot more than others of the same age

Ask if: F39 = Yes

F40e

(Over the last 6 months, and by comparison with other young people of the same age, has NAME CHILD worried about:)

Bad things happening to others: family friends, pets, the world (e.g. wars)

(5) No more than others of the same age
(6) A little more than others of the same age
(7) A lot more than others of the same age

Ask if: F39 = Yes

F40f

(Over the last 6 months, and by comparison with other young people of the same age, has NAME CHILD worried about:)

The future: e.g. getting a job, boy/girlfriend, moving out

(5) No more than others of the same age
(6) A little more than others of the same age
(7) A lot more than others of the same age

Ask if: F39 = Yes

F40g

(Over the last 6 months, and by comparison with other young people of the same age, has NAME CHILD worried about:)

Making and keeping friends

(5) No more than others of the same age
(6) A little more than others of the same age
(7) A lot more than others of the same age

ASK IF: F39 = Yes

F40h

(Over the last 6 months, and by comparison with other young people of the same age, has NAME CHILD worried about:)

Death and dying

(5)   No more than others of the same age
(6)   A little more than others of the same age
(7)   A lot more than others of the same age

ASK IF: F39 = Yes

F40i

(Over the last 6 months, and by comparison with other young people of the same age, has NAME CHILD worried about:)
Being bullied or teased

(5)   No more than others of the same age
(6)   A little more than others of the same age
(7)   A lot more than others of the same age

ASK IF: F39 = Yes

F40j

(Over the last 6 months, and by comparison with other young people of the same age, has NAME CHILD worried about:) His/her appearance or weight

(5)   No more than others of the same age
(6)   A little more than others of the same age
(7)   A lot more than others of the same age

ASK IF: F39 = Yes

F40k

Has s/he worried about anything else?

(1)   Yes
(2)   No

ASK IF: F39 = Yes AND F40k = Yes

F40l

What else has s/he worried about?

ASK IF: F39 = Yes AND F40k = Yes

F40m

How much does s/he worry about this?

(5)   No more than others of the same age
(6)   A little more than others of the same age
(7)   A lot more than others of the same age

F42

Over the last 6 months has s/he worried excessively on more days than not?

(1)   Yes
(2)   No

F43

Does s/he find it difficult to control the worry?

(1)   Yes
(2)   No

F44

Does worrying lead to him/her feeling restless, keyed up, on edge or unable to relax?

(1)   Yes
(2)   No

ASK IF: F44 = Yes

F44a

Has this been true for more days than not in the last 6 months?

(1)   Yes
(2)   No

F45

Does worrying lead to him/her feeling tired or worn out more easily?

(1)   Yes
(2)   No

ASK IF: F45 = Yes

F45a

Has this been true for more days than not in the last 6 months?

(1)   Yes
(2)   No

F46

Does worrying lead to difficulties in concentrating or his/her mind going blank?

(1)   Yes
(2)   No

ASK IF: F46 = Yes

F46a

Has this been true for more days than not in the last 6 months?

(1)   Yes
(2)   No

F47

Does worrying make him/her irritable?

(1)   Yes
(2)   No

Ask if: F47 = Yes

F47a

Has this been true for more days than not in the last 6 months?

(1) Yes
(2) No

F48

Does worrying lead to muscle tension?

(1) Yes
(2) No

Ask if: F48 = Yes

F48a

Has this been true for more days than not in the last 6 months?

(1) Yes
(2) No

F49

Does worrying interfere with his/her sleep, e.g. difficulty in falling or staying asleep or restless, unsatisfying sleep?

(1) Yes
(2) No

Ask if: F49 = Yes

F49a

Has this been true for more days than not in the last 6 months?

(1) Yes
(2) No

F50

How upset or distressed is NAME CHILD as a result of all his/her various worries?
RUNNING PROMPT

(5) Not at all
(6) Only a little
(7) Quite a lot
(8) Or a great deal?

F51a

Have his/her worries interfered with ...

How well s/he gets on with you and the rest of the family?

(5) Not at all
(6) Only a little
(7) Quite a lot
(8) Or a great deal

F51b

(Have they interfered with ...)
making and keeping friends?

(5) Not at all
(6) Only a little
(7) Quite a lot
(8) Or a great deal

F51c

(Have they interfered with ...)
learning new things (or classwork)?

(5) Not at all
(6) Only a little
(7) Quite a lot
(8) Or a great deal

F51d

(Have they interfered with ...)
playing, hobbies, sports or other leisure activities?

(5) Not at all
(6) Only a little
(7) Quite a lot
(8) Or a great deal

F52

Have these worries put a burden on you or the family as a whole...

(5) Not at all
(6) Only a little
(7) Quite a lot
(8) Or a great deal?

Depression

DepIntr

This section of the interview is about NAME CHILD's mood.

G1

In the last 4 weeks, have there been times when NAME CHILD has been very sad, miserable, unhappy or tearful?

(1) Yes
(2) No

Ask if: G1 = Yes

G3

Over the last 4 weeks, has there been a period when s/he has been really miserable nearly every day?

(1)   Yes
(2)   No

Ask if: G1 = Yes

G4

During the time when s/he has been miserable, has s/he been really miserable for most of the day?
(i.e. for more hours than not)

(1)   Yes
(2)   No

Ask if: G1 = Yes

G5

When s/he has been miserable, could s/he be cheered up...

(1)   easily
(2)   with difficulty/only briefly
(3)   or not at all?

Ask if: G1 = Yes

G6

Over the last 4 weeks, the period of being miserable has lasted...

(1)   less than two weeks
(2)   or two weeks or more?

G8

In the last 4 weeks, have there been times when NAME CHILD has been grumpy or irritable in a way that was out of character for him/her?

(1)   Yes
(2)   No

Ask if: G8 = Yes

G10

Over the last 4 weeks, has there been a period when s/he has been really grumpy or irritable nearly every day?

(1)   Yes
(2)   No

Ask if: G8 = Yes

G11

During the period when s/he has been grumpy or irritable, has s/he been like that for most of the day? (i.e. for more hours than not)

(1)   Yes
(2)   No

Ask if: G8 = Yes

G12

Has the irritability been improved by particular activities, by friends coming round or by anything else?

(1)   Easily
(2)   With difficulty/only briefly
(3)   Not at all?

Ask if: G8 = Yes

G13

Over the last 4 weeks, has the period of being really irritable lasted...

(1)   Less than two weeks
(2)   Or two weeks or more?

G15

In the last 4 weeks, have there been times when NAME CHILD has lost interest in everything, or nearly everything that s/he normally enjoys doing?

(1)   Yes
(2)   No

Ask if: G15 = Yes

G17

Over the last 4 weeks, has there been a period when this lack of interest has been present nearly every day?

(1)   Yes
(2)   No

Ask if: G15 = Yes

G18

During those days when s/he has lost interest in things, has s/he been like this for most of each day? (i.e. for more hours than not)

(1)   Yes
(2)   No

Ask if: G15 = Yes

G19

Over the last 4 weeks, this loss of interest has lasted...

(1)   Less than two weeks
(2)   Or two weeks or more?

Ask if: G15 = Yes

G20

Has this loss of interest been present during the same period when s/he has been really miserable/irritable for most of the time?

(1)   Yes
(2)   No

289

G21a

During the period when NAME CHILD was sad, irritable or lacking in interest

. . . did s/he lack energy and seem tired all the time?

(1)   Yes
(2)   No

G21ba

(During the period when NAME CHILD was sad, irritable or lacking in interest)

. . . was s/he eating much more or much less than normal?

(1)   Yes
(2)   No

G21b

(During the period when NAME CHILD was sad, irritable or lacking in interest)

. . . did s/he either lose or gain a lot of weight?

(1)   Yes
(2)   No

G21c

(During the time when NAME CHILD was sad, irritable or lacking in interest)

. . . did s/he find it hard to get to sleep or to stay asleep?

(1)   Yes
(2)   No

G21d

(During the period when NAME CHILD was sad, irritable or lacking in interest)

. . .did s/he sleep too much?

(1)   Yes
(2)   No

G21e

(During the period when NAME CHILD was sad, irritable or lacking in interest)

. . . was s/he agitated or restless for much of the time?

(1)   Yes
(2)   No

G21f

(During the period when NAME CHILD was sad, irritable or lacking in interest)

. . . did s/he feel worthless or unnecessarily guilty for much of the time?

(1)   Yes
(2)   No

G21g

(During the period when NAME CHILD was sad, irritable or lacking in interest)

. . . did s/he find it unusually hard to concentrate or to think things out?

(1)   Yes
(2)   No

G21h

(During the period when NAME CHILD was sad, irritable or lacking in interest)

. . . did s/he think about death a lot?

(1)   Yes
(2)   No

G21i

(During the time when NAME CHILD was sad, irritable or lacking in interest)

. . . did s/he ever talk about harming himself/herself or killing himself/herself?

(1)   Yes
(2)   No

G21j

(During the period when NAME CHILD was sad, irritable or lacking in interest)

. . . did s/he ever try to harm himself/herself or kill himself/herself?

(1)   Yes
(2)   No

Aₛₖ ɪꜰ: *G21j = No*

G21k

Over the whole of his/her lifetime has s/he ever tried to harm himself/herself or kill himself/herself?

(1)   Yes
(2)   No
(3)   Don't know

G22

How much has NAME CHILD's sadness, irritability or loss of interest upset or distressed him/her?

(5)   Not at all
(6)   Only a little
(7)   Quite a lot
(8)   Or a great deal?

G23a

Has his/her sadness, irritability or loss of interest interfered with

...

how well s/he gets on with you and the rest of the family?

(5)   Not at all
(6)   Only a little
(7)   Quite a lot
(8)   Or a great deal

G23b

(Has this interfered with ...)
making and keeping friends?

(5)   Not at all
(6)   Only a little
(7)   Quite a lot
(8)   Or a great deal

G23c

(Has this interfered with ...)
learning new things (or classwork)?

(5)   Not at all
(6)   Only a little
(7)   Quite a lot
(8)   Or a great deal

G23d

(Has this interfered with ...)
playing, hobbies, sports or other leisure activities?

(5)   Not at all
(6)   Only a little
(7)   Quite a lot
(8)   Or a great deal

G24

Has his/her sadness, irritability or loss of interest put a burden on you or the family as a whole?

(5)   Not at all
(6)   Only a little
(7)   Quite a lot
(8)   Or a great deal?

Self Harm

G25

Over the last 4 weeks, has s/he talked about deliberately harming or hurting himself/herself?

(1)   Yes
(2)   No

G26

Over the last 4 weeks, has s/he ever tried to harm or hurt himself/herself?

(1)   Yes
(2)   No

ASK IF: G26 = No

G27

Over the whole of his/her lifetime, has s/he ever tried to harm or hurt himself/herself?

(1)   Yes
(2)   No
(3)   Don't know

Attention and Activity

AttnIntr

This section of the interview is about NAME CHILD's level of activity and concentration over the last six months.
Nearly all young people are overactive or lose concentration at times, but what I would like to know is how NAME CHILD compares with other young people of his/her age?
I am interested in how s/he is usually – not on the occasional 'off day'.

H1

Allowing for his/her age, do you think that NAME CHILD definitely has some problems with overactivity or poor concentration?

(1)   Yes
(2)   No

H2Intr

I would now like to go through some more detailed questions about how NAME CHILD has usually been over the last six months? I will start with questions about how active s/he has been

H2a

Does s/he often fidget?

(5)   No more than others of the same age
(6)   A little more than others of the same age
(7)   A lot more than others of the same age

H2b

Is it hard for him/her to stay sitting down for long?

(5)   No more than others of the same age
(6)   A little more than others of the same age
(7)   A lot more than others of the same age

H2c

Does s/he run or climb about when s/he shouldn't?

(5)   No more than others of the same age
(6)   A little more than others of the same age
(7)   A lot more than others of the same age

H2d

Does s/he find it hard to play or take part in other leisure activities without making a lot of noise?

(5)   No more than others of the same age
(6)   A little more than others of the same age
(7)   A lot more than others of the same age

H2e

If s/he is rushing about, does s/he find it hard to calm down when someone asks him/her to?

(5)   No more than others of the same age
(6)   A little more than others of the same age
(7)   A lot more than others of the same age

H3a

Does s/he often blurt out an answer before s/he had heard the question properly?

(5)   No more than others of the same age
(6)   A little more than others of the same age
(7)   A lot more than others of the same age

H3b

Is it hard for him/her to wait his/her turn?

(5)   No more than others of the same age
(6)   A little more than others of the same age
(7)   A lot more than others of the same age

H3c

Does s/he often butt in on other people's conversations or games?

(5)   No more than others of the same age
(6)   A little more than others of the same age
(7)   A lot more than others of the same age

H3d

Does s/he often go on talking even if s/he has been asked to stop or no one is listening?

(5)   No more than others of the same age
(6)   A little more than others of the same age
(7)   A lot more than others of the same age

H4a

Does s/he often make careless mistakes or fail to pay attention to what s/he is supposed to be doing?

(5)   No more than others of the same age
(6)   A little more than others of the same age
(7)   A lot more than others of the same age

H4b

Does s/he often seem to lose interest in what s/he is doing?

(5)   No more than others of the same age
(6)   A little more than others of the same age
(7)   A lot more than others of the same age

H4c

Does s/he often not listen to what people are saying to him/her?

(5)   No more than others of the same age
(6)   A little more than others of the same age
(7)   A lot more than others of the same age

H4d

Does s/he often not finish a job properly?

(5)   No more than others of the same age
(6)   A little more than others of the same age
(7)   A lot more than others of the same age

H4e

Is it often hard for him/her to get himself/herself organised to do something?

(5)   No more than others of the same age
(6)   A little more than others of the same age
(7)   A lot more than others of the same age

H4f

Does s/he often try to get out of things s/he would have to think about, such as homework?

(5)   No more than others of the same age
(6)   A little more than others of the same age
(7)   A lot more than others of the same age

H4g

Does s/he often lose things s/he needs for school or games?

(5)   No more than others of the same age
(6)   A little more than others of the same age
(7)   A lot more than others of the same age

H4h

Is s/he easily distracted?

(5)   No more than others of the same age
(6)   A little more than others of the same age
(7)   A lot more than others of the same age

H4i

Is s/he often forgetful?

(5)   No more than others of the same age
(6)   A little more than others of the same age
(7)   A lot more than others of the same age

H5a

Have NAME CHILD's teachers complained, over the past 6 months
of problems with being fidgety, restlessness or overactivity

(5)   No
(6)   A little
(7)   A lot
(8)   SPONTANEOUS: Not at school

H5b

(Have NAME CHILD's teachers complained over the last six months of problems with...)

Poor concentration or being easily distracted?

(5)   No
(6)   A little
(7)   A lot
(8)   SPONTANEOUS: Not at school

H5c

(Have NAME CHILD's teachers complained over the last six months of problems with...)

 Acting without thinking about what s/he was doing, frequently butting in, or not waiting his/her turn?

(5)   No
(6)   A little
(7)   A lot
(8)   SPONTANEOUS: Not at school

H7

Have NAME CHILD's difficulties with activity or concentration, been there for at least 6 months?

(1)   Yes
(2)   No

H8

What age did they start at?
IF 'ALWAYS' OR SINCE BIRTH, ENTER 00

H9

How much have NAME CHILD's difficulties with activity and concentration upset or distressed him/her

(5)   Not at all
(6)   Only a little
(7)   Quite a lot
(8)   Or a great deal?

H10a

(How much have NAME CHILD's difficulties with concentration and activity
 interfered with ...)

...how well s/he gets on with you and the rest of the family?

(5)   Not at all
(6)   Only a little
(7)   Quite a lot
(8)   Or a great deal

H10b

(Have they interfered with ...)

...making and keeping friends?

(5)   Not at all
(6)   Only a little
(7)   Quite a lot
(8)   Or a great deal

H10c

(Have they interfered with ...)

...learning new things (or class work)?

(5)   Not at all
(6)   Only a little
(7)   Quite a lot
(8)   Or a great deal

H10d

(Have they interfered with ...)

...playing, hobbies, sports or other leisure activities?

(5)   Not at all
(6)   Only a little
(7)   Quite a lot
(8)   Or a great deal

H11

Have these difficulties with activity or concentration put a burden on you or the family as a whole?

(5)   Not at all
(6)   Only a little
(7)   Quite a lot
(8)   Or a great deal?

Awkward and Troublesome Behaviour

AwkIntr

This next section of the interview is about behaviour. Nearly all children are awkward and difficult at times – not doing what they are told, being irritable or annoying, having temper outbursts and so on. What I would like to know is how NAME CHILD compares with other young people of the same age.

I am interested in how s/he is usually, and not just on occasional 'off days'.

I1

Thinking about the last 6 months, how does NAME CHILD's behaviour compare with other young of the same age...

(1)   Less troublesome than average
(2)   About average
(3)   Or more troublesome than average

I2Intr

Some young people are awkward or annoying with just one person – perhaps with yourself or just one brother or sister. Others are troublesome with a range of adults or children. The following questions are about how NAME CHILD is in general, and not just with one person.

I2a

Over the last 6 months and compared with other young people of the same age.
Has s/he often had temper outbursts?

(5)   No more than others of the same age
(6)   A little more than others of the same age
(7)   A lot more than others of the same age

I2b

(Over the last 6 months and compared with other young people of the same age.)
Has s/he often argued with grown-ups?

(5)   No more than others of the same age
(6)   A little more than others of the same age
(7)   A lot more than others of the same age

I2c

(Over the last 6 months and compared with other young people of the same age.)
Has s/he often taken no notice of rules, or refused to do as s/he is told?

(5)   No more than others of the same age
(6)   A little more than others of the same age
(7)   A lot more than others of the same age

I2d

(Over the last six months and compared with other young people of the same age.)
Has s/he often seemed to do things to annoy other people on purpose?

(5)   No more than others of the same age
(6)   A little more than others of the same age
(7)   A lot more than others of the same age

I2e

(Over the last six months and compared with other young people of the same age.)
Has s/he often blamed others for his/her own mistakes or bad behaviour?

(5)   No more than others of the same age
(6)   A little more than others of the same age
(7)   A lot more than others of the same age

I2f

(Over the last six months and compared with other young people of the same age.)
Has s/he often been touchy and easily annoyed?

(5)   No more than others of the same age
(6)   A little more than others of the same age
(7)   A lot more than others of the same age

I2g

(Over the last six months and compared with other young people of the same age.)
Has s/he often been angry and resentful?

(5)   No more than others of the same age
(6)   A little more than others of the same age
(7)   A lot more than others of the same age

I2h

(Over the last six months and compared with other young people of the same age.)
Has s/he often been spiteful?

(5)   No more than others of the same age
(6)   A little more than others of the same age
(7)   A lot more than others of the same age

I2i

(Over the last six months and compared with other young people of the same age.)
Has s/he often tried to get his/her own back on people?

(5)   No more than others of the same age
(6)   A little more than others of the same age
(7)   A lot more than others of the same age

I3

Have NAME CHILD's teachers complained over the last 6 months of problems with this kind of awkward behaviour or disruptiveness in class?

(5)   No
(6)   A little
(7)   A Lot
(8)   DNA: No longer at school

I4

Has NAME CHILD's awkward behaviour been there for at least 6 months?

(1)   Yes
(2)   No

Ask if: I4 = Yes

I5

How old was s/he when this sort of awkward behaviour began?

I6Intr

Has NAME CHILD's awkward behaviour interfered with ...

I6a

how well s/he gets on with you and the rest of the family?

(5)   Not at all
(6)   Only a little
(7)   Quite a lot
(8)   Or a great deal

I6b

...making and keeping friends?

(5)   Not at all
(6)   Only a little
(7)   Quite a lot
(8)   Or a great deal

I6c

...learning new things (or class work)?

(5)   Not at all
(6)   Only a little
(7)   Quite a lot
(8)   Or a great deal

I6d

... playing, hobbies, sports or other leisure activities?

(5)   Not at all
(6)   Only a little
(7)   Quite a lot
(8)   Or a great deal

I7

Has his/her awkward behaviour put a burden on you or the family as a whole?

(5)   Not at all
(6)   Only a little
(7)   Quite a lot
(8)   Or a great deal?

I8Intr

I'm now going to ask about behaviour that sometimes gets young people into trouble, including dangerous, aggressive or antisocial behaviour. Please answer according to how s/he has been over the last year – I'm switching to the past 12 months for this set of questions. As before, I am interested in how s/he is usually, and not just on occasional 'off days'.

As far as you know, over the last 12 months.....

I8a

Has s/he often told lies in order to get things or favours from others, or to get out of having to do things s/he is supposed to do?

(5)   No
(6)   Perhaps
(7)   Definitely

Ask if: I8a = Definitely

I8aa

Has this been going on for the last 6 months?

(1)   Yes
(2)   No

I8b

Has s/he often started fights?
(other than with brothers or sisters)

(5)   No
(6)   Perhaps
(7)   Definitely

Ask if: I8b = Definitely

I8ba

Has this been going on for the last 6 months?

(1)   Yes
(2)   No

I8c

Has s/he often bullied or threatened people?

(5)   No
(6)   Perhaps
(7)   Definitely

Ask if: I8c = Def

I8ca

Has this been going on for the last 6 months?

(1)   Yes
(2)   No

I8d

Has s/he often stayed out after dark much later than s/he was supposed to?

(5)   No
(6)   Perhaps
(7)   Definitely

Ask if: I8d = Definitely

I8da

Has this been going on for the last 6 months?

(1)   Yes
(2)   No

I8e

Has s/he stolen from the house, or from other people's houses, or from shops or school?
(This doesn't include very minor thefts, e.g. stealing his/her pencil or food from the fridge)

(5)   No
(6)   Perhaps
(7)   Definitely

Ask if: I8e = Definitely

I8ea

Has this been going on for the last 6 months?

(1)   Yes
(2)   No

I8f

Has s/he run away from home more than once or ever stayed away all night without your permission?

(5)   No
(6)   Perhaps
(7)   Definitely

Ask if:: I8f = Definitely

I8fa

Has this been going on for the last 6 months?

(1)   Yes
(2)   No

I8g

Has s/he often played truant ('bunked off') from school?

(5)   No
(6)   Perhaps
(7)   Definitely
(8)   DNA: no longer at school

Ask if: I8g = Definitely

I8ga

Has this been going on for the last 6 months?

(1)   Yes
(2)   No

Ask if: Child is aged 13 or over AND I8g = Definitely

I9

Did s/he start playing truant ('bunking off') from school before s/he was 13?

(1)   Yes
(2)   No

I10Intr

May I now ask you about a list of less common but potentially more serious behaviours.
I have to ask everyone all these questions even when they are not likely to apply.
As far as you know, have any of the following happened even once in the last 12 months...?

I10a

Has s/he used a weapon or anything that could seriously hurt someone? (e.g. a bat, brick, broken bottle, knife, gun)?

(1)   Yes
(2)   No

Ask if: I10a = Yes

I10aa

Has this happened in the past 6 months?

(1)   Yes
(2)   No

I10b

Has s/he really hurt someone or been physically cruel to them? (e.g. has tied up, cut or burned someone)?

(1)   Yes
(2)   No

Ask if: I10b = Yes

I10ba

Has this happened in the past 6 months?

(1)   Yes
(2)   No

I10c

Has s/he been really cruel on purpose to animals and birds?

(1)   Yes
(2)   No

Ask if: I10c = Yes

I10ca

Has this happened in the past 6 months?

(1)   Yes
(2)   No

I10d

Has s/he deliberately started a fire?
(This is only if s/he intended to cause severe damage. This question is not about lighting camp fires, or burning individual matches or
pieces of paper)

(1)   Yes
(2)   No

Ask if: I10d = Yes

I10da

Has this happened in the past 6 months?

(1)   Yes
(2)   No

I10e

Has s/he deliberately destroyed someone else's property?
(This question is not about fire setting or very minor acts, eg. destroying sister's drawing. It does include things such as smashing car windows or school vandalism)

(1)   Yes
(2)   No

Ask if: I10e = Yes

I10ea

Has this happened in the past 6 months?

(1)   Yes
(2)   No

I10f

Has s/he been involved in stealing on the streets, e.g. snatching a handbag or mugging?

(1)   Yes
(2)   No

Ask if: I10f = Yes

I10fa

Has this happened in the past 6 months?

(1)   Yes
(2)   No

I10g

Has s/he tried to force someone to have sexual activity against their will?

(1)   Yes
(2)   No

Ask if: I10g = Yes

I10ga

Has this happened in the past 6 months?

(1)   Yes
(2)   No

I10h

Has s/he broken into a house, any other building, or a car?

(1)   Yes
(2)   No

Ask if: I10h = Yes

I10ha

Has this happened in the past 6 months?

(1)   Yes
(2)   No

I11

Have NAME CHILD's teachers complained of troublesome behaviour over the last 6 months?

(1)   Yes
(2)   No
(3)   DNA Not at school

I12

Has his/her troublesome behaviour been present for at least 6 months?

(1)   Yes
(2)   No

I11a

Has NAME CHILD ever been in trouble with the police?

(1)   Yes
(2)   No

Ask if: I11a = Yes

I11b

Please give a short description of this trouble.

I13a

(Has NAME CHILD's troublesome behaviour interfered with....)
how well s/he gets on with you and the rest of the family ?

(5)   Not at all
(6)   Only a little
(7)   Quite a lot
(8)   Or a great deal

I13b

(Has NAME CHILD's troublesome behaviour interfered with....)
making and keeping friends

(5)   Not at all
(6)   Only a little
(7)   Quite a lot
(8)   Or a great deal

I13c

(Has this interfered with...)
learning or class work?

(5)   Not at all
(6)   Only a little
(7)   Quite a lot
(8)   Or a great deal

I13d

(Has this interfered with...)
playing, hobbies, sports or other leisure activities?

(5)   Not at all
(6)   Only a little
(7)   Quite a lot
(8)   Or a great deal

I14

Has his/her troublesome behaviour put a burden on you or the family as a whole

(5)   Not at all
(6)   Only a little
(7)   Quite a lot
(8)   Or a great deal?

Eating disorders

ASK IF: Child is over 7 years old

P1Intr

> I am now going to ask you some questions about NAME CHILD's eating habits
> and how s/he feels about him/herself.

ASK IF: Child is over 7 years old

P1a

> Has NAME CHILD ever thought s/he was fat even when other people said s/he was very thin?

> (1) Yes
> (2) No

ASK IF: Child is over 7 years old

P1b

> Would NAME CHILD be ashamed if other people knew how much s/he eats?

> (1) Yes
> (2) No

ASK IF: Child is over 7 years old

P1c

> Has NAME CHILD ever deliberately made him/herself sick (throw up)?

> (1) Yes
> (2) No

ASK IF: Child is over 7 years old

P1d

> Do worries about eating (what? where? how much?) really interfere with his/her life?

> (1) Yes
> (2) No

ASK IF: Child is over 7 years old

P1e

> If NAME CHILD eats too much, does s/he blame him/herself a lot?

> (1) Yes
> (2) No

ASK IF: Child is over 7 years old

P2a

> How tall is NAME CHILD? (approximately)

> (1) Feet
> (2) CM

ASK IF: P2a = Feet

Feet

> INTERVIEWER: RECORD HOW MANY WHOLE FEET NAME CHILD IS.

ASK IF: P2a = Feet

Inches

> INTERVIEWER: RECORD HOW MANY ADDITIONAL INCHES NAME CHILD IS.

ASK IF: P2a = CM

Cent

> INTERVIEWER: NAME CHILD's HEIGHT IN CENTIMETRES.

ASK IF: Child is over 7 years old

P2b

> How much does NAME CHILD weigh? (approximately)

> INTERVIEWER: PLEASE STATE WHETHER YOU WILL GIVE WEIGHT IN
> STONES & POUNDS OR IN KILOGRAMS
> (1) Stones
> (2) Kilos

ASK IF: ASK IF: Child is over 7 years old P2b = Stones

Stones

> INTERVIEWER: RECORD HOW MANY WHOLE STONES NAME CHILD IS.

ASK IF: P2b = Stones

Pounds

> RECORD HOW MANY ADDITIONAL POUNDS NAME CHILD IS.

ASK IF: P2b = Stones

P2cStone

> What was his/her lowest weight in the last 12 months?

> PLEASE ENTER TOTAL NUMBER OF STONES

ASK IF: P2b = Stones

P2cPound

> PLEASE ENTER TOTAL NUMBER OF POUNDS

Ask if: *P2b = Stones*

P2dStone

What was his/her highest weight ever?

EXCLUDE ANY TIMES WHEN CHILD HAS BEEN PREGNANT

Ask if: *P2b = Stones*

P2dPound

PLEASE ENTER TOTAL NUMBER OF POUNDS

Ask if: *P2b = Kilos*

Kilos

INTERVIEWER: ENTER NAME CHILD's WEIGHT IN KILOGRAMS.

Ask if: *P2b = Kilos*

P2c

What was his/her lowest weight in the last 12 months?

PLEASE GIVE WEIGHT IN KILOGRAMS

Ask if: *P2b = Kilos*

P2d

What was his/her highest weight ever?

PLEASE GIVE WEIGHT IN KILOGRAMS

EXCLUDE ANY TIMES WHEN CHILD HAS BEEN PREGNANT

Ask if: *Child is over 7 years old*

P3

At present, would you describe NAME CHILD as very thin, thin, average, plump or fat?

(1) Very thin
(2) Thin
(3) Average
(4) Plump
(5) Fat

Ask if: *P3 = very thin or thin*

P4

Has s/he been like this for the last 5 years, or is s/he thinner now than s/he used to be?

(1) Even thinner in the past
(2) Always like this
(3) A little thinner now
(4) A lot thinner now

Ask if: *Child is over 7 years old*

P5

At present, would s/he describe him/herself as very thin, thin, average, plump or fat?

(1) Very thin
(2) Thin
(3) Average
(4) Plump
(5) Fat
(6) SPONTANEOUS ONLY – Child probably wouldn't think about this or DNA

Ask if: *Child is over 7 years old*

P6

Have you or other people – family, a friend, a doctor – been seriously concerned that his/her weight has been bad for his/her physical health?

(1) Yes
(2) No

Ask if: *Child is over 7 years old*

P7

What does NAME CHILD think? Does s/he think that his/her weight is bad for his/her physical health?

(1) Yes
(2) No
(3) SPONTANEOUS ONLY – Child probably wouldn't think about this or DNA

Ask if: *Child is over 7 years old*

P8

Is NAME CHILD afraid of gaining weight or getting fat?

(5) No
(6) A little
(7) A Lot

Ask if: *P8 = A Lot*

P9

Does the thought of gaining weight or getting fat really terrify him/her?

(1) Yes
(2) No

Ask if: *Child is over 7 years old*

P10

If a doctor told NAME CHILD that s/he needed to put on five pounds (two kilograms), would s/he find this easy, difficult or impossible to accept?

(1) Easy
(2) Difficult
(3) Impossible

Ask if: *Child is over 7 years old*

P11

Does NAME CHILD try to avoid eating the sorts of food that will make him/her fat?

(5) No
(6) A little
(7) A Lot

Ask if: *Child is over 7 years old P11 = A Lot*

P12

How often does NAME CHILD succeed in this?

(1) Never
(2) Sometimes
(3) Most of the time
(4) Always

Ask if: *Child is over 7 years old*

P13

Does NAME CHILD spend a lot of him/her time thinking about food?

(1) Yes
(2) No

Ask if: *Child is over 7 years old*

P14

Sometimes people say that they have such a strong desire for food, and that this desire is so hard to resist, that it is like the way an addict feels about drugs or alcohol.

Does this apply to NAME CHILD?

(5) No
(6) A little
(7) A Lot

Ask if: *Child is over 7 years old*

P15Intr

Sometimes people lose control over what they eat, and then they eat a very large amount of food in a short time. For example, they may open the fridge and eat as much as they can find – eating and eating until they feel physically ill. This usually happens when people are by themselves.

Ask if: *Child is over 7 years old*

P15

Does this happen to NAME CHILD?

(1) Yes
(2) No

Ask if: *Child is over 7 years old P15 = Yes*

P16

Over the last three months, how often on average has this happened?
Would you say...

(1) It hasn't happened
(2) it has happened occasionally
(3) about once a week
(4) or twice a week or more

Ask if: *P15 = Yes*

P17

When this happens, does NAME CHILD have a sense of having lost control over his/her eating?

(1) Yes
(2) No

Ask if: *Child is over 7 years old*

P18a

Over the last three months, has NAME CHILD been...

...eating less at meals

in order to avoid putting on weight?

WHEN 'NO' CHECK IF CHILD TRIES BUT IS NOT ALLOWED

(1) No
(2) Tries but is not allowed
(3) A little
(4) A lot

Ask if: *Child is over 7 years old*

P18b

...skipping meals?

(in order to avoid putting on weight?)

WHEN 'NO' CHECK IF CHILD TRIES BUT IS NOT ALLOWED

(1) No
(2) Tries but is not allowed
(3) A little
(4) A lot

Ask if: Child is over 7 years old

P18c

...going without food for long periods, e.g. all day or most of the day?

(in order to avoid putting on weight?)

WHEN 'NO' CHECK IF CHILD TRIES BUT IS NOT ALLOWED

(1)　No
(2)　Tries but is not allowed
(3)　A little
(4)　A lot

Ask if: Child is over 7 years old

P18d

...hiding or throwing away food that others give him/her?

(in order to avoid putting on weight?)

WHEN 'NO' CHECK IF CHILD TRIES BUT IS NOT ALLOWED

(1)　No
(2)　Tries but is not allowed
(3)　A little
(4)　A lot

Ask if: Child is over 7 years old

P18e

...exercising more?

(in order to avoid putting on weight?)

WHEN 'NO' CHECK IF CHILD TRIES BUT IS NOT ALLOWED

(1)　No
(2)　Tries but is not allowed
(3)　A little
(4)　A lot

Ask if: Child is over 7 years old

P18f

...making him/herself sick (vomiting)?

(in order to avoid putting on weight?)

WHEN 'NO' CHECK IF CHILD TRIES BUT IS NOT ALLOWED

(1)　No
(2)　Tries but is not allowed
(3)　A little
(4)　A lot

Ask if: Child is over 7 years old

P18g

...taking pills or medicines in order to lose weight?

(in order to avoid putting on weight?)

WHEN 'NO' CHECK IF CHILD TRIES BUT IS NOT ALLOWED

(1)　No
(2)　Tries but is not allowed
(3)　A little
(4)　A lot

Ask if: P18g = 2, 3, or 4

P18ga

DIETING, WEIGHT AND BODY SHAPE – PARENT

Please describe what pills or medicine NAME CHILD has been taking.

Ask if: Child is over 7 years old

P18h

Over the last three months, has NAME CHILD been doing other things in order to avoid putting on weight?

WHEN 'NO' CHECK IF CHILD TRIES BUT IS NOT ALLOWED

(1)　No
(2)　Tries but is not allowed
(3)　A little
(4)　A lot

Ask if: P18h = 2, 3, 4

P18ha

Please describe the other things that NAME CHILD has been doing to
avoid weight gain

Ask if: P18a = A Lot OR P18b = A Lot OR P18c = A Lot OR P18d = A Lot OR P18e = A Lot OR P18f = A Lot OR P18g = A Lot OR P18h = A Lot AND P15 = Yes

P19

You told me earlier about the times when NAME CHILD loses control and eats too much. After s/he does this, does s/he normally then P18Text to stop him/herself putting on weight?

(1)　Yes
(2)　No

Asᴋ ɪꜰ: *the child is female and over age 9*

P20

Has she had any periods in the last three months?

(1)   Yes
(2)   No

Asᴋ ɪꜰ: *the child is female and over age 9 AND P20 = No*

P21

Has she ever had any period?

(1)   Yes
(2)   No

Asᴋ ɪꜰ: *the child is female and over age 9 Aɴᴅ: (P20 = Yes) OR (P21 = Yes)*

P22

Is she taking any hormone pills or injections? (INCLUDING CONTRACEPTIVES)

(1)   Yes
(2)   No

Asᴋ ɪꜰ: *the child is female and over age 9 Aɴᴅ: (P20 = Yes) OR (P21 = Yes)*

P23

Please describe how her periods have been in general, and how they have been recently.

Asᴋ ɪꜰ: *P20 = No*

P24

Why do you think she has not had any period in the last 3 months?

Asᴋ ɪꜰ: *the child is female and over age 9 Aɴᴅ: (P20 = Yes) OR (P21 = Yes) P22 = Yes*

P25

Please describe what effects the hormone pills or injections have on NAME CHILD's periods.

Asᴋ ɪꜰ: *P3 = Very OR P5 = Very OR P9 = Yes OR P10 = Impossible OR P14 = A Lot OR P15 = Yes OR P18a = A Lot OR P18b = A Lot OR P18c = A Lot OR P18d = A Lot OR P18e = A Lot OR P18f = A Lot OR P18g = A Lot OR P18h = A Lot*

P26

You have told me about NAME CHILD's eating pattern and concern about weight or body shape. How upset or distressed is s/he by this?

(5)   Not at all
(6)   A little
(7)   A medium amount
(8)   A great deal

Asᴋ ɪꜰ: *P3 = Very OR P5 = Very OR P9 = Yes OR P10 = Impossible OR P14 = A Lot OR P15 = Yes OR P18a = A Lot OR P18b = A Lot OR P18c = A Lot OR P18d = A Lot OR P18e = A Lot OR P18f = A Lot OR P18g = A Lot OR P18h = A Lot*

P27a

How much have NAME CHILD's eating pattern or concern about weight and body shape interfered with...

...how well s/he gets on with you and the rest of the family?

(5)   Not at all
(6)   A little
(7)   A medium amount
(8)   A great deal

Asᴋ ɪꜰ: *P3 = Very OR P5 = Very OR P9 = Yes OR P10 = Impossible OR P14 = A Lot OR P15 = Yes OR P18a = A Lot OR P18b = A Lot OR P18c = A Lot OR P18d = A Lot OR P18e = A Lot OR P18f = A Lot OR P18g = A Lot OR P18h = A Lot*

P27b

(How much have NAME CHILD's eating pattern or concern about weight and body shape interfered with...)

...making and keeping friends?

(5)   Not at all
(6)   A little
(7)   A medium amount
(8)   A great deal

Asᴋ ɪꜰ: *P3 = Very OR P5 = Very OR P9 = Yes OR P10 = Impossible OR P14 = A Lot OR P15 = Yes OR P18a = A Lot OR P18b = A Lot OR P18c = A Lot OR P18d = A Lot OR P18e = A Lot OR P18f = A Lot OR P18g = A Lot OR P18h = A Lot*

P27c

(How much have NAME CHILD's eating pattern or concern about weight and body shape interfered with...)

...learning or class work?

(5)   Not at all
(6)   A little
(7)   A medium amount
(8)   A great deal

Asᴋ ɪꜰ: *P3 = Very OR P5 = Very OR P9 = Yes OR P10 = Impossible OR P14 = A Lot OR P15 = Yes OR P18a = A Lot OR P18b = A Lot OR P18c = A Lot OR P18d = A Lot OR P18e = A Lot OR P18f = A Lot OR P18g = A Lot OR P18h = A Lot*

P27d

(How much have NAME CHILD's eating pattern or concern about weight and body shape interfered with...)

...playing, hobbies, sports or other leisure activities?

(5)   Not at all
(6)   A little
(7)   A medium amount
(8)   A great deal

ASK IF: P3 = Very OR P5 = Very OR P9 = Yes OR P10 = Impossible OR P14 = A Lot OR P15 = Yes OR P18a = A Lot OR P18b = A Lot OR P18c = A Lot OR P18d = A Lot OR P18e = A Lot OR P18f = A Lot OR P18g = A Lot OR P18h = A Lot

P28

Has her eating pattern or concern about weight or body shape put a burden on you or the family as a whole?

(5)   Not at all
(6)   A little
(7)   A medium amount
(8)   A great deal

Tics

TicIntr

I am now going to ask you about any tics or habits that NAME CHILD has.

Q1

Over the last year, has NAME CHILD had any tic movements or twitches that s/he couldn't seem to control – such as excessive eye blinking, facial grimaces, nose twitches or head nodding?

(1)   Yes
(2)   No

Q2

Over the last year, has s/he had any tic noises or sounds that s/he couldn't seem to control – such as excessive sniffing, coughing or throat clearing?

(1)   Yes
(2)   No

Q3Intr

What doctors mean by 'motor tics' are repeated movements that are sudden and rapid, that follow more or less the same pattern every time, and that occur without the person really wanting them to.

Thinking about the whole of NAME CHILD's life, has s/he ever had motor tics involving any of the following types of repeated movement...

Q3a

Excessive blinking of eyes?

(1)   Yes
(2)   No

Q3b

Raising of eyebrows?

(1)   Yes
(2)   No

Q3c

Squinting of eyes?

(1)   Yes
(2)   No

Q3d

Rolling eyes up, down or sideways?

(1)   Yes
(2)   No

Q3e

Twitching of nose?

(1)   Yes
(2)   No

Q3f

Flaring of nostrils?

(1)   Yes
(2)   No

Q3g

Pouting of mouth (as if giving a kiss)?

(1)   Yes
(2)   No

Q3h

Stretching mouth wide open?

(1)   Yes
(2)   No

Q3i

Nodding of head?

(1)   Yes
(2)   No

Q3j

Screwing up of face?

(1)   Yes
(2)   No

Q3k

Touching chin to shoulder?

(1)   Yes
(2)   No

Q3l

Stretching neck?

(1)   Yes
(2)   No

Q3m

Shrugging shoulder?

(1)   Yes
(2)   No

Q3n

Jerking movement of arm or leg?

(1)   Yes
(2)   No

Q3o

Other motor tics?

(1)   Yes
(2)   No

ASK IF: *Q3o = Yes*

Q3oa

Please describe these.

Q4Intr

Sometimes, movements that look like tics turn out to have some other explanation. For example, some children squint because they need to wear glasses or change to stronger glasses. Similarly some children have nose and eye problems during the hay fever season.

ASK IF: *Q3a = Yes OR Q3b = Yes OR Q3c = Yes OR Q3d = Yes OR Q3e = Yes OR 3f = Yes OR Q3g = Yes OR Q3h = Yes OR Q3i = Yes OR Q3j = Yes OR Q3k = Yes OR Q3l = Yes OR Q3m = Yes OR Q3n = Yes OR Q3o = Yes*

Q4

Do you think that any of NAME CHILD's movements could have been caused by other things?

(1)   Yes
(2)   No

ASK IF: *Q4 = Yes*

Q5

Please describe what other things might have caused NAME CHILD's movements.

Q6Intr

We are now going to move on from motor tics to vocal tics. These are sounds that come from the mouth, nose or throat. They are sudden and rapid, they follow more or less the same pattern every time, and they occur without the person really wanting them to.

Thinking about the whole of NAME CHILD's life, has s/he ever had vocal tics involving any of the following types of repeated sounds?

Q6a

Throat clearing?

(1)   Yes
(2)   No

Q6b

Excessive sniffing?

(1)   Yes
(2)   No

Q6c

Coughing as a habit?

(1)   Yes
(2)   No

Q6d

Gulping?

(1)   Yes
(2)   No

Q6e

(Thinking about the whole of NAME CHILD's life, has s/he ever had vocal tics involving any of the following types of repeated sounds...)

High-pitched squeaks?

(1)   Yes
(2)   No

Q6f

Making little noises, e.g. 'Ah', 'Eh', 'Eee'?

(1)   Yes
(2)   No

Q6g

Sucking noises?

(1)   Yes
(2)   No

Q6h

Burping, not just when eating or drinking?

(1)   Yes
(2)   No

Q6i

A word said repeatedly and out of context?

(1)   Yes
(2)   No

Q6j

Swearing, without meaning to and without being annoyed?

(1)   Yes
(2)   No

Q6k

Other vocal tics?

(1)   Yes
(2)   No

Ask if: Q6k = Yes

Q6ka

Please describe.

Ask if: Q6a = Yes OR Q6b = Yes OR Q6c = Yes OR Q6d = Yes OR Q6e = Yes OR Q6f = Yes OR Q6g = Yes OR Q6h = Yes OR Q6i = Yes OR Q6j = Yes OR Q6k = Yes

Q7Intr

Sometimes, sounds that seem like tics turn out to have some other explanation. For example, some children clear their throat when they are nervous or cough a lot because they have a tickly throat with a cold or hay fever.

Ask if: Q6a = Yes OR Q6b = Yes OR Q6c = Yes OR Q6d = Yes OR Q6e = Yes OR Q6f = Yes OR Q6g = Yes OR Q6h = Yes OR Q6i = Yes OR Q6j = Yes OR Q6k = Yes

Q7

Do you think that any of NAME CHILD's sounds could have been caused by other things?

(1)   Yes
(2)   No

Ask if: Q7 = Yes

Q8

Please describe what other things might have caused NAME CHILD's sounds.

ᴀsᴋ ɪғ:

Q3a,Q3b,Q3c,Q3d,Q3e,Q3f,Q3g,Q3h,Q3I,Q3j,Q3k,Q3l,Q3m,Q3n,Q3o,Q6a,Q6b,Q6c,Q6d,Q6e,Q6f,Q6g,Q6h,Q6I,Q6j OR Q6k = yes

Q9

Do/Did the tics go away when s/he is asleep?

(1)   Yes
(2)   No

ᴀsᴋ ɪғ: Q3a,Q3b,Q3c,Q3d,Q3e,Q3f,Q3g,Q3h,Q3I,Q3j,Q3k,Q3l,Q3m,Q3n,Q3o,Q6a,Q6b,Q6c,Q6d,Q6e,Q6f,Q6g,Q6h,Q6I,Q6j OR Q6k = yes

Q10

Do/Did the tics sometimes worsen when s/he relaxes, e.g. while watching TV after a busy day at school?

(1)   Yes
(2)   No

ᴀsᴋ ɪғ: Q3a,Q3b,Q3c,Q3d,Q3e,Q3f,Q3g,Q3h,Q3I,Q3j,Q3k,Q3l,Q3m,Q3n,Q3o,Q6a,Q6b,Q6c,Q6d,Q6e,Q6f,Q6g,Q6h,Q6I,Q6j OR Q6k = yes

Q11

If NAME CHILD tries really hard, can/could s/he stop the tics from happening?

(1)   Yes
(2)   No

ᴀsᴋ ɪғ: Q11 = Yes

Q12

If s/he uses/used her will power to keep the tics under control for a while, does/did s/he get a rebound later, e.g. fewer tics when visitors come, but an extra burst of them later when they've gone?

(1)   Yes
(2)   No

ᴀsᴋ ɪғ: Q3a,Q3b,Q3c,Q3d,Q3e,Q3f,Q3g,Q3h,Q3I,Q3j,Q3k,Q3l,Q3m,Q3n,Q3o,Q6a,Q6b,Q6c,Q6d,Q6e,Q6f,Q6g,Q6h,Q6I,Q6j OR Q6k = yes

Q13

How old was s/he when the tic(s) first began?

ᴀsᴋ ɪғ: Q3a,Q3b,Q3c,Q3d,Q3e,Q3f,Q3g,Q3h,Q3I,Q3j,Q3k,Q3l,Q3m,Q3n,Q3o,Q6a,Q6b,Q6c,Q6d,Q6e,Q6f,Q6g,Q6h,Q6I,Q6j OR Q6k = yes

Q14

Over the last year, has NAME CHILD had any bad weeks for tics?
(Just to remind you, that means at least one week when s/he had many tics a day, either every day that week, or most days that week.)

(1)   Yes
(2)   No

ᴀsᴋ ɪғ: Q14 = Yes

Q15

When did NAME CHILD first start having bad weeks for tics?

(1)   Less than a month ago
(2)   1 month to 11 months ago
(3)   At least a year ago

ᴀsᴋ ɪғ: Q14 = Yes ᴀɴᴅ: Q15 = 2 or 3

Q16

Over the last year, roughly how many weeks have been bad weeks for tics...

(1)   well under half of them
(2)   about half of them
(3)   well over half of then
(4)   or, all or nearly all of them?

ᴀsᴋ ɪғ: Q14 = Yes ᴀɴᴅ: Q15 = 2 or 3

Q17

Over the last year, has NAME CHILD had a period of at least 4 weeks in a row that were bad weeks for tics?

(1)   Yes
(2)   No

ᴀsᴋ ɪғ: ᴀsᴋ ɪғ: Q14 = Yes ᴀɴᴅ: Q15 = 2 or 3 ᴀɴᴅ: Q17 = Yes

Q18

Have the last 4 weeks been bad weeks for tics?

(1)   Yes
(2)   No

ᴀsᴋ ɪғ: Q14 = Yes ᴀɴᴅ: Q15 = 2 or 3

Q19Intr

Some children/young people have tics week in, week out – though the pattern and number of tics isn't necessarily the same every week.

Other children/young people have weeks or months when the tics go away completely.

Ask if: Q14 = Yes *And:* Q15 = 2 or 3

Q19

Over the last year, has NAME CHILD had any tic-free periods lasting weeks or months?

(1) Yes
(2) No

Ask if: Q14 = Yes *And:* Q15 = 2 or 3 *And:* Q19 = Yes

Q20

What has been the longest tic-free period this year?

(1) Up to two months
(2) More than 2 months but less than 3 months
(3) More than 3 months

Ask if: Q14 = Yes

Q21

How upset or distressed is NAME CHILD as a result of all his/her tics?

(5) Not at all
(6) A little
(7) A medium amount
(8) A great deal

Ask if: Q14 = Yes

Q22a

Have his/her tics interfered with...

...how well s/he gets on with you and the rest of the family?

(5) Not at all
(6) A little
(7) A medium amount
(8) A great deal

Ask if: Q14 = Yes

Q22b

(Have his/her tics interfered with...)

...making and keeping friends?

(5) Not at all
(6) A little
(7) A medium amount
(8) A great deal

Ask if: Q14 = Yes

Q22c

Have his/her tics interfered with...

...learning or class work?

(5) Not at all
(6) A little
(7) A medium amount
(8) A great deal

Ask if: Q14 = Yes

Q22d

Have his/her tics interfered with...

...playing, hobbies, sport or other leisure activities?

(5) Not at all
(6) A little
(7) A medium amount
(8) A great deal

Ask if: Q14 = Yes

Q23

Have the tics put a burden on you or the family as a whole?

(5) Not at all
(6) A little
(7) A medium amount
(8) A great deal

Personality

PersIntr

I am now going to ask you about NAME CHILD's personality. I am going to read out several statements and for each one I would like you tell me whether it's Not true, Partly true or Certainly true for NAME CHILD

I have to ask everyone all these questions even though many of them may seem inappropriate for your child.

Occupy

Good at keeping him/herself occupied

(5) Not true
(6) Partly true
(7) Certainly true

Reckless

Often does reckless things without thinking of the danger or the consequences for him/herself or others

(5) Not true
(6) Partly true
(7) Certainly true

GoodImp

Makes a good first impression but people tend to see through him/her after they get to know him/her

(5) Not true
(6) Partly true
(7) Certainly true

Friends

Keeps friends

(5) Not true
(6) Partly true
(7) Certainly true

Shallow

Shallow and fast-changing emotions

(5) Not true
(6) Partly true
(7) Certainly true

TooFull

Too full of him/herself or his/her own abilities

(5) Not true
(6) Partly true
(7) Certainly true

Sorry

Is usually genuinely sorry if s/he has hurt someone or acted badly

(5) Not true
(6) Partly true
(7) Certainly true

Black

Often uses emotional blackmail to get his/her own way

(5) Not true
(6) Partly true
(7) Certainly true

NoScare

Not troubled in situations that worry or scare other children/young people of his/her age

(5) Not true
(6) Partly true
(7) Certainly true

Cold

Can seem cold-blooded or callous

(5) Not true
(6) Partly true
(7) Certainly true

Promise

Keeps promises

(5) Not true
(6) Partly true
(7) Certainly true

NoTrust

Difficulty trusting others

(5) Not true
(6) Partly true
(7) Certainly true

Genuine

Genuine in his/her expression of emotions

(5) Not true
(6) Partly true
(7) Certainly true

Tries

Usually tries his/her best

(5) Not true
(6) Partly true
(7) Certainly true

Less Common Disorders

L5

Apart from the things you have already told me about, are there any other aspects of NAME CHILD's psychological development that really concern you?

(1) Yes
(2) No

L6

Apart from the things you have already told me about, are there any other aspects of NAME CHILD's psychological development that really concern his/her teachers?

(1) Yes
(2) No

Significant Problems

Intro

You have told me about: ENTER PROBLEMS

I'd now like to hear a bit more about these difficulties in your own words.

SigProb

FURTHER DETAILS – ADULT INTERVIEW
LIST OF PROBLEMS:

INTERVIEWER: Please try and cover all areas of difficulty, but it is a good idea to let the parent choose which order to cover them in, starting with the area that concerns them most.
Use the prompt cards to cover each area of difficulty.
Below are details of which card you will need for each problem.

A. Separation anxiety, Specific phobia
B. Social phobia, Panic/Agoraphobia, Post traumatic stress
C. Obsessions and compulsions, Generalised anxiety
D. Depression, Deliberate self-harm
E. Hyperactivity, Awkward or troublesome behaviour
F. Dieting, weight and body shape, Tics
G. Less common disorders, Interviewer comments

OPEN

Anxiety

Does NAME CHILD experience any of the following symptoms when he/she feels anxious, nervous or tense

(1) Heart racing or pounding?
(2) Hands sweating or shaking?
(3) Feeling dizzy?
(4) Difficulty getting his/her breath?
(5) Butterflies in stomach?
(6) Dry mouth?
(7) Nausea or feeling as though s/he wanted to be sick?
(8) OR are you not aware of him/her having any of the above?

Service Use

Whhelp

Here is a list of people who parents and young people often turn to when they want advice and treatment about a young person's emotions, behaviour or concentration difficulties.
In the past year, have you, or NAME CHILD, been in contact with any of these people because of worries about his/her emotions, behaviour or concentration?

(1) Someone in your family or a close friend
(2) Telephone help line
(3) Self help group
(4) Internet
(5) Social worker
(6) A teacher (including Head of Year, Head-teacher or Special educational Needs Co-ordinator)
(7) Someone working in special educational services (for example educational psychologist, Educational Social Worker or School Counsellor)
(8) Your GP, family doctor or practice nurse
(9) Someone specialising in child mental health (for example child psychiatrist or child psychologist)
(10) Someone specialising in adult mental health (for example psychiatrist, psychologist or community psychiatric nurse)
(11) Someone specialising in children's physical health (for example a hospital or community paediatrician)
(12) Other – please describe
(13) None of these

Ask if: Whhelp = 12

WhhelpO

Who else have you sought advice from?

Ask if: Whhelp = social worker

LinkDesc

Now talking about
Social worker

Can you describe what they did?

OPEN

Ask if: Whhelp = social worker

LinkAdv

Still talking about
the Social worker

Was the advice or help offered for NAME CHILD 's emotional, behavioural or concentration difficulties..

(1) very helpful,
(2) helpful,
(3) made no difference,
(4) unhelpful or
(5) very unhelpful?

Ask if: Whhelp = teacher

TeacDesc

Now talking about
A teacher (including Head of Year, Head-teacher or Special educational Needs Co-ordinator)

Can you describe what they did?

OPEN

Ask if: Whhelp = teacher

TeacAdv

Still talking about
A teacher (including Head of Year, Head-teacher or Special educational Needs Co-ordinator)

Was the advice or help offered for NAME CHILD 's emotional, behavioural or concentration difficulties..

(1)   very helpful,
(2)   helpful,
(3)   made no difference,
(4)   unhelpful or
(5)   very unhelpful?

Ask if: Whhelp = special educational services

SpecDesc

Now talking about
Someone working in special educational services (for example educational psychologist, Educational Social Worker or School Counsellor)

Can you describe what they did?

OPEN

Ask if: Whhelp = special educational services

SpecAdv

Still talking about
Someone working in special educational services (for example educational psychologist, Educational Social Worker or School Counsellor)

Was the advice or help offered for NAME CHILD 's emotional, behavioural or concentration difficulties..

(1)   very helpful,
(2)   helpful,
(3)   made no difference,
(4)   unhelpful or
(5)   very unhelpful?

Ask if: Whhelp = GP, family doctor or practice nurse

GPDesc

Now talking about
Your GP, family doctor or practice nurse

Can you describe what they did?

OPEN

Ask if: Whhelp = GP, family doctor or practice nurse

GPAdv

Still talking about
Your GP, family doctor or practice nurse

Was the advice or help offered for NAME CHILD 's emotional, behavioural or concentration difficulties..

(1)   very helpful,
(2)   helpful,
(3)   made no difference,
(4)   unhelpful or
(5)   very unhelpful?

Ask if: Whhelp = child mental health specialist

ChdDesc

Now talking about
Someone specialising in child mental health (for example child psychiatrist or child psychologist)

Can you describe what they did?

OPEN

Ask if: Whhelp = child mental health specialist

ChdAdv

Still talking about
Someone specialising in child mental health (for example child psychiatrist or child psychologist)

Was the advice or help offered for NAME CHILD 's emotional, behavioural or concentration difficulties..

(1)   very helpful,
(2)   helpful,
(3)   made no difference,
(4)   unhelpful or
(5)   very unhelpful?

Ask if: Whhelp = adult mental health specialist

AdltDesc

Now talking about
Someone specialising in adult mental health (for example psychiatrist, psychologist or community psychiatric nurse)

Can you describe what they did?

OPEN

Ask if: Whhelp = adult mental health specialist

AdltAdv

Still talking about
Someone specialising in adult mental health (for example psychiatrist, psychologist or community psychiatric nurse)

Was the advice or help offered for NAME CHILD 's emotional, behavioural or concentration difficulties...

(1)　Very helpful,
(2)　Helpful,
(3)　Made no difference,
(4)　Unhelpful or
(5)　Very unhelpful?

Ask if: Whhelp = child physical health specialist

CPhyDesc

Now talking about
Someone specialising in children's physical health (for example a hospital or community paediatrician)

Can you describe what they did?

OPEN

Ask if: Whhelp = child physical health specialist

CPhyAdv

Still talking about
Someone specialising in children's physical health (for example a hospital or community paediatrician)

Was the advice or help offered for NAME CHILD 's emotional, behavioural or concentration difficulties..

(1)　Very helpful,
(2)　Helpful,
(3)　Made no difference,
(4)　Unhelpful or
(5)　Very unhelpful?

Ask if: Whhelp = other type of help

OthSDesc

Now talking about
the other type of help you mentioned

Can you describe what they did?
OPEN

Ask if: Whhelp = other type of help

OthSAdv

Still talking about
the other type of help you mentioned

Was the advice or help offered for NAME CHILD 's emotional, behavioural or concentration difficulties..

(1)　Very helpful,
(2)　Helpful,
(3)　Made no difference,
(4)　Unhelpful or
(5)　Very unhelpful?

SpecIntr1

You have said that you were worried about your child's emotions, behaviour or concentration, and you haven't seen a specialist about your worries in the past year.

By specialist services we mean Mental health services, Social services, Special Educational resources and Paediatrics (people specialising in children's physical health).

There are many good reasons for not seeing specialist services about your concerns as they are often not needed, but sometimes people don't get to specialist services because there are barriers in their way.

NoSpec1

I am going to show you a list of things that may have stopped you from
seeing a specialist in the last 12 months. Please say whether any of the following applied to you.

(1)　Didn't know of any services for these types of problems
(2)　Hard to persuade GP, teacher or other professional to refer me
(3)　Was referred but specialist services were reluctant to see us
(4)　Didn't like what the specialist services offered us
(5)　Didn't think that specialists would be able to help
(6)　Worried about what other people may think of us
(7)　Worried that my child might be taken away from me
(8)　NONE OF THESE

NoSpec2

Here is another list of things that may have stopped you from seeing a specialist in the last 12 months. Please say whether any of these things applied to you.

(1)　Had a bad experience with specialist services in the past
(2)　Difficult to arrange appointments for times we could manage
(3)　The specialist was too far away or too hard to get to
(4)　Couldn't afford to lose pay because of time off work or travel to specialist
(5)　Took so long for appointment to come through that by the time it arrived there seemed little point in going
(6)　Worried about privacy, confidentiality or child being left with permanent record
(7)　Other reason
(8)　NONE OF THESE

Ask if: NoSpec2 = other

OthSpec

Please specify other reason(s) you did not see a specialist.

SpecIntr2

You are seeing/have seen specialist services about your child's emotions, behaviour or concentration.

By specialist services we mean Mental health services, Social services, Special Educational resources and Paediatrics (people specialising in children's physical health).

Some families get to see a specialist without any difficulty but other families do meet some obstacles and we are interested in finding out about these.

SeenSpec1

I am going to show you a list of statements. Please say whether any of the following applied to you.

(1) Didn't know of any services for these types of problems
(2) Hard to persuade GP, teacher or other professional to refer me
(3) Was referred but specialist services were reluctant to see us
(4) Didn't like what the specialist services offered us
(5) Didn't think that specialists would be able to help
(6) Worried about what other people may think of us
(7) Worried that my child might be taken away from me
(8) NONE OF THESE

SeenSpec2

I am now going to show you another list of statements. Please say whether any of these things applied to you.

(1) Had a bad experience with specialist services in the past
(2) Difficult to arrange appointments for times we could manage
(3) The specialist was too far away or too hard to get to
(4) Couldn't afford to lose pay because of time off work or travel to specialist
(5) Took so long for appointment to come through that by the time it arrived there seemed little point in going
(6) Worried about privacy, confidentiality or child being left with permanent record
(7) Other reason
(8) NONE OF THESE

ASK IF: SeenSpec2 = other

OthSpec2

Please describe any other obstacles you encountered.

ASK IF: Whhelp = social worker

LinkWait

Now talking about:

Social Worker

How long did you wait to see the specialist

(1) Less than 6 weeks
(2) Six to nine weeks
(3) 10 weeks to six months
(4) More than 6 months

ASK IF: Whhelp = social worker

LinkAcpt

Still talking about:

Social Worker

Was this length of time acceptable?

(1) Yes
(2) No
(3) Don't know

ASK IF: Whhelp = social worker

LinkStop

Did you or NAME CHILD decide not to go on seeing a Social Worker (about your concerns for your child's emotions, behaviour or concentration) while they were still sending you appointments?

(1) Yes
(2) No

ASK IF: LinkStop = Yes

LinkWhy

Please describe your reasons for deciding to stop seeing the specialist.

ASK IF: Whhelp = special educational services

SpecWait

Now talking about:

Someone working in special educational services (for example educational psychologist, Educational Social Worker or School Counsellor)

How long did you wait to see the specialist

(1) Less than 6 weeks
(2) Six to nine weeks
(3) 10 weeks to six months
(4) More than 6 months

Ask if: Whhelp = special educational services

SpecAcpt

Still talking about:
Someone working in special educational services (for example educational psychologist, Educational Social Worker or School Counsellor)

Was this length of time acceptable?

(1)   Yes
(2)   No
(3)   Don't know

Ask if: Whhelp = special educational services

SpecStop

Did you or NAME CHILD decide not to go on seeing
Someone working in special educational services (for example educational psychologist, Educational Social Worker or School Counsellor) (about your concerns for your child's emotions, behaviour or concentration) while they were still sending you appointments?

(1)   Yes
(2)   No

Ask if: SpecStop = Yes

SpecWhy

Please describe your reasons for deciding to stop seeing the specialist.

Ask if: Whhelp = child mental health specialist

ChdWait

Now talking about:

Someone specialising in child mental health (for example child psychiatrist or child psychologist)

How long did you wait to see the specialist

(1)   Less than 6 weeks
(2)   Six to nine weeks
(3)   10 weeks to six months
(4)   More than 6 months

Ask if: Whhelp = child mental health specialist

ChdAcpt

Still talking about:
Someone specialising in child mental health (for example child psychiatrist or child psychologist)

Was this length of time acceptable?

(1)   Yes
(2)   No
(3)   Don't know

Ask if: Whhelp = child mental health specialist

ChdStop

Did you or NAME CHILD decide not to go on seeing
Someone specialising in child mental health (for example child psychiatrist or child psychologist) (about your concerns for your child's emotions, behaviour or concentration) while they were still sending you appointments?

(1)   Yes
(2)   No

Ask if: ChdStop = Yes

ChdWhy

Please describe your reasons for deciding to stop seeing the specialist.

Ask if: Whhelp = adult mental health specialist

AdltWait

Now talking about:
Someone specialising in adult mental health (for example psychiatrist, psychologist or community psychiatric nurse)

How long did you wait to see the specialist

(1)   Less than 6 weeks
(2)   Six to nine weeks
(3)   10 weeks to six months
(4)   More than 6 months

Ask if: Whhelp = adult mental health specialist

AdltAcpt

Still talking about:
Someone specialising in adult mental health (for example psychiatrist, psychologist or community psychiatric nurse)

Was this length of time acceptable?

(1)   Yes
(2)   No
(3)   Don't know

Ask if: Whhelp = adult mental health specialist

AdltStop

Did you or NAME CHILD decide not to go on seeing a
Someone specialising in adult mental health (for example psychiatrist, psychologist or community psychiatric nurse) (about your concerns for your child's emotions, behaviour or concentration) while they were still sending you appointments?

(1)   Yes
(2)   No

Ask if: AdltStop = Yes

AdltWhy

Please describe your reasons for deciding to stop seeing the specialist.

ASK IF: *Whhelp = child physical health specialist*

CPhyWait

Now talking about:
Someone specialising in children's physical health (for example a hospital or community paediatrician)

How long did you wait to see the specialist

(1)   Less than 6 weeks
(2)   Six to nine weeks
(3)   10 weeks to six months
(4)   More than 6 months

ASK IF: *Whhelp = child physical health specialist*

CPhyAcpt

Still talking about:
Someone specialising in children's physical health (for example a hospital or community paediatrician)

Was this length of time acceptable?

(1)   Yes
(2)   No
(3)   Don't know

ASK IF: *Whhelp = child physical health specialist*

CPhyStop

Did you or NAME CHILD decide not to go on seeing a
Someone specialising in children's physical health (for example a hospital or community paediatrician) (about your concerns for your child's emotions, behaviour or concentration) while they were still sending you appointments?

(1)   Yes
(2)   No

ASK IF: *CPhyStop = Yes*

CPhyWhy

Please describe your reasons for deciding to stop seeing the specialist.

Better

However pleased you have been with specialist services, there is usually room for some improvement. What do you think could be done to make them better?

Hospital

In the past 12 months has NAME CHILD had to stay in hospital overnight or attend a hospital for several hours each day for a while due to his/her emotions, behaviour or concentration difficulties?

(1)   Yes
(2)   No

ASK IF: *Hospital = Yes*

HospInfo

Can you tell me a little more about this.
PROMPTS: Number of in-patient (overnight) stays and day patient visits?
Duration of each inpatient stay? What were the visits for? What advice treatment did you get?

SeenYth

(Has NAME CHILD been seen by)

.........youth justice worker/probation worker

(1)   Yes
(2)   No
(3)   Don't know

ASK IF: *SeenYth = Yes*

TrtYth

What sort of help, advice or treatment did they give?

ASK IF: *SeenYth = Yes*

YthSHlp

Was it helpful?

ASK IF: *SeenYth = Yes*

YthConv

Has NAME CHILD received a caution or conviction?

(1)   Yes
(2)   No
(3)   Don't know

ASK IF: *YthConv = Yes*

WhyConv

When did NAME CHILD receive this caution or conviction?

ASK IF: *YthConv = Yes*

WhatConv

What was this caution or conviction for?

Stressful Life Events

StrsIntr

I would now like to ask about things that may have happened or problems that you or NAME CHILD may have faced.

K1

Since NAME CHILD was born, have you had a separation due to marital difficulties or broken off a steady relationship?

(1)   Yes
(2)   No

K2

Since NAME CHILD was born, have you (or a partner) had a major financial crisis, such as losing the equivalent of 3 months income?

(1)   Yes
(2)   No

K3

Since NAME CHILD was born, have you (or a partner) had a problem with the police involving a court appearance?

(1)   Yes
(2)   No

K8

Since NAME CHILD was born, have you (or a partner) had a serious physical illness such as cancer or a major heart attack?

(1)   Yes
(2)   No

K9

Since NAME CHILD was born, have you (or a partner) had a serious mental illness such as schizophrenia or major depression?

(1)   Yes
(2)   No

K6

Now turning to things that have happened to NAME CHILD. At any stage in his/her life, has a parent, brother or sister of his/hers died?

(1)   Yes
(2)   No

K7

At any stage in his/her life, has a close friend of his/hers died?

(1)   Yes
(2)   No

K4

Has s/he ever had a serious illness which required a stay in hospital

(1)   Yes
(2)   No

K5

Has s/he ever been in a serious accident or badly hurt in an accident?

(1)   Yes
(2)   No

Ask if: Child is aged 13 or over

K10

In the past year has one of NAME CHILD's close friendship ended, for example, permanently falling out with a best friend or breaking off a steady relationship with a boy or girl friend?

(1)   Yes
(2)   No

Ask if: Child is aged under 13

K11

In the past year has one of NAME CHILD's close friendship ended, for example, permanently falling out with a best friend?

(1)   Yes
(2)   No

School Exclusions

HowSch

How many different schools has NAME CHILD ever attended?

1..50

School

Is NAME CHILD still in full-time education?

(1)   Yes
(2)   No

ASK IF: *School = Yes*

Picked

Over the last year, has NAME CHILD been stressed because s/he feels s/he has been unfairly picked on by a teacher?

(5)   No
(6)   A little
(7)   A Lot

ASK IF: *Picked = A Lot*

FlyWall

It's difficult for you to know because you're not a fly on the classroom wall, but what do you make of this?

ExcEver

Has NAME CHILD ever been excluded from school?

(1)   Yes
(2)   No

ASK IF: *ExcEver = Yes*

ExcNum

How many times has NAME CHILD been excluded from school?

ASK IF: *ExcEver = Yes*

ExcLst

When was NAME CHILD (last) excluded?

ASK IF: *ExcEver = Yes*

WhyExc

Why was NAME CHILD excluded from school on this last occasion?

ASK IF: *ExcEver = Yes*

ExcFix

Was the exclusion fixed term (suspension) or permanent?

(1)   Fixed-term exclusion/suspension
(2)   Permanent exclusion
(3)   Not sure

ASK IF: *ExcFix = 1*

FixLong

How long was NAME CHILD suspended from school?
ENTER NUMBER OF DAYS

ASK IF: *ExcEver = Yes*

AftExc

What sort of educational provision did NAME CHILD have after being excluded?

(1)   Move to other school
(2)   Home tutoring
(3)   Referral unit
(4)   Special school
(5)   None

ASK IF: *ExcEver = Yes*

HelpExc

Did NAME CHILD receive any of these types of extra help after being excluded?

(1)   Behaviour management training
(2)   Social skills
(3)   Cognitive behavioural therapy
(4)   Parent management training
(5)   Family therapy
(6)   Receive NO extra help
(7)   Other – PLEASE SPECIFY

ASK IF: *(HelpExc = Other*

HelpOth

What other type of extra help did NAME CHILD receive?

Ask if: School = Yes

MisSch

Has NAME CHILD missed school for any other reason in the past term?

(1) Yes
(2) No

Ask if: MisSch = Yes

LongMis

How many days did NAME CHILD miss school last term?
PLEASE ENTER NUMBER OF DAYS

Ask if: MisSch = Yes

WhyMis

Why did NAME CHILD miss school?

(1) Short term illness
(2) Long term illness
(3) Refused to attend school
(4) Has a school phobia
(5) Other – PLEASE SPECIFY

Ask if: WhyMis = 5

OthMis

What was the other reason for missing school?

Ask if: WhyMis 2, 3, 4 or 5

EduProv

Did NAME CHILD receive any educational provision while s/he was unable to attend school?

(1) Yes
(2) No

Ask if: EduProv = Yes

WhatEdu

What type of educational provision did NAME CHILD receive?

(1) Home tutoring
(2) Individual or group tuition as an inpatient within hospital school
(3) Education within a pupil referral unit
(4) Other PLEASE SPECIFY

Ask if: WhatEdu = other

OthEduc

What other type educational provision did NAME CHILD receive?

SchProj

Has NAME CHILD taken part in any 'out of school projects' or any schemes in school to help him/her manage their behaviour, make friends or reading? Some example are listed on this card

(1) Homework clubs
(2) Out of school clubs
(3) Friendship clubs
(4) Nurture Groups
(5) Behaviour management groups
(6) Social skills group
(7) Anger management group
(8) Therapeutic groups
(9) Other – PLEASE SPECIFY
(10) No projects/schemes attended

Ask if: SchProj = other

ProjOth

What other type of school project has NAME CHILD been involved with?

LookAft

Has NAME CHILD ever spent any time being 'looked after' by social services?

(1) Yes
(2) No

Ask if: LookAft = Yes

LookNum

How many times has NAME CHILD been 'looked after'?

Ask if: LookAft = Yes

LastLook

How long was NAME CHILD 'looked after' on the most recent ocassion?
PLEASE ENTER NUMBER OF WEEKS

Ask if: LookAft = Yes

MoveSch

Did NAME CHILD move schools as a result of being 'looked after'?
IF MORE THAN ONE OCASSION PLEASE THINK ABOUT THE MOST RECENT TIME

(1) Yes
(2) No

Strengths

NIntro

I have been asking you a lot of questions about difficulties and problems.
I now want to ask you about NAME CHILD's good points or strengths.
I am going to read through a list of descriptions and I would like you to tell me whether or not they apply to NAME CHILD.

N1a

...generous

(5)   No
(6)   A little
(7)   A Lot

N1b

...lively

(5)   No
(6)   A little
(7)   A Lot

N1c

...keen to learn

(5)   No
(6)   A little
(7)   A Lot

N1d

...affectionate

(5)   No
(6)   A little
(7)   A Lot

N1e

...reliable and responsible

(5)   No
(6)   A little
(7)   A Lot

N1f

...easy going

(5)   No
(6)   A little
(7)   A Lot

N1g

...good fun, good sense of humour

(5)   No
(6)   A little
(7)   A Lot

N1h

...interested in many things

(5)   No
(6)   A little
(7)   A Lot

N1i

...caring, kind-hearted

(5)   No
(6)   A little
(7)   A Lot

N1j

...bounces back quickly after set-backs

(5)   No
(6)   A little
(7)   A Lot

N1k

...grateful, appreciative of what s/he gets

(5)   No
(6)   A little
(7)   A Lot

N1l

...independent

(5)   No
(6)   A little
(7)   A Lot

N2Intr

I now want to ask you about the things that NAME CHILD's
does that really please you.
I am going to read through a list of activities and I would like you
to tell me whether or not NAME CHILD does them.

N2a

...helps around the home

(5)   No
(6)   A little
(7)   A Lot

N2b

...gets on well with the rest of the family

(5) No
(6) A little
(7) A Lot

N2c

...does homework without needing to be reminded

(5) No
(6) A little
(7) A Lot

N2d

...creative activities: art, acting, music, making things

(5) No
(6) A little
(7) A Lot

N2e

...likes to be involved in family activities

(5) No
(6) A little
(7) A Lot

N2f

...takes care of his/her appearance

(5) No
(6) A little
(7) A Lot

N2g

...good at school work

(5) No
(6) A little
(7) A Lot

N2h

...polite

(5) No
(6) A little
(7) A Lot

N2i

...good at sport

(5) No
(6) A little
(7) A Lot

N2j

...keeps his/her bedroom tidy

(5) No
(6) A little
(7) A Lot

N2k

...good with friends

(5) No
(6) A little
(7) A Lot

N2l

...well behaved

(5) No
(6) A little
(7) A Lot

N3

Does NAME CHILD have any other good points you particularly want to mention?

(1) Yes
(2) No

Ask if: N3 = Yes

N3a

Please describe NAME CHILD's other good points.

Lrndifa

Compared with an average child of the same age, is his/her READING.....

(1) Above average
(2) Average
(3) has some difficulty
(4) or marked difficulty?

Lrndifb

Compared with an average child of the same age, is his/her MATHEMATICS .....

(1)   Above average
(2)   Average
(3)   has some difficulty
(4)   or marked difficulty?

Lrndifc

Compared with an average child of the same age, is his/her SPELLING.....

(1)   Above average
(2)   Average
(3)   has some difficulty
(4)   or marked difficulty?

Parent's self completion questionnaire

SCIntr

I would now like to you to take the computer and answer the next set of questions yourself.

HthIntr

We would like to know how your health has been in general, over the past few weeks. Please answer ALL the questions by entering the number next to the answer which describes how you have been feeling recently

GH1

Have you recently been able to concentrate on whatever you're doing?
ENTER THE NUMBER NEXT TO YOUR ANSWER

(1)   Better than usual
(2)   Same as usual
(3)   Less than usual
(4)   Much less than usual

GH2

Have you recently lost much sleep over worry?

(1)   Not at all
(2)   No more than usual
(3)   Rather more than usual
(4)   Much more than usual

GH3

Have you recently felt that you are playing a useful part in things?

(1)   More so than usual
(2)   Same as usual
(3)   Less so than usual
(4)   Much less useful

GH4

Have you recently felt capable of making decisions about things?

(1)   More so than usual
(2)   Same as usual
(3)   Less so than usual
(4)   Much less capable

GH5

Have you recently felt constantly under strain?

(1)   Not at all
(2)   No more than usual
(3)   Rather more than usual
(4)   Much more than usual

GH6

Have you recently felt you couldn't overcome your difficulties?

(1)   Not at all
(2)   No more than usual
(3)   Rather more than usual
(4)   Much more than usual

GH7

Have you recently been able to enjoy your normal day-to-day activities?

(1)   More so than usual
(2)   Same as usual
(3)   Less so than usual
(4)   Much less than usual

GH8

Have you recently been able to face up to your problems?

(1)   More so than usual
(2)   Same as usual
(3)   Less able than usual
(4)   Much less able

GH9

Have you recently been feeling unhappy and depressed?

(1)   Not at all
(2)   No more than usual
(3)   Rather more than usual
(4)   Much more than usual

GH10

Have you recently been losing confidence in yourself?

(1)   Not at all
(2)   No more than usual
(3)   Rather more than usual
(4)   Much more than usual

GH11

Have you recently been thinking of yourself as a worthless person?

(1)   Not at all
(2)   No more than usual
(3)   Rather more than usual
(4)   Much more than usual

GH12

Have you recently been feeling reasonably happy, all things considered?

(1)   More so than usual
(2)   Same as usual
(3)   Less so than usual
(4)   Much lessthan usual

FamIntr

We would like to know how your family gets on together.

FF1

Planning family activities is difficult because we misunderstand each other

(1)   Strongly agree
(2)   Agree
(3)   Disagree
(4)   Strongly disagree

FF2

In times of crisis we can turn to each other for support

(1)   Strongly agree
(2)   Agree
(3)   Disagree
(4)   Strongly disagree

FF3

We cannot talk to each other about the sadness we feel

(1)   Strongly agree
(2)   Agree
(3)   Disagree
(4)   Strongly disagree

FF4

Individuals are accepted for what they are

(1)   Strongly agree
(2)   Agree
(3)   Disagree
(4)   Strongly disagree

FF5

We avoid discussing our fears and concerns

(1)   Strongly agree
(2)   Agree
(3)   Disagree
(4)   Strongly disagree

FF6

We can express feelings to each other

(1)   Strongly agree
(2)   Agree
(3)   Disagree
(4)   Strongly disagree

FF7

There is lots of bad feeling in the family

(1)   Strongly agree
(2)   Agree
(3)   Disagree
(4)   Strongly disagree

FF8

We feel accepted for what we are

(1)   Strongly agree
(2)   Agree
(3)   Disagree
(4)   Strongly disagree

FF9

Making decisions is a problem for our family

(1)   Strongly agree
(2)   Agree
(3)   Disagree
(4)   Strongly disagree

FF10

We are able to make decisions on how to solve problems

(1)   Strongly agree
(2)   Agree
(3)   Disagree
(4)   Strongly disagree

FF11

We don't get along well together

(1)   Strongly agree
(2)   Agree
(3)   Disagree
(4)   Strongly disagree

FF12

We confide in each other

(1)   Strongly agree
(2)   Agree
(3)   Disagree
(4)   Strongly disagree

Argue1

When the adults in the house get into arguments with one another, the
children may see or hear what is going on.
Has NAME CHILD witnessed one of these arguments?

(1)   Yes
(2)   No

ASK IF: *Argue1 = Yes*

Argue2

Were the arguments between the adults...

(1)   without verbal or physical aggression
(2)   with verbal aggression
(3)   with physical aggression

Education

SchLeft

Now thinking about yourself....
 At what age did YOU finish your continuous full-time education
at school or college?

AnyQuals

Have you got any qualifications of any sort?

(1)   Yes
(2)   No

ASK IF: *AnyQuals = Yes*

HiQuals

Please look at this card and tell me whether you have passed any
of the qualifications listed. Look down the list and tell me the
first one you come to that you have passed

(1)   Degree level qualification
(2)   Teaching qualification or HNC/HND,BEC/TEC Higher,
        BTEC Higher
(3)   'A'Levels/SCE Higher or ONC/OND/BEC/TEC not higher
        or City & Guilds Advanced Final Level
(4)   AS level
(5)   'O'Level passes (Grade A–C if after 1975)
        or City & Guilds Craft/Ord level
        or GCSE (Grades A–C)
(6)   CSE Grades 2–5
        GCE 'O'level (Grades D & E if after 1975)
        GCSE (Grades D,E,F,G)
        NVQs
(7)   CSE ungraded
(8)   Other qualifications (specify)
(9)   No qualifications

ASK IF: *HiQuals = Other*

OthQuals

What other qualification do you have?

Employment status

Wrking

Did you do any paid work in the 7 days ending Sunday the
DATE, either as an employee or as self-employed?

(1)   Yes
(2)   No

ASK IF: *Wrking = No* **AND** *parent is aged under 65* **AND**
Male

SchemeET

Were you on a government scheme for employment training?

(1)   Yes
(2)   No

ASK IF: *SchemeET = No*

JbAway

Did you have a job or business that you were away from?

(1)   Yes
(2)   No
(3)   Waiting to take up a new job/business already obtained

Ask if: JbAway = 2 OR 3

OwnBus

Did you do any unpaid work in that week for any business that you own?

(1)　　Yes
(2)　　No

Ask if: OwnBus = No

RelBus

...or that a relative owns?

(1)　　Yes
(2)　　No

Ask if: RelBus = No

Looked

Thinking of the 4 weeks ending Sunday the DMDLSUN, were you looking for any kind of paid work or government training scheme at any time in those 4 weeks?

(1)　　Yes
(2)　　No

Ask if: Looked = Yes

StartJ

If a job or a place on a government scheme had been available in the week ending Sunday the DATE, would you have been able to start within 2 weeks?

(1)　　Yes
(2)　　No

Ask if: Looked = No OR StartJ = No

YInAct

What was the main reason you did not seek any work in the last 4 weeks/would not be able to start in the next 2 weeks?

(1)　　Student
(2)　　Looking after the family/home
(3)　　Temporarily sick or injured
(4)　　Long-term sick or disabled
(5)　　Retired from paid work
(6)　　None of these

PEverwk

Has your partner ever had a paid job, apart from casual or holiday work?

(1)　　Yes
(2)　　No

Ask if: PEverwk = Yes

PDtJbL

When did you leave your last PAID job?

IndD

What did the firm/organisation you worked for mainly make or do (at the place where you worked)?

Ask if: PEverwk = Yes

OccT

What was your (main) job?

Ask if: PEverwk = Yes

OccD

What did you mainly do in your job?

Ask if: PEverwk = Yes

Stat

Were you working as an employee or were you self-employed HELP<F9>?

(1)　　Employee
(2)　　Self-employed

Ask if: Stat = Emp

Manage

Did you have any managerial duties, or were you supervising any other employees?

(1)　　Manager
(2)　　Foreman/supervisor
(3)　　Not manager/supervisor

Ask if: Stat = Emp

EmpNo

How many employees were there at the place where you worked?

(1)　　1–24
(2)　　25 or more

Ask if:: Stat = Self Employed

Solo

Were you working on your own or did you have employees?

(1)　　on own/with partner(s) but no employees
(2)　　with employees

Ask if: Solo = With Employees

SENo

How many people did you employ at the place where you worked?

(1)　　1–24
(2)　　25 or more

FtPtWk

In your (main) job were you working:

(1)   full time
(2)   or part time?

Ask if: PartYN = Yes

Partner

I'd now like to ask about you partner's employment status

Partner's employment status

Ask if: PartYN = Yes

PWrking

Did your partner do any paid work in the 7 days ending Sunday the DATE, either as an employee or as self-employed?

(1)   Yes
(2)   No

Ask if: PWrking = No And: partner is aged under 65

PSchemET

Was s/he on a government scheme for employment training?

(1)   Yes
(2)   No

Ask if: (PSchemET = No)

PJbAway

Did he/she have a job or business that s/he was away from?

(1)   Yes
(2)   No
(3)   Waiting to take up a new job/business already obtained

Ask if: PJbAway = Waiting

POwnBus

Did s/he do any unpaid work in that week for any business that s/he owns? (HLP<F9>)

(1)   Yes
(2)   No

Ask if: POwnBus = No

PRelBus

...or that a relative owns?

(1)   Yes
(2)   No

Ask if: PRelBus = No

PLooked

Thinking of the 4 weeks ending Sunday the DATE, was your partner looking for any kind of paid work or government training scheme at any time in those 4 weeks?

(1)   Yes
(2)   No

Ask if: PLooked = Yes

PStartJ

If a job or a place on a government scheme had been available in the week ending Sunday the DMDLSUN, would s/he have been able to start within 2 weeks?

(1)   Yes
(2)   No

Ask if: PLooked = No OR PStartJ = No

PYInAct

What was the main reason s/he did not seek any work in the last 4 weeks/would not be able to start in the next 2 weeks?

(1)   Student
(2)   Looking after the family/home
(3)   Temporarily sick or injured
(4)   Long-term sick or disabled
(5)   Retired from paid work
(6)   None of these

Ask if: partner is unemployed

PEverwk

Has your partner ever had a paid job, apart from casual or holiday work?

(1)   Yes
(2)   No

Ask if: PEverwk = Yes

PDtJbL

When did s/he leave their last PAID job?

Ask if: PEverwk = Yes

PIndD

What did the firm/organisation your partner worked for mainly make or do (at the place where s/he worked)?

POccT

What was your partner's (main) job ?

POccD

What did s/he mainly do in his/her job?

ASK IF: PEverwk = Yes

PStat

Was s/he working as an employee or was he self-employed ?

(1)   Employee
(2)   Self-employed

ASK IF: PStat = Employee

PManage

Did s/he have any managerial duties, or was s/he supervising any other employees?

(1)   Manager
(2)   Foreman/supervisor
(3)   Not manager/supervisor

PEmpNo

How many employees were there at the place where s/he worked?

(1)   1–24
(2)   25 or more

ASK IF: PStat = Self Employed

PSolo

Was s/he working on their own or did s/he have employees?

(1)   on own/with partner(s) but no employees
(2)   with employees

ASK IF: PSolo = With Employees

PSENo

How many people did s/he employ at the place where s/he worked?

(1)   1–24
(2)   25 or more

PFtPtWk

In your partner's (main) job was s/he working:

(1)   full time
(2)   or part time?

Individual Benefits/Tax Credits

Intro

Looking at this card, are you at present receiving any state benefits in your own right: that is, where you are the named recipient?

ASK IF: Aged 16+

Ben1Q

(1)   Child Benefit
(2)   Guardian's Allowance
(3)   Carer's Allowance (Formerly – Invalid Care Allowance)
(4)   Retirement pension (National Insurance), or Old Person's pension
(5)   Widow's Pension, Bereavement Allowance or Widowed Parent's (formerly Widowed Mother's) Allowance
(6)   War disablement pension or War Widow's Pension (and any related allowances)
(7)   Severe disablement allowance
(8)   None of these

ASK IF: Aged 16+

DisBen

(1)   CARE COMPONENT of Disability Living Allowance
(2)   MOBILITY COMPONENT of Disability Living Allowance
(3)   Attendance Allowance
(4)   None of these

ASK IF: Receives Attendance Allowance

AttAll

(1)   Together with pension
(2)   Separate payment

ASK IF: Aged 16+

Ben2Q

(1)   Job Seekers' Allowance(JSA)
(2)   PC_Txt
(3)   Income Support MIG_Txt
(4)   Incapacity Benefit
(5)   Statutory Sick Pay
(6)   Industrial Injury Disablement Benefit
(7)   None of these

ASK IF: Aged 16+

TxCred

(1)   Working Tax Credit (excluding any childcare tax credit)
(2)   Child Tax Credit (including any childcare tax credit)
(3)   None of these

ASK IF: Woman between 16 and 55

MatAll

(1)   Maternity Allowance
(2)   Statutory maternity pay from your employer or former employer
(3)   Neither of these

Ben12m

    (1)   A grant from the Social Fund for funeral expenses

    (2)   A grant from Social Fund for maternity expenses/ Sure Start Maternity Grant

    (3)   A Social Fund loan or Community Care grant

    (4)   None of these

Ask if: Person 60 or over

Winter

In the last 12 months have you received a winter fuel payment in your own right?

    (1)   Yes

    (2)   No

Ask if: Aged 16+

Ben6m

    (1)   A Back to Work bonus

    (2)   'Extended payment' of Housing Benefit/rent rebate , or Council Tax Benefit (4 week payment only)

    (3)   Widow's payment or Bereavement Payment – lump sum

    (4)   Child Maintenance Bonus

    (5)   Lone Parent's Benefit Run-On

    (6)   Any National Insurance or State benefit not mentioned earlier

    (7)   None of these

Income

IncKind

(In addition to these)
This card shows a number of (other) possible sources of income. Can you tell me which different kinds of income you personally receive?

    (1)   Earned income/salary

    (2)   Income from self-employment

    (3)   Pension from a former employer

    (4)   Interest from savings, building society, investment dividends from shares etc.

    (5)   Other kinds of regular allowances from outside the household (e.g. alimony, annuity, educational grant)

    (6)   Any other source

    (7)   None of these

    (9)   Refused

Ask if: IncKind = 6

IncOther

What is this other source of income?

GrossInc

Could you please look at this card and tell me which group represents your own personal gross income from all sources mentioned?
By gross income, I mean income from all sources before deductions for income tax, National Insurance etc.

    (1)   Less than 1000

    (2)   1,000 – 1,999

    (3)   2,000 – 2,999

    (4)   3,000 – 3,999

    (5)   4,000 – 4,999

    (6)   5,000 – 5,999

    (7)   6,000 – 6,999

    (8)   7,000 – 7,999

    (9)   8,000 – 8,999

    (10)   9,000 – 9,999

    (11)   10,000 – 10,999

    (12)   11,000 – 11,999

    (13)   12,000 – 12,999

    (14)   13,000 – 13,999

    (15)   14,000 – 14,999

    (16)   15,000 – 17,499

    (17)   17,500 – 19,999

    (18)   20,000 – 24,999

    (19)   25,000 – 29,999

    (20)   30,000 – 39,999

    (21)   40,000 or more

    (22)   No source of income

    (23)   Refused

HHldInc

Could you look at this card again and tell me which group represents your household's gross income from all sources mentioned.

    (1)   Less than 1000

    (2)   1,000 – 1,999

    (3)   2,000 – 2,999

    (4)   3,000 – 3,999

    (5)   4,000 – 4,999

    (6)   5,000 – 5,999

    (7)   6,000 – 6,999

    (8)   7,000 – 7,999

    (9)   8,000 – 8,999

    (10)   9,000 – 9,999

    (11)   10,000 – 10,999

    (12)   11,000 – 11,999

    (13)   12,000 – 12,999

    (14)   13,000 – 13,999

    (15)   14,000 – 14,999

    (16)   15,000 – 17,499

    (17)   17,500 – 19,999

    (18)   20,000 – 24,999

    (19)   25,000 – 29,999

    (20)   30,000 – 39,999

    (21)   40,000 or more

    (22)   No source of income

    (23)   Refused

Strengths and Difficulties Questionnaire – other children in household

OthChild

I now want to ask you some questions about the other children in the household.
Apart from NAME CHILD, are there any other children aged between 5 and 16 in the household?

(1)   Yes
(2)   No

Ask if: OthChild = Yes

ChldNum

EXCLUDING NAME CHILD, PLEASE ENTER THE NUMBER OF CHILDREN AGED BETWEEN 5 AND 16 IN THE HOUSEHOLD

Ask if: OthChild = Yes

SDQIntr

I am now going to ask you a few questions about each of the children in your family aged between 5 and 16. This is to give us an idea of the strengths and difficulties of the children in your family, so that we can get an overall picture of NAME CHILD's family life

And: OthChild = Yes

IntrSDQ

I would now like to ask you some questions about DMNAMES[ChldSDQ]'s personality and behaviour.

And: OthChild = Yes

SectnD

For each item that I am going to read out can you please tell me whether it is 'not true', 'partly true' or 'certainly true' for CHILD NAME – over the past six months

And: OthChild = Yes

D4

Considerate of other people's feelings

(5)   Not true
(6)   Partly true
(7)   Certainly true

And: OthChild = Yes

D5

Restless, overactive, cannot stay still for long

(5)   Not true
(6)   Partly true
(7)   Certainly true

And: OthChild = Yes

D6

Often complains of headaches, stomach aches or sickness

(5)   Not true
(6)   Partly true
(7)   Certainly true

And: OthChild = Yes

D7

Shares readily with other children (treats, toys, pencils etc)

(5)   Not true
(6)   Partly true
(7)   Certainly true

And: OthChild = Yes

D8

Often has temper tantrums or hot tempers

(5)   Not true
(6)   Partly true
(7)   Certainly true

And: OthChild = Yes

D9

Rather solitary, tends to play alone

(5)   Not true
(6)   Partly true
(7)   Certainly true

And: OthChild = Yes

D10

Generally obedient, usually does what adults request

(5)   Not true
(6)   Partly true
(7)   Certainly true

And: OthChild = Yes

D11

Many worries, often seems worried

(5)   Not true
(6)   Partly true
(7)   Certainly true

And: OthChild = Yes

D12

Helpful if someone is hurt, upset or feeling ill

(5)   Not true
(6)   Partly true
(7)   Certainly true

---

1. Questions D4–D31 are copyrighted © to Professor Robert Goodman, Department of Child and Adolescent Psychiatry, De Crespigny Park, London SE5 8AF.

AND: OthChild = Yes

D13

Constantly fidgeting or squirming

(5) Not true
(6) Partly true
(7) Certainly true

AND: OthChild = Yes

D14

Has at least one good friend

(5) Not true
(6) Partly true
(7) Certainly true

AND: OthChild = Yes

D15

Often fights with other children or bullies them

(5) Not true
(6) Partly true
(7) Certainly true

AND: OthChild = Yes

D16

Often unhappy, down-hearted or tearful

(5) Not true
(6) Partly true
(7) Certainly true

AND: OthChild = Yes

D17

Generally liked by other children

(5) Not true
(6) Partly true
(7) Certainly true

AND: OthChild = Yes

D18

Easily distracted, concentration wanders

(5) Not true
(6) Partly true
(7) Certainly true

AND: OthChild = Yes

D19

Nervous or clingy in new situations, easily loses confidence

(5) Not true
(6) Partly true
(7) Certainly true

AND: OthChild = Yes

D20

Kind to younger children

(5) Not true
(6) Partly true
(7) Certainly true

AND: OthChild = Yes

D21

Often lies or cheats

(5) Not true
(6) Partly true
(7) Certainly true

AND: OthChild = Yes

D22

Picked on or bullied by other children

(5) Not true
(6) Partly true
(7) Certainly true

AND: OthChild = Yes

D23

Often volunteers to help others (parents, teachers, other children)

(5) Not true
(6) Partly true
(7) Certainly true

AND: OthChild = Yes

D24

Thinks things out before acting

(5) Not true
(6) Partly true
(7) Certainly true

AND: OthChild = Yes

D25

Steals from home, school or elsewhere

(5) Not true
(6) Partly true
(7) Certainly true

AND: OthChild = Yes

D26

Gets on better with adults than with other children

(5) Not true
(6) Partly true
(7) Certainly true

1. Questions D4–D31 are copyrighted © to Professor Robert Goodman, Department of Child and Adolescent Psychiatry, De Crespigny Park, London SE5 8AF.

AND: OthChild = Yes

D27

Many fears, easily scared

(5)　Not true
(6)　Partly true
(7)　Certainly true

AND: OthChild = Yes

D28

Sees tasks through to the end, good attention span?

(5)　Not true
(6)　Partly true
(7)　Certainly true

AND: OthChild = Yes

D29

Overall, do you think that NAME CHILD has difficulties in one or more of the following areas: emotions, concentration, behaviour or getting on with other people?

(5)　No
(6)　Yes: minor difficulties
(7)　Yes: definite difficulties
(8)　Yes: severe difficulties

ASK IF: D29 = 6, 7 or 8

D29a

How long have these difficulties been present?

(1)　Less than a month
(2)　One to five months
(3)　Six to eleven months
(4)　A year or more

ASK IF: D29 = 6, 7 or 8

D29b

Do the difficulties upset or distress NAME CHILD

(5)　not at all
(6)　only a little
(7)　quite a lot
(8)　or a great deal?

ASK IF: D29 = 6, 7 or 8

D30

(Do the difficulties interfere with NAME CHILD's everyday life in terms of his or her...)
...home life?

(5)　not at all
(6)　only a little
(7)　quite a lot
(8)　a great deal

ASK IF: D29 = 6, 7 or 8

D30a

(Do the difficulties interfere with NAME CHILD]'s everyday life in terms of his or her...)
... friendships?

(5)　not at all
(6)　only a little
(7)　quite a lot
(8)　a great deal

ASK IF: D29 = 6, 7 or 8

D30b

(Do the difficulties interfere with NAME CHILD's everyday life in terms of his or her...)
... classroom learning?

(5)　not at all
(6)　only a little
(7)　quite a lot
(8)　a great deal

ASK IF: D29 = 6, 7 or 8

D30c

(Do the difficulties interfere with NAME CHILD's everyday life in terms
of his or her...)
...leisure activities?

(5)　not at all
(6)　only a little
(7)　quite a lot
(8)　a great deal

ASK IF: D29 = 6, 7 or 8

D31

Do the difficulties put a burden on you or the family as a whole?

(5)　not at all
(6)　only a little
(7)　quite a lot
(8)　a great deal

YOUNG PERSON'S INTERVIEW

(Face-to-face interview with 11- to 16-year-olds)

Strengths and Difficulties Questionnaire

ASK: If child is aged 11 or over

IntrSDQ

This section is about your personality and behaviour. This is to give us an overall view of your strengths and difficulties.

SectnB

For each item that I am going to read out, can you please tell me whether
it is 'not true', 'partly true' or 'certainly true' for you.

---

1. Questions D4–D31 are copyrighted © to Professor Robert Goodman, Department of Child and Adolescent Psychiatry, De Crespigny Park, London SE5 8AF.

CB4[3]

I try to be nice to other people, I care about their feelings

(5)   Not true
(6)   Partly true
(7)   Certainly true

CB5

I am restless, I cannot stay still for long

(5)   Not true
(6)   Partly true
(7)   Certainly true

CB6

I get a lot of headaches, stomach aches or sickness

(5)   Not true
(6)   Partly true
(7)   Certainly true

CB7

I usually share with others (food, games, pens etc.)

(5)   Not true
(6)   Partly true
(7)   Certainly true

CB8

I get very angry and often lose my temper

(5)   Not true
(6)   Partly true
(7)   Certainly true

CB9

I am usually on my own, I generally play alone or keep to myself

(5)   Not true
(6)   Partly true
(7)   Certainly true

CB10

I usually do as I am told

(5)   Not true
(6)   Partly true
(7)   Certainly true

CB11

I worry a lot

(5)   Not true
(6)   Partly true
(7)   Certainly true

CB12

I am helpful if someone is hurt, upset or feeling ill

(5)   Not true
(6)   Partly true
(7)   Certainly true

CB13

I am constantly fidgeting or squirming

(5)   Not true
(6)   Partly true
(7)   Certainly true

CB14

I have at least one good friend

(5)   Not true
(6)   Partly true
(7)   Certainly true

CB15

I fight a lot. I can make other people do what I want

(5)   Not true
(6)   Partly true
(7)   Certainly true

CB16

I am often unhappy, down-hearted or tearful

(5)   Not true
(6)   Partly true
(7)   Certainly true

CB17

Other people my age generally like me

(5)   Not true
(6)   Partly true
(7)   Certainly true

---

3. *Questions CB4–CB34 are copyrighted © to Professor Robert Goodman, Department of Child and Adolescent Psychiatry, De Crespigny Park, London SE5 8AF.*

CB18

I am easily distracted, I find it difficult to concentrate

(5) Not true
(6) Partly true
(7) Certainly true

CB19

I am nervous in new situations. I easily lose my confidence

(5) Not true
(6) Partly true
(7) Certainly true

CB20

I am kind to younger children

(5) Not true
(6) Partly true
(7) Certainly true

CB21

I am often accused of lying or cheating

(5) Not true
(6) Partly true
(7) Certainly true

CB22

Other children or young people pick on me or bully me

(5) Not true
(6) Partly true
(7) Certainly true

CB23

I often volunteer to help others (parents, teachers, other children)

(5) Not true
(6) Partly true
(7) Certainly true

CB24

I think before I do things

(5) Not true
(6) Partly true
(7) Certainly true

CB25

I take things that are not mine from home, school or elsewhere

(5) Not true
(6) Partly true
(7) Certainly true

CB26

I get on better with adults than with people of my own age

(5) Not true
(6) Partly true
(7) Certainly true

CB27

I have many fears, I am easily scared

(5) Not true
(6) Partly true
(7) Certainly true

CB28

I finish the work I'm doing, my attention is good

(5) Not true
(6) Partly true
(7) Certainly true

CB29

Overall, do you think that you have difficulties in one or more of the following areas: emotions, concentration, behaviour or getting on with other people?

(5) No
(6) Yes: minor difficulties
(7) Yes: definite difficulties
(8) Yes: severe difficulties

Ask if: CB29 6, 7, or 8

Cb29a

How long have these difficulties been present?

(1) Less than a month
(2) One to five months
(3) Six to eleven months
(4) A year or more

Ask if: CB29 6, 7, or 8

CB29b

Do the difficulties upset or distress you..

(5) not at all
(6) only a little
(7) quite a lot
(8) or a great deal?

3. Questions CB4–CB34 are copyrighted © to Professor Robert Goodman, Department of Child and Adolescent Psychiatry, De Crespigny Park, London SE5 8AF.

ASK IF: CB29 6, 7, or 8

Cb30

Do the difficulties interfere with your everyday life in terms of
...your home life?

(5) Not at all
(6) Only a little
(7) Quite a lot
(8) A great deal

ASK IF: CB29 6, 7, or 8

Cb30a

(Do the difficulties interfere with your everyday life in terms of)
... your friendships?

(5) Not at all
(6) Only a little
(7) Quite a lot
(8) A great deal

ASK IF: CB29 6, 7, or 8

Cb30b

(Do the difficulties interfere with your everyday life in terms of
your)
...classroom learning?

(5) Not at all
(6) Only a little
(7) Quite a lot
(8) A great deal

ASK IF: CB29 6, 7, or 8

Cb30c

(Do the difficulties interfere with your everyday life in terms of
your)
...leisure activities?

(5) Not at all
(6) Only a little
(7) Quite a lot
(8) A great deal

ASK IF: CB29 6, 7, or 8

Cb31

Do the difficulties make it harder for those around you such as
your family, friends and teachers?

(5) Not at all
(6) Only a little
(7) Quite a lot
(8) A great deal

EntRat

INTERVIEWER – Thinking about how the child responded to
the SDQ, do you think s/he would be able to understand the rest
of the interview?

(1) Yes
(2) No
(3) Not sure

Separation Anxiety

CIntroF

Many young people are particularly attached to one adult or a few
key adults, looking to them for security, and turning to them
when upset or hurt. They can be mum and dad, grandparents,
favourite teachers, neighbours etc.

C1

Which adults are you specially attached to?

(1) Mother (biological or adoptive)
(2) Father (biological or adoptive
(3) Another mother figure (stepmother, father's partner)
(4) Another father figure (stepfather, mother's partner)
(5) One or more grandparents
(6) One or more adult relatives (e.g. aunt, uncle, grown-up
brother or sister)
(7) Childminder, nanny, au pair
(8) One or more teachers
(9) One or more other adult non-relative (e.g. Social worker,
family friend or neighbour)
(10) Not specially attached to any adult

ASK IF: C1 = 10

C1a

Are you specially attached to any of the following children or
young people?

(1) One or more brothers, sisters or other young relatives
(2) One or more friends
(3) Not specially attached to anyone

ASK IF: C1a = 3

Livewit1

Do any of these people live with you?

(1) Yes
(2) No

ASK IF: C1a = 1 or 2

CInt1

You've just told us who you are specially attached to….. From
now on, I am going to refer to these people as your 'attachment
figures'.

ASK IF: C1a = 1 or 2

CInt2

What I'd like to know next is how much you worry about being
separated from your 'attachment figures'. Most young people
have worries of this sort, but I'd like to know how you compare
with other people of your age. I am interested in how you are
usually – not on the occasional off day.

---

3. Questions CB4–CB34 are copyrighted © to Professor Robert Goodman, Department of Child and Adolescent Psychiatry, De Crespigny Park, London SE5 8AF.

ASK IF: *Cla = 1 or 2*

C2

Overall, in the last 4 weeks, have you been particularly worried about being separated from your 'attachment figures'?

(1)   Yes
(2)   No

CF2a

...have you worried about something unpleasant happening to (your attachment figures), or about losing them?

(5)   No more than other young people of my age
(6)   A little more than other young people of my age
(7)   A lot more than other young people of my age

CF2b

(Thinking about the last 4 weeks and comparing yourself with other people of your age...)
...have you worried unrealistically that you might be taken away from (your 'attachment figures') for example, by being kidnapped, taken to hospital or killed?

(5)   No more than other young people of my age
(6)   A little more than other young people of my age
(7)   A lot more than other young people of my age

CF2c

...have you not wanted to go to school in case something nasty happened to (your 'attachment figures' who live with you) while you were at school?

(5)   No more than other young people of my age
(6)   A little more than other young people of my age
(7)   A lot more than other young people of my age
(8)   SPONTANEOUS: Not at school

CF2d

...have you worried about sleeping alone?

(5)   No more than other young people of my age
(6)   A little more than other young people of my age
(7)   A lot more than other young people of my age

CF2e

...have you come out of your bedroom at night to check on, or to sleep near your 'attachment figures' (who live with you)?

(5)   No more than other young people of my age
(6)   A little more than other young people of my age
(7)   A lot more than other young people of my age

CF2f

...have you worried about sleeping in a strange place?

(5)   No more than other young people of my age
(6)   A little more than other young people of my age
(7)   A lot more than other young people of my age

CF2h

...have you been afraid of being alone at home if your ('attachment figures' who live with you)pop out for a moment?

(5)   No more than other young people of my age
(6)   A little more than other young people of my age
(7)   A lot more than other young people of my age

CF2i

...have you had repeated nightmares or bad dreams about being separated from your 'attachment figures'?

(5)   No more than other young people of my age
(6)   A little more than other young people of my age
(7)   A lot more than other young people of my age

CF2j

...have you had headaches, stomach aches or felt sick when you had to leave (your 'attachment figures') or when you knew it was about to happen?

(5)   No more than other young people of my age
(6)   A little more than other young people of my age
(7)   A lot more than other young people of my age

CF2k

...has being apart, or the thought of being apart, from (your 'attachment figures')led to worry, crying, angry outbursts, clinginess or misery?

(5)   No more than other young people of my age
(6)   A little more than other young people of my age
(7)   A lot more than other young people of my age

CF3

Have your worries about separation been there for at least 4 weeks?

(1)   Yes
(2)   No

CF3a

How old were you when your worries about separation began?

CF4

How much have these worries upset or distressed you...

- (5) Not at all
- (6) Only a little
- (7) Quite a lot
- (8) Or A great deal?

CF5Intr

I also want to ask you about the extent to which these worries have interfered with your day to day life.

CF5a

Have these worries interfered with...
How well you get on with the rest of the family...?

- (5) Not at all
- (6) Only a little
- (7) Quite a lot
- (8) A great deal

CF5b

....making and keeping friends?

- (5) Not at all
- (6) Only a little
- (7) Quite a lot
- (8) A great deal

CF5c

...learning new things (or class work)?

- (5) Not at all
- (6) Only a little
- (7) Quite a lot
- (8) A great deal

CF5d

...playing, hobbies, sports or other leisure activities?

- (5) Not at all
- (6) Only a little
- (7) Quite a lot
- (8) A great deal

CF5e

Have these worries made it harder for those around you (family, friends, teachers etc.)?

- (5) Not at all
- (6) Only a little
- (7) Quite a lot
- (8) A great deal

Specific phobias

CF6Intr

This section of the interview is about some things or situations that young people are often scared of, even though they aren't really a danger to them. I'd like to know what you are scared of. I am interested in how you are usually – not on the occasional 'off day'.
Not all fears are covered in this section – some are covered in other sections, e.g. fear of social situations, dirt, separation, crowds.

CF7

Are you PARTICULARLY scared about any of the things or situations on this list?

- (1) Animals: Dogs, spiders, bees and wasps, mice and rats, snakes, or any other bird, animal or insect
- (2) Some aspect of the natural environment, e.g. Storms, thunder, heights or water
- (3) The dark
- (4) Loud noises, e.g. fire alarms, fireworks
- (5) Blood-injection-Injury – Set off by the sight of blood or injury or by an injection, or by some other medical procedure
- (6) Dentists or Doctors
- (7) Vomiting, choking or getting particular diseases, e.g. Cancer or AIDS
- (8) Using particular types of transport, e.g. cars, buses, boats, planes, ordinary trains, underground trains, bridges
- (9) Small enclosed spaces, e.g. lifts, tunnels
- (10) Using the toilet, e.g. at school or in someone else's house
- (11) Specific types of people, e.g. clowns, people with beards, with crash helmets, in fancy dress, dressed as Santa Claus
- (12) Imaginary or supernatural beings, e.g. monsters, ghosts, aliens, witches
- (13) Any other specific fear (specify)
- (99) Not particularly scared of anything

Ask if: CF7 = 13

CF7Oth

What are these other fears?

Ask if: responded to C7F

CF7a

Are these fears a real nuisance to you, or to anyone else?

- (5) No
- (6) Perhaps
- (7) Definitely

Ask if: CF7a = Definitely

CF8

How long has this fear (or the most severe of these fears) been present?

- (1) less than a month
- (2) At least one month but less than 6 months
- (3) Six months or more

Ask if: CF7a = Definitely

CF9

When you come up against the things you are afraid of, or when you think you are about to come up against them, do you become anxious or upset?

(5) No
(6) A little
(7) A Lot

Ask if: CF9 = A Lot

CF9a

Do you become anxious or upset every time, or almost every time, you come up against the things you are afraid of?

(1) Yes
(2) No

Ask if: CF9 = A Lot

CF10

How often do your fears result in you becoming upset like this ...
IF THE CHILD IS AFRAID OF SOMETHING THAT IS ONLY THERE FOR PART OF THE YEAR (E.G. WASPS), THIS QUESTION IS ABOUT THAT PARTICULAR SEASON.

(1) Many times a day
(2) Most days
(3) Most weeks
(4) Or every now and then?

Ask if: CF7a = Definitely

CF11

Do your fears lead to you avoiding the things you are afraid of...

(5) No
(6) A little
(7) A Lot

Ask if: CF11 = A Lot

CF11a

Does this avoidance interfere with your daily life?

(5) No, not at all
(6) a little
(7) or a lot?

Ask if: CF7a = Definitely

CF11b

Do other people think that your fears are over the top or unreasonable?

(5) No
(6) Perhaps
(7) Definitely

Ask if: CF7a = Definitely

CF11bb

And what about you? Do you think your fears are over the top or unreasonable?

(5) No
(6) Perhaps
(7) Definitely

Ask if: CF7a = Definitely

CF11c

Are you upset about having this fear?

(5) No
(6) Perhaps
(7) Definitely

Ask if: CF7a = Definitely

CF12

Have your fears made it harder for those around you (family, friends, teachers etc.)...

(5) not at all
(6) only a little
(7) quite a lot
(8) or a great deal?

Social Phobias

CF13intr

I am interested in whether you are particularly afraid of social situations.
This is as compared with other people of you own age, and is not counting the occasional 'off day' or ordinary shyness.

CF13

Overall, do you particularly fear or avoid social situations that involve a lot of people, meeting new people or doing things in front of other people?

(1) Yes
(2) No

CF14Intr

Have you been particularly afraid of any of the following social situations over the last 4 weeks?

CF14a

Have you been particularly afraid of any of the following social situations over the last 4 weeks...
. . . meeting new people?

(5) No
(6) A little
(7) A Lot

CF14b

...meeting a lot of people, such as at a party?

(5)   No
(6)   A little
(7)   A Lot

CF14c

. . .eating in front of others?

(5)   No
(6)   A little
(7)   A Lot

CF14d

. . .speaking with other young people around (or in class)?

(5)   No
(6)   A little
(7)   A Lot

CF14e

. . .reading out loud in front of others?

(5)   No
(6)   A little
(7)   A Lot

CF14f

. . .writing in front of others?

(5)   No
(6)   A little
(7)   A Lot

CF15

Most young people are attached to a few key adults, feeling more secure when they are around. Some young people are only afraid of social situations if they don't have one of these key adults around. Other young people are afraid of social situations even when they are with one of these key adults.
 Which is true for you?

(1)   mostly fine in social situations as long as key adults are around
(2)   Social fears are marked even when key adults are around

Ask if: CF15 = 2

CF16

Are you just afraid with adults, or are you also afraid in situations that involve a lot of young people, or meeting new people of your age?

(1)   Just with adults
(2)   just with young people
(3)   With both adults and young people

Ask if: CF15 = 2

CF17

Outside of these social situations, are you able to get on well enough with the adults and young people you know best?

(1)   Yes
(2)   No

Ask if: CF15 = 2

CF18

Is the main reason you dislike social situations because you are afraid you will act in a way that will be embarrassing or show you up?

(5)   No
(6)   Perhaps
(7)   Definitely

Ask if: CF15 = 2 *And:* CF14d = A LOT OR CF14d = A Little OR CF14e = A Lot OR CF14e = A Little OR CF14f = A Lot OR CF14f = A Little

CF18a

Do you dislike social situations because of specific problems with speaking, reading or writing?

(5)   No
(6)   Perhaps
(7)   Definitely

Ask if: CF15 = 2

CF19

How long has this fear of social situations been present?

(1)   Less than a month
(2)   At least one month but less than six months
(3)   Six months or more

Ask if: CF15 = 2

CF20

How old were you when your fear of social situations began?

Ask if: CF15 = 2

CFblush

When you are in one of the social situations you are afraid of, do you normally...
...blush (go red) or shake (tremble)?

(1)   Yes
(2)   No

Ask if: CF15 = 2

CFSick

...feel afraid that you are going to be sick (throw up)?

(1)   Yes
(2)   No

Ask if: CF15 = 2

CFShort

...need to rush off to the toilet or worry that you might be caught short?

(1)   Yes
(2)   No

Ask if: CF15 = 2

CF21

When you are in one of the social situations you are afraid of, or when you think you are about to come up against one of these situations, do you become anxious or upset?

(5)   No
(6)   A little
(7)   A Lot

Ask if: CF15 = 2 And: CF21 = A Lot

CF22

How often does your fear of social situations result in you becoming upset like this..

(1)   Many times a day
(2)   Most days
(3)   Most weeks
(4)   Or every now and then?

Ask if: CF15 = 2

CF23

Does your fear lead to you avoiding social situations...

(5)   No
(6)   A little
(7)   A Lot

Ask if: CF15 = 2 And: CF23 = A Lot

CF23a

Does this avoidance interfere with your daily life?

(5)   No
(6)   A little
(7)   A Lot

Ask if: CF15 = 2

CF23b

Do you think that your fear of social situations is over the top or unreasonable?

(5)   No
(6)   Perhaps
(7)   Definitely

Ask if: CF15 = 2

CF23c

Are you upset about having this fear?

(5)   No
(6)   Perhaps
(7)   Definitely

Ask if: CF15 = 2

CF24

Has your fear of social situations made it harder for those around you (family, friends or teachers)...

(5)   Not at all
(6)   Only a little
(7)   Quite a lot
(8)   Or a great deal?

Panic Attacks and Agoraphobia

CF25Intr

Many young people have times when they get very anxious or worked up about silly little things, but some get severe panics that come out of the blue – they just don't seem to have any trigger at all.

CF25

In the last 4 weeks have you had a panic attack when you suddenly became very panicky for no reason at all, without even a little thing to set you off?

(1)   Yes
(2)   No

Ask if: CF25 = Yes

CFStart

Can I just check..
Do your panics start very suddenly?

(1)   Yes
(2)   No

Ask if: CF25 = Yes

CFPeak

Do they reach a peak within a few minutes (up to 10)?

(1)   Yes
(2)   No

Ask if: CF25 = Yes

CFHowLng

Do they last at least a few minutes?

(1)   Yes
(2)   No

Ask if: CF25 = Yes

CHeart

When you are feeling panicky, do you also feel...
...your heart racing, fluttering or pounding away?

(1)   Yes
(2)   No

Ask if: CF25 = Yes

CFSweat

(When you are feeling panicky, do you also feel...)
...sweaty?

(1)   Yes
(2)   No

Ask if: CF25 = Yes

CFTremb

(When you are feeling panicky, do you also feel...)
...trembly or shaky?

(1)   Yes
(2)   No

Ask if: CF25 = Yes

CFMouth

(When you are feeling panicky, do you also feel...)
...that your mouth is dry?

(1)   Yes
(2)   No

Ask if: CF25 = Yes

CFBreath

(When you are feeling panicky, do you also feel...)
...that it is hard to get your breath or that you are suffocating?

(1)   Yes
(2)   No

Ask if: CF25 = Yes

CFChoke

(When you are feeling panicky, do you also feel...)
...that you are choking?

(1)   Yes
(2)   No

Ask if: CF25 = Yes

CFPain

(When you are feeling panicky, do you also feel...)
...pain or an uncomfortable feeling in your chest?

(1)   Yes
(2)   No

Ask if: CF25 = Yes

CFsick

(When you are feeling panicky, do you also feel...)
...that you want to be sick (throw up) or that your stomach is turning over?

(1)   Yes
(2)   No

Ask if: CF25 = Yes

CFDizz

(When you are feeling panicky, do you also feel...)
...dizzy, unsteady, faint or light-headed? =

(1)   Yes
(2)   No

Ask if: CF25 = Yes

CFunreal

(When you are feeling panicky, do you also feel...)
...as though things around you were unreal or you were not really there?

(1)　Yes
(2)　No

Ask if: CF25 = Yes

CFCrazy

(When you are feeling panicky, do you also feel...)
...afraid that you might lose control, go crazy or pass out?

(1)　Yes
(2)　No

Ask if: CF25 = Yes

CFDie

(When you are feeling panicky, do you also feel...)
...afraid you might die?

(1)　Yes
(2)　No

Ask if: CF25 = Yes

CFCold

(When you are feeling panicky, do you also feel...)
...hot or cold all over?

(1)　Yes
(2)　No

Ask if: CF25 = Yes

CFNumb

(When you are feeling panicky, do you also feel...)
...numbness or tingling feelings in your body?

(1)　Yes
(2)　No

CF26

Over the last 4 weeks have you been very afraid of, or tried to avoid, the things on this card?

(1)　Crowds
(2)　Public places
(3)　Travelling alone (if you ever do)
(4)　Being far from home
(9)　None of the above

Ask if: CF26 = 1, 2, 3 or 4

CF27

Is this fear or avoidance of .... mostly because you are afraid that if you had a panic attack or something like that (such as dizziness or diarrhoea), you would find it difficult or embarrassing to get away, or would not be able to get the help you need?

(1)　Yes
(2)　No

CF27a

Have these panic attacks and/or avoidance of specific situations upset or distressed you...

(5)　not at all
(6)　only a little
(7)　quite a lot
(8)　a great deal

CF27b

Have these panic attacks and/or avoidance of specific situations interfered with...
How well you get on with the rest of the family?

(5)　not at all
(6)　only a little
(7)　quite a lot
(8)　a great deal

CF27c

....making and keeping friends?

(5)　not at all
(6)　only a little
(7)　quite a lot
(8)　a great deal

CF27d

...learning new things (or class work)?

(5)　not at all
(6)　only a little
(7)　quite a lot
(8)　a great deal

CF27e

...playing, hobbies, sports or other leisure activities?

(5)　not at all
(6)　only a little
(7)　quite a lot
(8)　a great deal

CF27f

Have panic attacks and/or avoidance or specific situations made it harder for those around you (family, friends, teachers etc.)?

(5)   Not at all
(6)   Only a little
(7)   Quite a lot
(8)   A great deal

Post Traumatic Stress Disorder

CE1

The next section is about events or situations that are exceptionally stressful, and that would really upset almost anyone. For example, being caught in a burning house, being abused, being in a serious car crash or seeing a member of your family or friends being mugged at gun point.

During your lifetime has anything like this happened to you?

(1)   Yes
(2)   No

ASK IF: CE1 = Yes

CE12a

Have you ever experienced any of the following?

(1)   A serious and frightening accident, e.g. being run over by a car, being in a bad car or train crash etc.
(2)   A bad fire, e.g. trapped in a burning building
(3)   Other disasters, e.g. kidnapping, earthquake, war
(4)   A severe attack or threat, e.g. by a mugger or gang
(5)   Severe physical abuse that you still remember
(6)   Sexual abuse
(7)   Rape
(8)   You witnessed severe domestic violence, e.g. saw your mother being badly beaten up at home
(9)   You saw a family member or friend severely attacked or threatened, e.g. by a mugger or a gang
(10)   You witnessed a sudden death, a suicide, an overdose, a serious accident, a heart attack etc.
(11)   Some other severe trauma (Please describe)

ASK IF: CE12a = 11

Othtrma1

Please describe this other trauma

ASK IF: CE12a = accident, fire, kidnap, attack, physical abuse, sexual abuse, rape, beaten, other attacked, witnessed death or other trauma.

CE1bIntr

I am now going to ask you how this event(s) has affected your behaviour and feelings.

If there is more than one event, I would like you to think about all of these.

ASK IF: CE12a = accident, fire, kidnap, attack, physical abuse, sexual abuse, rape, beaten, other attacked, witnessed death or other trauma.

CE1b

At the time, were you very upset or badly affected by it in some way?

(1)   Yes
(2)   No

ASK IF: CE12a = accident, fire, kidnap, attack, physical abuse, sexual abuse, rape, beaten, other attacked, witnessed death or other trauma.

CE2

At present, is it affecting your behaviour, feelings or concentration?

(1)   Yes
(2)   No

ASK IF: CE2 = Yes

CE2a

Over the last 4 weeks, have you...

...'relived' the event with vivid memories (flashbacks) of it?

(5)   No
(6)   A little
(7)   A Lot

ASK IF: CE2 = Yes

CE2b

...had a lot of upsetting dreams of the event?

(5)   No
(6)   A little
(7)   A Lot

ASK IF: CE2 = Yes

CE2c

...got upset if anything happened that reminded you of it?

(5)   No
(6)   A little
(7)   A Lot

ASK IF: CE2 = Yes

CE2d

...tried to avoid thinking or talking about anything to do with the event?

(5)   No
(6)   A little
(7)   A Lot

Ask if: CE2 = Yes

CE2e

...tried to avoid activities places or people that remind you of the event?

(5)   No
(6)   A little
(7)   A Lot

Ask if: CE2 = Yes

CE2f

...blocked out important details of the event from your memory?

(5)   No
(6)   A little
(7)   A Lot

Ask if: CE2 = Yes

CE2g

...shown much less interest in activities you used to enjoy?

(5)   No
(6)   A little
(7)   A Lot

Ask if: CE2 = Yes

CE2h

...felt cut off or distant from others?

(5)   No
(6)   A little
(7)   A Lot

Ask if: CE2 = Yes

CE2i

...expressed a smaller range of feelings than in the past, e.g. no longer able to express loving feelings?

(5)   No
(6)   A little
(7)   A Lot

Ask if: CE2 = Yes

CE2j

...felt less confidence in the future?

(5)   No
(6)   A little
(7)   A Lot

Ask if: CE2 = Yes

CE2k

...had problems sleeping?

(5)   No
(6)   A little
(7)   A Lot

Ask if: CE2 = Yes

CE2l

...felt irritable or angry?

(5)   No
(6)   A little
(7)   A Lot

Ask if: CE2 = Yes

CE2m

...had difficulty concentrating?

(5)   No
(6)   A little
(7)   A Lot

Ask if: CE2 = Yes

CE2n

...always been on the alert for possible dangers?

(5)   No
(6)   A little
(7)   A Lot

Ask if: CE2 = Yes

CE2o

...jumped at little noises or easily startled in other ways?

(5)   No
(6)   A little
(7)   A Lot

CE3

You have told me about .....

How long after the stressful event did these other problems begin?

(1)   Within six months
(2)   More than six months after the event

CE4

How long have you been having these problems?

(1)   Less than a month
(2)   At least one month but less than three months
(3)   Three months or more

CE5

How upset or distressed are you by the problems that the stressful event(s) triggered off...

(5)   not at all
(6)   only a little
(7)   quite a lot
(8)   or a great deal?

CE6a

...how well you get on with the rest of the family?

(5) Not at all
(6) Only a little
(7) Quite a lot
(8) A great deal

CE6b

...making and keeping friends?

(5) Not at all
(6) Only a little
(7) Quite a lot
(8) A great deal

CE6c

...learning new things (or class work)?

(5) Not at all
(6) Only a little
(7) Quite a lot
(8) A great deal

CE6d

...playing, hobbies, sports or other leisure activities?

(5) Not at all
(6) Only a little
(7) Quite a lot
(8) A great deal

CE7

Have these problems made it harder for those around you (family, friends, teachers etc.)...

(5) Not at all
(6) Only a little
(7) Quite a lot
(8) Or a great deal?

Compulsions and Obsessions

CF28Intr

Many young people have some rituals or superstitions, e.g. not stepping on the cracks in the pavement, having to go through a special goodnight ritual, having to wear lucky clothes for exams or needing a lucky mascot for school sports matches. It is also common for young people to go through phases when they seem obsessed by one particular subject or activity, e.g cars, a pop group, a football team. But what I want to know is whether you have rituals or obsessions that go beyond this.

CF28

Do you have rituals or obsessions that upset you, waste a lot of your time, or interfere with your ability to get on with everyday life?

(1) Yes
(2) No

CF29Intr

Over the last 4 weeks have you had any of the following rituals (doing any of the following things over and over again even though you have already done them or don't need to do them at all)?

CF29a

Excessive cleaning; hand washing, baths, showers, toothbrushing etc.?

(5) No
(6) A little
(7) A Lot

CF29b

Other special measures to avoid dirt, germs or poisons?

(5) No
(6) A little
(7) A Lot

CF29c

Excessive checking: electric switches, gas taps, locks, doors, the oven?

(5) No
(6) A little
(7) A Lot

CF29d

Repeating the same simple activity many times in a row for no reason, e.g. repeatedly standing up or sitting down or going backwards and forwards through a doorway?

(5) No
(6) A little
(7) A Lot

CF29e

Touching things or people in particular ways?

(5) No
(6) A little
(7) A Lot

CF29f

Arranging things so they are just so, or exactly symmetrical?

(5)   No
(6)   A little
(7)   A Lot

CF29g

Counting to particular lucky numbers or avoiding unlucky numbers?

(5)   No
(6)   A little
(7)   A Lot

CF31a

Over the last 4 weeks, have you been obsessively worrying about dirt, germs or poisons – not being able to get thoughts about them out of your mind?

(5)   No
(6)   A little
(7)   A Lot

CF31b

Over the last 4 weeks, have you been obsessed by the worry that something terrible will happen to yourself or to others – illnesses, accidents, fires etc.?

(5)   No
(6)   A little
(7)   A Lot

Ask if: *CF31b = A Lot*

CF32

Is this obsession about something terrible happening to yourself or others just one part of a general concern about being separated from your key attachment figures, or is it a problem in its own right?

(1)   Part of separation anxiety
(2)   A problem in it's own right

CF33

Have your rituals or obsessions been present on most days for a period of at least 2 weeks?

(1)   Yes
(2)   No

CF34

Do you think that your rituals or obsessions are over the top or unreasonable?

(5)   No
(6)   Sometimes
(7)   Definitely

CF35

Do you try to resist the rituals or obsessions?

(5)   No
(6)   Perhaps
(7)   Definitely

CF36

Do the rituals or obsessions upset you...

(5)   No, I enjoy them
(6)   Neutral, I neither enjoy them nor become upset
(7)   They upset me a little
(8)   They upset me a lot?

CF37

Do the rituals or obsessions use up at least an hour a day on average?

(1)   Yes
(2)   No

CF38a

Have the the rituals or obsessions interfered with ...
...how well you get on with the rest of the family?

(5)   Not at all
(6)   Only a little
(7)   Quite a lot
(8)   A great deal

CF38b

...making and keeping friends?

(5)   Not at all
(6)   Only a little
(7)   Quite a lot
(8)   A great deal

CF38c

...learning new things (or class work)?

(5)   Not at all
(6)   Only a little
(7)   Quite a lot
(8)   A great deal

CF38d

...playing, hobbies, sports or other leisure activities?

(5)   Not at all
(6)   Only a little
(7)   Quite a lot
(8)   A great deal

CF38e

Have the rituals or obsessions made it harder for those around you (family, friends, teachers etc.)?

(5)   Not at all
(6)   Only a little
(7)   Quite a lot
(8)   A great deal

Generalised Anxiety

CF39

This section is about worrying.

Do you ever worry?

(1)   Yes
(2)   No

Ask if: CF39 = Yes

CF40Int

Some young people worry about just a few things, sometimes related to specific fears, obsessions or separation anxieties. Other young people worry about many different aspects of their lives. They may have specific fears, obsessions or separation anxieties, but they also have a wide range of worries about many things.

Ask if: CF39 = Yes

CF40

Are you a worrier in general?

(1)   Yes, I worry in general
(2)   No, I have just a few specific worries

Ask if: CF40 = Yes

CF40a

Over the last 6 months, have you worried so much about so many things that it has really upset you or interfered with your life?

(5)   No
(6)   Perhaps
(7)   Definitely

Ask if: CF40 = Yes

CF41a

Thinking of the last 6 months and by comparing yourself with other people of your age, have you worried about:

 Past behaviour: Did I do that wrong? Have I upset someone? Have they forgiven me?

(5)   No more than other young people of my age
(6)   A little more than other young people of my age
(7)   A lot more than other young people of my age

Ask if: CF40 = Yes

CF41b

School work, homework or examinations

(5)   No more than other children of my age
(6)   A little more than other children of my age
(7)   A lot more than other children of my age
(8)   SPONTANEOUS: Not at school

Ask if: CF40 = Yes

CF41c

Disasters: Burglaries, muggings, fires, bombs etc.

(5)   No more than other young people of my age
(6)   A little more than other young people of my age
(7)   A lot more than other young people of my age

Ask if: CF40 = Yes

CF41d

Your own health

(5)   No more than other young people of my age
(6)   A little more than other young people of my age
(7)   A lot more than other young people of my age

Ask if: CF40 = Yes

CF41e

Bad things happening to others: family, friends, pets, the world (e.g. wars)

(5)   No more than other young people of my age
(6)   A little more than other young people of my age
(7)   A lot more than other young people of my age

Ask if: CF40 = Yes

CF41f

The future: e.g. changing school, moving house, getting a job, getting a boy/girlfriend

(5)   No more than other young people of my age
(6)   A little more than other young people of my age
(7)   A lot more than other young people of my age

Ask if: CF40 = Yes

CF41fa

Making and keeping friends

(5) No more than other young people of my age
(6) A little more than other young people of my age
(7) A lot more than other young people of my age

Ask if: CF40 = Yes

CF41fb

Death and dying

(5) No more than other young people of my age
(6) A little more than other young people of my age
(7) A lot more than other young people of my age

Ask if: CF40 = Yes

CF41fc

Being bullied or teased

(5) No more than other young people of my age
(6) A little more than other young people of my age
(7) A lot more than other young people of my age

Ask if: CF40 = Yes

CF41fd

Your appearance or weight

(5) No more than other young people of my age
(6) A little more than other young people of my age
(7) A lot more than other young people of my age

Ask if: CF40 = Yes

CF41g

Do you worry about anything else?

(1) Yes
(2) No

Ask if: CF41g = Yes

CF41ga

What else do you worry about?

Ask if: CF41g = Yes

CF41gb

How much do you worry about this?

(5) No more than other young people of my age
(6) A little more than other young people of my age
(7) A lot more than other young people of my age

CF43

Over the last 6 months have you been really worried on more days than not?

(1) Yes
(2) No

CF44

Do you find it difficult to control the worry?

(1) Yes
(2) No

CF45

Does worrying lead to you feeling restless, keyed up, tense, on edge or unable to relax?

(1) Yes
(2) No

Ask if: CF45 = Yes

CF45a

Has this been true for more days than not in the last six months?

(1) Yes
(2) No

CF46

Does worrying lead to you feeling tired or 'worn out' more easily?

(1) Yes
(2) No

Ask if: CF46 = Yes

CF46a

Has this been true for more days than not in the last six months?

(1) Yes
(2) No

CF47

Does worrying lead to difficulties in concentrating or to your mind going blank?

(1) Yes
(2) No

Ask if: CF47 = Yes

CF47a

Has this been true for more days than not in the last six months?

(1) Yes
(2) No

CF48

Does worrying make you feel irritable?

(1) Yes
(2) No

ASK IF: *CF48 = Yes*

CF48a

Has this been true for more days than not in the last six months?

(1) Yes
(2) No

CF49

Does worrying lead to you feeling tense in your whole body?

(1) Yes
(2) No

ASK IF: *CF49 = Yes*

CF49a

Has this been true for more days than not in the last six months?

(1) Yes
(2) No

CF50

Does worrying interfere with your sleep, e.g difficulty in falling or staying asleep, or restless, unsatisfying sleep?

(1) Yes
(2) No

ASK IF: *CF50 = Yes*

CF50a

Has this been true for more days than not in the last six months?

(1) Yes
(2) No

CF51

How upset or distressed are you as a result of all you worries...

(5) Not at all
(6) Only a little
(7) Quite a lot
(8) Or a great deal?

CF52Intr

I now want to ask you about the extent to which these worries have interfered with your day to day life.

CF52a

Have your worries interfered with ...
...how well you get on with the rest of the family?

(5) Not at all
(6) Only a little
(7) Quite a lot
(8) A great deal

CF52b

...making and keeping friends?

(5) Not at all
(6) Only a little
(7) Quite a lot
(8) A great deal

CF52c

...learning new things (or class work)?

(5) Not at all
(6) Only a little
(7) Quite a lot
(8) A great deal

CF52d

...playing, hobbies, sports or other leisure activities?

(5) Not at all
(6) Only a little
(7) Quite a lot
(8) A great deal

CF53

Have these worries made it harder for those around you (family friends, teachers etc)

(5) Not at all
(6) Only a little
(7) Quite a lot
(8) Or a great deal?

Depression

CDepInt

This next section of the interview is about your mood.

CG1

In the last 4 weeks, have there been times when you have been very sad, miserable, unhappy or tearful?

(1) Yes
(2) No

ASK IF: *CG1 = Yes*

CG3

Over the last 4 weeks has there been a period when you were really miserable nearly every day?

(1) Yes
(2) No

Ask if: CG1 = Yes

CG4

During the time when you were really miserable were you really miserable for most of the day? (i.e. more hours than not)

(1)   Yes
(2)   No

Ask if: CG1 = Yes

CG5

When you were miserable, could you be cheered up...

(1)   Easily
(2)   With difficulty/only briefly
(3)   Or not at all?

Ask if: CG1 = Yes

CG6

Over the last 4 weeks, the period of feeling really miserable has lasted...

(1)   Less than two weeks
(2)   Two weeks or more

CG8

In the last 4 weeks, have there been times when you have been grumpy or irritable in a way that was out of character for you?

(1)   Yes
(2)   No

Ask if: CG8 = Yes

CG10

Over the last 4 weeks, has there been a period when you were really irritable nearly every day?

(1)   Yes
(2)   No

Ask if: CG8 = Yes

CG11

During the period when you were grumpy or irritable, were you like that for most of the day? (i.e. more hours than not)

(1)   Yes
(2)   No

Ask if: CG8 = Yes

CG12

Has the irritability been improved by particular activities, by friends coming around or by anything else...

(1)   Easily
(2)   With difficulty/only briefly
(3)   Or not at all?

Ask if: CG8 = Yes

CG13

Over the last 4 weeks, has the period of being really irritable lasted..

(1)   less than two weeks
(2)   or two weeks or more?

CG15

In the last 4 weeks, have there been times when you lost interest in everything, or nearly everything that you normally enjoy doing?

(1)   Yes
(2)   No

Ask if: CG15 = Yes

CG17

Over the last 4 weeks, has there been a period when this lack of interest has been present nearly every day?

(1)   Yes
(2)   No

Ask if: CG15 = Yes

CG18

During these days when you lost interest in things, were you like this for most of each day? (i.e. more hours than not)

(1)   Yes
(2)   No

Ask if: CG15 = Yes

CG19

Over the last 4 weeks, has the period of being really miserable lasted...

(1)   Less than two weeks
(2)   Or two weeks or more?

CG20

Has this loss of interest been present during the same period when you have been really miserable or irritable for most of the time?

(1)   Yes
(2)   No

CG21a

During the period when you were sad, miserable or lacking in interest...
...did you lack energy and feel tired all the time?

(1)   Yes
(2)   No

CG21b

(During the period when you were sad, miserable or lacking in interest...) ...were you eating much more or much less than normal?

(1) Yes
(2) No

CG21ba

(During the period when you were sad, miserable or lacking in interest...) ...did you either lose or gain a lot of weight?

(1) Yes
(2) No

CG21c

(During the period when you were sad, miserable or lacking in interest...) ...did you find it hard to get to sleep or to stay asleep

(1) Yes
(2) No

CG21d

(During the period when you were sad, miserable or lacking in interest...) ...did you sleep too much?

(1) Yes
(2) No

CG21e

(During the period when you were sad, miserable or lacking in interest...) ...were you agitated or restless for much of the time?

(1) Yes
(2) No

CG21f

(During the period when you were sad, miserable or lacking in interest...) ...did you feel worthless or unnecessarily guilty for much of the time?

(1) Yes
(2) No

CG21g

(During the period when you were sad, miserable or lacking in interest...) ...did you find it unusually hard to concentrate or to think things out?

(1) Yes
(2) No

CG21h

(During the period when you were sad, miserable or lacking in interest...) ...did you think about death a lot?

(1) Yes
(2) No

CG21i

(During the period when you were sad, miserable or lacking in interest...) ...did you ever talk about harming yourself or killing yourself?

(1) Yes
(2) No

CG21j

(During the period when you were sad, miserable or lacking in interest...) ...did you ever try to harm yourself or kill yourself?

(1) Yes
(2) No

ASK IF: CG21j = No

CG21k

Over the whole of your lifetime have you ever tried to harm yourself or kill yourself?

(1) Yes
(2) No

CG22

How much has your sadness, irritability or loss of interest upset or distressed you?

(5) Not at all
(6) Only a little
(7) Quite a lot
(8) Or a great deal?

CG23Intr

I also want to ask you about the extent to which feeling LC1Dep has interfered with your day to day life.

CG23a

(Has your sadness, irritability or loss of interest interfered with...) ...how well you get on with the rest of your family?

(5) Not at all
(6) Only a little
(7) Quite a lot
(8) A great deal

CG23b

(Has your sadness, irritability or loss of interest interfered with...)
...making and keeping friends?

(5)   Not at all
(6)   Only a little
(7)   Quite a lot
(8)   A great deal

CG23c

(Has your sadness, irritability or loss of interest interfered with...)
...learning new things (or class work)?

(5)   Not at all
(6)   Only a little
(7)   Quite a lot
(8)   A great deal

CG23d

(Has your sadness, irritability or loss of interest interfered with...)
...playing, hobbies, sports or other leisure activities?

(5)   Not at all
(6)   Only a little
(7)   Quite a lot
(8)   A great deal

CG24

Has your sadness, irritability or loss of interest made it harder for those around you (family, friends, teachers etc...

(5)   Not at all
(6)   Only a little
(7)   Quite a lot
(8)   Or a great deal?

CG25

Over the last 4 weeks have you thought about harming or hurting yourself?

(1)   Yes
(2)   No

CG26

Over the last 4 weeks, have you ever tried to harm or hurt yourself?

(1)   Yes
(2)   No

Ask if: *CG26 = No*

CG27

Over the whole of your lifetime, have you ever tried to harm or hurt yourself?

(1)   Yes
(2)   No

Attention and Activity

AttnInt

This section of the interview is about attention and activity.

CH1

Do your teachers complain about you having problems with overactivity or poor concentration?

(5)   No
(6)   A little
(7)   A Lot
(8)   DNA not at school

CH2

Do your family complain about you having problems with overactivity or poor concentration?

(5)   No
(6)   A little
(7)   A Lot

CH3

And what do you think? Do you think you have real problems with overactivity or poor concentration?

(5)   No
(6)   A little
(7)   A Lot

Awkward and Troublesome Behaviour

CI1

This next section is about behaviour that sometimes gets young people into trouble with parents, teachers or other adults.

Do your teachers complain about you being awkward or troublesome?

(5) No
(6) A little
(7) A Lot
(8) DNA not at school

CI2

Do your family complain about you being awkward or troublesome?

(5) No
(6) A little
(7) A Lot

CI3

And what do you think? Do you think you are awkward or troublesome?

(5) No
(6) A little
(7) A Lot

CFrIntr

I am now going to ask you a couple of questions about your friends.

CFr9a

Do you have any friends?

(1) Yes
(2) No

ASK IF: *CFr9a = Yes*

CFr9

Overall, do your parents/carers approve of your friends?

(1) Yes
(2) No

ASK IF: *CFr9a = Yes*

CFr10

Are many of your friends the sorts of people who often get into trouble for bad behaviour?

(1) Not at all
(2) a few are like that
(3) many are like that
(4) or all are like that?

Eating Disorders

CP1Intr

I am now going to ask you some questions about your eating habits and how you feel about yourself.

CP1a

Have you ever thought you were fat even when other people told you that you were very thin?

(1) Yes
(2) No

CP1b

Would you be ashamed if other people knew how much you eat?

(1) Yes
(2) No

CP1c

Have you ever deliberately made yourself sick (throw up)?

(1) Yes
(2) No

CP1d

Do worries about eating (what? where? how much?) really interfere with your life?

(1) Yes
(2) No

CP1e

If you eat too much, do you blame yourself a lot?

(1) Yes
(2) No

CP2a

How tall are you? (approximately)

(1) Feet
(2) CM

Ask if: CP2a = Feet

CFeet

INTERVIEWER: RECORD HOW MANY WHOLE FEET NAME CHILD IS.

Ask if: CP2a = Feet

CInches

INTERVIEWER: RECORD HOW MANY ADDITIONAL INCHES NAME CHILD IS.

Ask if: CP2a = CM

CCent

INTERVIEWER: NAME CHILD's HEIGHT IN CENTIMETRES.

CP2b

How much do you weigh? (approximately)

(1) Stones
(2) Kilos

Ask if: CP2b = Stones

CStones

INTERVIEWER: RECORD HOW MANY WHOLE STONES NAME CHILD IS.

Ask if: CP2b = Stones

CPounds

RECORD HOW MANY ADDITIONAL POUNDS NAME CHILD IS.

Ask if: CP2b = Stones

CP2cSton

What was his/her lowest weight in the last 12 months?

Ask if: CP2b = Stones

CP2cPoun

PLEASE ENTER TOTAL NUMBER OF POUNDS

Ask if: CP2b = Stones

CP2dSton

What was his/her highest weight ever?

Ask if: CP2b = Stones

CP2dPoun

PLEASE ENTER TOTAL NUMBER OF POUNDS

Ask if: CP2b = Kilos

CKilos

INTERVIEWER: ENTER NAME CHILD's WEIGHT IN KILOGRAMS.

Ask if: CP2b = Kilos

CP2c

What was your lowest weight in the last 12 months?

Ask if: CP2b = Kilos

CP2d

What was your highest weight ever?

CP3

At present, would you describe yourself as very thin, thin, average, plump or fat?

(1) Very thin
(2) Thin
(3) Average
(4) Plump
(5) Fat

Ask if: CP3 = Very thin OR Thin

CP4

Have you been like this for the last 5 years, or are you thinner now than you used to be?

(1) Even thinner in the past
(2) Always like this
(3) A little thinner now
(4) A lot thinner now

CP5

How would other people, such as your friends and family, describe you at present – as very thin, thin, average, plump or fat?

(1) Very thin
(2) Thin
(3) Average
(4) Plump
(5) Fat

CP6

Have other people, such as your family, a friend, or a doctor, been seriously concerned that your weight has been bad for your physical health?

(1)   Yes
(2)   No

CP7

What do you think? Do you think that your weight has been bad for your physical health?

(1)   Yes
(2)   No

CP8

Are you afraid of gaining weight or getting fat?

(5)   No
(6)   A little
(7)   A Lot

ASK IF: *CP8 = A Lot*

CP9

Does the thought of gaining weight or getting fat really terrify you?

(1)   Yes
(2)   No

ASK IF: *CF40 = Yes*

CP10

If a doctor told you that you needed to put on five pounds (two kilograms), would you find this easy, difficult or impossible to accept?

(1)   Easy
(2)   Difficult
(3)   Impossible

CP11

Do you try to avoid eating the sorts of food that will make you fat?

(5)   No
(6)   A little
(7)   A Lot

ASK IF: *CP11 = A Lot*

CP12

How often do you succeed in this?

(1)   Never
(2)   Sometimes
(3)   Most of the time
(4)   Always

CP13

Do you spend a lot of your time thinking about food?

(1)   Yes
(2)   No

CP14

Sometimes people say that they have such a strong desire for food, and
that this desire is so hard to resist, that it is like the way an addict feels about drugs or alcohol.

Does this apply to you?

(5)   No
(6)   A little
(7)   A Lot

CP15

Sometimes people lose control over what they eat, and then they eat a very large amount of food in a short time. For example, they may open the fridge and eat as much as they can find – eating and eating until they feel physically ill.
This usually happens when people are by themselves.

Does this happen to you?

(1)   Yes
(2)   No

ASK IF: *CP15 = Yes*

CP16

Over the last three months, how often on average has this happened? Has it...

(1)   Not happened
(2)   happened occasionally
(3)   happened about once a week
(4)   or happened twice a week or more?

ASK IF: *CP15 = Yes*

CP17

When this happens, do you have a sense of having lost control over
your eating?

(1) Yes
(2) No

CP18a

In order to avoid putting on weight over the last three months,
have you been...

...eating less at meals?

IF NO CHECK IF CHILD TRIES BUT IS NOT ALLOWED

(5) No
(6) Tries but is not allowed
(7) A little
(8) A lot

ASK IF: `(QSelect2.ChldAg > 10) AND (ChldNow = Yes)`
AND: `(QC1SDQ.EntRat = Yes) OR (QC1SDQ.EntRat =`
`notsure)`

CP18b

...skipping meals?

(5) No
(6) Tries but is not allowed
(7) A little
(8) A lot

CP18c

...going without food for long periods, e.g. all day or most of the
day?

(5) No
(6) Tries but is not allowed
(7) A little
(8) A lot

CP18d

...hiding or throwing away food that others give you?

(5) No
(6) Tries but is not allowed
(7) A little
(8) A lot

CP18e

...exercising more?

(5) No
(6) Tries but is not allowed
(7) A little
(8) A lot

CP18f

...making your self sick (vomit)?

(5) No
(6) Tries but is not allowed
(7) A little
(8) A lot

CP18g

...taking pills or medicines in order to lose weight?

(5) No
(6) Tries but is not allowed
(7) A little
(8) A lot

ASK IF: `CP18g = 6, 7, 8`

CP18ga

Please describe what pills or medicines you have been taking.

CP18h

...doing other things?

(5) No
(6) Tries but is not allowed
(7) A little
(8) A lot

ASK IF: `CP18h 6, 7, 8`

CP18ha

Please describe the other things you have done to avoid weight
gain.

ASK IF: `CP18a = A Lot OR CP18b = A Lot OR CP18c = A`
`Lot OR CP18d = A Lot OR CP18e = A Lot OR CP18f`
`= A Lot OR CP18g = A Lot OR CP18h = A Lot AND`
`CP15 = Yes`

CP19

You told me earlier about the times when you lose control and eat
too much. After you do this, do you normally then CP18Text to
stop yourself putting on weight?

(1) Yes
(2) No

ASK IF: `child is female and aged over 9`

CP20

Have you had any periods in the last three months?

(1) Yes
(2) No

Ask if: CP20 = No

CP21

Have you ever had any period?

(1)　Yes
(2)　No

Ask if: CP20 = Yes OR CP21 = Yes

CP22

Are you taking any hormone pills or injections?

(1)　Yes
(2)　No

Ask if: CP20 = Yes OR CP21 = Yes

CP23

Please describe how your periods have been in general, and how they have been recently.

Ask if: CP20 = No

CP24

Why do you think you have not had any period in the last 3 months?

Ask if: CP22 = Yes

CP25

Please describe what effects the hormone pills or injections have on your periods.

Ask if: CP3 = Very OR CP5 = Very OR CP9 = Yes OR CP10 = Impossible OR CP14 = A Lot OR cP15 = Yes OR cP18a = A Lot) OR CP18b = A Lot OR CP18c = A Lot OR CP18d = A Lot OR CP18e = A Lot OR CP18f = A Lot OR CP18g = A Lot OR CP18h = A Lot

CP26

You have told me about your eating pattern and concern about weight or body shape. How upset or distressed are you by this?

(5)　Not at all
(6)　A little
(7)　A medium amount
(8)　A great deal

Ask if: CP3 = Very OR CP5 = Very OR CP9 = Yes OR CP10 = Impossible OR CP14 = A Lot OR cP15 = Yes OR cP18a = A Lot) OR CP18b = A Lot OR CP18c = A Lot OR CP18d = A Lot OR CP18e = A Lot OR CP18f = A Lot OR CP18g = A Lot OR CP18h = A Lot

CP27a

How much has your eating pattern or concern about weight and body shape interfered with...

...how well you get on with you and the rest of the family?

(5)　Not at all
(6)　A little
(7)　A medium amount
(8)　A great deal

Ask if: CP3 = Very OR CP5 = Very OR CP9 = Yes OR CP10 = Impossible OR CP14 = A Lot OR cP15 = Yes OR cP18a = A Lot) OR CP18b = A Lot OR CP18c = A Lot OR CP18d = A Lot OR CP18e = A Lot OR CP18f = A Lot OR CP18g = A Lot OR CP18h = A Lot

CP27b

...making and keeping friends?

(5)　Not at all
(6)　A little
(7)　A medium amount
(8)　A great deal

Ask if: CP3 = Very OR CP5 = Very OR CP9 = Yes OR CP10 = Impossible OR CP14 = A Lot OR cP15 = Yes OR cP18a = A Lot) OR CP18b = A Lot OR CP18c = A Lot OR CP18d = A Lot OR CP18e = A Lot OR CP18f = A Lot OR CP18g = A Lot OR CP18h = A Lot

CP27c

...learning or classwork?

(5)　Not at all
(6)　A little
(7)　A medium amount
(8)　A great deal

Ask if: CP3 = Very OR CP5 = Very OR CP9 = Yes OR CP10 = Impossible OR CP14 = A Lot OR cP15 = Yes OR cP18a = A Lot) OR CP18b = A Lot OR CP18c = A Lot OR CP18d = A Lot OR CP18e = A Lot OR CP18f = A Lot OR CP18g = A Lot OR CP18h = A Lot

CP27d

...playing, hobbies, sports or other leisure activities?

(5)　Not at all
(6)　A little
(7)　A medium amount
(8)　A great deal

Ask if: *CP3 = Very OR CP5 = Very OR CP9 = Yes OR CP10 = Impossible OR CP14 = A Lot OR cP15 = Yes OR cP18a = A Lot) OR CP18b = A Lot OR CP18c = A Lot OR CP18d = A Lot OR CP18e = A Lot OR CP18f = A Lot OR CP18g = A Lot OR CP18h = A Lot*

CP28

Has your eating pattern or concern about weight or body shape made
it harder for those around you(family, friends, teachers etc.)?

(5)   Not at all
(6)   A little
(7)   A medium amount
(8)   A great deal

Less Common Disorders

LessInt

This next section is about a variety of different aspects of behaviour and development.

CL1

Do you have any tics or twitches that you can't seem to control?

(1)   Yes
(2)   No

CL3

Have you had any out-of-ordinary experiences, such as seeing or hearing things, or having unusual ideas, that have worried you?

(1)   Yes
(2)   No

CL4

Apart from the things you have already told me about, is there anything else about your feelings or behaviour that really concerns you or anyone else?

(1)   Yes
(2)   No

Significant Problems

CSigPrb

FURTHER DETAILS – YOUNG PERSON INTERVIEW
LIST OF PROBLEMS:
INTERVIEWER: Please try and cover all areas of difficulty, but it is a good idea to let the parent choose which order to cover them in, starting with the area that concerns them most.
Use the prompt cards to cover each area of difficulty.
Below are details of which card you will need for each problem.

A. Separation anxiety, Specific phobia
B. Social phobia, Panic/Agoraphobia, Post traumatic stress
C. Obsessions and compulsions, Generalised anxiety
D. Depression, Deliberate self-harm
E. Hyperactivity, Awkward or troublesome behaviour
F. Dieting, weight and body shape, Tics
G. Less common disorders, Interviewer comments

OPEN

CAnxity

Do you experience any of the following when you feel anxious, nervous or tense

(1)   Heart racing or pounding?
(2)   Hands sweating or shaking?
(3)   Feeling dizzy?
(4)   Difficulty getting my breath?
(5)   Butterflies in stomach?
(6)   Dry mouth?
(7)   Nausea or feeling as though I wanted to be sick?
(8)   or none of the above?

Social Support

CloseInt

The next few questions are about people you feel close to, including relatives and friends

Numrel

How many relatives do you live with?

Liverel

How many relatives who live with you do you feel close to?

(1)   None
(2)   One
(3)   Two or more

Othrel

How many relatives who do not live with you do you feel close to?

(1)   None
(2)   One
(3)   Two or more

Friend

How many friends would you describe as close, or good, friends?

(1)   None
(2)   One
(3)   Two or more

ThinkInt

I would now like you to think about your family and friends (by family I mean those that live with you, as well as those who live elsewhere). Here are some comments that people have made about their family and friends. Please say how true you think they are for you.

Happy

There are people I know who do things to make me happy.

(5)   Not true
(6)   Partly true
(7)   Certainly true

Loved

There are people I know who make me feel loved.

(5)   Not true
(6)   Partly true
(7)   Certainly true

Rely

There are people I know who can be relied on no matter what happens.

(5)   Not true
(6)   Partly true
(7)   Certainly true

Care

There are people I know who would see that I am taken care of if I need to be.

(5)   Not true
(6)   Partly true
(7)   Certainly true

Accept

There are people I know who accept me just as I am.

(5)   Not true
(6)   Partly true
(7)   Certainly true

FeelImp

There are people I know who make me feel an important part of their lives.

(5)   Not true
(6)   Partly true
(7)   Certainly true

Support

There are people I know who give me support and encouragement.

(5)   Not true
(6)   Partly true
(7)   Certainly true

Social Life

YIntro

I am now going to ask you some questions about your life, the sorts of things you do and what you think about things. As before there are NO right or wrong answers to ANY of the questions. All of the young people we talk to will give different answers and I am only interested in knowing what YOU think about things.

Yintro1

I would like to start by asking you some questions about your neighbourhood.

YEnjo

Would you say that this is a neighbourhood that you enjoy living in...

(1)   A lot
(2)   A little
(3)   Or not one you enjoy living in?
(4)   JUST MOVED HERE
(5)   DON'T KNOW

YSafe

And how safe would you feel walking ALONE in this neighbourhood during the daytime? Would you feel...

(1)   Very safe
(2)   fairly safe
(3)   a bit unsafe
(4)   or very unsafe?
(5)   NEVER GO OUT ALONE

Ask if: (YSafe = 3 or 4

YUnsaf

Why would you feel unsafe?

(1)   Stranger danger/abduction/kidnapping
(2)   Children/teenagers/bullying
(3)   Cars/traffic
(4)   Dogs
(5)   OTHER (SPECIFY)

YGoout

Do you ever go to the local shops or to a local park on your own?

(1)   Yes
(2)   No

YTrust

Would you say that ....

(1)   MANY of the people in your neighbourhood can be trusted,
(2)   SOME can be trusted,
(3)   A FEW can be trusted,
(4)   or that none of the people in your neighbourhood can be trusted?
(5)   SPONTANEOUSLY ONLY: JUST MOVED HERE

YLost

Suppose you lost a bag with some money in it in this neighbourhood. And suppose it had your address in it. How likely is it that it would be returned to you with nothing missing? Would you say that it is...

(1)   very likely,
(2)   quite likely,
(3)   not very likely,
(4)   or not at all likely?

YIntro8

Now I want to ask you about any help you give in the home and any help you give to relatives who don't live with you.

YFam

On this card are things that SOME young people might do in the home or for other relatives.
If you don't do any of these things you can say 'NONE OF THESE'.

(1)   Doing shopping for someone
(2)   Cooking or helping to prepare family meals
(3)   Cleaning, hoovering or gardening
(4)   Washing or ironing clothes
(5)   Decorating or repairs
(6)   Baby sitting or caring for children
(7)   Writing letters or filling in forms for someone who has problems reading or writing
(8)   Taking care of someone who is sick
(9)   Helping out in a family business
(10)   Anything else
(11)   NONE OF THESE

Ask if: Yfam not equal to none

YFamoft

How often do you do ACTIVITY? Would you say...

(1)   Every day,
(2)   at least once a week,
(3)   at least once a month,
(4)   or less often?
(5)   Other

YIntro9

Now I want to ask you about any help you may have given to people who are NOT related to you. This could be help for a friend, neighbour or someone else.

Yhlp

Do you ever do any of these things for other people, apart from relatives?

(1)   Doing shopping for someone
(2)   Cooking or helping to prepare meals
(3)   Cleaning, hoovering or gardening
(4)   Washing or ironing clothes
(5)   Decorating or repairs
(6)   Baby sitting or caring for children
(7)   Writing letters or filling in forms for someone who has problems reading or writing
(8)   Taking care of someone who is sick
(9)   Anything else
(10)   NONE OF THESE

Ask if: Yhlp = 1-9

YhlpOft

Do you do give some kind of help...

(1)   Every day,
(2)   at least once a week,
(3)   at least once a month,
(4)   or less often?
(5)   Other

Ask if: `YhlpOft = Other`

YOthOFT3

INTERVIEWER – CODE THE APPROXIMATE NUMBER OF TIMES ACTIVITIES DONE IN LAST 12 MONTHS

Ask if: `Yhlp = 1-9`

Yifpaid

And when you have given this help, have you ....

(1) Always received money,
(2) Or sometimes received money,
(3) Or have you never received any money

Ask if: `Yhlp = 1-9`

YPdwk

Is there any PAID work that you do regularly?
By regularly, I mean at least once a month

(1) Yes
(2) No

Ask if: `YPdwk = Yes`

Ywhtwk

What type of paid work do you do regularly?

(1) Family business
(2) Newspaper round/delivery
(3) Shop/restaurant
(4) Building/decorating/gardening
(5) Household chores (paid)
(6) OTHER – SPECIFY

Ask if: `Other IN Ywhtwk`

YPdwhat

INTERVIEWER: PLEASE RECORD OTHER TYPE OF PAID WORK DONE

Ask if: `YPdwk = Yes`

ypDOFT

And how often do you do this paid work. At least once a week or less often?

(1) At least once a week
(2) Less often

Ask if: `School = Yes`

YIntro7A

Now some questions about any clubs or groups you've been involved with in the last 12 months.
In a minute, I am going to show you a card with some types of clubs or groups you might have been involved with in the last year, that is, since DATE.
I'm going to start with clubs or groups at your school.
If there are any that you don't understand I can help you with some examples.
INCLUDES PREVIOUS SCHOOL IF THEY HAVE CHANGED SCHOOLS WITHIN LAST YEAR

Ask if: `School = Yes`

YPartA

In the last year, that is, since DATE, have you taken part in any of these clubs or groups AT YOUR SCHOOL? This could mean in school hours or after school or in the school holidays.

(1) School holiday playschemes
(2) Environmental clubs/groups
(3) Sports clubs/teams
(4) Political clubs/groups
(5) Debating clubs/groups
(6) School/student councils
(7) Computer clubs/groups
(8) Art, drama, dance or music clubs/groups
(9) Human rights groups
(10) Religious groups or organisations
(11) Youth clubs
(12) Student Union
(13) After-school clubs
(14) Groups for extra teaching or special lessons
(15) Animal (welfare) groups
(16) Voluntary groups helping people
(17) Safety, First Aid groups
(18) Local community or neighbourhood groups
(19) NONE OF THESE

Ask if: `School = Yes`

YIntro7b

Now I'd like you to think about any groups, clubs or organisations that you've been involved with OUTSIDE OF SCHOOL during the last 12 months. I mean things you've done in the evenings, or at weekends or in the school holidays.

Ask if: `School = Yes`

YPartB

In the last year, that is, since DMDLYEAR, have you taken part in any of these clubs or groups DURING THE EVENINGS OR WEEKENDS OR SCHOOL HOLIDAYS (apart from the things you told me you had done at your school)
Remember, if there are any that you don't understand I can help you with some examples.

(1)   School holiday playschemes
(2)   Environmental clubs/groups
(3)   Sports clubs/teams
(4)   Political clubs/groups
(5)   Debating clubs/groups
(6)   Computer clubs/groups
(7)   Art, drama, dance or music clubs/groups
(8)   Human rights groups
(9)   Religious groups or organisations
(10)   Youth clubs
(11)   Animal (welfare) groups
(12)   Voluntary groups helping people
(13)   Safety, First Aid groups
(14)   Local community or neighbourhood groups
(15)   OTHER CLUBS/GROUPS
(16)   NONE OF THESE

Ask if: School = Yes

YDomor

Do any of these things stop you from ACTIVITY in groups IN YOUR FREE TIME?

(1)   I have no way of getting to the clubs or groups
(2)   There are no good groups or clubs locally
(3)   I can't afford to join clubs
(4)   I wouldn't feel safe travelling to and from clubs
(5)   There are no clubs or groups that I'm interested in
(6)   I'm too busy
(7)   I don't want to
(8)   I don't have time after my homework
(9)   I am not allowed
(10)   OTHER REASONS
(11)   None of these

Yunpaid

Now I would like you to look at this showcard.
In the last 12 months, that is, since DATE, have you given help to any groups, clubs or organisations in any of the ways shown on this card?

(1)   Collected or raised money for a group or club
(2)   Taken part in a sponsored activity for a group or club
(3)   Been part of a committee for a group or club
(4)   Helped to organise or run an event
(5)   Given any other help to a group or club
(6)   NONE OF THESE

Educational Attainment

Ask if: child aged 15 or over

EduIntr

I am now going to ask you about exams that you have passed or been entered for.

Ask if: child aged 15 or over

CAnyQual

Have you got any qualifications of any sort?

(1)   Yes
(2)   No

Ask if: CAnyQual = Yes

CHiQuals

Please look at this card and tell me whether you have passed any of the qualifications listed. Look down the list and tell me the first one you come to that you have passed

(1)   'A'Levels/SCE Higher
       or ONC/OND/BEC/TEC not higher
       or Certificate of Sixth Year Studies (CSYS)
       or City & Guilds Advanced Final Level
(2)   AS level
(3)   GCSE (Grades A–C)
       or SCE Standard – Credit level
       or City & Guilds Craft/Ord Level
(4)   GCSE (Grades D–G)
       or SCE Standard – General or Foundation level
       or NVQ's/SVQ's
(5)   Other qualifications (specify)
(6)   No qualifications

Ask if: CHiQuals = Other

cOthQual

What other qualification do you have?

Ask if: CHiQuals = 1–5

AgeQual

How old were you when you gained this qualification?

Ask if: child aged 15 or over

HiEnter

EDUCATIONAL ATTAINMENT – YOUNG PERSON INTERVIEW

What is the highest educational exam you have been entered for? Please look down the list and tell me the first one you come to that you have been entered for.
SHOW CARD 13a

(1)   'A'Levels/SCE Higher
       or ONC/OND/BEC/TEC not higher
       or Certificate of Sixth Year Studies (CSYS)
       or City & Guilds Advanced Final Level
(2)   AS level
(3)   GCSE's
       or SCE Standard
       or City and Guilds
       or NVQ's/SVQ's
(4)   Other qualifications (specify)
(5)   Not entered for any examinations

Ask if: HiEnter = Other

COthQua2

What other qualification have you been entered for?

Ask if: child aged 14 or under

CSchLeft

Are you still in continuous full-time education at school or college?

(1)   Yes
(2)   No

Ask if: CSchLeft = No

WhyLeft

Why did you leave school?

HowSch2

How many different schools have you ever attended?

Child Self Completion Questionnaire

CSCIntr

I would now like you to take the computer and answer the next set of questions yourself

Confid

Take your time to read each question carefully in turn and answer it as best you can.
REMEMBER THAT WE ARE ONLY INTERESTED IN YOUR OPINION. THIS IS NOT A TEST

CN1Intr

You have been asked a lot of questions about difficulties and problems.
Now there are some questions about your good points or strengths.
Next you will see some things which other young people have said about themselves.

Please say whether they apply to you by choosing 1 for 'No', 2 for 'A little'
or 3 for 'A lot'..

CN1a

Does the following description apply to you?

...generous

CN1b

...out-going, sociable

CN1c

...nice personality

CN1d

...reliable and responsible

CN1e

...easy-going

CN1f

...good fun, good sense of humour

CN1g

...caring, kind-hearted

CN1h

...independent

CN2Intr

Next you will see some things that other young people have said they have done that they are really proud of.
Please say whether they apply to you by choosing 1 for 'No', 2 for 'A little'
or 3 for 'A lot'..

CN2a

...good at sport

CN2b

...good with friends

CN2c

...helpful at home

CN2d

...good at music

CN2e

...well behaved

CN2f

...good with computers

CN2g

...good at drama, acting

CN2h

...raising money for charity, helping others

CN2i

...good at art, making things

CN2j

...polite

CN2k

...good at school work

CN2l

Are there any other good points about you that you particularly want to mention?

(1)　No
(2)　Yes

ASK IF: CN2l = Yes

CN2la

PLEASE TYPE IN ANY OTHER GOOD POINTS OR THINGS THAT YOU ARE PROUD OF THAT YOU WOULD LIKE TO MENTION.

Child self completion– Troublesome Behaviour

AwkIntr

The next set of questions is about your behaviour.

C3A4a

Thinking of the last year, have you often told lies to get things or favours from others, or to get out of having to do things you are supposed to do?

(1)　No
(2)　Perhaps
(3)　Definitely

ASK IF: C3A4a = Definitely

C3A4aa

Has this been going on for the last 6 months?

(1)　No
(2)　Yes

C3A4b

Have you often started fights in the past year?

(1)　No
(2)　Perhaps
(3)　Definitely

ASK IF: C3A4b = Definitely

C3A4ba

Has this been going on for the last 6 months?

(1)　No
(2)　Yes

C3A4c

During the past year, have you often bullied or threatened people?

(1)　No
(2)　Perhaps
(3)　Definitely

ASK IF: C3A4c = Definitely

C3A4ca

Has this been going on for the last 6 months?

(1)　No
(2)　Yes

C3A4d

Thinking of the past year, have you often stayed out later than you were supposed to?

(1) No
(2) Perhaps
(3) Definitely

ASK IF: C3A4d = Definitely

C3A4da

Has this been going on for the last 6 months?

(1) No
(2) Yes

C3A4e

Have you stolen valuable things from your house or other people's houses, shops or school in the past year?

(1) No
(2) Perhaps
(3) Definitely

ASK IF: C3A4e = Definitely

C3A4ea

Has this been going on for the last 6 months?

(1) No
(2) Yes

C3A4f

Have you run away from home more than once or ever stayed away all night without permission in the past year?

(1) No
(2) Perhaps
(3) Definitely

ASK IF: C3A4f = Definitely

C3A4fa

Has this been going on for the last 6 months?

(1) No
(2) Yes

C3A4g

Thinking of the past year, have you often played truant ('bunked off') from school?

(1) No
(2) Perhaps
(3) Definitely

ASK IF: C3A4g = Definitely

C3A4ga

Has this been going on for the last 6 months?

(1) No
(2) Yes

ASK IF: C3A4g = Definitely AND: child is over age 12

C3A5

Did you start playing truant ('bunking off') from school before you were 13 years old?

(1) No
(2) Yes

C3A6a

The next few questions are about some other behaviours that sometimes get people into trouble.
We have to ask everyone these questions even when they are not likely to apply.
In the past year, have you ever used a weapon against another person (e.g. a bat, brick, broken bottle, knife, gun)?

(1) No
(2) Yes

ASK IF: C3A6a = Yes

C3A6aa

Has this happened in the last 6 months?

(1) No
(2) Yes

C3A6b

In the past year, have you really hurt someone or been physically cruel to them, for example, tied up, cut or burned someone?

(1) No
(2) Yes

ASK IF: C3A6b = Yes

C3A6ba

Has this happened in the last 6 months?

(1) No
(2) Yes

C3A6c

Have you been really cruel to animals or birds on purpose in the past year (eg. tied them up, cut or burnt them)?

(1) No
(2) Yes

Ask if: C3A6c = Yes

C3A6ca

Has this happened in the last 6 months?

(1)　No
(2)　Yes

C3A6d

Have you deliberately started a fire in the past year?
(DO NOT INCLUDE BURNING INDIVIDUAL MATCHES
OR PIECES OF PAPER, CAMP FIRES ETC.)

(1)　No
(2)　Yes

Ask if: C3A6d = Yes

C3A6da

Has this happened in the last 6 months?

(1)　No
(2)　Yes

C3A6e

Thinking of the past year, have you deliberately destroyed
someone else's property?

(e.g. smashing car windows or destroying school property)
PRESS 1 FOR 'NO' OR 2 FOR 'YES'

(1)　No
(2)　Yes

Ask if: C3A6e = Yes

C3A6ea

Has this happened in the last 6 months?

(1)　No
(2)　Yes

C3A6f

Have you been involved in stealing from someone in the street?

(1)　No
(2)　Yes

Ask if: C3A6f = Yes

C3A6fa

Has this happened in the last 6 months?

(1)　No
(2)　Yes

C3A6g

During the past year have you tried to force someone into sexual
activity against their will?

(1)　No
(2)　Yes

Ask if: C3A6g = Yes

C3A6ga

Has this happened in the last 6 months?

(1)　No
(2)　Yes

C3A6h

Have you broken into a house, another building or a car in the
past year?

(1)　No
(2)　Yes

Ask if: C3A6h = Yes

C3A6ha

Has this happened in the last 6 months?

(1)　No
(2)　Yes

C3A7

Have you ever been in trouble with the police?

(1)　No
(2)　Yes

Ask if: C3A7 = Yes

C3A7a

Please type in why you were in trouble with the police.

Ask if: (C3A7 = Yes)

C3A8a

You have told me about some behaviours that have got you into
trouble. Have these interfered with how well you get on with the
others at home?

(1)　Not at all
(2)　A little
(3)　Quite a lot
(4)　A great deal

Ask if: *(C3A7 = Yes)*

C3A8b

Have these interfered with making and keeping friends?

(1) Not at all
(2) A little
(3) Quite a lot
(4) A great deal

Ask if: *(C3A7 = Yes)*

C3A8c

Have these interfered with learning or class work?

(1) Not at all
(2) A little
(3) Quite a lot
(4) A great deal

Ask if: *C3A7 = Yes*

C3A8d

Have these interfered with playing, hobbies, sports or other leisure activities?

(1) Not at all
(2) A little
(3) Quite a lot
(4) A great deal

Ask if: *C3A7 = Yes*

C3A9

Has your behaviour made it harder for those around you (the others at (in the) home, friends, family, or teachers etc.)?

(1) Not at all
(2) A little
(3) Quite a lot
(4) A great deal

Child self completion – Smoking

SmkIntro

Here are some questions about smoking

C3E1

Do you smoke cigarettes at all these days?

(1) No
(2) Yes

C3E2

Now read all the following statements carefully and type in the number next to the one which best describes you.

(1) I have never smoked
(2) I have only tried smoking once
(3) I used to smoke cigarettes but I never smoke now
(4) I sometimes smoke cigarettes now, but I don't smoke as many as one a week
(5) I usually smoke between 1 – 6 cigarettes a week
(6) I usually smoke more than 6 cigarettes a week

Ask if: *C3E2 = Never*

C3E3

Just to check, read the statements below carefully and type in the number next to the one which best describes you.

(1) I have never tried smoking a cigarette, not even a puff or two
(2) I did once have a puff or two of a cigarette, but I never smoke now
(3) I do sometimes smoke cigarettes

Ask if: *C3E3 = 2 or 3 OR C3E2 = UsuSmok = 5, 6*

C3E3a

About how many cigarettes a day do you usually smoke?

IF YOU SMOKE LESS THAN 1, TYPE 0

Ask if: *C3E3 = 2 or 3 OR C3E2 = UsuSmok = 5, 6*

C3E3b

How old were you when you started smoking at least one cigarette a week?

Ask if: *C3E3 = 2 or 3 OR C3E2 = UsuSmok = 5, 6*

C3E3c

Thinking about the last time you smoked, where were you when you smoked?

(1) At home
(2) Someone else's home
(3) In a pub/pubs
(4) In a restaurant
(5) In a night club/club
(6) Outside in a public place (e.g. park, street)
(7) Other

Ask if: *C3E3 = 2 or 3 OR C3E2 = UsuSmok = 5, 6*

C3E3d

Still thinking about the last time you smoked, with how many people were you when you smoked?

(1) Alone
(2) One other person
(3) Two to five people
(4) Six to ten people
(5) More than 10 people

Ask if: C3E3d = 2, 3, 4 or 5

C3E3e

And with whom were you when you smoked?

YOU CAN TYPE AS MANY NUMBERS AS YOU WANT.
PRESS THE SPACE BAR BETWEEN EACH NUMBER THAT
YOU TYPE IN

(1) Boyfriend or girlfriend
(2) With a friend/friends
(3) With family
(4) Other

Ask if: C3E3a > 9

C3E4

Do you ever feel like cutting down or stopping smoking?

(1) No
(2) Yes

Ask if: C3E3a > 9

C3E5

Do you feel annoyed if other people criticise your smoking?

(1) No
(2) Yes

Ask if: C3E3a > 9

C3E6

Is smoking getting in the way of things you would really like to
do?
(e.g. by using money you'd rather have for other things)

(1) No
(2) Yes

Ask if: C3E3a > 9

C3E7

Do you have a really strong need for cigarettes to get through the
day?

(1) No
(2) Yes

Ask if: C3E3a > 9

C3E8

Do you get into trouble as a result of smoking?
(e.g. trouble at school, at home, starting fires)

(1) No
(2) Yes

Child self-completion – Drinking

DrnkIntr

Now there are some questions about drinking

C3F1

Have you ever had a proper alcoholic drink – a whole drink not
just a sip?

(1) No
(2) Yes

Ask if: C3F1 = Yes

C3F2

How often do you usually have an alcoholic drink?

(1) Almost every day
(2) About twice a week
(3) About once a week
(4) About once a fortnight
(5) About once a month
(6) Only a few times a year
(7) I never drink alcohol

Ask if: C3F1 = Yes

C3F3

When did you last have an alcoholic drink?

(1) Today
(2) Yesterday
(3) Some other time during the last week
(4) One week, but less than two weeks ago
(5) Two weeks, but less than four weeks ago
(6) One month, but less than six months ago
(7) Six months ago or more

Ask if: C3F1 = Yes And: C3F3 = 1-6

C3F4

Thinking about the last time you had an alcoholic drink, where
did you have this drink?

(1) At home
(2) Someone else's home
(3) In a pub/pubs
(4) In a restaurant
(5) In a night club/club
(6) Outside in a public place (e.g. park, street)
(7) Other

ASK IF: *C3F1 = Yes* AND: *C3F3 = 1-6*

C3F5

Still thinking about the last time you had an alcoholic drink, with how many people did you have this drink?

(1)   Alone
(2)   One other person
(3)   Two to five people
(4)   Six to ten people
(5)   More than 10 people

ASK IF: *C3F5 = 2-5*

C3F6

And with whom did you have your drink?

(1)   Boyfriend or girlfriend
(2)   With a friend/friends
(3)   With family
(4)   Other

ASK IF: *C3F1 = Yes* AND: *C3F2 1, 2, 3*

C3F7

Do you ever feel like cutting down or stopping your drinking?

(1)   No
(2)   Yes

ASK IF: *C3F1 = Yes* AND: *C3F2 1, 2, 3*

C3F8

Do you feel annoyed if other people criticise your drinking?

(1)   No
(2)   Yes

ASK IF: *C3F1 = Yes* AND: *C3F2 1, 2, 3*

C3F9

Is drinking getting in the way of things you would really like to do? (e.g. by using money you'd rather have for other things, stopping you get a qualification or job)

(1)   No
(2)   Yes

ASK IF: *C3F1 = Yes* AND: *C3F2 1, 2, 3*

C3F10

Do you have a really strong need for alcoholic drinks to get through the day?

(1)   No
(2)   Yes

ASK IF: *C3F1 = Yes* AND: *C3F2 1, 2, 3*

C3F11

Do you get into trouble as a result of drinking? (e.g. trouble at school, at home, with the police, accidents, fights)

(1)   No
(2)   Yes

Child self completion – Drugs

CanIntr

The next set of questions are about drugs

The first few questions are about marijuana and hashish. Marijuana is also called cannabis, hash, dope, grass, ganja, kif. Marijuana is usually smoked either in cigarettes, called joints, or in a pipe.

C3C1

Have you ever had a chance to try marijuana or hashish? Having a 'chance to try' means that cannabis was available to you if you wanted to use it or not?

(1)   No
(2)   Yes

C3c2

Have you ever, even once, used cannabis?

(1)   No
(2)   Yes
(3)   Never heard of cannabis/don't know

ASK IF: *C3c2 = Yes*

C3c3

Have you ever used cannabis more than 5 times in your life?

(1)   No
(2)   Yes

ASK IF: *C3c2 = Yes*

C3C4

About how old were you the first time you used cannabis, even once?

ASK IF: *C3c2 = Yes*

C3C5

About how often have you used cannabis in the past year?

(1)   About daily
(2)   2 or 3 times a week
(3)   About once a week
(4)   About once a month
(5)   Only a once or twice in past year
(6)   Not at all in past year

ASK IF: C3C5 = 1–5

C3CWhere

Thinking about the last time you had cannabis, where did you have it?

(1)   At home
(2)   Someone else's home
(3)   In a pub/pubs
(4)   In a restaurant
(5)   In a night club/club
(6)   Outside in a public place (e.g. park, street)
(7)   Other

ASK IF: C3C5 = 1–5

C3CHow

Still thinking about the last time you had cannabis, with how many people did you have it?

(1)   Alone
(2)   One other person
(3)   Two to five people
(4)   Six to ten people
(5)   More than 10 people

ASK IF: C3CHow = 2, 3, 4, 5

C3CWho

And with whom did you have cannabis?

(1)   Boyfriend or girlfriend
(2)   With a friend/friends
(3)   With family
(4)   Other

ASK IF: C3C5 = 1, 2, 3

C3Ca6

Have you ever been concerned or worried about using it?

(1)   No
(2)   Yes

ASK IF: C3C5 = 1, 2, 3

C3C7

Has using cannabis ever made you feel ill?

(1)   No
(2)   Yes

ASK IF: C3C5 = 1, 2, 3

C3C8

Has anyone expressed concern about you using cannabis -

(1)   No
(2)   Yes

ASK IF: C3C5 = 1, 2, 3

C3C9

Do you feel like cutting down or stopping your use of cannabis?

(1)   No
(2)   Yes

ASK IF: C3C5 = 1, 2, 3

C3C10

Do you feel annoyed if other people criticise your use of cannabis?

(1)   No
(2)   Yes

ASK IF: C3C5 = 1, 2, 3

C3C11

Is using cannabis getting in the way of things you would really like to do?
(e.g. by using money you'd rather have for other things or stopping you get a qualification or job)

(1)   No
(2)   Yes

ASK IF: C3C5 = 1, 2, 3

C3C12

Do you have a really strong need for cannabis to get through the day?

(1)   No
(2)   Yes

ASK IF: C3C5 = 1, 2, 3

C3C13

Do you get into trouble as a result of using cannabis?
(e.g. trouble at school, at home, with police, accidents)

(1)   No
(2)   Yes

C3G2

Have you ever used any other drug?

(1)   No
(2)   Yes

Ask if: C3G2 = Yes

C3G3

Have you ever used inhalants (these are liquids or sprays that people
 sniff or inhale to get high or make them feel good such as
 solvents, sprays, glue or amylnitrate)?

(1)   No
(2)   Yes
(3)   Never heard of inhalants/don't know

Ask if: C3G3 = Yes

C3G3a

Have you ever used inhalants more than 5 times in your life?

(1)   No
(2)   Yes

Ask if: C3G2 = Yes

C3G4

Have you ever used ECSTASY?

(1)   No
(2)   Yes
(3)   Never heard of ecstasy/don't know

Ask if: C3G4 = Yes

C3G4a

Have you ever used ecstasy more than 5 times in your life?

(1)   No
(2)   Yes

Ask if: C3G2 = Yes

C3G5

Have you ever used AMPHETAMINES (SPEED)

(1)   No
(2)   Yes
(3)   Never heard of amphetamines/don't know

Ask if: C3G5 = Yes

C3G5a

Have you ever used amphetamines (speed) more than 5 times in
your life?

(1)   No
(2)   Yes

Ask if: C3G2 = Yes

C3G6

Have you ever used LSD (ACID)?

(1)   No
(2)   Yes
(3)   Never heard of LSD/don't know

Ask if: C3G6 = Yes

C3G6a

Have you ever used LSD (Acid) more than 5 times in your life?

(1)   No
(2)   Yes

Ask if: C3G2 = Yes

C3G7

Have you ever used TRANQUILLISERS
(VALIUM,TEMAZAPAN)?

(1)   No
(2)   Yes
(3)   Never heard of tranquillisers/don't know

Ask if: C3G7 = Yes

C3G7a

Have you ever used Tranquillisers (valium, temazapan) more than
5 times
 in your life?

(1)   No
(2)   Yes

Ask if: C3G2 = Yes

C3G8

Have you ever used COCAINE (CRACK)?

(1)   No
(2)   Yes
(3)   Never heard of cocaine/don't know

Ask if: C3G8 = Yes

C3G8a

Have you ever used cocaine (crack) more than 5 times in your
life?

(1)   No
(2)   Yes

Ask if: C3G2 = Yes

C3G9

Have you ever used HEROIN (METHADONE)?

(1)   No
(2)   Yes
(3)   Never heard of heroin/don't know

Ask if: C3G9 = Yes

C3G9a

Have you ever used Heroin (methadone) more than 5 times in
your life?

(1)   No
(2)   Yes

C3DgHlp3

Have you ever had help or treatment because you were taking drugs?

(1)   No
(2)   Yes

Ask if: C3DgHlp3 = Yes

C3DgWho

Who did you get help from?

Ask if: C3DgHlp3 = No

C3DgHlp2

If you felt that you needed help or treatment because you were using drugs,
would you know where to go?

(1)   No
(2)   Yes

Ask if: C3DgHlp3 = No

C3DgHlp1

Have you ever felt that you needed to get help or treatment because you were
using drugs?

(1)   No
(2)   Yes

C3DrgInf

Would you know where to go if you wanted to get more information about drugs?

(1)   No
(2)   Yes

national StaTiSTiCS

IN CONFIDENCE

Survey of the health, development and emotional well-being of young people

Questionnaire for teachers and tutors

Stick serial number label here

7 digit number (COLS 1-7)

1 letter (COL 8)

How to fill in this questionnaire

1. Please read each question carefully.

2. All questions can be answered by putting a tick in the box next to the answer that applies to the child.

    For example

Not true	Partly true	Certainly true
☐	☐	☐

3. Sometimes you are asked to write a number in a box.

    For example   Enter number of days⟶ **4**

4. It would help if you could answer all the questions as best you can, even if you are not absolutely certain or you think the question seems a little odd.

5. The answers in the questionnaire should be your opinion only and not the collective opinions of several staff members.

A1. Compared with an average child of the same age, how does he or she fare in the following areas:

	Above average	Average	Some difficulty	Marked difficulty	
(a) Reading?	1	2	3	4	COL 9
(b) Mathematics?	1	2	3	4	COL 10
(c) Spelling?	1	2	3	4	COL 11

A2. Although "mental age" is a crude measure that cannot take account of a child being better in some areas than others, it would be helpful if you could answer the following question:

In terms of overall intellectual and scholastic ability, roughly what age level is he or she at?

Enter age level → **Go to Question A3**

2 digits
COLS 12-13

A3. How many days was the child absent during the last whole term?
(Enter to nearest half day, e.g. 4.5 or 7.0)

Enter number of days
If don't know enter '99'
If none enter '00'

→ **Go to Question A3a**

3 digits in format ##.#
COLS 14-16

A3a. Of these absences, how many were unauthorised absences?
(Enter to nearest half day, e.g. 4.5 or 7.0)

Enter number of days
If don't know enter '99'
If none enter '00'

→ **Go to Question A4**

3 digits in format ##.#
COLS 17-19

A4. Does the child have officially recognised special needs?

Yes 1 → **Go to Question A4a**
No 2 → **Go to Section B**

COL 20

A4a. Does the child have a written statement (record) of SEN?

Yes 1 → **Go to Question A5**
No 2

COL 21

A5. Are these special needs related to…………
(Please tick all that apply)

	Yes	No	
(a) **Cognition and Learning Needs** • Specific Learning Difficulty (SpLD) • Moderate Learning Difficulty (MLD) • Severe Learning Difficulty (SLD) • Profound and Multiple Learning Difficulty (PMLD)	1	2	COL 22
(b) **Behaviour, Emotional and Social Development Needs** • Behaviour, Emotional and Social Difficulty (BESD)	1	2	COL 23
(c) **Communication and Interaction Needs** • Speech, language and communication needs • Autistic Spectrum Disorder (ASD)	1	2	COL 24
(d) **Sensory and/or Physical Needs** • Visual Impairment (VI) • Hearing Impairment (HI) • Multi-Sensory Impairment (MSI) • Physical Disability (PD)	1	2	COL 25
(e) **Other (Please specify)** ………………………………… …………………………………	1	2	COL 26

Section B   Strengths and Difficulties Questionnaire[1]

For each item, please tick a box under one of the headings:
Not True, Partly True or Certainly True

Over the past six months:

	Not true	Partly true	Certainly true	
B1. Considerate of other people's feelings......	1	2	3	COL 27
B2. Restless, overactive, cannot stay still for long............	1	2	3	COL 28
B3. Often complains of headaches, stomach aches or sickness............	1	2	3	COL 29
B4. Shares readily with other children (treats, toys, pencils etc)............	1	2	3	COL 30
B5. Often has temper tantrums or hot tempers	1	2	3	COL 31
B6. Rather solitary, tends to play alone...........	1	2	3	COL 32
B7. Generally obedient, usually does what adults request............	1	2	3	COL 33
B8. Many worries, often seems worried...........	1	2	3	COL 34
B9. Helpful if someone is hurt, upset or feeling ill............	1	2	3	COL 35
B10. Constantly fidgeting or squirming............	1	2	3	COL 36
B11. Has at least one good friend............	1	2	3	COL 37
B12. Often fights with other children or bullies them............	1	2	3	COL 38

For each item, please tick a box under one of the headings:
Not True, Partly True or Certainly True

Over the past six months:

	Not true	Partly true	Certainly true	
B13. Often unhappy, downhearted or tearful............	1	2	3	COL 39
B14. Generally liked by other children	1	2	3	COL 40
B15. Easily distracted, concentration wanders...	1	2	3	COL 41
B16. Nervous or clingy in new situations, easily loses confidence............	1	2	3	COL 42
B17. Kind to younger children............	1	2	3	COL 43
B18. Often lies or cheats............	1	2	3	COL 44
B19. Picked on or bullied by other children......	1	2	3	COL 45
B20. Often volunteers to help others (parents, teachers, other children)............	1	2	3	COL 46
B21. Thinks things out before acting............	1	2	3	COL 47
B22. Steals from home, school or elsewhere......	1	2	3	COL 48
B23. Gets on better with adults than with other children............	1	2	3	COL 49
B24. Many fears, easily scared............	1	2	3	COL 50
B25. Sees tasks through to the end, good attention span............	1	2	3	COL 51

1. *The Strength and Difficulties Questionnaire (Questions B1–B29) is copyrighted © to Professor Robert Goodman, Department of Child and Adolescent Psychiatry, De Crespigny Park, London SE5 8AF.*

B26. Overall, do you think that this child has difficulties in on or more of the following areas: Emotions, concentration, behaviour or getting on with other people?

No.............................	1	→ **Go to Section C**
Yes: minor difficulties..........	2	
Yes: definite difficulties.........	3	→ **Go to Question B26(a)**
Yes: severe difficulties..........	4	

COL 52

(a) How long have these difficulties been present?

Less than a month................	1
1 – 5 months	2
6 – 12 months	3
A year or more	4

COL 53

	Not at all	Only a little	Quite a lot	A great deal	
B27. Do the difficulties upset or distress the child?..........	1	2	3	4	COL 54
B28. Do the difficulties interfere with the child's everyday life in terms of his or her......					
peer relationships?......	1	2	3	4	COL 55
classroom learning?.....	1	2	3	4	COL 56
B29. Do the difficulties put a burden on you or the class as a whole?..	1	2	3	4	COL 57

Please go to Section C

Section C   Emotions

For each item, please tick a box under one of the headings:
Not true, Partly true or Certainly true

	Not true	Partly true	Certainly true	
C1. Excessive worries...................	1	2	3	COL 58
C2. Marked tension or inability to relax......	1	2	3	COL 59
C3. Excessive concern about his/her own abilities, e.g. academic, sporting or social......	1	2	3	COL 60
C4. Particularly anxious about speaking to class or reading aloud......	1	2	3	COL 61
C5. Reluctant to separate from family to come to school......	1	2	3	COL 62
C6. Unhappy, sad or depressed......	1	2	3	COL 63
C7. Has lost interest in carrying out usual activities......	1	2	3	COL 64
C8. Feels worthless or inferior......	1	2	3	COL 65
C9. Concentration affected by worries or misery......	1	2	3	COL 66
C10. Other emotional difficulties e.g. marked fears, panic attacks, obsessions or compulsions......	1 → **Go to C11**	2 → **Go to C10a**	3	COL 67

C10a. Please describe these briefly

Section D   Attention, Activity and Impulsiveness

D1. When s/he is doing something in class that s/he enjoys and is good at, whether reading or drawing or making a model or whatever, how long does s/he typically stay on that task?

Less than 2 minutes......... | 1 |

2 – 4 minutes................. | 2 |

5 – 9 minutes................. | 3 | COL 73

10 – 19 minutes .... | 4 |

20 minutes or more.......... | 5 |

Please review your answers to questions C1 to C10 about worries, misery and so on.

If you have ticked 'CERAINLY TRUE' to any of the questions C1 to C10 – Please go to Question C11. If not, go to Section D.

	Not at all	Only a little	Quite a lot	A great deal	
C11. Do the difficulties upset or distress the child?.........	1	2	3	4	COL 68
C12. Do the difficulties interfere with the child's everyday life in terms of his or her......					
peer relationships?......	1	2	3	4	COL 69
classroom learning?......	1	2	3	4	COL 70
C13. Do the difficulties put a burden on you or the class as a whole?..	1	2	3	4	COL 71

C14. Do you have any further comments about this child's emotional state?

Yes | 1 | ➤ **Go to Question C14a**

No | 2 | ➤ **Go to Section D**   COL 72

C14a. If there are serious concerns in this area, please say how long the child has had these problems, and what, if anything, might have triggered them.

Please go to Section D

For each item, please tick a box under one of the headings:
Not true, Partly true or Certainly true

		Not true	Partly true	Certainly true	
D2.	Makes careless mistakes.	1	2	3	COL 74
D3.	Fails to pay attention.	1	2	3	COL 75
D4.	Loses interest in what s/he is doing.	1	2	3	COL 76
D5.	Doesn't seem to listen.	1	2	3	COL 77
D6.	Fails to finish things s/he starts.	1	2	3	COL 78
D7.	Disorganised.	1	2	3	COL 79
D8.	Tries to avoid tasks that require thought.	1	2	3	COL 80
D9.	Loses things.	1	2	3	COL 81
D10.	Easily distracted.	1	2	3	COL 82
D11.	Forgetful.	1	2	3	COL 83
D12.	Fidgets.	1	2	3	COL 84
D13.	Can't stay seated when required to do so.	1	2	3	COL 85
D14.	Runs or climbs about when s/he shouldn't.	1	2	3	COL 86
D15.	Has difficulty playing quietly.	1	2	3	COL 87
D16.	Finds it hard to calm down when asked to do so.	1	2	3	COL 88
D17.	Interrupts, blurts out answers to questions.	1	2	3	COL 89
D18.	Hard for him/her to wait their turn.	1	2	3	COL 90
D19.	Interrupts or butts in on others.	1	2	3	COL 91
D20.	Goes on talking if asked to stop.	1	2	3	COL 92

Please review your answers to questions D2 to D20 on attention and activity.

If you have ticked 'CERAINLY TRUE' to any of the questions D2 to D20 – Please go to Question D21. If not, go to Section E.

		Not at all	Only a little	Quite a lot	A great deal	
D21.	Do the difficulties upset or distress the child?	1	2	3	4	COL 93
D22.	Do the difficulties interfere with the child's everyday life in terms of his or her......					
	peer relationships?	1	2	3	4	COL 94
	classroom learning?	1	2	3	4	COL 95
D23.	Do the difficulties put a burden on you or the class as a whole?..	1	2	3	4	COL 96

D24. Do you have any further comments about this child in relation to attention, or activity and impulsiveness?

Yes → **Go to Question D24a**

No → **Go to Section E**

COL 97

D24a. Please describe. If there are serious concerns in this area, please say how long the child has had these problems and what, if anything, might have triggered them.

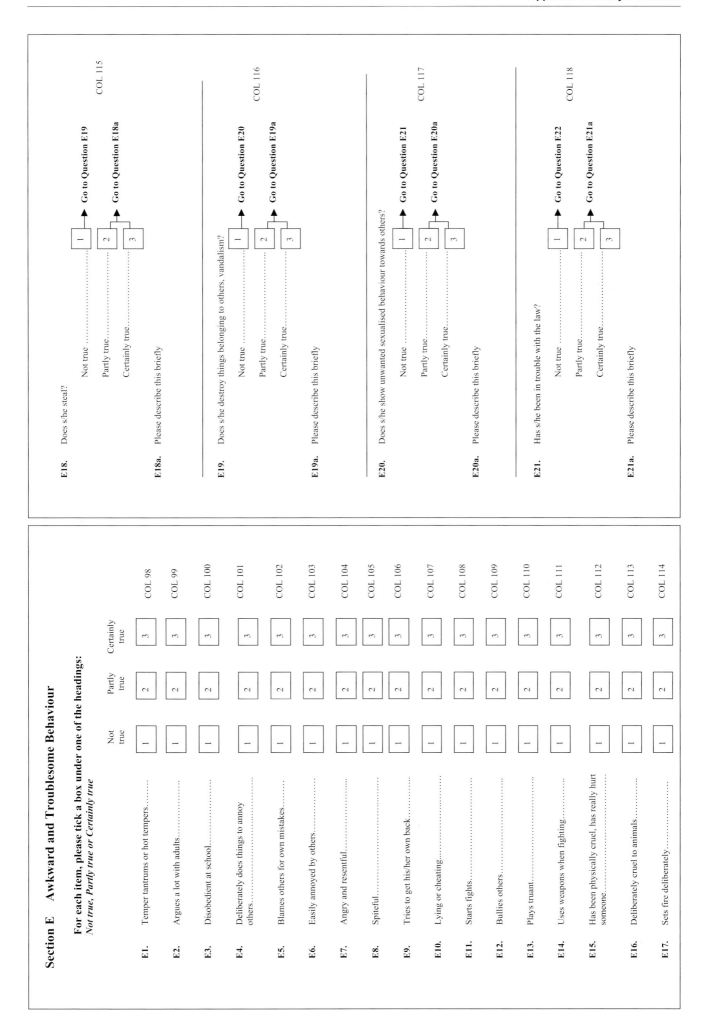

Section E   Awkward and Troublesome Behaviour

For each item, please tick a box under one of the headings:
Not true, Partly true or Certainly true

	Not true	Partly true	Certainly true	
E1. Temper tantrums or hot tempers	1	2	3	COL 98
E2. Argues a lot with adults	1	2	3	COL 99
E3. Disobedient at school	1	2	3	COL 100
E4. Deliberately does things to annoy others	1	2	3	COL 101
E5. Blames others for own mistakes	1	2	3	COL 102
E6. Easily annoyed by others	1	2	3	COL 103
E7. Angry and resentful	1	2	3	COL 104
E8. Spiteful	1	2	3	COL 105
E9. Tries to get his/her own back	1	2	3	COL 106
E10. Lying or cheating	1	2	3	COL 107
E11. Starts fights	1	2	3	COL 108
E12. Bullies others	1	2	3	COL 109
E13. Plays truant	1	2	3	COL 110
E14. Uses weapons when fighting	1	2	3	COL 111
E15. Has been physically cruel, has really hurt someone	1	2	3	COL 112
E16. Deliberately cruel to animals	1	2	3	COL 113
E17. Sets fire deliberately	1	2	3	COL 114

E18. Does s/he steal?

Not true .... 1 → **Go to Question E19**
Partly true 2
Certainly true .... 3 → **Go to Question E18a**

COL 115

E18a. Please describe this briefly

E19. Does s/he destroy things belonging to others, vandalism?

Not true .... 1 → **Go to Question E20**
Partly true 2
Certainly true .... 3 → **Go to Question E19a**

COL 116

E19a. Please describe this briefly

E20. Does s/he show unwanted sexualised behaviour towards others?

Not true .... 1 → **Go to Question E21**
Partly true 2
Certainly true .... 3 → **Go to Question E20a**

COL 117

E20a. Please describe this briefly

E21. Has s/he been in trouble with the law?

Not true .... 1 → **Go to Question E22**
Partly true 2
Certainly true .... 3 → **Go to Question E21a**

COL 118

E21a. Please describe this briefly

Section F   Personality

For each item, please tick a box under one of the headings:
Not true, Partly true or Certainly true

	Not true	Partly true	Certainly true	
F1. Good at keeping him/herself occupied ….	1	2	3	COL 124
F2. Often does reckless things without thinking of the danger or the consequences for him/herself or others	1	2	3	COL 125
F3. Makes a good first impression but people change their minds after they get to know him/her	1	2	3	COL 126
F4. Keeps friends	1	2	3	COL 127
F5. Has shallow and fast-changing emotions ……	1	2	3	COL 128
F6. Too full of him/herself or his/her own abilities	1	2	3	COL 129
F7. Is usually genuinely sorry if s/he has hurt someone or acted badly ……	1	2	3	COL 130
F8. Often uses emotional blackmail to get his/her own way …	1	2	3	COL 131
F9. Fearless in situations that should worry or scare children/young people of his/her age. …	1	2	3	COL 132
F10. Can seem cold blooded or callous ………	1	2	3	COL 133
F11. Keeps promises ………	1	2	3	COL 134
F12. Has difficulty trusting others ……	1	2	3	COL 135
F13. Genuine in his/her expression of emotions ….	1	2	3	COL 136
F14. Usually tries his/her best………	1	2	3	COL 137

Please go to Section G

Please review your answers to questions E1 to E21 on awkward and troublesome behaviour.

**If you have ticked 'CERAINLY TRUE' to any of the questions E1 to E21 –
Please go to Question E22. If not, go to Section F.**

	Not at all	Only a little	Quite a lot	A great deal	
E22. Do the difficulties upset or distress the child?……	1	2	3	4	COL 119
E23. Do the difficulties interfere with the child's everyday life in terms of his or her……					
peer relationships?……	1	2	3	4	COL 120
classroom learning?……	1	2	3	4	COL 121
E24. Do the difficulties put a burden on you or the class as a whole?…	1	2	3	4	COL 122

E25. Do you have any further comments about this child's awkward and troublesome behaviour?

Yes 1 → **Go to Question E25a**
COL 123
No 2 → **Go to Section F**

E25a. Please describe. If there are serious concerns in this area, please say how long the child has had these problems and what, if anything, might have triggered them.

Please go to Section F

Section H   Help from School

H1.   During this school year, has s/he had any specific help for emotional or behavioural problems from teachers, educational psychologists, or other professionals working within the school setting.

Yes [1] ——► **Go to Question H1a**

No [2] ——► **END**   COL 143

H1a.   Please describe briefly what sort of help was provided, by whom, and for what:

Thank you very much for your help

Please return the questionnaire in the pre-paid envelope as soon as possible

national STATISTICS

Office for National Statistics
1 Drummond Gate
London
SW1V 2QQ

Section G   Other concerns

For each item, please tick a box under one of the headings:
Not true, Partly true or Certainly true

	Not true	Partly true	Certainly true	
G1. Tics, twitches, involuntary grunts or noises...............	[1]	[2]	[3]	COL 138
G2. Diets to excess................	[1]	[2]	[3]	COL 139

G3.   Has s/he been diagnosed with an autistic spectrum disorder, or do you have concerns that s/he may have one?

Yes [1]

No [2]   COL 140

G4.   Do you have any other concerns about the child's psychological development?

Yes [1] ——► **Go to Question G4a**

No [2] ——► **Go to Question G5**   COL 141

G4a.   Please describe this briefly

G5.   Do you have any further comments about him/her in general?

Yes [1] ——► **Go to Question G5a**

No [2] ——► **Go to Section G**   COL 142

G5a.   Please describe

Please go to Section H

PA359

IN CONFIDENCE

Survey of the health, development and emotional well-being of young people in Great Britain

Follow-up questionnaire for parents

How to fill in this questionnaire

1. Please read each question carefully.

2. Most questions can be answered by putting a tick in the box next to the answer that applies.

For example…

Not true	Partly true	Certainly true
☐	✔	☐

3. Sometimes you are asked to write your answer in a box.

For example…

like this...

4. Please try to answer all the questions as best as you can even if you are not absolutely certain or you think the question does not really apply to your child.

1

---

31. It is now about 6 months since you took part in our survey.

During this last 6 months, have you used any of the following sources of help or advice about your child's emotions, concentration or behaviour? Please tick as many as apply:

(If you know for certain that your child has used one of these services but without your involvement, please tick the relevant box for that too.)

Yes

☐ Someone in your family or a close friend

☐ Books or magazines

☐ The Internet

☐ Telephone help-line

☐ Self-help group

☐ A teacher (e.g. class teacher, head of year, special educational needs coordinator)

☐ Someone working in special educational services (e.g. an educational psychologist, an education welfare officer or a behavioural support teacher)

☐ Your GP, family doctor, or health visitor

☐ Someone specialising in mental health (e.g. a counsellor, psychologist or psychiatrist)

☐ Someone specialising in children's general health (e.g. a paediatrician, school doctor or school nurse)

☐ Someone from social services (e.g. a social worker)

☐ Someone else – please say who:

Thank you very much for your help.
Please return this questionnaire in the pre-paid envelope provided.

D0069 6/04

4

Please indicate how much the following statements apply to how your child has been over the LAST MONTH.

	Not true	Partly true	Certainly true
1. Considerate of other people's feelings	☐	☐	☐
2. Restless, overactive, cannot stay still for long	☐	☐	☐
3. Often complains of headaches, stomach aches or sickness	☐	☐	☐
4. Shares readily with other children (treats, toys, pencils etc.)	☐	☐	☐
5. Often has temper tantrums or hot tempers	☐	☐	☐
6. Rather solitary, tends to play alone	☐	☐	☐
7. Generally obedient, usually does what adults request	☐	☐	☐
8. Many worries, often seems worried	☐	☐	☐
9. Helpful if someone is hurt, upset or feeling ill	☐	☐	☐
10. Constantly fidgeting or squirming	☐	☐	☐
11. Has at least one good friend	☐	☐	☐
12. Often fights with other children or bullies them	☐	☐	☐
13. Often unhappy, down-hearted or tearful	☐	☐	☐
14. Generally liked by other children	☐	☐	☐
15. Easily distracted, concentration wanders	☐	☐	☐
16. Nervous or clingy in new situations, easily loses confidence	☐	☐	☐
17. Kind to younger children	☐	☐	☐
18. Often lies or cheats	☐	☐	☐
19. Picked on or bullied by other children	☐	☐	☐
20. Often volunteers to help others (parents, teachers, other children)	☐	☐	☐
21. Thinks things out before acting	☐	☐	☐
22. Steals from home, school or elsewhere	☐	☐	☐
23. Gets on better with adults than with other children	☐	☐	☐
24. Many fears, easily scared	☐	☐	☐
25. Sees tasks through to the end, good attention span	☐	☐	☐

2

26. **Compared with 6 months ago (when we visited you), is your child's behaviour, concentration and emotional adjustment now:**

Much worse	A bit worse	About the same	A bit better	Much better
☐	☐	☐	☐	☐

27. **Over the LAST MONTH, has your child had difficulties in one or more of the following areas: emotions, concentration, behaviour or being able to get on with other people?**

No	Yes - minor difficulties	Yes - definite difficulties	Yes - severe difficulties
☐	☐	☐	☐

▷ IF YOU ANSWERED 'YES' TO THIS QUESTION, PLEASE CONTINUE WITH **QUESTIONS 28 - 30** on this page

▷ IF YOU ANSWERED 'NO' PLEASE CONTINUE WITH **QUESTION 31** on the last page

28. **Do the difficulties upset or distress your child?**

Not at all	Only a little	Quite a lot	A great deal
☐	☐	☐	☐

29. **Do the difficulties interfere with your child's everyday life in the following areas?**

	Not at all	Only a little	Quite a lot	A great deal
Home life	☐	☐	☐	☐
Friendships	☐	☐	☐	☐
Classroom learning	☐	☐	☐	☐
Leisure activities	☐	☐	☐	☐

30. **Do the difficulties put a burden on you or the family as a whole?**

Not at all	Only a little	Quite a lot	A great deal
☐	☐	☐	☐

3

Glossary of terms

Acorn

The Acorn classification is a means of classifying areas according to various Census characteristics (geographic and demographic), devised by CACI limited. An ACORN code is assigned to each Census Enumeration District (ED) which is then copied to all postcodes within the ED. The classification consists of 56 area types. These can be collapsed into 17 higher level groups and five top level categories as shown below. Analyses in this report use the five category classification. The categories, groups and area types are shown below.

Category	Group	Type
Wealthy achievers	Wealthy executives	1 Affluent mature professionals, large houses
		2 Affluent working families with mortgages
		3 Villages with wealthy commuters
		4 Well-off managers, larger houses
	Affluent greys	5 Older affluent professionals
		6 Farming communities
		7 Old people, detached houses
		8 Mature couples, smaller detached houses
	Flourishing families	9 Larger families, prosperous suburbs
		10 Well-off working families with mortgages
		11 Well-off managers, detached houses
		12 Large families and houses in rural areas
Urban prosperity	Prosperous professionals	13 Well-off professionals, larger houses and converted flats
		14 Older professionals in detached houses and apartments
	Educated urbanites	15 Affluent, urban professionals, flats
		16 Prosperous young professionals, flats
		17 Young educated workers, flats
		18 Multi-ethnic young, converted flats
		19 Suburban privately renting professionals
	Aspiring singles	20 Student flats and cosmopolitan sharers
		21 Singles & sharers, multi-ethnic areas
		22 Low income singles
		23 Student terraces
Comfortably off	Starting out	24 Young couples, flats and terraces
		25 White collar singles/sharers, terraces
	Secure families	26 Younger white-collar couples with mortgages
		27 Middle income home owning areas
		28 Working families with mortgages
		29 Mature families in suburban semis
		30 Established home owning workers
		31 Home owning Asian family areas
	Settled suburbia	32 Retired home owners
		33 Middle income, older couples
		34 Lower income people, semis
	Prudent pensioners	35 Elderly singles, purpose built flats
		36 Older people, flats

Moderate Means	Asian communities	37 Crowded Asian terraces
		38 Low income Asian families
	Post industrial families	39 Skilled older family terraces
		40 Young family workers
	Blue collar roots	41 Skilled workers, semis and terraces
		42 Home owning, terraces
		43 Older rented terraces
Hard Pressed	Struggling families	44 Low income larger families, semis
		45 Older people, low income, small semis
		46 Low income, routine jobs, unemployment
		47 Low rise terraced estates of poorly-off workers
		48 Low incomes, high unemployment, single parents
		49 Large families, many children, poorly educated
	Burdened singles	50 Council flats, single elderly people
		51 Council terraces, unemployment, many singles
		52 Council flats, single parents, unemployment
	High rise hardship	53 Old people in high rise flats
		54 Singles & single parents, high rise estates
	Inner city adversity	55 Multi-ethnic purpose built estates
		56 Multi-ethnic crowded flats

Burden of mental disorders

The burden of the child's problem is a measure of the consequences of the symptoms in terms of whether they cause distress to the family by making the parents worried, depressed, tired or physically ill.

Case vignettes

The case vignette approach for analysing survey data uses clinician ratings based on a review of all the information of each subject. This information includes not only the questionnaires and structured interviews but also any additional comments made by the interviewers, and the transcripts of informants' comments to open-ended questions particularly those which ask about the child's significant problems.

Education level of parent

Educational level was based on the highest educational qualification obtained and was grouped as follows:

Degree (or degree level qualification)

Teaching qualification
HNC/HND, BEC/TEC Higher, BTEC Higher
City and Guilds Full Technological Certificate
Nursing qualifications: (SRN,SCM,RGN,RM,RHV,Midwife)

A-levels/SCE higher
ONC/OND/BEC/TEC/not higher
City and Guilds Advanced/Final level

GCE O-level (grades A–C if after 1975)
GCSE (grades A–C)
CSE (grade 1)
SCE Ordinary (bands A–C)
Standard grade (levels 1–3)
SLC Lower SUPE Lower or Ordinary
School certificate or Matric
City and Guilds Craft/Ordinary level

GCE O-level (grades D–E if after 1975)
GCSE (grades D–G)
CSE (grades 2–5)
SCE Ordinary (bands D–E)
Standard grade (levels 4–5)
Clerical or commercial qualifications
Apprenticeship
Other qualifications

CSE ungraded

No qualifications

Ethnic Group

Household members were classified into fifteen groups. For analysis purposes these fifteen groups were subsumed under 5 headings:

White (White British, any other white background)

Black (Black Caribbean, Black African, Any other black background, Mixed white and black)

Indian

Pakistani or Bangladeshi

Other (Chinese, Other Asian background, Mixed white and Asian, Other mixed background, Any other ethnic group)

Exclusion from school

Exclusions can be either fixed term (previously called 'suspension') or permanent (previously referred to as 'expulsion'). A fixed term exclusion means that the child must leave the school premises and not return before the period of the fixed term is over. In the case of permanent exclusions they should never return to school unless there is a successful appeal.

Household

This survey used the standard household definition that is used in most surveys carried out by ONS and is comparable with the 2001 Census definition. A household is defined as a single person or group of people who have the accommodation as their only or main residence and who either share one meal a day or share the living accommodation.

Impact of mental disorders

Impact refers to the consequences of the disorder for the child in terms of social impairment and distress. Social impairment refers to the extent to which the disorder interferes with the child's everyday life in terms of his or her home life, friendships, classroom learning or leisure activities.

Marital status

Two questions were asked to obtain the marital status of the interviewed parent. The first asked: "Are you single, that is never married, married and living with your husband/wife, married and separated from your husband/wife, divorced or widowed?" The second question, which was asked of everyone except those married and living with husband/wife, was "May I just check, are you living with someone else as a couple?" The stability of the cohabitation was not assessed.

Mental disorders

The questionnaires used in this survey were based on both the ICD10 and DSM-IV diagnostic research criteria, but this report uses the term 'mental disorders' as defined by the ICD-10 to imply a clinically recognisable set of symptoms or behaviour associated in most cases with considerable distress and substantial interference with personal functions.

Reconstituted families

Reconstituted families are those where two separate families of a parent and a child, or children, have joined together so that the reconstituted family is made up of a couple and two sets of children of different parentage. Reconstituted families are referred to in the tables as containing step-children.

Socio-economic classification

From April 2001 the National Statistics Socio-economic Classification (NS-SEC) was introduced for all official statistics and surveys. It replaced Social Class based on occupation and Socio-economic Groups (SEG). Full details can be found in *The National Statistics Socio-economic Classification User Manual 2002*, ONS 2002.

Descriptive definition

	NS-SEC categories
Large employers and higher managerial occupations	L1, L2
Higher professional occupations	L3
Lower managerial and professional occupations	L4, L5, L6
Intermediate occupations	L7
Small employers and own account workers	L8, L9
Lower supervisory and technical occupations	L10, L11
Semi-routine occupations	L12
Routine occupations	L13
Never worked and long-term unemployed	L14
Full-time students	L15

The two residual categories: L16 (occupation not stated or inadequately described) and L17 (not classifiable for other reasons) are excluded when the classification is collapsed into its analytical classes.

Tenure

Tenure is classified into 3 categories:

Owned includes buying with a mortgage and owned outright, that is, bought without a mortgage or loan or with a mortgage or loan which has been paid off. It also includes co-ownership and shared ownership schemes.

Social sector renting include rented from local authorities, New Town corporations or commissions and Scottish Homes, and housing associations which include co-operatives and property owned by charitable trusts.

Private renting includes renting from organisations (property company, employer or other organisation) and from individuals (relative, friend, employer or other individual).

Working status

Working adults

People were counted as working if they did any work for pay or profit in the week ending the last Sunday prior to interview. Self-employed persons were considered to be working if they worked in their own business for the purpose of making a profit. Anyone on a Government scheme that was employer-based was also 'working last week'

Unemployed adults

This category includes those who were waiting to take up a job that had already been obtained, those who were looking for work, and people who intended to look for work but who were prevented by temporary ill-health, sickness or injury.

Economically inactive adults

This category covers all other groups including students at school or college, those who were permanently unable to work, retired people and those looking after the home or family.